DEEP IN THE

Heart

OF

MUMBAI

Rhonda Erwin

Deep in the Heart of Mumbai is a work of nonfiction.

First Edition

I have tried to recreate events, locales, and conversations from my memories of them. I may have changed some identifying characteristics and details, such as physical properties, occupations, places of residence, and names in order to maintain subject anonymity. My memories are my own, and I have recalled the stories recorded here to the best of my ability.

For more information, please contact:
Mascot Books
620 Herndon Parkway, Suite 320
Herndon, VA 20170
info@mascotbooks.com
www.mascotbooks.com

Library of Congress Control Number: 2018902082

CPSIA Code: PBANG0418A
ISBN-13: 978-1-68401-937-3
Printed in the United States of America

To my Maharajas

Grant Odell and Matthew Avery.

Have the courage to follow your heart

and intuition...it will make all the difference.

"There are thousands of lives in one single life."

—SVANI PRAJNANPAD—

The smell of jasmine fills the air as I stroll past the tennis courts and enter Taamra—the feng shui–inspired ayurvedic spa at the Taj Exotica Hotel in Goa.

Instantly, I'm smitten with the Eastern simplicity—high ceilings, low lighting, burning lotus-shaped candles—and even more so by the silence.

Quickly, though, my thoughts are interrupted when Ritvik greets me. In freshly pressed white *kurta pajamas*, he jumps into an explanation of how the philosophy of Jiva is naturally inspired by ancient Indian healing wisdom.

"Madam, wellness is a state of physical and psychological well-being, a contented state of consciousness that is achieved through Ayurveda, which is a way of life based on the deep understanding of mind, body, and spirit."

Then he mumbles something about determining my *dosha* and rattles on about space, fire, air, water, and earth. "Madam, after your treatment, there will be a *sari*-draping demonstration in the yoga room. Perhaps this is something of interest to you?"

"I don't own a *sari*."

"Very well, Madam," he replies. "Please remove all of your clothes, place them in the basket behind the door, and lie down on this plank. Do take a moment to relax, and to breathe, and then your *Abhyanga* will begin in a matter of minutes."

Frantically, I look around. "Um. I think there must be a mistake. I'm here for a massage. Just a basic massage, like the kind of rubdown that will make me forget where I am, at least for ninety minutes."

Ritvik smiles. "Yes, Madam. Your husband scheduled the very best pampering session for you today. Do not worry, Madam. *Abhyanga* is not only reflexology, Madam. It is a program where oil is applied using gentle strokes in a downward direction all over your body. The benefits are fine appetite, alertness, reduced stress, and glowing skin."

For a split second, I wonder if it will make the diarrhea disappear, but I'm too afraid to ask. I also contemplate if the last benefit is an afterthought considering the way he studied my face, which has been absorbing the massive amounts of pollutants in the air. Frankly, my skin began a colossal revolution back in the States the minute we agreed to move to Mumbai with our two boys—both under the age of five.

I scour the room for a towel or a blanket to crawl under once I get naked, but there is nothing in sight.

Ritvik is standing in front of me grinning and nodding while bobbing his head side to side. I don't know what this head wiggle means. I think he senses my hesitation.

"Don't worry, Madam. Once your entire body is covered, our therapist will bathe you with a soothing combination of herbal paste and medicated water."

"S-T-A-A-A-N! STANLEY ERWIN!" I scream out, hoping he's still within earshot. "S-T-A-A-A-N!"

He dutifully appears and finds Ritvik and me in a standoff.

"I'm not precisely sure what you signed me up for, but it's not going to happen. Tell this person or whomever you need to tell—slowly, in English— I'm not participating."

I storm off, but Ritvik catches me before I can escape. Flustered and short of breath, he blurts out, "Madam, very funny. Madam. *P-l-e-a-s-e* wait. I spoke to your husband."

I stop.

"I don't think anything is comical right now."

"Madam, this is common misunderstanding and it happens especially today."

Finally, Stanley pipes up. "Rhonda, I accidentally booked you into the Indian spa by mistake. Not the western spa. How hilarious would that have been if you had actually gone through with it? You could cross it off your bucket list!"

"*Bucket list?*" I shriek. "Do you think I want a complete stranger to lubricate me from head to toe and then scrub me clean?"

N-E-V-E-R!

"You've lost your mind. I've spent the past few days in a country I never wanted to see—much less *move to* in several months. What about the scent of urine that knocks me off my feet every day and the heat and the stares? How about the diesel fumes that rush into my mouth whenever I speak? Did I mention the honking? How about the nausea from the traffic? I doubt I'll ever produce a normal bowel movement again after all the tea and curry I've consumed. And now you want to add groping to the list?"

Ritvik isn't certain what to do. He's probably never heard a woman speak to her husband like I just did.

He sighs and bows his head, folds his hands at his chest, and turns to face me, "*Namaste.*"

Then very cautiously, he adds, "Please allow me. If you don't mind me saying, Madam, if the 5,000-year-old Ayurveda system in my country won't help you, we have many, many gods, and I'm most positive you can find one who can."

1

Brrrrring! Brrrrring! Brrrrring! Stan's cell phone is ringing and I'm trying to get ten more minutes of beauty rest. Who on Earth is calling at this hour?

"It's for you, Madam," he says with a smirk.

"Madam? Hello, Madam, how's the trip going?" says Channing.

I giggle at the "Madam" reference.

I've known Channing for six years. I met her when she dated one of Stan's employees, and eventually we decided we liked each other more than we liked him.

"I'm thinking of you. I read a travel article about India. It's a *Lonely Planet* hotspot. I phoned because you've been rather quiet."

"Channing, I can assure you there's nothing lonely about India. I feel as though I fell off the turnip truck, or worse yet, I'm Alice and I've done a swan dive down the rabbit hole and there's no turning back. There are people *everywhere*. I think Stanley said eighteen million people live Mumbai. Who knows? I've stopped counting.

"What I do know is I've traveled to more than twenty-one countries, some of those with you, and I have never, and I mean never, experienced anything like this. First of all, everyone keeps calling me 'madam,' like someone who manages prostitutes in a brothel. Who knew it's what female foreigners are called in this country?"

Channing laughs. "Only you would make the comparison, Madam Rhonda. Seriously, it can't be that bad, can it?"

"I bought a few trinkets and three wooden elephants at Central Cottage Industries Emporium, a government-regulated shop. The clerk hand-punched the prices into an old push-key cash register and then issued me a handwritten receipt. Another employee stamped 'paid' on it and instructed me to take it to the delivery window. I showed the slip of paper to a young clerk while he wrapped my items in a large sheet of brown paper. Once he finished, he looped white kite string around the package and politely asked me to put my finger in the middle so he could tie the knot. I walked to the door with my stash, but the security guard, who saw the whole transaction go down, needed to initial my receipt before he would allow me to exit the building."

She laughs some more.

"I think it was a test," I say. "It's India saying: you can't handle this, maybe a move isn't a splendid idea."

"The only beef I've seen are the cows on the road and they're considered holy, according to Ricky, Stan's Hindu company driver. Yesterday, we left our hotel, the Taj Mahal Palace, only to sit in traffic for a solid hour without moving once! I can't describe the sight of beggars knocking at the car windows asking for food or the women with babies in their arms begging for rupees. And don't get me started on the honking. Channing, yesterday I saw a man pull his penis out of his pants and urinate on the sidewalk right in front of me while I shopped at a bangle stall. But the good news is I can buy Diet Pepsi by the case. Thank God I can get my caffeine fix!"

Channing laughs again. "Well, it does sound interesting, Madam. Do you like *anything* so far?"

Hmm.

"Come to think of it? Yes. Yes, there is one thing I like so far about Mumbai—color. It is everywhere—teal, hot-pink, yellow, green, blue, purple—and we all need more color in our lives."

Waving his arms, Stanley motions for me to get off the phone so we can start our day. "Gotta go, Chan. Thanks for calling."

Obviously eavesdropping on my conversation, Stanley smarts off, "My high expectations of you are dwindling. Enlighten me, Madam. What are your *real* thoughts on India?"

I take a lingering look at my husband. We met in a program created by the Greater Austin Chamber of Commerce called "Leadership Austin." Their mission is to provide leadership training to those with a passion for the community. We've been married ten years. Our sons, Grant and Matthew—ages four and nine months—are back home in the care of friends and have no idea their world is about to radically change.

Thank goodness the company decided to give me one visit to scope out the country and help select housing and schools before we agree to leave our beautiful three-year-old custom home in the Eanes School district.

Stanley calmly says, "We need to be candid. We've traveled to Kenya and Russia and many exotic places, and while Mumbai isn't paradise, it could be a great adventure for our family."

I take a second to breathe as a flashback of the Goa spa mishap races across my mind.

But then I spat, "Okay, I'll be straight-forward. Who stops to buy pleated khakis on the way to an international flight? Then, who screams at his wife when American Airlines wants twenty-five dollars for an overweight bag? And more so, who goes off on a Maudie's employee when the salsa runs out and demands a five-dollar refund for a taco when your flight is boarding and you're guaranteed brunch in first class?"

Really?

"Then you flipped your lid when you discovered that your secretary and American Express Corporate Travel booked our seats on opposite sides of the plane!

"And while you may have spent the past year traveling to India forming business relationships from Chennai to Hyderabad and Delhi to Bangalore, since we landed, you've been acting like you've never set foot on Indian soil. You keep putting the cart before the horse. If you act like this now, how are you going to handle the pressure once we move?"

He tries to interrupt me, but I hold him off. I'm second-guessing this decision. "To be truthful, I thought you asked if I wanted Indian food for dinner the day you shouted out from your study while on that conference call. I said yes to tandoori chicken as in, 'Yes, I'll go to Clay Pit for dinner.' I didn't mean, 'Yes, I'll go to Mumbai to get it.' Did you notice our airline tickets said Mumbai but our luggage tags read BOM—as in Bombay?

"Can't you see this country is having an identity crisis? Maybe you're having your own identity crisis, too!

"Roaming the globe for fun is one thing, but moving to a developing country is seeming more and more asinine. I feel like a child and we don't live here yet. For goodness' sake, I'm one of five in my family who earned a college degree. And now—according to the Foreigner Regional Registration Office yesterday—I'll never work or earn money in this country.

"After my parents' divorce, my mother made me swear I would never depend on a man for financial means because leaning on any man would make for disappointment. My dependency on you was tremendously difficult when I stopped working full-time to raise our boys, but not being able to earn any money when my children are in school rocks my world.

"Ricky speaks little English, but he speaks enough for me to see he clearly thinks you're the important one. He's said a total of seven words to me. He's mad I keep sitting up front instead of in the backseat, but I can't help the carsickness. I'm not sure this male-dominated country is ready for a madam from Texas. I'm terrified I won't have enough patience to survive. I mean, I just want to know why it takes so long to do the simplest things!"

I hold up my hand for more time and continue my rant.

"Besides the stench and poverty, I can't get past the insane amounts of paperwork required for every transaction. I've collected thirty-seven pieces of paper in the last three days. India is drowning in red tape.

"You should have warned me about the killer jet lag and the Indian bathrooms. Frankly, most of the time I don't know where I am, much less where I'm going. Just because Trammell Crow Company formed a joint relationship with Meghraj Chesterton to explore development and investment opportunities, I'm not sure I can handle moving here for five years."

We emerge from the Taj Mahal Palace Hotel as a unified front. I'm grateful for the cloud coverage. It's stifling hot. I'm wearing capri pants because I refuse to show my legs in public. Ricky, right on time for our nine o'clock pickup, zips the Skoda, an elegant gray four-door sedan, around to the front and stops. As we descend the marble steps from the lobby, he springs out of the car and greets Stan. "*Namaste*, Boss."

Then he opens the backseat door and I climb in. Stanley follows. Once the door is shut and locked, we drive straight into the blaring traffic. Unexpectedly, Stanley reaches over and squeezes my hand.

"Madam, I promise to be more supportive," he says. "We can do this!"

As we drive parallel to the harbor, I notice a white foreigner in Nike workout clothes stretching his arms and legs against a concrete pillar, preparing for what looks like a morning jog. I laugh out loud when two locals walk up beside him and start imitating his every move. *Oh my God, it's too much.* The foreigner isn't sure what to do. He continues stretching for a few seconds and then runs off, leaving the men puzzled.

We drive past a number of beautiful but filthy Victorian buildings. I can only visualize what India must have looked like during colonial times. I don't see any auto rickshaws—the yellow and black beetles I spotted in Goa—but I sure can hear the taxis and Tata Indigos honking.

I like this area. We briefly discussed living in Colaba, the city's southernmost peninsula, packed with restaurants, museums, markets, and crumbling mansions. But it's too far from the Dhirubhai Ambani International School (DAIS) or the American School of Bombay (ASB) in Kurla West (an industrial area), where we're hoping Grant will attend school.

Stanley informs me it could take thirty minutes to one hour—possibly two hours—to drive north today, but considering our appointment is before noon we should make decent time regardless.

We stop at a red light and a young girl, perhaps twelve, taps on my window. She's dirty beyond belief and is dressed in rags. She puts her fingers up to her mouth repeatedly. Ricky honks the horn and waves her on. She slowly steps back from the car as the light changes, never once taking her eyes off me.

Stanley points out a series of deteriorated houses and shacks over to my right and tells me it's called Kamthipura, Mumbai's oldest and Asia's second-largest red-light district. We pass Chhatrapati Shivaji Terminus, formerly known as the Victoria Terminus Station, and I wonder if the girl who knocked on my window lives and works in Kamthipura.

Ricky races on the newly paved stretches of highway, but we hit the honking wall of traffic once we reach the suburbs. The stopping and starting movements through numerous intersections make me ill. I begin to see more cows along with those cute rickshaws, and I notice billboards advertising Bollywood movies. I watch a woman throw up out of a double decker BEST bus window as it makes a sharp right turn in front of our Skoda. A family of six on a motorbike pulls up beside us at the intersection one block before the DAIS. The woman sitting sideways on the scooter in a blue-gray *sari* smiles at me. I grin back.

Girija Dhawan, administrative officer of DAIS, greets us in the lobby and gives us a very short tour of several classrooms. The children are wearing lackluster uniforms, and I don't see one foreign student in the population. DAIS, a K-12 school founded in 2003, is the country's top international school. Girija is cordial, but once she reviews the admission log, she informs us Grant will never attend the school as long as we live in India. The school is at capacity and given the sibling-to-student ratio as well as the alumni factor, there's no space—period. She instructs us to go elsewhere, and bids us good luck on our move.

Ricky seems shocked to see us outside so promptly and races toward the car in the parking lot. He motions to Stanley for us to stay put. We're not accustomed to waiting for a driver because we drive ourselves everywhere—all over Texas, all over the USA.

Once again, Ricky opens the backseat door and I climb in and Stanley follows. Now we're set to meet Ms. Beena Gupta, Director of the Eurokids Preschool.

I look out the back window as we leave, feeling somewhat grateful Grant won't be attending DAIS. I ask Stan, "Why in the world did we need to drive all the way here when she could have simply told us "no" over the telephone?"

Driving back to the residential area of Bandra West, it's lunchtime and the traffic is horrendous. I think there are more cars on the road than there is space available. All types of vehicles and domestic cows are competing for the right-of-way. I watch a garbage truck clip the back wheel of a rickshaw and continue down the road as it crashes into a telephone poll. Locals carry on as usual.

Despite the chaos, this area pulses with positive energy.

Ms. Gupta is waiting for us in front of the building. After an exchange of greetings, she opens the large lock on the gate surrounding the daycare center housing thirty-five children and several Hindu teachers and staff. I'm trying to keep an open mind, but again, I do not see an expat child.

After a short tour of the facilities, I collect an admission application. There will be an opening for Matthew upon our arrival to the city in several months. I simply need to deliver the paperwork, a deposit in rupees, and my baby. They will handle the rest. All the classrooms are spotless, but as we approach the gate to leave, I smell tar.

I peek over my left shoulder and there's a tall, skinny construction worker mixing blacktop in a metal container over an open fire two feet from where all the children are playing on a plastic jungle gym. Children could easily burn themselves on the pot, or even worse, fall into the flames. Ms. Gupta assures us this work only occurs several weeks once a year so the roof doesn't leak during monsoon.

We complete two more facility tours at Jolly Dwarfs Playschool and Kangaroo Kids before heading to China Gate for lunch with Raj and Sunita, leasing agents who work for Trammell Crow Meghraj Property Consultants.

They're very pleasant and want to know how I'm finding India so far. I don't want to embarrass Stan. I lie and tell them it's incredible.

Raj announces he's the creator of our trip's agenda. He took all of my concerns and requests and worked very, very hard. He doesn't address me as Madam and neither does Sunita. The young thirtysomething professionals hang on to each sentence Stanley says, making very little direct eye contact with me.

A waiter appears to take our drink order. I'm pleased they serve diet soda. I didn't drink enough tea this morning, and I'll need more caffeine to make it through this afternoon.

In response to my query, Raj points to the "loo" signage, and I excuse myself. I head to the bathroom. I'm overjoyed there's a Western toilet.

In a traditional Indian bathroom, you position yourself directly over an opening in the floor. It is centered between two footpads on each side of the hole, a little more than a shoulder's width apart, where you place your feet. You crouch and bend your knees into a semi-sitting position and perform your task. Then you wash your private parts with your left hand using the spray hose. Sometimes there will be a spigot to turn on, while other times there will simply be a bucket full of water to dip from. I wash my hands profusely and see my puffy image looking back at me in the mirror. The humidity is killing me. My cystic acne is lurking in the shadows from all the stress.

Back at the table, Raj and Sunita ask if we can split several dishes between the four of us. I'm startled by their thriftiness. Stanley is on the same level as the president of Meghraj, their boss, and I'm not sure they would ever ask him to share. But perhaps this is a sign our "foreignness" is not such a big deal after all.

I inquire about the Hunan chicken entrée, but Stanley informs me Raj and Sunita are vegetarians.

My cold can of Diet Pepsi arrives and is placed beside the empty glass.

"Madam, would you care for ice cubes?" the waiter asks.

"Yes, I would love ice."

He looks perplexed. He looks at Sunita and then Raj and then me.

"How many do you wish, Madam?"

I watch him take the lid off the bucket of ice and pull a set of tongs out of the pocket of his short apron. Then he plops one cube in my glass. I glance around the table, not sure what to do. Is this it? I don't want to insult anyone.

Finally I say, "Can I get four more cubes of ice, please?" For a millisecond, I thought the clouds parted and I heard angels sing, because he politely placed exactly four more ice cubes in my glass—not a cube more—and handed me a straw.

Raj and Sunita are texting and can't be bothered about my drama. Stanley, sitting across from me, is checking his email. I don't have a phone because Stanley didn't want me to incur high international fees on our US bill. Literally, I'm out of touch.

The fried rice, *hakka* noodles, and crispy vegetable spring rolls arrive hot and fresh. Lunch conversation is casual, but it dawns on me the company entrusted our trip coordination to young, entry-level employees who do not have children and who are unmarried. I'm not elated.

Exactly one hour and thirty minutes after our arrival, we open our fortune cookies and Raj pays the bill.

My fortune reads: *You create your own stage. The audience is waiting.*

We say happy trails to Sunita and spend the afternoon with Raj and Ricky exploring Lilavati Hospital, Otters Club, Hinduja Hospital, and Jaslok Hospital, slowly making our way down south. Back near the Gateway, Ricky drops us a block from the hotel (yes, there was traffic congestion), and takes Raj back to the office.

The throbbing headache I've had since we landed eases as soon as the elevator doors open. Up in our suite, there is a large gorgeous, floral arrangement and a chilled bottle of imported Chardonnay on a British Colonial antique desk with a sweet handwritten note from Farhat Jamal and the staff at the Taj Mahal Palace Hotel, who want to make sure I feel welcomed.

"Yee-haw! My headache just vanished! I *really* like this place."

After a long, hot bath and a short nap, I dress for a casual dinner in dress slacks because I just don't understand what type of clothes I need to wear to garner respect as a foreigner. Ritu, an Indian friend in Houston, warned me to cover up, but I'm getting a lot of unwanted attention even though I'm not showing my shoulders or legs.

Stanley tells me Sunita booked us at Indigo, a popular international restaurant she thinks I might like. As long they serve alcohol, I say, this madam will certainly enjoy herself tonight.

There's a lot of commotion among the doormen who watch us leave the lobby on foot and go out into the sea of locals. A light breeze is blowing at the Gateway of India. I ignore all the gypsy kids begging for rupees and don't comment on the number of stares we're receiving. We walk several blocks from the Taj to the restaurant for our 8 p.m. dinner reservation.

Arriving at Indigo feels like strutting into a Napa eatery, and we are overjoyed. Once the door shuts behind us, we can no longer detect the smell of burning plastic in the air. However, I notice two things: we're the only customers in the restaurant, and there are menu cards at our place settings detailing the evening's course selections—lobster salad with green peppercorn dressing, pan-roasted grouper with warm artichoke salad, three-mushroom risotto with toasted almonds and bleu cheese, and flourless chocolate cake with Rocky Road ice cream. I pick up my card and it reads, "Mr. Stanley Erwin & Friend."

Good grief.

Well for now, I'll simply revel in the prime seating, enjoy a full staff waiting on us hand and foot, and make a toast in honor of our new uncharted journey—but only after the martini cart departs our table.

Stanley gets somber. "Rhon, I'm willing to give you all the support you need. Let's move. I know it will be challenging, but think of all the memories we'll create. You can buy anything you want for the flat—that's if we find one," he laughs. "We're a team."

I'm anxious and overwhelmed, and I'm not sure I can depend on strangers—a huge problem for a control freak, but I hear myself agree to the adventure. If he can run a company of 150 employees in Austin, certainly I can manage one household in India.

If he can do it, I can do it. If he can do it, I can do it.

Dinner was magnificent, and I make a mental note to thank Sunita for the recommendation if I ever see her again. We pay the bill and return to the hotel.

While Stanley flips the TV channels to catch up on international news, I get ready for bed. I keep reminding him that I'm extremely independent, and I feel like I've stepped back in time.

"Honestly, perhaps this isn't the ideal expat assignment for me," I sigh as I crawl into bed, knowing this decision is b-i-g. I'm giving him one last chance to jump ship.

Stanley pays no attention to me and begins to work on his computer, so I flip open the *InStyle* magazine I bought in the Dallas/Fort Worth International Airport.

I glance at the summer crop tops and tiny shorts, doubting I can wear ninety-nine percent of these clothes in Mumbai. My mind begins to wander, and I flip ahead to the horoscope page. It reads:

> *Aquarius (January 20–February 18): So many planets are on your side, urging you out of your comfort zone, that you can't help but make all sorts of discoveries about what is now possible. Don't hold back. Don't hold on to old ways or habits. Don't be afraid to let go. Don't be afraid to start again. Your future is so bright, you'll have to wear shades.*

2

Portuguese navigator and explorer Vasco da Gama discovered the direct sea route to India in the late fifteenth century. I discovered it via Swiss Air Flight 6314.

It hasn't been pretty. Less than nine hours from Zürich, I landed in one of the most contradictory places on earth. While the jet lag has subsided, my ears continue to ring.

I want the honking to cease. I've seen beggars, women in magenta and orange *saris*, poor people missing arms or legs or both, happy children playing with sticks and rocks, a funeral, a Bollywood film in production on a side street near our hotel, and food cooked right on the sidewalk on a piece of hot rusted tin—all before lunchtime.

On top of that, I had my left breast squeezed tightly as I sat in a rickshaw stopped at a red light. A male bystander felt me up as the light changed. I never saw his face.

Stan, mortified, was speechless. I took it in stride.

"It could have been worse. He could have grabbed my Louis Vuitton tote bag and run off to the train station. Maybe the guy just needed a quick feel."

While all this goes against Stan's "sell" of India as a safe city to raise our boys for the next five years, I'm thankful I birthed boys. I can't imagine a young girl growing up in a male-dominated world and dealing with dowry nonsense.

Apart from the atrocious traffic and complimentary boob rub, I do love calling Stanley "Boss" and riding in a rickshaw.

We're in Khar West to view another rental property and on the spur of the moment, flag down a rickshaw to take a spin around the neighborhood.

Actually, we made Ricky speak Hindi to the driver, who was sprawled across his backseat napping under the palms near the building complex, and ask if he might take us for a cruise. I guess he was desperate because he got up, wiggled his head, and started the engine when Stanley gave him fifty rupees. Ricky didn't appear too keen on the idea. He probably can't understand why we wanted to ride around the block sweating in a tin can when our fancy Skoda with air conditioning awaited. Nevertheless, Ricky did as instructed and appeared confident the driver would take us and return.

For our part, it was a test to see what street living entailed. We dared ourselves to venture out of our comfort zone, on our own terms.

The minute we took off, the wind begins to blow, and I can't stop laughing. I feel thirteen years old again, riding my blue-and-white-banana-seat bicycle at lightning speed down Glenvale Drive as far from my parent's one-story starter home in north Houston as I could go.

Wheee!

People share the road with wildlife, all going about their own business. Locals buzz by us on shiny motorcycles and scooters.

Stanley sees a makeshift temple and a sugarcane stall. We watch while a young man shoves large pieces of sugarcane through a press of some sort as a teenager turns a hand crank. Juice pours out the back and a small boy, not more than six years old, raises glasses to catch the liquid. I doubt the process is sanitary, but my stomach growls just watching the locals suck down what is clearly the drink of choice.

We watch a skinny white-haired man walk a rather healthy-looking cow. Vegetable vendors are selling onions, garlic, and potatoes in open, dirty wooden carts. We stop at a red light and wait for one of the double-decker BEST buses to pass so we can make a left turn.

Stanley shouts above the din, "It's India's version of Capital Metro, but without air conditioning." A fellow rickshaw driver zips up to the intersection and stops alongside us. I peek out from behind the black vinyl rooftop canopy and he smiles at me. His teeth are red and rotten, and I wonder if he is spitting up blood. He seems chipper and Stanley tells me the color is from *paan*, a stimulant—like tobacco. Many local men chew on it during the workday.

We continue down the dirt road alongside Khar Gymkhana and begin to make our way back to Ricky and the housing complex.

As the driver stops to let us out, I notice his calloused and cracked bare feet. He has six toes on the right foot and five on the left. He does the head wiggle and I give him fifty more rupees because he didn't have to take us but he did. And, it was big fun.

Ricky does the head wiggle too and guides us to the car. I noticed he'd wiped the windshield down and all the dust was gone. I wondered if it was ever possible to rid everything of the dust.

Stanley takes me to a Subway for lunch, and I can't believe how similar the storefront and interior of the restaurant are to Subways in the States. Somehow I accidentally get in the vegetarian line instead of the non-vegetarian line and try to order a ham and turkey on wheat. You should have seen the stares—the nerve of NV people in line with the V people! Scandalous!

Stanley tells me to pay more attention to my surroundings. "Anuj told me food directly correlates with religion. If you're Muslim, you don't eat pork. If you're Hindu, you're raised either V or NV. Some folks are Jain and eat vegetables—just not root vegetables."

Did I say my head was still spinning? What are root vegetables? And for the record, shouldn't Subway have two completely separate storefronts, one for V people and one for NV people, similar to a kosher kitchen or a non-kosher kitchen?

"Rhonda, there are Parsis, Christians, and Jews here. And Buddhism has a large following too, but you have to read about different ethnic groups and their belief systems so you don't offend anyone."

Seriously?

I just want my sandwich—NV, please, and a Diet Pepsi with a straw—so I shut up and twiddle my thumbs. Waiting in line at Subway is like watching paint dry on a rainy day. I've never seen so many people put so many items on two pieces of bread. A new little voice inside me says, *Patience, Madam,* but I want to scream.

After lunch, we head directly to the American School of Bombay.

Anne Wichstorm, Director of Admission, discusses enrollment and gives us a short tour of the campus. Think large, open classrooms, lots of natural light, global studies in various languages, and diversity within grade levels. Students are every color, shape, and size and from all over the world.

Anne-from-Norway gives Stan-and-Rhonda-from-Texas campus specs: twenty-three percent of the students are American. The majority of students are from Germany, France, and Sweden, and the rest are from Asia and the UK. A small percent are locals, but the school no longer accepts non-expatriate students living in Mumbai. A few years back, an influx of middle-class Indian families inundated the school with applications. In order to provide space for expat children who didn't want to attend the French or German private schools in south Bombay, they modified the admission rule. Enrollment tops out at four hundred students, pre-K to high school. A nurse is on staff every day and a general practitioner doctor visits on Fridays.

We enroll Grant in pre-kindergarten. Classes run 8 a.m. to noon, Monday through Friday, and the two pre-K classrooms have a maximum of twenty students each with a main teacher (American, British, or French) and an Indian assistant. Their day includes music, arts, crafts, playtime, foreign language, physical education, and technology.

Upon graduation, Grant will advance to kindergarten, where classes are held 8 a.m. to 3 p.m., Monday through Friday. Swim lessons are offered for a small fee and Grant is welcome to ride the ASB bus to school. *Bus? What bus?* He has to ride a bus to school in the traffic? A bus like the I-saw-the-woman-throw-up-out-of-the-window bus?

Anne shows us the fleet of buses, which are at least modern, in the parking lot. Sensing my stress level rising, Stanley jumps in and says, "I will deliver Grant to school on my way to the office and Rhonda, with a driver, will pick him up in the afternoon."

Before we depart, Anne says we'll receive a final confirmation letter in July and accepts our company check for the tuition deposit. She will be in touch and bids us goodbye.

Stanley returns to the topic of transportation before we reach the car. "Rhonda, Anne doesn't know you fell asleep on the bus on the way home your first day of kinder. She doesn't know that the driver and the driving assistant didn't realize you were on the bus until you woke up at the depot and shouted out to them, nearly giving them a heart attack. She doesn't know your mother, worried sick, picked you up and from that moment on, you became an official 'car rider' until you graduated high school."

Trust me, Grant will do the same.

3

"With nearly 200 members, the American Women's Club of Bombay is a nonprofit group aiming to provide support and assistance to its members as well as to promote friendship within both the American and the wider expat communities through social, cultural, and philanthropic activities," Stanley reads off of Google.

He adds with a smirk, "It's the Junior League of India, Madam!"

Oh dear.

I must say, Stan the Man was very forward-thinking on my behalf. He's been communicating with Alix, a member of the AWC, and so I'm invited to attend the weekly coffee in Bandra today.

We finish breakfast poolside while a peacock cry pierces the morning and shatters the quiet of the landscaped lawn filled with mango trees. I don't even flinch a muscle because my head no longer feels like it's going to implode with frustration. I'm getting my bearings now that I've got a little experience under my belt.

Plus, after three cups of Darjeeling and crunchy toast with marmalade, I'm high on palace life. Grant is enrolled in ASB. Moreover, I'm sporting one very sassy beaded hot-pink tunic I found in a shop near the hotel and a pair of Bollywood-inspired hoops I bought from a street vendor for seventy-five rupees.

With my mojo replenished, Ricky and I head to the home of Jessica Turner, who lives in Jivesh Terraces, Bandra. Upon arrival, Ricky personally escorts me to the third floor and tells me slowly in English that he will return in exactly two hours, as per the instructions given by Boss.

I exhale and laugh.

I feel giddy removing my shoes before entering the flat, and Alix warmly introduces herself, putting me at ease. I'm sure it's apparent I'm the new kid in town. My eyes scan the room and see this is certainly a far cry from expat wives' clubs of the past that I've read about on the internet.

These women have lived all over the globe and combined have international stints in Egypt, Japan, Australia, Britain, Singapore, South Africa,

Malaysia, Indonesia, France, and Canada.

Alix informs the group I'm on my first expat assignment. I rapidly chirp back that I survived a Spanish immersion program one summer during college in San Miguel de Allende, eager to show I'm not a complete novice. I don't dare mention I cried for the first forty-eight hours. Not because of homesickness, but because they truly never spoke English except on the first day of class to tell you, in English, they won't ever speak English to you again, so you'd better study hard and learn Spanish.

I'm instantly welcomed into the Bombay sisterhood. A copy of *Namaskar Mumbai: At Home in India* is thrust into my hands. It's a guide of expat resources, and Alix leads me toward five women who have small children at ASB and who say all positive things about it.

A mother from France tells me grade-school ASB children play together every week and the majority of families go outside the city on weekends. I wonder, *Where do they go, given the traffic?*

A mother from Australia tells me, "Sundays are best spent at any of the five-star-hotel boozy brunches or late-night dinners, but remember, millions of other people are out doing the same thing."

Got it.

A member from Britain tells me it's common for AWC women to eat out and shop during the week to avoid traffic but then stay in on the weekend.

"I play the same tune back in Texas," I tell her.

She nods.

I say politely, "Could you give me brief tidbits on being an expat, if possible?"

While she hands Alix a handful of rupees for a local charity supporting underprivileged women and babies, she doesn't skip a beat.

"You can't purchase goods over the internet. Customs officials open everything and steal it, but the brilliant thing is you can bring anything you want back in a suitcase.

"Want someone to blow dry your hair? Just call the salon and within minutes, someone arrives to perform the service.

"There are no tampons with applicators, so bring the mother load in your crate.

"You can pay someone to shine all your shoes all day long.

"The local tailor can make a knock-off of any designer dress you wish.

"If you fancy plants, you can hire a gardener.

"Anything sold in India can be delivered to your flat. You run out of cereal, call the corner grocery store. Dry cleaners, clothing stores, restaurants—everyone delivers anything for almost nothing. You run out of wine, call the wine shop and they deliver. Actually, you never, ever need to leave your flat. The city will come to you—"

I cut her off. "Did you just tell me I could get wine delivered to my flat?"

She laughs. "Yes. I hosted a party and we ran out of vodka and wine, so I called the liquor shop and minutes later the order appeared. Several hours later, we ran out again…and you guessed it…another delivery arrived—along with ice!"

Who knew I had to move to India to get grape juice delivery?

Alix and two other British members cornered me. The talk was stern but they meant well.

"There is a large expat community in Mumbai, and you will find we're very supportive. Mumbai is a bit of culture shock, but, on the whole, it's a good place to live. Overall, if you survive it, you can live anywhere, including Antarctica.

"Don't ever expect to drive. It's a bit restrictive relying on a driver all the time, so find yourself a brilliant one. The upside is that you'll never have to worry about parking."

I love positive attitudes!

"Accommodations are mainly in apartments and are very expensive. Finding appropriate housing can be a problem, and the wheels move slowly. It's the hardest part of relocation. Once you find a place to live, the worst is over.

"You can find most things you need to buy in Mumbai—for a price.

"It's going to take you a good six months to get up and running in order to be familiar with a routine and know your whereabouts.

"While the city never sleeps, it takes a little longer for things to happen. Learn to be patient."

(They actually repeated this one several times.)

"You must hire servants to cook and clean. Realize you will need to rely on other people or you absolutely won't survive."

Damn it!

Hesitant after so much insight and assistance, I muster the gall to announce I have a unique list of questions for them. I knew this would be my only opportunity to get bona fide answers from women who deal with India daily. I'd started a running list in Austin. By the time the plane touched down at the Chhatrapati Shivaji International Airport, it was complete at forty-one questions.

Without any faltering, they say, "Show us the list now and we'll answer every question before you go."

Oh my God! I take the cocktail napkins out of my tote bag:

1. What vaccinations should our family get?
2. Can you recommend a pediatrician?
3. Can you recommend a dentist?
4. Where are the decent grocery stores?
5. Are diapers and infant formula sold in stores?
6. Do we have to drink bottled water?
7. What is available for kids to do during the week or on weekends?
8. Is Christmas celebrated?
9. What do families generally do on weekends?

10. Where can I purchase beef and bacon?
11. Do we need to join a gym to exercise?
12. Do I need to dress more conservatively than I normally do?
13. Do most Indians speak English?
14. How do I hire a nanny?
15. How do I find a driver?
16. How do I hire a cook?
17. Can I get California Chardonnay in India?
18. Can you recommend a hair stylist?
19. Are movies at the theater shown in English or with English subtitles?
20. What is the best hospital in the city?
21. Can you recommend a place for a pedicure and manicure?
22. Where can I buy milk?
23. Where can I purchase seafood?
24. Are there any good sushi restaurants in the city?
25. Where is the best area to live if you have small children?
26. Any tips for setting up a flat?
27. Can I get drapes sewn and installed?
28. Should we purchase one or two cars?
29. What is a typical day? (This question garnered the most laughs!)
30. What cell service do you recommend?
31. Can I hire a decorator?
32. Any tips on managing servants?
33. Can you recommend a club to join?
34. Do you know a good yoga instructor?
35. Can you recommend a tennis instructor?
36. Where can I purchase a Christmas tree?
37. Can you recommend other cities and places to visit in India?
38. Explain bargaining in the market.
39. Are there stores that carry regular clothes to purchase for my family or should I stock up before the move?
40. Can I find quality shoes for kids?
41. Am I crazy to move to India with two small children? (Yes!)

Jackpot! They answer each question thoughtfully and sincerely while I take notes. They even throw in a bonus question: "Madam, want to know how much you pay for a Rolling Stones ticket when they're in town? Eight hundred rupees—about twenty US dollars for general seats."

Comical.

"Thanks to your generosity, I gained a greatest hits list. *Namaste.*"

Wait! Did I just speak Hindi?

When I see Ricky at the door, I scramble to gather a few email addresses and then we leave.

Over lunch at the Grand Hyatt Hotel outside of Bandra in Santa Cruz (a nearby neighborhood), I tell Stanley AWC is a lifeboat, critical to my survival in a place I know very little about. I'll join this group the minute I land back in the city.

We discuss properties and spend the rest of the day combing neighborhoods with Ricky. On a previous business trip, Stanley was smart enough to video a series of thirty-five flats and bungalows to show me, so we narrowed our search while still in Austin and sent reviews to Raj.

Once I arrive, we hit the ground running and very, very quickly are able to narrow the choices even further. There just aren't high construction standards and anything goes. Some complexes are either unfinished, or the individual units have already been leased.

Come to find out, it was slim pickins', friends.

After viewing twenty-five properties—I kid you not—only two condominiums meet our standards.

Condo Number One

- A three-bedroom with a study and three baths
- A small ocean view
- A workout facility planned but not yet complete
- A parking area Stanley thinks our boys could play in—a concrete jungle
- An onsite pool, which would save us money; we could forego the expense of joining a members-only club or a five-star hotel for entertainment purposes such as dining, swimming, and fitness

I think back to the AWC meeting and one of the women's words of wisdom: if you have small children, make your home a palace, because there is absolutely nothing for little kids to do in a city full of typhoid fever, polio, measles, and dengue fever.

Trust me, I heard her loud and clear. Matthew isn't even a year old, so he can't receive the crucial vaccinations for yellow fever, Hepatitis A/B, or whooping cough before we leave the States. I stress over this fact. But for now, our move seems to be inevitable, so I put the horrid what-if thoughts on the back burner. I just don't know what else to do.

Condo Number Two

- No pool but 3,000 square feet our boys could roam freely in
- A view of an official cricket field and luscious beautiful palms—the Khar Gymkhana Club
- A planned fitness center, approved for the ground floor near the car park

What's not to love about it? I tell Stanley I envision cocktails on the balcony watching matches (although I know nothing about cricket) and lazy afternoon naps on a window seat. Remember, I'm told I can hire a local seamstress or tailor to sew drapes and seat cushions who will deliver and install them to boot. I catch myself daydreaming, my thoughts drifting to fabric swatches...

Good God! I haven't even found a place to live yet! Quickly, I put the decorating thoughts on the backburner too.

Ricky is driving us south. Traffic is mind-boggling. We get back to the Taj, shower, and backtrack twenty minutes to The Club Mumbai we passed on the way to the hotel. Stan's business partner, Anuj, a member, has reserved a table for dinner and drinks.

I want to strangle myself when Chinese food is ordered again. Anuj is vegetarian like Sunita and Raj.

I whisper to Stan, "This is the fifth time we're eating Chinese food. We're official members of the veggie cult, but I'm eating Stubbs BBQ the minute I get back to Austin!"

He grins.

Anuj is polite and full of pertinent information. I'm disappointed his wife, Priti, is a no-show. They have two children older than our boys, and I want her valuable input before our departure. She grew up in Mumbai and they live in an affluent area of the city called "Juhu."

Dinner is a little buttoned-up and boring, so I take a leap of faith and ask Anuj to speak on behalf of Priti. Boy, do the floodgates open.

First thing out of his mouth is, "You need to join 'The Club.'"

"You mean *this* club?"

Stanley kicks me under the table.

Anuj is polite. "It's a leading private club providing world-class fitness, recreation, and hospitality combined with unrivaled service and efficiency."

"Efficiency? In what?"

Stanley kicks me again under the table.

I take a long sip of my Bombay Sapphire gin and tonic.

He continues with a hint of a British accent, "India handles fifty percent of the world's trade and has expensive real estate, comparable only to Tokyo and New York. Understand it is extremely difficult to find accommodation, but we are doing our best. We will find something."

He takes a few bites of fried rice and a sip of Kingfisher, the popular local beer, and continues.

"Rhonda, servants are a must and the number of servants you hire should coordinate with the size of the flat and duties. You will need servants to open your door, shop in the markets, clean the food, wash the laundry, iron all the clothes. The low cost of living *(I thought he just said otherwise?)* is a reason high-castes have servants. The other reason is some kitchens don't have dishwashers or state-of-the-art appliances. *(Red flag)* Stanley will need to hire many servants. For example, I employ a servant whose sole duty is to wash my car each day. It's the way life is in Mumbai, Rhonda. You'll adapt."

Hmm.

While Stanley and Anuj talk about a deal, I take another sip of my gin and tonic. I feel homesick. I miss my boys. I want beef tacos and guacamole. I want a margarita with salt and I want chips and salsa, not Chinese food again, but I'm determined to finish the night on a positive note.

Dinner lasts roughly two hours. Stanley and Anuj end up discussing more business again over dessert. I order another gin and tonic and head to the bathroom, or should I say, "loo."

The stalls are empty. I look at my image in the mirror. I feel mellow, but my complexion looks blotchy, probably from the mix of sweltering outdoor heat and indoor air conditioning and now, alcohol.

A well-dressed Indian woman walks in and I introduce myself. Then I throw caution to the wind and say, "May I ask you a question about childcare in India?" Frantically, I ramble on and on about the lack of facilities for babies, about the scary tar at Eurokids, and tell her perhaps I should import an American nanny for several months just for peace of mind while I get settled...clearly the gin has given me a boost of abruptness...could this be a bright idea?

She steps forward, looks me up and down, and then her facial expression changes to disgust.

"I don't understand why you would bring a nanny from the States when you can pay a low-caste nanny forty dollars a month to care for your baby," she says. "American nannies are overrated." And on that note she slips into a stall and locks the door.

Silence. Then I hear a loud flush.

Anuj pays for dinner. We say our goodbyes and I thank him for the chocolates and coffee-table book on India he presents as parting gifts. I'm collecting quite the stash of textiles and souvenirs.

Anuj points to his Meghraj driver, introduced as Ganesh, who will take us back to our hotel. He's younger than Ricky and smiles at me when he opens the backseat door.

We make decent time in traffic, but when we're caught at a red light, a thin woman dressed in a cheap-looking *sari* walks up to Stan's window and starts banging on it, asking for rupees. It's dark, but the Thums Up (an Indian cola brand) electric sign flashes sporadically from a storefront. I can see she's wearing red lipstick and bangles. I do a double take and ask Stanley if it's a man dressed like a woman.

Before he can answer, Ganesh pipes up, "Madam, this is a eunuch. It is good luck for you to see a eunuch your first visit to India. Very, very good luck, Madam." I look at Stanley when the light changes to green. What is a lucky eunuch?

The handsome doormen at the Taj welcome a blissful me back to the hotel. My new little voice says again, *Remember, Madam...patience.*

Back in the room, Stanley showers and checks the BBC for news, then he powers on his computer.

I'm tired and delirious but I open the guide. There are all types of activities and groups I can join: Hopping Bunnies, Mumbai Mums, Aadhaar, Powai Mah-Jongg, Craft Club, Book Club.

Interesting.

I grab the remote and flip channels to soap operas, Bollywood videos and Zee TV. Nothing looks entertaining on this side of the globe tonight, so we call the boys. While they have no concept of time, it's good to hear their little voices receiving the royal treatment in our absence: cheese pizza and movies.

Before bed, I take a soothing, hot bubble bath and try not to reflect on the fact that not one of the properties we've toured has a tub.

Maybe I can get one delivered.

4

W-H-A-C-K!

"Oh, dear God! I am sorry. I'm really, really sorry," I say to the bony Indian man wearing a turban and a thin piece of fabric around his waist like a sarong. I just hit him with my car door. He rubs his arm, checking to see if it's broken, wiggles his head, and continues down the street without saying a word.

Stanley and Raj laugh. Ricky doesn't seem amused. Raj reminds me I have to let Ricky open the car door because he gets out first to look around for people in the street, passing cars, or lorries. A main responsibility of the driver is safety.

"I bet that hurt. Poor guy."

I feel bad. I had thrown the door open because I'm impatient and tired of waiting for Ricky to open Stan's door first and then come around to my side of the car and open mine.

But I switch gears and ask Raj about the sarong. He grins at me and says, "Rhonda, it's called a *lungi* and it can be worn as a skirt or a turban."

I say, "Do you wear one?" He looks shocked.

"No, Rhonda, men from southern India wear the *lungi* or *surkha*. My family is from northern India."

Today is our final day to tour residential properties, grocery stores, hospitals, children's shops, and malls. It's a supersized list, but Raj is confident we can accomplish every task—it's going to be one long day.

Currently we've stopped at the Navi Mumbai coastline, watching the Arabian Sea and inhaling the nastiest air I've ever smelled in my entire life. I cover my mouth, gagging. This complex (a third option) facing the water is Stan's favorite property. He wants to live on the tenth floor in this building because it has an ocean view.

The stench is too much. My nostrils are burning. I sprint back to the car, jump in, and shut the door. No point in viewing an apartment I won't live in.

Finally, Ricky cracks a smile as he walks toward the car.

Stanley and Raj discuss the odor, looking for the source. I peer out the window and see women wearing brightly colored *saris* and lots of gold jewelry. I notice the men are wearing a piece of fabric like the man I hit with my door, except it's drawn through the legs and knotted at the back so I can't see their underwear. But what I do see are thousands of dried fish spread out over several hundred blankets out in the open fields to my left behind the building.

I might vomit.

Stanley and Raj dash back inside the car. Ricky climbs back in too and starts the engine.

He speaks Hindi to Raj and I watch as his facial expression changes from cool to startled. Then Raj speaks English to us: "Ricky spoke to the Kolis, and it's the season for drying fish and shrimp to sell in the markets."

"Who are the Kolis?"

"It's the name of the community of men and women who live in this area, some of the original inhabitants of the city. The season starts in May."

"Several months ago when I scoured this property there were no fish in sight," Stanley says. "How come no one told me about the stench? I almost signed a year's lease on the spot."

Raj does the head wiggle. I laugh this time. Does this mean he knew about the fish and ignored it, or he didn't know about the fish and doesn't want to appear ignorant? This cultural mannerism is irritating me.

I exclaim, "Oh, wait! I met a woman at the AWC coffee and she warned me about this place. I'm just now putting two and two together. She said she wasn't told about the drying season either and they have to light a bunch of candles and make the best of it for the three months."

Stanley shouts, "Three months?"

"Wait a minute...there was one more woman who talked about these fish. She loves her flat so much she never leaves during the smelly months. She has everything delivered, but she doesn't have children. She also leaves during monsoon and doesn't return until the coast is clear, literally. She said it's a steep price to pay for a view."

Frankly, I can't imagine looking directly out over water day after day after day.

Stan, frustrated, looks at me. "I thought we had found the perfect place."

"Glad we're here this month. Can you even fathom?"

Secretly, I am thrilled beyond belief. The video tour of the condo showed a gigantic outdoor balcony with a gap large enough for a small child to easily crawl under and fall down ten levels onto the rocks. Stanley urged me to overlook this issue because Matthew would be watched like a hawk. *I don't think so.*

Raj calls ahead to a broker who wants to show us a new property several blocks over in Bandra, away from the foul odor. Before he hangs up, he informs Stanley we can mark it off the list. The families who live in the building are vegetarians and we eat beef. They don't want us on the premises.

We depart for Santa Cruz and tour the Asian Heart Hospital. It resembles a hospital in the States and gets my vote if the boys have an emergency. While Lilavati Hospital is closer to Khar West and Bandra, it doesn't even compare.

The traffic is roaring and so is the honking. At every traffic signal, muddy kids are banging on the windows for rupees.

We head to Olive Bar and Kitchen—one of the most popular Bollywood restaurants in the city, Raj tells us. Ricky drops us at the front gate and we're ushered up the steps and into a lush courtyard. We don't know anything about Bollywood actors. The only famous Indian actor we could possibly identify is former Miss World, Aishwarya Rai.

We sit indoors because of the heat and are enjoying the air conditioning. The place has a Mediterranean vibe and it's full of beautiful people. I don't see a tunic in sight. I don't see Miss Rai, either.

Everything on the menu and on plates around the room looks scrumptious. I want to do a happy dance when I spot a classic Caesar salad with grilled chicken and bacon listed under lunch entries. I need that salad. Not only will I get my poultry fix, but also, as a windfall, pork! Plus, I'm ordering white wine from France—none of that Indian wine for me today.

"Are you fine with me ordering meat?" I ask. Raj says yes and thanks me for double-checking. Then he orders the cherry tomato, mozzarella, and basil pizza along with juice because he doesn't drink alcohol. Stanley orders pan-seared sea bass with crab butter and a martini.

We frown at Stan. "How can you possibly eat seafood after smelling dried fish and shrimp?"

He shrugs. "I forgot. I'm starving."

The discussion turns to monsoon season. "Last year, it rained so hard and so fast people were trapped in their cars, their homes, at work, and in schools," Raj says. "Trains and buses couldn't run. There was no electricity for three to five days in various parts of the city."

I add, "One of the manicurists in the Taj spa told me all the employees were stranded in the hotel for three days. Hey, I would love to be stranded at the Taj for three days!"

Raj doesn't acknowledge the humor. "Rhonda, it rained ninety-four centimeters in one day. The mobile service was down and 400 people died."

Stanley adds, "That's a little over three feet. It set a world record. Anuj told me he slept at the office along with a number of other employees because the city was at a standstill. Water was up over the cars and buses."

I feel like a complete ass, but I'd never read or heard of this disaster. India never registered on my radar until now.

Thankfully, the waiter delivers our entrées and we can change the subject. As lunch conversation steers toward malls and shops, Raj calls Ricky to bring the car around and Stanley picks up the tab.

We glance at the agenda again. We need to knock out the remaining places in north Mumbai so we can get back down south and finish up. I don't ask how Raj knows about the children's shops, but I keep silent. I've caused enough drama today.

We stop by Kiddy Kids Department Store and the guys sit in the car while I pop inside and take inventory. We all do the same at West View Baby Shop, Shree Ram Medical Store, and Hari Om General Store.

Sunita calls and speaks to Raj on his phone and we're off to Fabindia to talk to a salesperson about drapes, fabric, and installation.

On the way, Ricky stops at a local park that has an airplane made of concrete that kids can climb in. There's no grass—just dirt—and it's locked up daily until about 4:30 p.m. (I make a mental note to ask the pediatrician about mosquitoes and malaria.) Then it's on to Rajesh Khanna Garden, which has a small train children can ride around the grounds for a small fee. But it's closed, too—until 6 p.m. We pass by one more park that Raj calls "Jogger's Park." No fence, a seaside track, two swing sets, and a large slide made of old metal.

I'm dissatisfied. Raj says the best parks are down south and spouts out names like Victoria Gardens and Kamala Nehru. He has to spell out the name of the last one—I can't even pronounce it. I add it to the growing list of places to visit when we move.

On we go. We pass a Kodak Express Store on a street called "Linking," a main road we sure have spent a lot of time on, and stop at Little Wonders (not much in terms of quality clothes or baby food). Visiting Mothercare, a UK-based store selling equipment, toys, and furniture, required a feat of magic. It's at a mall called High Street Phoenix. Between the traffic to enter the complex and the parking dilemma, Ricky at last manages to drop us near the front entrance.

We jump out and Raj reminds Stanley to text when we're ready to leave, as Ricky will pull the car around from the car park. Raj disappears into the crowd towards a store selling men's jeans. Mothercare has the gold mine, but it's extremely expensive. Still, it's better than nothing because I haven't seen anything I could buy in the other shops except poorly-made polyester clothes. Basically, I will need to purchase the baby stuff in Austin and bring it with me.

We pop into Big Bazaar. Stanley tells me it's the largest hypermarket in India, a tad similar to Sam's Club, but on a less significant level.

Two stops are left on the agenda: Breach Candy Club and Bhaghem Bombay.

Breach Candy, another private club, has the country's largest India-shaped swimming pool and houses three restaurants, a state-of-the-art gym, a reading room, three outdoor tennis courts, a basketball court, and a volleyball court. Raj instructs us to sign in as guests and he pays 600 rupees so we can tour the facility. He speaks Hindi to the front desk staffer and I can't take my eyes off the sign stating: "No servants allowed past this point, under

NO circumstances."

A senior-level staffer greets us to discuss membership requirements, the approval process, and annual fees. They seem fairly open to offering us a membership because we're not permanent residents.

I scan the property and it's a European playground—wealthy locals and expatriates galore. I see bikini-clad women sipping cocktails and the salty air whips my hair into massive tangles. It's right on the seafront and it has two kiddy pools. I love this place and the boys will love it as well. Two words come to mind: open space.

Stanley reminds me of the traffic and drive time it will require to get here by car during the week, and more importantly, on the weekends. If we lived south it would be a no-brainer to apply for membership; however, we've set our sights on north Mumbai. It's not a smart move to join.

My heart sinks.

The sun is setting. We order a gin and tonic, a vodka tonic, and mango juice for Raj and plop down into chairs. No dead fish odor. The prices are cheap. I can't believe the variety of kid-friendly food offered, too. This is my kind of place. It's not fancy by any means. Heck, it's not a country club by American standards—it's a beach club. But I didn't grow up with money and my parents could never have afforded to join anything.

I gaze over the Breach Candy paperwork. The club was created under British rule and still has some charm. Lashing waves crash against the shore and it's such a pleasant reprieve from the noise. Raj orders cheese *naans* for us to share and we're smitten when they arrive.

Boy, it's been a whirlwind day!

"I can't believe I leave tomorrow night. It's been eight adventurous days— and tomorrow will make it a total of nine days in your country. I've seen things I've briefly read about in newspapers. I can't stand the honking, and the poverty is worse than I've witnessed in Mexico and Africa." (I skip over the men urinating on the streets.) "It's complex to grasp it all. I'm relieved I took plenty of photos and kept a journal full of notes."

We list our top four condos, in order of preference, and we'll make a final offer on a place once Stan's work contract is signed in two weeks. Anuj advised us to stay clear of buildings near temples or schools since there are a lot of religious holidays and festivals. It's common to get trapped in your flat for long periods of time with road closures when these events happen.

Our last stop is a little retail therapy at Bhaghem Bombay. Raj chats with Harish "Harry" Chellani, whose family has owned the store since the late sixties. After exchanging firm handshakes, Harry sells us more trinkets for the expanding collection of handicrafts I will haul back as gifts for family, employees, and friends.

I notice he sells ornaments perfect for Christmas, and I promise to buy a few packs in several months when I arrive in the city.

We say farewell and he hands us business cards. He doesn't want me to forget where his shop is located in south Mumbai.

Trust me, I won't.

Another two hours stuck in atrocious traffic and Ricky deposits us at the Taj. We gather our shopping bags, and I thank Raj for his assistance. He assures me he's here to help with anything we need.

Inside the suite, we collapse on the bed.

"My senses are dead," I tell Stan. "I'm taking a long, hot shower and putting on pajamas. I can't imagine going out again into...(I point in the direction of the Gateway of India) 'the zoo.' Can we just order room service tonight?"

"Sounds like a magnificent idea, Madam," he says with a smile.

Two glove-wearing butlers deliver dinner. The entrées are exceptional, the imported wine chilled, and the dessert sweet. Within minutes of a quick call to the food and beverage department, all carts and trays are removed.

Full and worn out, I crawl into bed and fall into a deep sleep, dreaming of a marigold-filled, fully furnished, child-friendly royal abode.

5

It's five o'clock in the morning and I'm awake, staring at the ceiling.

Stanley is in full-snore mode as I roll out of bed, pull the drapes back, and peer out the window. I spot a woman wearing a purple tunic, red MC Hammer pants, and yellow sneakers walking along the sidewalk across from the Gateway to India.

I'm a big runner and the only other joggers I've seen are tourists, I presume. I'm delighted to see a local fitness buff. Stanley and I had discussed joining the JW Marriott Club in order to gain access to a gym and a private pool, but the fitness facility is in the basement.

I open a Diet Pepsi, compliments of Ganesh, who stopped at a random store the other night since I drink it like water. I won't ever forget strutting up to that particular corner shack...a Bob Seger song played in my head while I watched the locals go about their nightly moves. A teenager bought one cigarette and then lit it with an orange Bic lighter tied to a piece of yellow string nailed to the store's side counter.

Two drunken male teenagers, arms wrapped around each other, bought five packs of *paan*, a mixture of betel leaf, lime, areca nut, clove, cardamom, mint, and tobacco. At first I thought they were buying condoms, but then I remembered Raj giving a rather extensive talk about the *paan* addiction. Also, we're told it's typical for Hindu men to walk around the city holding hands or showing affection to one another as a sign of friendship.

Who knew?

In my hotel room, I take another big sip of Diet Pepsi and study the room service breakfast menu. Then I grab a journal and pen out of my handbag as my OCD kicks in.

I need to make a list of everything the AWC ladies told me to pack, even though I haven't signed on the dotted line:

- Documents: photocopies of photographs, the boys' vaccination
  records, and birth certificates. Don't bring originals since acquiring

replacements while living abroad if documents are lost or stolen is lengthy.
- Clothes and shoes: infant and small children's necessities are extremely limited.
- General items:
  - hand sanitizer, children's medicine (cold, allergy, flu), face-cleansing gel, Q-tips
  - high-end wine openers and cooking knives
  - wine and hard liquor (the maximum amount allowed by the shipping gods)
  - linens (pillowcases, sheets, pillows)
  - pots, pans, cooking utensils, cutting boards
  - garbage bags, Ziplocs
  - cosmetics, perfume, hairspray, shampoo, conditioner, toothpaste
  - feminine hygiene products, panty liners, Playtex tampons
  - Tylenol, Alka-Seltzer, Tums, vitamins, Visine, Preparation H
  - a safe for valuables
  - a calendar, notebooks, acid-free scrapbooks, tape, art supplies
  - shaving mirror for shower, razors, shaving cream
  - DVDs, children's books in English
  - diapers, wipes
  - laptops, cameras, power-surge protectors, adapters, iPod Minis
  - duct tape, tool kit, extension cords, batteries and SIM cards for cameras
  - tennis rackets, tennis balls
  - rain gear
  - cleaning supplies, paper towels
  - canned artichokes, canned shrimp, canned smoked oysters
  - boxed rice, boxed stuffing, Kraft Macaroni & Cheese, power bars
  - gifts for the boys for birthdays and holidays for a year
  - business cards detailing our India contact information
  - SANITY!

Stanley suddenly stirs but continues snoozing. I peek out the window again and the city is stirring too. I can almost smell rain through the glass.

Then, I write a vocabulary list of British equivalents used in India:
- car for hire—rental car
- cash bin—ATM
- chemist—pharmacist
- daily—newspaper
- function—event
- holiday—vacation
- lift—elevator
- loo—bathroom
- mobile—cell phone

- shop—store
- starters—appetizers
- takeaway—takeout
- taxi—cab
- trainers—sneakers or tennis shoes
- trolley— shopping cart

My train of thought is interrupted by an alarm. Stanley has set his phone for 6:30 a.m. to speak to his boss in Dallas before I leave. He will stay behind for more than a week to handle work commitments. He springs up and sprints to the shower. Just as quickly, he's out and talking rapidly about something to do with international business.

Breakfast arrives and our thoughts drift to a game plan: lease our house...sell our cars...move in August, but spend time during monsoon back in Texas...travel internationally during school holidays.

We take a quick moment to call the boys to tell them goodnight.

Stanley takes a call from Shobhit on his cell phone. He excuses himself from the table and then promptly returns to say he's hiring an MBA student to work in the office and a new secretary. In his mind, our trip is over and he's focused on work.

Curious, I inquire what an MBA student in the land of call centers might make?

"Exactly 12,000 US dollars, Madam."

Shocked, I think back to my first job out of college as the director of public relations for the YMCA of Austin. I earned $20,500 my first year of employment while I tried to pay back student loans.

"Well, you both know what it's like to live without a lot of things."

With breakfast finished, we leave the hotel to start my last day in India, but we immediately pop into a shop behind the Taj to avoid the gypsies hounding us for rupees and the vendors wanting us to purchase everything from large balloons to coloring books to plastic necklaces.

I'm in luck—it's a small food store. Jars of baby food are triple the US prices. The owner speaks perfect English to me when I inquire about where to purchase milk, bacon, and beef. He shows me the non-refrigerated Nestlé boxes of skim or whole milk. Then he shows me a tiny refrigerator filled with processed cheese and local butter. I can purchase sliced pork at any five-star hotel for many, many rupees. I should get eggs delivered to my flat and this would be the best, very best way to go.

(For the record, I don't drink milk. I gave it up at the age of two, but my boys love it. I will need to purchase boxed milk by the truckload along with bottled water.)

My head is spinning when we leave the store, but with contact information in hand I feel validated. We stop by a few small stalls where Stanley barters for shirts and belts. We move on and slip into a pharmacy and discover we can purchase most medications without a prescription.

Priceless.

We pass a small furniture store and venture in. The owner has a binder he presents with photos of various patio stools and tables made of wicker or wood that we can order. Most of the ethnic sofas and chairs in the showroom are exceedingly uncomfortable. I take his business card as we leave.

We flag down a taxi, jump in, and hand the driver a business card from the Taj concierge. He takes us directly to an antique store selling high-end British Colonial pieces. Overrated. We leave sorely disappointed.

I have no idea how I will furnish a flat. It makes no sense for us to bring any furniture to India because Trammell Crow Company will give us a generous moving allowance for purchasing household goods. But where do you buy durable, comfortable furniture in Mumbai?

We're told monsoon starts in Goa. The daily light showers become full-force winds, and gusts of water pound each coastal town before heading north. I can see how the city needs a big power wash, because dirt and dust cover every square inch of space. But we don't know what to anticipate. I'm terrified to think of life in a flat with a four-year-old and an infant during the torrential rains.

Famished, we treat ourselves to a sushi lunch at Wasabi by Morimoto. The authentic culinary treasures from the repertoires of Iron Chef Morimoto are flown down from Japan. The food is astonishing, and, unlike other local establishments we've visited on this excursion, there are no Willy Nelson tunes and no theme from *Titanic* playing in the background through shady speakers.

Before Stanley finishes his sake, I broach the subject of bringing along an American nanny to help with the transition for the first several months. I conjured up this idea before I left but didn't bring up the subject until I could propose it to a few friends in Austin and women at the AWC coffee. They were optimistic about the scheme but were concerned about how exactly I would need to refer to this person due to the caste system.

Stanley doesn't know why I need a babysitter for anything. Clearly, Stanley doesn't get it. Then it dawns on me that I will need reinforcements, but that debate is for another time. The rest of the afternoon we spend visiting the Prince of Wales Museum. After I purchase the last pair of *jootis* (Indian handcrafted leather slippers locally tanned using vegetable dyes) for less than three dollars and more cheap bangles, we retire back to the suite.

While Stanley checks me in to my 1:50 a.m. flight to Zürich on Swiss Air, I drop my shopping bags and confirm my spa treatment on the room phone.

"What? I thought you hated the Jiva spa, Madam!"

"Listen, Stanley. I'm back and forth like a crazy person about this venture and I'm rolling the dice simply because I can't deal with the magnitude of it all. One second I'm out and the next I'm back in the game.

"I thought hard during this expedition about quality of life, and if I'm frazzled every day all day *without* the boys, I don't think I can handle the complexity of life *with* them. It's a yo-yo of extreme highs and lows.

"Heck, I didn't know life could be this tense anywhere, even though I'm praying every day for understanding to any god who will listen and respond.

"So take note. Do comprehend you're asking me to move across the world and set up a homestead while you spend seventy-five percent of your time in the office and flying to other cities. Hear me when I say the enormous scale of challenges frustrates me.

"I'm making one final attempt to relax. I pray it will unwind the ball of stress in my temples and the knot in my stomach."

You could have heard a pin drop.

At exactly 5 p.m., I depart the suite en route to the spa for the ultimate *champi* (Indian head massage). Duration: forty-five minutes.

Kiran, a spa employee, greets me in the small lobby. He leads me to a separate room where I'm told to change into a comfy robe and place my clothing and shoes into an upscale cabinet.

He senses my nervousness and leaves the room while I muster up nerve to proceed. I don't see any teak planks in sight, and I'm highly impressed by the fifteen burning candles plus the fragrant incense. The lights are dim and the room temperature is perfect. I stretch out onto a cozy massage table and unwind.

However, for some reason I can still hear the honking and congestion on the streets. We must be somewhere near the rear of the property, but I like what I see and a part of me really wants this experiment to be successful.

I'm snuggled up under a light silk and cotton throw, and Kiran reenters the room. He greets me again and discusses my treatment. He's calm and his demeanor puts me at ease. He tells me he's the top *champi* masseur and he knows this is my first visit to India.

Hmm.

I start to speak, but he motions for silence while he explains the ingredients (*amla, brahmi, jatamansi,* curry leaves, and *neem*) he's mixing together in a bowl, which he declares will transmit long-lasting and enriching benefits to my hair and scalp.

I hope the benefits will last during the flight home.

Kiran says the massage will also release muscular tension from the neck and shoulders, creating a deep sense of relaxation and joy.

I giggle.

Lowering my voice, I say, "Did you just proclaim you'll give me joy? This country might be the perfect place for me yet."

He cracks a smile, but I can tell he's a man of integrity, and he means business, so I never utter another sound.

Immediately, he rings a small bell.

Silence.

Then he gets to work.

He drips warm oil on my forehead and repeats the process over and over as the tension gently releases. Then, he places manly hands on my shoulders and rubs generously.

Honestly, I could do this forever.

Music begins to play softly in the background and Kiran performs magic on me. I feel warmth, comfort. He drips and weaves fragrant oil into my head of long hair and slowly his large hands carry out precise moves, extracting every ounce of tension that wants to linger. I no longer take notice of any outside noise; just the beating of my own heart.

I inhale. I exhale.

I inhale. I exhale.

I don't wiggle. I don't cough.

I inhale. I exhale.

I inhale. I exhale.

I don't think about all the other things I could be doing, like I usually do during massages.

I inhale. I exhale.

I inhale. I exhale.

I find myself letting go. This process continues until I can't control my own thoughts.

I inhale. I exhale.

I am just in this moment.

I inhale. I exhale.

I inhale. I exhale.

I feel the sensation of floating outside of my body.

I inhale. I exhale.

I inhale. I exhale.

I look down. I do not recognize the girl on the table. She is a shell of her former self.

I inhale. I exhale.

I inhale. I exhale.

I inhale. I exhale.

I inhale. I exhale.

I am at peace.

I inhale. I exhale.

I inhale. I exhale.

Kiran gently nudges me.

I inhale. I exhale.

I inhale. I exhale.

I can't move. In fact, I don't flinch.

I inhale. I exhale.

I inhale. I exhale.

Kiran gently nudges me, again.

I open my eyes. I'm back on the table and the treatment is over. I sit up, not sure of what just transpired, but I feel a sense of stillness I haven't felt in a very long time. Did I just surrender to a higher power?

Kiran grins and bows.

"I might be moving here in three months, and, while I'm opposed to the transition, something is forcing me to take note. All signs are pointing me to your India."

His response: "Madam, we all take various roads, but amid the chaos, there is harmony."

I'm taken aback. "Wait, is this an intervention?"

Kiran looks confused.

"*Namaste*, Madam."

"*Namaste*, Kiran."

I don't want to change out of my robe. I slowly pick up my clothes in the women's lounge and sashay to the elevator as hotel guests stare.

Stan, finishing up several emails, is in shock when I glide into the suite—glowing from head to toe.

"Well, how did it go?"

Calmly I declare, "Lying on that massage table, I thought about my life, realizing I have never truthfully found out what personally makes my heart sing since I became a stay-at-home mother."

"Wow, you got that from your head massage appointment?"

"Actually, I've tried to live my life without regrets, but at times I wish I'd acted with greater courage. But I didn't. What I'm trying to say is when we had our boys, your life didn't change, but mine sure did.

"India is forcing me to slow down, to live in the moment—which I haven't done in years. You want to know what I think about it?"

Stanley shrugs.

"Bring it on!"

6

Five hours and 34,000 feet into my nine-hour flight to Zürich on Swiss Air 6315, the Ambien wears off. I'm displeased—everyone in business class, including a flight attendant, is asleep.

We land and the Kloten Airport is sterile. It's sophisticated and bustling, but apparently casual and lethargic in the wee morning hours on weekends. There is not a single employee in sight to serve breakfast of any kind. (I could not stomach the airplane curry.)

I swiftly head to my next gate, board the plane, drink two glasses of champagne, and pop the other half of the sleeping pill.

En route to Dallas, I'm seated beside an Indian businessman who works for Dell. I only guess this because he's wearing a Dell golf shirt, sporting a Dell backpack, and he's rapidly typing on a Dell computer before we taxi down the runway.

I don't share with him that Stanley attended Michael Dell's bachelor party and hired Susan Lieberman to work for Trammell Crow Company out of concern the talking might begin. However, he pays me no attention until he wakes up to find me straddled across his lap in an attempt to go to the bathroom. While sneaking out from the window seat over the various chargers and Dell apparatuses plugged in, including into my outlets, I've snagged something. It's his headset cord.

Awkward.

The minute I return to my seat, I re-wrap my pashmina around my body and lose contact with reality.

Channing picks me up from Austin-Bergstrom International Airport. She's chipper and wants to talk all things India. She's normally very calm, but she wants to know *everything* about my trip. Pronto. She has no clue my senses are thrashed to a pulp and my immune system is hanging on for dear life.

She badgers me until I finally give in on the way to my house.

"I spoke in tongues," I said. "Bombay and Mumbai...I don't know what to call the city...I said *bathroom* but it was the *loo*...I was a complete stress ball, but then there were moments of clarity—like I sure could roll with the thought of having a cook, a driver, a nanny, a tennis instructor, and a yoga master...But as I've said before, I don't know how to find these people...I met AWC members so hopefully I'll gain a few new friends...I think I might need to talk about food a lot and that doesn't make me happy...Stanley will be gone working all the time...But I know there is an education for us in living abroad...Oh, I had two panic attacks—one after I was just about molested in a spa, of all places...You know me, normally I'm a cheerleader for worldwide travel, but moving to a developing country won't be a picnic—"

Channing cuts me off. "Cheer-Spice, go for it. If anyone can do it, you can. Have faith in yourself. Stanley will take care of the finances, and you will take care of the rest. I'm betting my money on you."

Then it dawns on me. Her life and the lives of all my other friends will proceed without me.

A mile from the neighborhood, she wants to know what fears I have about moving.

"Channing, I will lose all privacy and freedom. I now fear for my safety since a stranger grabbed my boob. Matthew and Grant might catch any number of diseases and die. I don't think anyone will visit, even if we do remain alive and well. It will be unbelievably lonely. The grandparents have already declared they will never set foot in Mumbai. Do I need to say more?"

Channing adds, "None of the grandparents visit Austin anyway, and you're certainly not going to catch diseases and die. And you said so yourself, there are millions of people in the city. Loneliness is a non-issue."

We arrive in Westlake, an affluent suburb on the west side of Austin, and, boy, summer is around the corner—it's a whopping 100 degrees. I might need back surgery after carrying my stuffed suitcases. It takes the two of us to drag them one by one inside the house.

"Thanks for picking me up, Channing," I say, giving her a hug. "Have a fun time at happy hour."

Bob and Sheri return my phone call later in the evening. They'll drop the boys off tomorrow before lunch, allowing me some down time to acclimate. I'm blessed by their friendship, too.

I unpack, wash clothes, and sort every gift into piles for various folks. Cyndie, one of my BFFs, kindly drops off Chardonnay and Stubbs BBQ for dinner because the refrigerator is empty. Super generous.

I no longer smell like India after a steamy hot shower and then a warm bubble bath, but of course she's still very much on my mind.

I'm trying to head off jet lag and stay up as late as I can. I send Stanley an email letting him know I'm safe and sound back in Texas and reply to one from my mother. She wants to know about my trip.

I can't comprehend why she's even inquiring. She loathes India, having garnered an opinion from reading *National Geographic* articles. I'm still upset she and my stepdad won't visit the grandkids while we're abroad.

I write:

> *The first two days were culture shock. It's like landing in Miami and Las Vegas rolled into one, but the strain on your senses is unimaginable. The smell of urine combined with the heat sucks the oxygen out of you. Every day, millions of humans are going (and going) back and forth on the roads. It takes hours and hours to do any small transaction, like purchasing a book or ordering lunch. There is a huge middle class forming, and locals make decent money, but cost of living is high. The government taxes food, liquor, and service. One of our boozy lunch bills had forty dollars' worth of taxes on it! Every day I saw shanty-lined streets, motorists sharing the roads with cows, auto rickshaws, beggars, motorbikes carrying entire families, food stalls on sidewalks, unfinished construction sites, and children begging for milk. I'm positive thousands of people stared at me daily as I inhaled the nastiest air pollution—probably equivalent to smoking four packs of cigarettes. I can't describe the honking, the nonstop, unbearable honking. However, I agree with Stan: the people are real nice.*

Then I hit SEND.

I set the alarm and snuggle into the comfort of my own bed. The second my head hits the pillow I'm fast asleep.

7

Jet lag is here. It barged into the bedroom, demanding my attention before the sun was up, and so I creep out from under the covers.

I decide to go for a morning jog around Town Lake on the hike and bike trail, one of the city's true gems. I need fresh air—motivation for the day.

Austin, the capital, is a paradox, because it isn't like the rest of Texas. It's "green," but old hippies now rub elbows with high-tech geeks. It's traditional but cutting edge, casual yet sophisticated, a college town, and home to state government. Plus, it's the only city in Texas with bragging rights for housing the best Chicken Shit Bingo (Jenny's Little Longhorn), the largest urban bat colony (Congress Avenue Bridge), and the longest-running music series in American television history (*Austin City Limits*).

Austinites two-step to their own tune, and we wouldn't have it any other way.

I park my car under Mopac Bridge off Stratford Drive, do a few stretches and some warm-up exercises like the man I saw near the Gateway of India. I select my "Hydrate" playlist and mosey on down the dirt trail.

I pass several friends jogging with their dogs. I wave but keep moving as the Pointer Sisters' "Jump (for My Love)" literally blares out of my ear buds. I'm so in love with Austin, and I just don't know if it's possible I will ever love India.

My pace suddenly slows to a crawl as "The Dance" by Garth Brooks begins to play, and the words take me back to high school prom and "country and western" dance nights during college at Midnight Rodeo.

I speed past a dog walker mismanaging seven pugs and hit my stride as the Psychedelic Furs play "Pretty in Pink." I can't help but chuckle out loud. This song takes me back to junior prom.

I race past the South Lamar Bridge and continue on to the First Street Bridge.

Stevie Nicks' "Stand Back" takes me to a new fitness level. I increase my speed. I have no idea at this point if I'm running to or away from our decision to move.

Thank God, Billy Idol kicks in for my final half-mile down the trail past the YMCA, and I'm "Dancing with Myself."

Before I know it, I'm home, showered, and on my way to Barnes & Noble. Barely missing a family of four deer crossing the street in my neighborhood, I'm on a mission before the boys get home, and I'm well aware I'm driving over the legal speed limit. I'm out of practice. Not sure I comprehend how Indian drivers weave around cows and pedestrians without causing fatal accidents, but I won't drive in India. Raj told me if you crash into a cow, you don't ever get to leave the country.

Lovely.

I whisk into the store and on to the travel section. I'm on a quest to find relevant material to tell me precisely what I need to do to make our move, but all I see are guidebooks. The selection of sources about traveling to Asia for fun is huge, including one book called *Holy Cow*, an expat novel about an Australian who moves to Delhi with her boyfriend.

I thumb through the pages and it looks interesting, but I'm married and I have a two small kids. I set the book down. (Little do I know that in six months I will recognize it at a tiny in-house shop at the Taj Mahal Palace Hotel and snap it up. I will madly read it over the course of four days searching for answers to all the unwritten arbitrary rules foreigners must follow.)

I flag down a salesperson and explain my situation. She is dumbfounded. She searches the racks of books and comes up with nothing. Quickly a light-bulb goes off and she sprints away and returns with *Culture Shock! India: A Survival Guide to Customs and Etiquette* by Gitanjali Kolanad.

It's all she's got. I pay for it and leave.

I get home with one hour to spare before Sheri drops off my little guys and so I leaf through the book.

It begins with first impressions. Been there, done that. Then it discusses practical aspects such as setting up your accommodation, utilities, telecommunications, and healthcare. Not there yet. Then it instructs all newcomers to immerse themselves into the food and language.

Well, maybe that diarrhea counted for something—right? And didn't I speak a little Hindi, once or twice?

"Getting the Message" is an informative section dedicated to the introduction of language. It states an estimated 28 million people speak English (or some version of it). The section also discusses calculation: a *lakh* is a hundred thousand dollars (written 1,00,000 instead of 100,000) and a *crore* is ten million dollars (written 1,00,00,000 instead of 10,000,000). Naturally, I'll need Stan's help to do currency conversion because I can do a lot of things, but finance is not one of them.

I examine the section called "Body Language." Printed on the page is "The Indian does not as a rule use toilet paper, and considers it a dirty habit. Rather, after using the toilet, water and the left hand are used to effect cleaning. Although the hand is then scrupulously washed, it is believed to retain something of its polluting quality." I hold up my left hand in front of my face and shake my head in disbelief.

One of the last sections, "India at a Glance," provides tidbits of basic information: climate, ethnic groups, industries, and exports. I'm feeling pretty fine about myself when I scan the "Do's and Don'ts" bullet points. It appears I didn't completely do a horrible job when in Rome.

Having said that, I focus and delve deeper into the "Culture Quiz" section.

> *Situation 7: While visiting a village in South India, you decide to take an evening stroll through the paddies. As you walk, squatting figures all around you stand up, looking decidedly uncomfortable. Should you be worried?*

> 1. No, they are just stretching their legs.
> 2. Yes, they're muggers, just waiting for the unsuspecting foreigner.
> 3. Not really, but you should still get out of there as quickly as you can.

Official Call: according to the author, the fields around a village are often used as toilets, and you have interrupted day laborers in the middle of a bodily function (which, given modesty, won't be completed until you scoot away).

I study it. I read it one more time. We won't be living in South India, but I suspect most certainly we will visit the region including Goa again.

Thankfully, at this moment and going forward, we know how to roll in a village.

> *Situation 8: An Indian friend takes you visiting to various neighbors. At each and every house, as soon as you enter, the hostess presents a tray with glasses of mango juice, chai, or just plain tap water. When you're offered a drink, you...*

> 1. Ask, "Has this water been boiled and filtered?"
> 2. Pray silently to the patron saint of hepatitis, cholera, and dysentery, and gulp it all down.
> 3. Take a glass, but never actually take a sip. Lift it up, put it down, bring it almost to your lips, but stop because you just thought of something to say, and perhaps carry on like that until your visit is over.

I'm baffled. The answer is: all of the above. I did all three on my visit, to the point where I finally told anyone who attempted to hand me any liquid, "I only drink Diet Pepsi," and it stopped the madness, although it did not stop the bowel explosions.

Now I have a pounding headache. I take two Advil tablets and shelve the book in my study. I swear off culture-shock talk until Stanley gets home in a week.

Sheri arrives with Grant and Matthew. It's wonderful to see my little guys. I bring in their suitcases and the huge haul of toys Sheri has bought for them. The boys give me hugs and kisses, and then Grant takes Matthew straight to the playroom with a few of the new toys.

I download with Sheri about the trip, which she already knows about given how much we checked in on the boys. Before she says her goodbyes, she wants to know one thing. "Did you approach Stanley about taking a nanny to help with the children while you set up the flat and get your bearings?"

"I did, and he didn't seem to think there's a need, so I pushed the notion aside."

"Well, we'll see about that. I'll talk to Bob and the four of us will have dinner in a few weeks."

I allow the boys to play a bit longer before we go to HEB, a local grocery store.

Once inside, Matthew gets locked into the flip-up child seat and Grant stuffs himself onto the tray underneath the cart, and off we go. A thought crosses my mind—if I had a driver, perhaps I could have left these dudes in the car to do a little solo shopping, eh?

We waltz down each aisle very slowly and I touch every fresh vegetable on the premises. Dare I say the strawberries look gorgeous? Oh, how I missed American grocery stores. I didn't see a fraction of the inventory and selection in Indian shops. When I start to drool at the deli-meat counter and then wig out over the sausage, steak, bison filets, seasoned chicken cutlets, lobster, and scallops at the meat/seafood counter, I know it's time to go.

Driving home, there's another near miss with a second family of deer. I cook a late lunch of chateaubriand, baked potatoes, green beans, and macaroni and cheese. For the finale, I bake homemade brownies for dessert. We feast like good-natured royalty.

By the time the boys finish an early-evening swim and a Disney movie, it's bedtime.

Madam is dog-tired.

Matthew goes down easily because Sheri has a crib in her house, since her grandkids visit often. She's kept him on a schedule—*hugely important* in the parenting world.

Grant brushes his teeth and then grabs a book from his bookshelf. I switch on the lamp on his nightstand and we both snuggle into the sheets. He's selected *Harold and the Purple Crayon* (one of my favorites).

We dive into the text, a parable about making your own way in the world. I know Grant is too young to understand the connection, but this story resonates with me because growing up I always felt alone. My parents struggled and finally divorced. For a long time, I believed I only had myself to rely on, but I'm here to tell you—that burden is grueling.

As I reach the end of the story, Grant is sleepy.

Harold remembers where his bedroom window was, when there was a moon. Then he drops off to sleep.

I turn the lamp off but leave the closet light on and give him a kiss goodnight. I set the security alarm and walk upstairs. I check on Matthew and he's snoring in the nursery.

Now I'm ready for bed. I change into my pajamas, remove my makeup, and apply tons of moisturizer. I look out the bathroom window and lo and behold, there is a large crescent-shaped moon shining brightly in the dark sky over the city tonight. I stare out the window.

I inhale. I exhale.

I inhale. I exhale.

Out of nowhere, I'm back in my pink-and-blue bedroom in yellow pajamas peering out from underneath Holly Hobbie drapes at the moon, listening to my parents argue down the hallway.

And then it dawns on me: everywhere Harold goes, every page he walks across, the moon goes with him. Harold wasn't alone. Maybe I'm not either.

8

It's been two months since the Bombay trip, and I feel like folks around me are living in a vacuum. Am I the only one except Stanley who understands the consequences of our actions? We're moving to a developing country and it seems the only two things our friends want to do are throw back cocktails in our honor and take us downtown to chow on lamb vindaloo. In their minds, we've signed up for an enormous Bollywood party and they're happily along for the ride—that is until we go, because no one mentions a visit while they're sober.

Fortunately, I enrolled the boys in a variety of summer camps while we work and take care of business.

The India to-do list is long, and this is one of those rare occasions when my OCD comes in handy. In fact, Stan's OCD and ADD kick into overdrive and we get the Erwin game plan down, playing to win, just like Bill Walsh and Joe Montana.

Under Madam's Jurisdiction

- Purchase a postal box
- Sign Grant's ASB enrollment letter and email it to Anne
- Order a forty-foot container to ship our goods
- Clean out the garage and attic ("Donate and Purge" is my theme song)
- Clean out every nook and cranny inside the house (if it hasn't been used in two years, it doesn't belong in the storage unit or crate. C'est la vie!)
- Price-shop storage unit facilities (we'll be renting for one to five years, so we need a year-to-year rental agreement)
- Prepare and schedule the house for a photo session for a brochure
- Mail a letter to the Headliner's Club (requesting approval for a leave of absence)

- Schedule doctor appointments
- Schedule dental appointments
- Schedule vaccination appointments with Pro Med clinic
- Order medications from the pharmacy (insurance has allowed a year's supply of prescriptions to be filled)
- Schedule baptism services for Matthew at Westlake Hills Presbyterian Church
- Ongoing sorting of things to store, pack, or donate

What Boss Covers

- Complete the TCC/India business plan
- Finalize a work agreement with Anuj
- Finalize tax agreements/contracts with Deloitte & Touche
- Research credit cards charging the least amount of interest on conversion rates
- Interview property managers
- Business trip to India (sign our housing contract, collect information on opening Citibank accounts, inquire about final registration with the Foreigner Regional Registration Office, inquire about cell phones)
- List the house in order to sell or lease
- Letter to American Consulate General (ACG—Approval of Non-Resident Status)
- Finalize a storage unit agreement
- Visit the Cooper Clinic in Dallas for a corporate health checkup
- Ongoing packing

Despite the temperatures having hit all-time highs (more than 105 degrees Fahrenheit), the first week of August brings reprieve from the sun and the boys finally enjoy cool pool time while late afternoon breezes flow.

Stanley returns from his business trip to India—the last one he will take from the River City, with great news: we have an official Indian residence. Turns out two favorites were undersold from us to French couples that agreed to higher rental terms, and so it came down to the fish flat or my beloved 3,000-square-foot flat overlooking Khar Gymkhana Club, the winner by default.

Score!

But the good news included rather harsh news: Stanley has yet to finalize his work agreement, despite signing a lease on behalf of the partnership for our new living space. Yes, you read that correctly. We're eradicating our belongings and vacating our house, and Stan's compensation package is still up in the air.

Later, he informs me he had no choice but to negotiate a lease. It was sign on the dotted line, or start the search over.

Maybe now this will light a fire under a few company butts.

Tick-tock. Tick-tock.

I'm perturbed beyond belief and it shows on my face. My pal cystic acne has returned with friends and is forcing me to visit my dermatologist, Dr. Ramsdell, on a weekly basis for cortisone shots, the only thing that makes them disappear without leaving scars.

For once I want to hear an update from Stanley—that *every t* is crossed and *every i* is dotted by the same business partners who wanted me to land at the airport at night so I couldn't see the poverty or filth.

"This is *our* life!" I yell. "When will they sign the contract? Because the ball is rolling, Boss!"

A week later, I'm out with Annika, a Swedish friend and former model. Her daughter Isabelle attended the Presbyterian preschool with Grant. As mothers, we've bonded during playdates, children's birthday parties, sushi lunches, dirty diapers, and five-o'clock happy hours, not necessarily in that order.

Over dinner at Manuel's downtown on South Congress, a contemporary setting serving dishes from Mexico's interior and coastal regions, we're chatting with co-owner Ahmad Modoni and sipping margaritas.

"Annika, I reminded Stanley that now Grant is enrolled in ASB, we're on the school calendar. A big reason I said okay to this was that we'd leave promptly in August. We have to go on my time frame, but the company is not cooperating. I'm furious about negotiations coming and going. Honestly, they've already paid a huge chunk of tuition and wired a year's rent for a flat. Why can't they get it together and settle his deal?"

"Calm thyself. It will all work out, honey," she says, taking a sip of her El Patrón margarita.

"No, you don't understand. Let me be clear. This is unfair. I don't want to start off being treated like my opinion and needs don't matter. No other company employees wanted to go to Bombay. Remember?"

"Honey, breathe."

"Okay, I'll be frank. Stan's bosses are much older. No one has kids in preschool or elementary school or even middle school. I'm bitter, because I'm the one making sacrifices and lying to the teachers about fall enrollment."

"Rhonda, please breathe. You've got to just take it one day at a time or you're going to have a stroke, girlfriend. It will all work out in the end like I keep saying. Grant's only in preschool and he won't miss much.

"Think about all the servants you're going to have, and that should erase the tension," she adds.

Fine.

We order another margarita, and Ahmad sends over complimentary flan. Over dessert, Annika suggests I throw a going-away party called Bombay or Bust.

Sounds ideal. Add that to my list, Swedish Babe. Because I sure need more to do.

The check arrives and before we leave, I share the latest update: "Buyers call every day talking price wars, but we can't pull the plug. We just don't want to lose our home in case the India deal tanks, so we re-listed the house as rental property. At least that makes me feel better."

And, on that note, we call it quits.

Stanley and I have kept up our nightly meetings after the boys go to bed to evaluate lists. He brings the Excel spreadsheets and elaborate graphs to the table; I bring rainbow-colored pens and a thick white legal pad—and somehow we conquer the ongoing task of organizing the move.

One evening I revisit the subject of taking an American nanny to India. One of our current sitters, Fiona, finalized her divorce a month ago and is looking for more full-time work. She would be a great candidate for our overseas job.

Stanley tries to talk over me, but I hold up my right hand. He stops. I give my twenty-five-second spiel on the benefits of a nanny and how it will change his life, and I tell him to think about it because I'm not backing down.

I also want to talk about what items to pack with our shoes, clothes, linens, and bedding when the crate arrives. An hour later, the list is complete:

~~~~~~

"Texas to India via the Houston Ship Channel"

- 5 cases toilet paper (Charmin 3-ply)
- 4 cases Bounty paper towels
- 5 cases Pampers Baby Fresh Baby Wipes
- 12 cases Huggies Snuggle & Dry Disposable Diapers (sizes 5, 6)
- 3 cases Ziploc sandwich bags
- 4 cases Ziploc quart bags
- 3 cases Ziploc gallon bags
- 2 Cases Tall Kitchen garbage bags
- 2 First Aid Kits
- 20 boxes Waterproof Band-Aids
- 52 boxes Playtex tampons
- 30 boxes panty liners
- 4 boxes Q-tips
- 2 gallons hand sanitizer
- 25 bars Dove soap
- 10 decorative paper napkin packages
- 100 plastic disposable plastic sippy cups
- 8 rolls plastic wrap
- 20 rolls aluminum foil
- 10 boxes SOS pads
- 4 cases Kleenex
- 25 Scotch-Brite sponges

- 5 boxes Depend Super Plus Absorbency Underwear, Small
- 100 clothespins
- 100 clothes hangers
- 2 outdoor clothing lines
- 1 ironing board
- 1 iron
- 4 gallons Mylanta
- 15 bottles Tums
- 10 bottles Tylenol
- 2 bottles fish oil
- 2 bottles multivitamins
- 15 tubes Colgate toothpaste
- 13 boxes Alka-Seltzer
- 10 boxes Preparation H
- 3 bottles Kaopectate
- 3 small toddler inflatable pools
- 4 pairs swim goggles
- 9 pool toys
- 2 life jackets (infant and toddler)
- 15 cans Off! Deep Woods insect repellent
- 4 bottles Bullfrog insect repellent
- 8 bottles insect repellent with DEET
- 12 bottles Banana Boat Ultra Mist Sport SPF 50
- 8 bottles Benadryl
- 15 bottles Coppertone Water Babies SPF 50

- 5 sticks Coppertone Water Babies SPF 55
- 10 bottles Coppertone sunscreen lotion SPF 8
- 8 cans Neutrogena Oil-Free Moisture with sunscreen
- 825 L'il Critters Gummy Vites
- 7 bottles Dimetapp Cold/Allergy Relief Liquid
- 10 bottles Tylenol Pain Reliever and Fever Reducer for Infants
- 10 bottles Caladryl
- 1 bottle hydrogen peroxide
- 5 bottles baby oil
- 8 cans Nutramigen formula
- 15 cans Nutramigen powder
- 8 bottles Olay Moisturizer SPF 15
- 3 bottles Neutrogena Oil-Free Makeup Remover
- 10 sticks Lady Speed Stick Antiperspirant
- 12 Gillette Venus razors
- 4 cans shaving cream
- 10 bottles Visine
- 5 bottles shampoo
- 8 bottles conditioner

- 1 case of red wine
- 1 case of California Chardonnay
- 3 bottles Tanqueray gin
- 3 bottles Bacardi white rum
- 3 bottles Absolut vodka
- 5 boxes of Barilla spaghetti
- 1 case of Kraft Mac and Cheese
- 40 jars Gerber baby food (various vegetables, fruits, 2nd Foods)
- 250 straws
- 200 toothpicks
- 4 boxes Lipton Tea bags
- 6 boxes Splenda
- 303 grams ground Saigon cinnamon
- 3 cases chicken Vienna sausages
- 1 *Necessities and Temptations Junior League of Austin Cookbook*
- 1 *Austin Entertains Junior League of Austin Cookbook*
- 2 sets of dishes (including salad plates, bowls, cups, saucers)
- 1 set silverware
- 1 set kitchen utensils
- 1 set pots and pans
- 6 potholders
- 24 wine glasses
- 3 wine openers
- 12 champagne glasses

- 1 Russian tea set (purchased in St. Petersburg)
- 15 bottles perfume
- 2 cutting boards
- 2 cases hairspray
- 3 bottles men's cologne
- 4 sticks Degree Antiperspirant
- 2 Mach3 Turbo razors
- 16 Mach3 Turbo refills
- 2 brooms
- 2 dust pans
- 1 plunger
- 5 flashlights
- 50 batteries (various sizes)
- 1 filing cabinet
- 1 iPod
- 1 iPod Mini
- 1 Camera
- 1 Dell laptop
- 1 OKI Printer
- 2 OKI C5150N printer cartridges
- 1 paper shredder
- 5 high-end adapters
- 2 power strips
- 1 caulking gun
- 1 drill
- 3 cans WD-40
- 5 rolls duct tape
- 3 rolls masking tape
- 1 large tool chest (screws, nails, tools, picture hangers, taping compound)
- 2 full-size bed frames

- 2 full-size mattresses
- 1 tan sectional
- 1 plaid recliner and ottoman
- 1 antique folding wine table
- 1 dining table
- 6 dining room chairs
- 1 rolling beverage cart
- 1 wine rack
- 1 highchair
- 1 travel highchair
- 1 inflatable cooler
- 1 Pottery Barn baby crib
- 1 Pottery Barn crib mattress
- 1 Pottery Barn rocking chair and ottoman
- 1 Pottery Barn nightstand
- 1 infant potty training chair
- 1 Graco 3-in-1 stroller
- 2 Pottery Barn monogrammed backpacks
- 2 Pottery Barn monogrammed lunch boxes
- 2 monogrammed water bottles
- 2 large boxes (toys)
- 1 large craft box (crayons, glue, markers, tape, stapler, staples, coloring books)
- 1 small box (stationery, cards, journals, photo albums, various paperbacks)

- 1 small box (various office supplies)
- 1 large box (board games, dice, poker chips, cards)
- 1 small box (photocopies of photographs)

- 1 large box (birthday and Christmas gifts for the boys)
- 400 DVDs
- 2 cameras
- 4 SIM cards

- 1 set golf clubs
- 2 tennis rackets
- 6 cans tennis balls
- 1 road bike
- 1 helmet
- 1 safe

Stanley reviews the inventory and has a few questions. "What's the point of taking Coppertone sunscreen SPF 8?"

I retaliate, "What's the purpose of taking a road bike?"

He moves on to the next question.

"What are toddler pools?"

"Well, since there's no tub in the flat, I bought two small inflatable baby pools so Matthew can take a bath from time to time in the shower stall."

I can tell he's impressed since he would have never thought of baby pools.

He has one final question. "Why on earth are you packing five boxes of Depends?

I'm completely amused. "Stanley, I'm packing the Depends for an emergency."

Oh Lord. He's doubled over in stitches. "No. No. Don't tell me. It's for the diarrhea."

I can barely speak. "Silly, it's in case Matthew takes a long time to potty train. I'm not kidding—once we run out of size six Huggies, the next step is to slap an adult small diaper on him. They don't carry extra-large diapers at Mothercare."

And on that note, he ends his interrogation.

The following day, the remaining Container Store plastic bins are labeled, packed, and stacked in the garage.

By the third week of August, Stan's contract negotiations are still dragging on. But I march forward as the forklift roars swiftly to the truck bed at the end of my driveway and sets our container upright. Matthew can't talk but he's gurgling. Grant says, "Mama, it's Bob the Builder." Tears are rolling slowly down my cheeks.

I can't fathom how our precious stuff can leave the premises without a final contract notarized by all parties, but it does.

Two days later, I catch one of those documentaries on CNN about colossal cargo ships that sail around the world with more than 18,000 containers piled twenty high. In my dream that night, my container is the first one to drop off into the deep blue sea after a perfect storm. I wake up around midnight and remember more than 10,000 crates are lost each year.

The next morning after breakfast, with the boys in tow, I deliver donations to Goodwill Central Texas and list our cars to sell in the *Austin American-Statesman*, the local newspaper. Remember, I've got a few trust issues and I hope one of those Hindu gods will help me through it all.

It's Thursday, and early in the evening we leave the boys with Fiona for a Young President's Organization (YPO) event at Tarry House, an Austin jewel of private clubs nestled in Tarrytown. Stanley has been a member of YPO for some time.

After cocktails, we're seated next to Brett Hatton, founder of Four Hands Home, a leading furniture design wholesaler with customers that include Pottery Barn, Restoration Hardware, and the Container Store, for dinner. We've known of Brett and his successes, but this is the first time we've spent quality time with him. He lived in India for three years after traveling the Silk Road—a network of trade routes linking the regions of the ancient world with commerce—before starting his company.

I mention our upcoming adventure, and instantly he takes out a business card, flips it over, writes down two email addresses, and hands it to me. He then inquires about our crate and furnishings.

"The company is giving us a healthy allowance to purchase household items, and we only crated a few things. I don't know how I will furnish the flat we leased. I toured Mumbai in May and I didn't see anything in terms of sturdy chairs or beds to buy."

With a stereotypical British accent, he says, "I love India. Isn't it amazing! The whole country is an assault on your senses and every day is a festival, Rhonda. Actually, I don't think I can explain the country. It has to be felt and it conjures up immense passion—either you love it or hate it. There is no middle ground."

The YPOers at the table are listening attentively.

This is the part where this man makes my day. No—makes my year.

"Rhonda, I just gave you two significant names: Laxman Chand and Cathy Nieddu.

"Laxman runs the Four Hands Home India operations in Jodhpur. Go visit him, stay at the Four Hands house for free, and shop till you drop in all the warehouses.

"Actually, do go visit our Austin showroom before you leave and tell them you want to see every piece of furniture made in India, then make a list of the pieces you want to purchase, and email it to Laxman. He will coordinate the delivery to your building in Mumbai.

"Then, please email Cathy and introduce yourself. Cathy and her husband, Roberto, have lived in Jodhpur for more than fifteen years. They own VJ Home, makers of global innovative wooden furniture, metalwork, and textiles. They live about fifteen minutes from the FH house, and they will help you select the remaining items you need. Rhonda, I can't even describe what's in store for you."

An hour later, Brett and I reconnect at the bar before the program ends.

"I'm terrified I can't survive this move. You know India like no other person in this room, and I worry about Grant and Matthew."

Calmly, Brett says, "Darling, the boys will be spoilt beyond belief."

"Seriously?"

"I promise."

Unexpectedly, I feel a slight chill in the room.

He takes a sip of his cocktail and says, "After you leave, if you need anything, please call Lax or Cathy or text me, and don't ever truly forget to see what an extraordinary encounter this is—not only for your family, but for you. In other words, have the time of your life, mate."

Then he asks, "Just curious. When is your birthday?"

"February 16."

Smirking, the handsome Brit takes his driver's license out of his wallet to show me we have the day in common.

"Actually, Madam, we were born to do India!"

9

Waiting for Japanese encephalitis and yellow fever vaccinations one morning in a small waiting room at Pro Med Medical Center off Highway 183, I confront any last-minute hesitation about Mumbai with gusto, because nothing says certainty like needles.

While I'm discussing ailments with Dr. Saeed, my anxiety disappears. I elaborate on my predicament, and she cracks up during the discussion of my Mumbai adventures.

"While on a May visit, I spoke to three ladies at an American Women's Club coffee who confessed to disliking all things India, and I can't get them off my mind."

"I admire your spunk. I see lots of travelers here at the clinic, and having a positive attitude will take you far. Remember to remain optimistic—always. It's a great travel rule. Most clients can't wait to go see amazing places, but they also can't wait to return home. You don't have that option."

For a split second, I'm mildly uncomfortable, because in the midst of being consumed by my passage to India, *that* fact never occurred to me.

I blink a little and swallow a big gulp of reality.

"Truthfully, I've been a big flake in the game; sometimes I'm on the team, then I'm back on the sidelines watching the game take place before me. But I'm going to be responsible. I know the train left the station a long time ago—with my stuff."

I giggle and say, "I grew up watching *Star Trek*, and all I can hear is the background music every time I talk about leaving. The ultimate voiceover… 'to explore strange, new worlds, to seek out new life and new civilizations, to boldly go where no man has gone before.'"

Laughing, she asks if it's really that awful—because she's never been to any part of Asia.

I hold steady while she finishes up with the last shot, then say, "Yes, it can be, but I know you understand it's about perspective. So when an Indian family who owned a gas station in South Austin bought my husband's Toyota Sequoia, I felt like destiny slapped me in the face and told me, 'Damn it! Stop the loony talk."

She clutches her stomach, hands me the malaria pills, and tells me my sense of humor will serve me well, because millions of travelers have already gone boldly before me—and survived.

I inquire about any additional mandatory shots after she glances at my World Health Organization International Certificate of Vaccination. Come to find out, she's the doctor who issued my injections and meds before a four-week trip to East Africa and the Seychelles I took with Stanley in 1999.

I inhale. I exhale.

I'm set to go.

I slide off the table as she launches into a lecture about the most predictable travel-related illness: traveler's diarrhea (TD). Health data indicates 30 to 70 percent of travelers will come to know this illness. Statistics state travelers and patrons are the largest contributors to TD risks due to poor hygiene practices in local eateries.

I let her know that I know *all* about TD, and I'm prepared for war, given my history with the new civilization.

She bids me goodbye and best of luck. I collect my chart and pay my fees.

When I insert the key into the ignition, I wonder if she thinks I'm naïve.

A youth memory flashes: I'm a child again, and I'm not packing luggage to move abroad. No, it's a completely different trip I'm remembering.

My mother is driving. She picks me up at school and takes me to my new home: an apartment in north Houston near Greenspoint Mall. It's a cheap two-bedroom, two-bath dwelling, but it's all we can afford. She took it upon herself to move whatever she thought we might want or need before my father arrived home from work. She was escaping an abusive relationship once and for all.

Is this why I'm a scatterbrain? Is this why I want to take everything except the kitchen sink, because this time I have the choice of what to pack?

Fiona is with Grant at swim lessons and Matthew is attending the Mother's Day Out program at St. John Neumann's Catholic Church (SJNCC) today.

I scarf down a Schlotzsky's Original sandwich I grab in a drive-thru and add more items on the to-do list so we can get down to final business.

Highlights include:

- Lease our house to a Mormon family of six
- Move our wine cellar inventory to Uncle Jim's ranch outside of Dallas
- Move all household bills to the management company (including pool and landscape maintenance)
- Sell the Mercedes S560
- Move all personal bills to online banking
- Prepare a final home-inventory list
- Submit receipts for all packing supplies to TCC for reimbursement
- Finalize our home insurance

- Change our Austin address to the new postal box
- Cancel the local newspaper
- Resign from Lifeworks and Leadership Austin boards
- Resign from the Junior League of Austin and take a leave of absence from the Bob Bullock Texas State History Museum docent program
- Complete final dental checkups
- Complete remaining vaccination appointments for Grant
- FedEx visa documents to India
- Email the Le Gardenia mailing address to friends (Le Gardenia is the building where we'll be living)

Whew!

Fiona arrives home with the boys. She puts Matthew down for a nap and Grant isn't far behind. After I give him a quick bath, he's down for the count as well.

Fiona picked up lunch from Schlotzsky's too, since Emler's Swim School is near the Pro Med Clinic, so we finish our gourmet sandwiches together. The conversation about her willingness to move turns serious. She's ready to go to Mumbai because she needs a fresh start. Her mother adores all things India, so she knows about the country, but has never been there herself.

She accepts our verbal agreement in terms of time commitment (three months), monthly earning plan (X amount per month in cash), and living expenses (all paid).

When I cooked up this nanny idea, I came to this decision lightly with relatively few other choices.

Selfish? You bet.

We hired Fiona three years ago to babysit Grant. She came to us highly recommended by an agency, and she had certification in CPR. She was thirty-something, aced a background check, and had no outstanding warrants for her arrest. In addition, her parents live in our community.

Fiona takes care of Grant religiously while I still occasionally nab a freelance public relations gig or volunteer opportunity—or simply when we need a night out. We also pay her to house-sit when we vacation out of the country. Now she helps out part-time with Matthew, who will celebrate his first birthday on August 26th.

To say we trust her with our most valuable assets is accurate. And as she witnessed our growth and changes, we certainly witnessed a natural progression in her life too—an engagement, a marriage, and finally a divorce.

Uncertain about her true agenda with regard to moving, I pay her for the day, as my inner voice whispers, *Caution,* and then adds, *Don't put all your eggs in one basket!*

Meanwhile, Stanley is on a six-day business trip to Des Moines with Trammell Crow partners and then on to Cupertino, California for three days to attend his twenty-fifth high school reunion.

My family arrives from Houston and Louisiana, Stanley is back, and we're hosting festivities for Matthew's birthday. We eat a lot of Cajun food—compliments of my stepdad's insane ability to make a downright unique roux.

The following weekend, the guests are gone. This gives us time to stock-pile extra furniture and rugs in our storage unit and to donate any items that didn't sell in a friend's garage sale to Goodwill. We say goodbye to our neigh-bors, load up the rental car and a friend's Suburban with our luggage, and head west on Highway 71 to temporary housing—Bob and Sheri's Barton Creek Lakeside guesthouse.

Brad, the caretaker, meets us and shows us through the gates and into our very own living quarters. Grant sprints off to the tennis court when he spies a Barbie Corvette, property of the granddaughter.

We unpack and make ourselves at home. Luckily, we're fortunate to have loving friends. I'm not joking—if it wasn't for their generosity, I'd be down at the Extended Stay America across from the main post office on Sixth Street.

I failed to mention, I'm barely speaking to Stanley right now. This is uncomfortable, given our situation. TCC has failed to finalize the business contract once again this week. And to top it all off, the reason we had to move out of our house is because the Mormons backed out on letting us sublease until we leave the city.

Maybe they got scared since the move date continues to…well, move.

August came and went, and now September is here.

To add fuel to the fire, my inner voice is yelling at me. She wants to know why we didn't lease the house to the Wilson brothers, as in Luke and Owen, who were in town filming a movie and contacted our property manager repeatedly.

Bob arrives to the cabana and we meet poolside for a delicious grilled tilapia and vegetable dinner. After dessert, I let Sheri know the Fiona deal is sealed. She won Boss over because, as a matriarch, she gets it, and what she says goes.

School has started: Grant at WHPP and Matthew back at SJNCC. We march on.

Over a long holiday weekend, Stanley and Grant attend a combined fam-ily reunion and Bombay Bon Voyage party at Uncle Jim and Aunt Carole's ranch. Every Erwin is in attendance, from Oklahoma to Texas. It's quite the upscale hoedown.

The three-day BBQ fest includes skeet, putt-putt golf, horseshoes, cards, cruising on the John Deere Gators across 1,300 acres, hand-feeding llamas, fishing for bass, chasing longhorns across the prairie on horseback, roasting marshmallows for s'mores, and sitting under a sky full of stars so radiant one can see deer and wild turkeys walking up to the feeders for late-night snacks.

Meanwhile, back at the guesthouse, Matthew has a 103-degree tempera-ture, so we've stayed behind. After-hours doctor appointments consume my weekend. Sincerely, I was bummed to miss the in-laws and relatives, though I'm elated Stanley got to have the ultimate going-away party deep in the heart of Texas.

By late Sunday afternoon, Stanley and Grant are home and tired. Mat-thew is feeling better and sits proudly in his high chair grinning while his big brother imitates every animal on the ranch. There's an *oink* here and an *oink* there, but in a matter of seconds, *o-i-n-ks* are echoing through the guesthouse and laughter is all around us. I can't wait to see the boys imitate animals in India.

Stanley gets up to serve seconds on the lasagna I baked and returns from the kitchen with two glasses of Veuve Clicquot champagne.

Surprise! TCC has finalized Stan's international employment agreement. Stop the oinking and cue the angels, please! Relief sweeps over me like a tidal wave and I throw back the glass of bubbly.

It's mind-boggling, but there's nothing stopping us now—except for bedtime.

After baths and story time, the boys easily go to sleep, unfazed by the magnitude of Daddy's announcement.

A group of friends gather the following Sunday to witness Matthew's baptism at Westlake Hills Presbyterian Church by the pastor who baptized me in the same church where we were married in 1996. During lunch fol-lowing the ceremony we discuss the exhilaration of rebirth, and I reflect on the pastor's words encouraging and ushering each of us to completely focus on the present.

With the end of September approaching, the hours are going by fast. However, before we move, we're flying to Nevis to celebrate our ten-year wedding anniversary with the boys—and Fiona. After I started talking to Stanley again, I convinced him to take her with us on a trial run. What bet-ter way to enjoy ourselves and discover how the dynamics work between her and our own family in close quarters before we head east?

Nevis, a small island in the Caribbean Sea, is part of the Leeward Islands chain of the West Indies. Pure paradise. Eight days of sand, sun, and fun.

The trial run went smoothly, but I'll admit we crossed a few lines; we've never hired a live-in nanny or taken a full-time babysitter on a trip. For the most part, we discovered our boys just wanted to be with us regardless of whether Fiona was around.

In discussing our situation with other friends who do have a live-in nanny on the payroll, we didn't set strong boundaries. Besides that, we allowed her to drink alcohol while she was on the clock.

Good Lord—Bad Parenting 101.

Feeling desperate, I take her anyway.

Channing and I meet for lunch. She has kindly offered to check our postal box from time to time to sort through statements and letters that might have missed our online change-of-address notice. I hand over the Christmas cards she promises to mail in December.

"Madam, you've got serious control issues," she says. "These could have waited, you know."

I grin. "One less thing I need to worry about. Now it's on your plate, girlfriend."

One evening, Bob and Stanley are at the Austin Golf Club for an event, and the boys are asleep.

In my pajamas, I meet Sheri out on the master deck overlooking Lake Travis, and we toast with two big pours of yummy Cakebread Chardonnay under the light of the moon. We talk about how my life is now inextricably tied to India. We've done this many times, just the two of us, with the baby monitor nearby. But tonight is very special because our time together is up.

"Your life will be affected in so many ways," she says. "Culturally, economically, and environmentally."

We both laugh when she says "environmentally."

She's an interior decorator, so we discuss color swatches, patterns, and decorating tips for Le Gardenia. I show her the inventory list and an email confirmation from Laxman. I ordered nine pieces of furniture to be shipped to our building within days of our arrival.

Then I ask Sheri if I can read her my horoscope for October:

> *Make sure your travel documents are up to date—this month you'll be on the road more than at home. Treat yourself to a sleek piece of luggage; pack a pair of skinny jeans and a soft tunic sweater. In addition to leisure getaways, a business may require international journeys late this month.*

She promises to visit.

"My mind is still constantly racing. I pray at some point I can de-stress and relax again once we're settled. I really gotta visit that *champi* guy at the Taj again…and find a yoga instructor…and a driver…and…"

"Sweetie, don't worry. You will. Bob and I have traveled all over the world. Just remember the golden rule: cook it, peel it, boil it…or forget it!"

We giggle in unison like high school girls.

"I'm telling you my mind is playing tricks on me, and I just don't know how to remember every little bit of advice and how to ask all the right questions. I'm sure I forgot to pack a million things. Then, I start to think about all the other stuff I have to pack over the next eight days. Sheri, my life is going to be in the toilet."

She corrects me. "Your life is going to be *on* the toilet!"

Then she gives me sweet reassurance. "If anyone can do this move, it's you, Rhonda. It's not the change that makes a difference. It's how you handle it for yourself and for your boys."

I file that advice away for another day.

I give Sheri a big bear hug and walk back to the guesthouse.

Once inside, I scan the Bombay party and the holiday card mailing lists on the kitchen counter. Overcome with emotions, reality sinks in.

It's time—for me to leave.

10

Nhava Sheva Intercontinental Terminal is the largest container port in India, located east of Mumbai in Maharashtra. Its name is derived from the two villages, Nhava and Sheva, which were on the premises before the government demolished them to build the facility that is now holding my crate hostage.

"Let me get this straight," I say calmly. "You think eight-year-old dented golf clubs, a Pottery Barn baby crib with multiple teeth marks on the rail, and a handful of three-year-old French country dining chairs with worn cushions are new? Are you high?"

Stanley cringes and looks the other way while the inspection officers look nervous.

We were in London thirteen days ago. Spending a few days in Britain's capital to break up the time change served us well. Our grand Anglo-Saxon itinerary included visits to the Victoria and Albert Museum, the London Eye, the National Gallery, the Tower of London, the Transport Museum, and, of course, the Texas Embassy.

We ate fish and vinegar chips, and we shopped till we dropped at Harrods.

Flying to Mumbai set us straight, though. It was the reality check for all things imperfect—like circling the airport for an hour before we could land.

Once on the ground, a mob of taxi drivers riddled with measles and whooping cough fought each other over who should escort our caravan: fourteen suitcases (minus my bag #15, which mistakenly got picked up by another person), a Trek bike, a play yard, one umbrella stroller, Grant's Dora the Explorer backpack, a toddler car seat, and five additional carry-on bags.

After waiting forty minutes for company drivers, Ricky and Ganesh (who were no-shows), I took matters into my own hands by waving US dollars to flag down an elderly gentleman who drove me, the boys, Fiona, and a few of the bags to the upscale Sun-n-Sand Hotel.

What the driver couldn't squeeze into the undersized yellow-and-black trunk, he meticulously tied onto the roof with mucky rope.

We left Stanley in the pickup area with his Lance Armstrong bike and the remaining luggage, on his cell phone, steadfast that the company drivers would eventually appear.

Today is a new day, and just like parenting, there will be major setbacks. I just need to trust my instincts and keep moving.

My driver, Naushad, sees me approaching the car and he starts the engine and jumps out to greet me.

The second I slam the door he turns the A/C on full blast.

I remove my *jootis*, recline the seat, and close my eyes.

We sit in silence.

Wait! I'm receiving a call on my fancy new Motorola phone.

"What? *Morphine?* Can you repeat what you just said? I don't think I heard you correctly."

Dr. Shah, the JW Marriott's resident doctor, now has my full attention.

"This in-house doctor you spoke of from the Sun-n-Sand Hotel did not advise the proper medication," he says. "Basically from the description of the symptoms and results you described, he gave you and Grant morphine shots to avoid pain, but nothing he prescribed orally is healthy. It's all narcotics and antibiotics for urinary tract infections, which you don't have, according to the lab reports. I threw it all in the trash bin.

"The chemist will deliver the new medicine to your flat for 700 rupees. Within forty-eight hours you and Grant should feel better. Please call if you require anything more. I'm here to help even if you're no longer a guest at the hotel, Ms. Erwin. And again, welcome to Bombay."

"Thank you very much, Dr. Shah."

I close my eyes again.

Time is passing very slowly until Naushad finally breaks the silence. "Madam, may I please ask you something, Madam?"

He sounds concerned.

"Sure."

Then it dawns on me he might not know what "sure" means, because he doesn't respond.

Slowly I say, "Naushad, ask me anything."

I hear a sigh of relief.

"Madam, where is Boss?"

I open my eyes and look over to my right.

"Boss? Oh, I left him to negotiate a deal with the inspectors, because they're trying to cheat us. They opened our crate and unwrapped used items but refuse to accept they're not new, and now they want $800 before they will release the crate. As far as I'm concerned, they can kiss my grits."

He looks mystified.

"Boss and I know the rules about what we must pay taxes on and how many new items we can bring into the country. I told the inspectors to keep it all. I can't remember if I gave them the finger or not, but I instructed Raj to help Boss figure it out. Then I discreetly walked away during their negotiations over a paper receipt. Now I'm here with you."

Naushad looks scared to death.

My phone rings again. It's Fiona checking in. Matthew is taking a nap in one of the suitcases and Grant is sitting in the toddler car seat watching a movie on the flat-screen TV in the living room.

Fiona says, "You should have seen the look on the neighbor's face when she stopped by the flat and saw our living conditions. I told her the crate is MIA and we eat out every meal or order Domino's."

I say a small prayer that one of the gods will help me find a cook and a yoga instructor to relieve the stress that continues to build.

Kudos to Laxman, who made sure the Four Hands Home order arrived promptly; but we don't have mattresses, and we're using nightstands as tray tables in the living area because we don't have a dining table.

I'm about to blow a gasket. Stanley insisted we move into Le Gardenia almost right away to save money. Meanwhile, our dishes and bedding reside in Nhava Sheva territory, except for the items we brought in our luggage like toys, clothes, and toiletries.

I'm still trying to grasp how we're truly saving rupees when I had to squander a lot of them at HyperCITY, Mumbai's version of Walmart, to purchase utensils, paper plates, toilet paper, a frying pan, paper towels, glasses, a pot, cleaning supplies, sheets, and basic food staples like lunchmeat, pasta, soup, and bread so we can function like civilized people.

Matthew and Grant don't seem to mind the situation; in fact, they love the open space in the flat. But they did get incredibly sad after they depleted the last of the Austin contraband—beef jerky and chicken Vienna sausages. The look on their sweet faces made me recall the FACES Pain-Rating Scale for birthing mothers. On a scale of zero to ten, I'm an eight: "Hurts a whole lot."

My inside voice poses a question while I'm contemplating my next move: *Is this the glorious adventure we imagined, Madam?*

"Well, if you count riding in the back of various Indian-made vehicles driven erratically along tiny streets, a harsh bout of food poisoning combined with a mysterious virus Grant and I contracted, as well as sleeping on cheap Indian pads bought in a local market on marble floors—heck no, this isn't the adventure I imagined. *So, zip it!*"

The bottom line is I *need* my crate, but we're not willing to pay bribe money to get it—it's a matter of principle.

I spot Stanley sprinting toward the car. Naushad jumps out and opens my door.

"Rhonda, I've been looking all over for you. I need you to walk with me to sign some paperwork so the crate will be released and delivered this weekend."

I climb out. "You didn't pay the money, did you?"

"No, I didn't, but Raj donated $200 in cash to the inspection fund and we declined a paper receipt. This is just the way things work here. Plus, Raj has agreed to meet the delivery team at Le Gardenia."

Naushad is all smiles.

Despite the unpredictable introduction to expat life, Stanley did do me a favor. He secured Naushad—an English-speaking driver from Auto Riders, a popular service company offering transportation to foreign businessmen.

The day Boss forced us to move into the flat, Naushad appeared in uniform and in a white Tata minivan at the JW Marriott doorsteps, where I moved after a short stint at Sun-n-Sand. Taking control like a four-star general, he jammed our things into the vehicle in record time without ever breaking a sweat, whipping our family into shape right then and there.

Now it's day fifteen and we're on Jet Air headed to Jodhpur for a three-day weekend. The smell of body odor is atrocious. After I buckle up, I unzip my purse, take out a bottle of Liz Claiborne perfume, and spray around me.

Stanley and the boys are seated two rows ahead, and I'm in a window seat reading *Elle* magazine. I turn directly to the horoscope page.

> *Aquarius (Jan. 20–Feb. 18): You'll be making fresh connections. Remember that other people don't know what you know. Avoid slipping into talk that is so specific to your work or culture that outsiders won't understand it.*

Hmm.

I'm looking out the window, contemplating the consequences of pulling the emergency latch on the exit door and ending it all here and now.

Quickly, the captain announces we will begin our descent into the Jodhpur Airport, a civil enclave facility in Rajasthan that shares its space with the Jodhpur Air Base of the Indian Air Force. Laxman made sure to share this with me so we wouldn't be caught off guard by the number of MiG fighter aircraft on the ground. What he should have warned us about is the aerosolized insecticide that the flight attendants sprayed down the aisle before we landed.

"*Aap kaise ho!*" says Laxman. "Welcome."

In unison we say, "*Namaste*, Laxy!"

He shrieks loudly, "Wow, you Indian family now!"

My inside voice says sarcastically, *Madam, you've mastered one phrase of the local language. That's talent.*

If Mumbai is India's most cosmopolitan city—an overpopulated melting pot of extremes from industry to Bollywood to religion, then Jodhpur reigns as Rajasthan's second-largest city: a desert town with a royal history, a vast fort, and a stunning palace.

Breathing in the dust and intense heat, Laxman loads our bags into the mid-size company Jeep, and I grasp the fact that city life is far, far behind us. We're speechless as we exit the airport on our way to the Four Hands house as we pass camel-driven carts, goats along the roadside, and envoys of bedazzled, big trucks carrying huge hay bales.

Monica, a pretty young woman clad in a light-green *sari*, greets us in the front yard with her arms placed at her chest. She bows and says, "*Namaste.*" She hands Laxman flower leis one by one from a wicker chair to give us. Then she can't resist reaching for Matthew, who easily goes into her arms.

Ushpal, the Four Hands cook, shyly and quickly makes introductions, and then collects the bags. In the wink of an eye, windows are shut, the air conditioning is turned on, bottled water sans ice is poured, and a vegetarian meal is presented in our honor: cheese pizza, salad, rice with vegetables, and *chapati*, an unleavened flatbread. Grant and Matthew squeal with delight the minute the tray holding the pizza hits the wooden dining table.

Cathy and Roberto have lived in Jodhpur for eleven years. She's Canadian and he's Italian. The two met in the city within months of moving to the country to further their passion for textiles, design, and adventure. They've graciously agreed to manage and coordinate our shopping efforts.

After lunch, we immediately set out to visit a variety of warehouses, including their own showrooms—VJ Home Studios. In addition, she announces: "We can custom make anything for you in terms of furniture and fabrics, mirrors, stone, and hardware…and our quality control team reviews each piece to make sure the products are delivered in flawless condition to your flat."

Perfect.

Laxman is our official driver and off we go into the unknown. An unarmed guard meets us at an anonymous-looking warehouse with no signage on the outskirts of the city. Once inside the compound, the wrought iron gates are closed behind us and we're given the signal to park. Laxman speaks Hindi to several workers. Unexpectedly, a manager appears, greeting us in perfect English. Then we're led to the first of many large buildings.

We have no clue what to expect, but Cathy guarantees a large selection of columns, doors, school desks, decorative pieces, armoires, benches, bookcases, and chairs—newly-crafted and genuine objects that once graced private homes.

Imagine, if you will, a starting pistol signaling the beginning of an Olympic track event.

The race is on!

I swear if you had told me I could furnish an entire house like a mansion for under $5,000 and that a shopping Mecca exists where everyone knows my name, I would have moved to India sight unseen.

At first we nervously and politely ask warehouse assistants to pull down items stacked on top of other pieces. We approve them and get pricing quotes before an assistant tags them with initials in white chalk. Laxman, following me at every turn, instructs me to survey the premises quickly. I can do one final approval before committing to buy, thus covering more territory in less time.

I've died and gone to a super-shopper's heaven.

Into the third building on the property, I turn to Laxman and say, "I have to visit Jodhpur again."

He laughs at first, but stops when I say, "No, I'm serious. I could do this in my sleep."

Maya, Cathy's assistant, greets us with chilled bottled water when we make a pit stop to browse the fabric side of the VJ Home business. Visualize mirrored pillow cushions, place mats, embroidered purses and artwork, scarves, silver jewelry, and bedspreads sewn from vintage *saris*.

Stanley encourages me to load up, and I do.

After lukewarm showers back at the house, we depart for dinner at the Nieddu homestead. We enter a walled compound surrounded by massive stone gates. Cathy and Roberto greet us.

We pinch ourselves.

The courtyard is lit with kerosene torches burning brightly along the U-shaped residence—former horse stables. In the center of the courtyard is a two-story Haveli, a large manor made from carved red sandstone; renovation plans are in the works.

Bianca—the Nieddu's adorable daughter, who is the same age as Grant— races up to us with her pals, a Great Dane and a German Shepherd who patrol the property. Within seconds, Bianca latches on to Grant and off they go to play with the pet bunnies. Fiona attends to Matthew and they disappear to explore Roberto's collection of vintage motorbikes and automobiles parked on the opposite side of the main living wing.

A poolside table illuminated by the light of a green swimming pool is set for a European dinner. Roberto introduces his Nepali cook when he serves plated imported Spanish *jamón* appetizers and Sula champagne.

Can this be real?

How can *anyone* have a problem living here? And furthermore, how can *I* hire a Nepali cook to move to Mumbai?

The evening is superb and I don't know about Stan, but I certainly enjoyed myself for the first time since our relocation.

Before we gather our belongings, the guys disappear into the office to review a prospective real estate venture and Laxman heads to the Jeep. I ask Fiona to collect the stroller and load up the boy's backpacks and shoes. *If she's the babysitter, why do I have to ask her to collect the things?* I wonder.

When we're alone, I ask Cathy for any final advice.

She's graciously given me sound suggestions throughout the evening, and I've been a sponge all night, but there may be things we forgot to discuss.

"The servants will establish a hierarchical system among themselves," Cathy says. "In other words, they will betray one another. You don't have to honor their way of doing things, but be very clear you're in charge. If not, they'll run all over you. Make sure you lock up all of your jewelry, money, and passports. And if you give servants an opportunity to steal from you, at least one of them will take you up on it."

"I only packed costume jewelry," I say, "Except for the cheap, thin gold wedding band and hoops I'm sporting. All my valuables—including my platinum and diamond wedding ring and band—are in a safe deposit box in Austin."

"This country is the Holy Grail for incredible gems—trust me, you will definitely acquire your fair share of fabulous finds. Just secure it when it's not on you."

"Will do."

She wants to know why I brought Fiona and I provide details.

"You should tell the servants she's your friend—not the nanny. She doesn't fit into the hierarchy because she's an American."

I agree to do that.

"Cathy, people often refer to Texas as a state of mind, and I'm beginning to see that India is a state of mind, too. Perhaps I need to forgo my Western biases."

She nods in agreement.

"Having said that, I just pray sanity returns to the asylum soon."

We both laugh.

I thank her for the royal dinner and for coordinating the next two days of ultimate shopping.

She gives me a hug and a final thought for the evening, "Madam, remember: if you can't change the circumstance, change your perception of it."

11

I'm in pajamas, feeling restless after too many long nights with little sleep, when I hear a loud knock. It's Raj—who oversaw the Erwin crate delivery without a hitch—with certified company documents for Stanley to PDF to Trammell Crow Company for reimbursement.

We chat briefly and he leaves.

Thankfully, we've finally unpacked most of our belongings and settled into our flat, which I dubbed the "Marble Palace" because everything in it is indeed made of marble.

Then there's another knock at the door and I find myself face-to-face with a person whose features resemble a Ninja Turtle, wearing funky eye-wear and holding a local Hindi newspaper. Confused, I take a sip of Diet Pepsi from a glass holding six petite ice cubes, to be exact. (This reminds me I need to get more bottled water to fill up the empty trays.)

Boss and Grant have gone already, and Matthew is snoring in his crib. Fiona is in the shower; and I'm staring into the face of an individual who clearly needs major dental work.

"Madam, I'm Vinay. Get dressed properly, and I'll see you downstairs. We need to roll before traffic gets worse," he says with a lisp, clearly thinking I should be pleased with his sudden appearance.

I watch, baffled, as he steps into the lift and disappears. "Where in the hell is Naushad?" I spout out sarcastically as I quietly shut the door and tiptoe down the hall.

I pass through the living room and slide open the glass door leading onto the balcony, pausing to admire the custom drapes and window-seat cushions Gautham, a Fab India employee, helped me design and purchase. Thank goodness, we have privacy. The duct tape and Reynolds aluminum foil is off every window.

I step out and shut the door behind me, inhaling a big breath of foul air, conscious once again of the multitude of pollutants I breathe daily. I sit down comfortably in one of our wooden patio chairs from VJ Home, coughing a little, then a lot, until the coughing begins to sound like sobbing.

I fight back tears.

Right after we landed, the sense of adventure I felt was replaced by a sense of major despair. Yes, I agreed to uproot my boys and had even, at the outset, been energized by the challenge of living in a foreign country. But I thought the move would be more on my terms.

I envisioned myself overcoming the language and cultural differences simultaneously and brilliantly setting up a home among the locals. But India has her own terms, and I never fathomed I'd desperately need so much help.

I believed finding a driver—conceivably Naushad—who could translate the language and keep my schedule flowing would be all I'd need to continue doing the things I love. I looked forward to volunteer opportunities, cooking lessons, and yoga while the boys were in school or with Fiona, but none of these things are happening yet. Newsflash: I don't actually know anyone, except Grant's teachers and a few mothers I met briefly at ASB.

Stanley says I shouldn't complain, because the "Easy-Bake Oven," the washing machine with two speeds, and a tiny dryer were delivered four days ago. I may not have a yogi, but I do have modern appliances.

Whatever.

I'm fed up by the amount of time I've spent receiving personal "presentations" from store managers who arrive at the flat to instruct me on how to operate each piece of equipment.

I'm bitter and I miss my friends. But, with the eleven-hour-thirty-minute time difference, they're inaccessible to me. No one is emailing, nor has there been a single card or package from the States.

I'm alone, feeling more irrelevant than I've ever felt in my life.

I'm so out of my league I want to shout, "Let's go! Let's go! L-E-T-S G-O!"

But I reel myself in. I need to stay strong for Grant and Matthew.

I hear laughter below me, and as I lean over the railing I see the building security guards joking around and sharing cigarettes with several drivers. When they notice me peering down, they look up, grinning—pleased to see the new madam out of the air conditioning and watching the cows stroll down our street. I'm not sure they know exactly what to make of me just yet, but their obvious interest makes me stop crying.

I also saw Vinay looking up sternly in my direction and pointing to his watch. I remember that I still need to get dressed. Casually, I sneak back inside, throw on white jeans and the pink tunic I bought on my first visit to the city months ago, and head downstairs, vaguely determined to face another day.

When I finally reach the car park, Vinay formally introduces himself and then informs me he's driving today because Naushad is on a very important job.

Yellow flag.

For a split second, it dawns on me that maybe I'm being put in my place—a recurring theme since moving. I'm stunned to learn of this reassignment because we signed a six-week contract with Auto Riders and then recently, an extension. Stanley specifically picked Naushad to be my driver, and now I'm told my business is not important enough?

I silently hope Naushad is not in trouble for the little fender bender we had after I ordered him to go the wrong way down a one-way street to explore a new children's store I discovered while reading *Time Out* magazine, a local entertainment and resource city guide…and I didn't admit to Boss that we also backed down a one-way street because of a traffic accident so I could buy toilet paper holders, towel racks, child-proof locks, and hooks at a shop Yvette, an ASB mum, suggested.

Once Vinay opens the door for me and I'm buckled up in the backseat, we drive out of the car park and into the ocean of endless traffic. I don't mind sitting up front with Naushad, but there's no way I'm sitting next to Vinay for all of the population to witness. Besides, I'm just beginning to conquer my motion sickness.

There's no Super Target here, and the day promises to be busy. My objective is to visit at least six stores, but I know from earlier missions you have to set your errand goal high but lower your overall expectations due to inner-city congestion and the language barrier. On a decent day, I can conquer two to three shops, max.

I still don't understand why a country that gives birth to millions of highly-trained, qualified doctors and computer science geniuses can't figure out the art of one-stop shopping. And I can't grasp why service company drivers know little about where I need to go to set up my household.

Newsflash: I have no clue where I am most of the time, so I just holler out "Stop!" whenever I see an interesting storefront.

Seriously.

We spend two hours running errands and Vinay never stops talking about "his India." I listen as long as I can to "my India this" and "my India that" until finally I raise my voice, and say, "Hey, Vinay! I'm still trying to figure out 'my India!'"

Naushad rarely speaks to me unless I speak to him first, and I haven't been speaking to Vinay. However, he continues to have entire conversations with himself at my expense over the course of the next two hours. I question whether or not I'm inadvertently encouraging these comments. Perhaps I'm inviting this bizarre dialogue.

"I need to go to Citibank and get rupees. I want to find a dry cleaner that accepts credit cards and delivers."

For reasons unknown, he feels very comfortable around me. But I feel very uncomfortable with him—he's someone I should ignore, according to Indian social customs and the caste system. I read in my guidebook that most Hindu madams don't even acknowledge a driver's presence.

Stan's at work and can't be bothered. Like I said, it's an isolated existence, unless you count interactions with Fiona or the building staff who don't speak English. After we pick up Grant from ASB at noon, I'm done with the crowded streets and the beggars banging on the car windows, staring at me when we stop at the intersections. I send a text message to Stanley to tell him I'm headed back to Le Gardenia. I have a giant headache and now the horrendous lunchtime traffic is in full force. I just can't get past all the honking. It's still *too much* honking!

The next morning I ask Stanley if he's called Auto Riders to inquire about the whereabouts of Naushad.

"Rhonda, I was told he is on an important assignment for several days and nothing more," he says. "It looks like you're stuck with Vinay. Be nice."

One afternoon, I unknowingly provoked Vinay by wearing my tennis skirt from the flat to Bandra Gymkhana Club to meet a new AWC friend for private tennis lessons. The look on his face when I walked down to the car park said it all.

"Madam, you do have very nice legs, but you're losing your dignity in my country because you're showing them to everyone."

Back in Austin, the other moms and I think nothing of wearing workout clothes around town. In fact, a lot of women proudly sport their post-workout, no-makeup glow and run errands—in coordinating outfits from their tennis match, yoga class, or run around the Town Lake hike and bike trail.

Now, I discover as a "Madam" I must carry myself in a certain manner. I had no clue local customs would consume me, an American.

Slowly, I'm learning to grasp I must abide by these rules in order to gain respect, but why didn't someone tell me these things in advance? How can every person be so fascinated with telling me how *I* need to act when everywhere I look the general population is so deprived and the city is disgustingly dirty?

I don't dare tell Vinay I once saw a man pull his penis out of his pants and urinate in front of me. One can only imagine the dialogue *that* would spark; but as far as I can see, Mumbai has way bigger issues than Madam losing her dignity by showing her legs in the hood.

I jerk the door away from him and slam it shut. Once he plops down in the front seat and starts the engine, I say, "Vinay, Madam will wear whatever she wants to wear, whenever she wants to wear it."

"Another thing, Madam, you better stop taking the photographs with the building staff, particularly the security team you refer to as the 'Sleepy People.' It's not acceptable for you to associate with the lower castes, and the residents in your building will start to look down upon you if this behavior continues, Madam."

I take a deep breath, trying to decide how to counter this ridiculous, backward-ass comment.

"Vinay, the security guards are 'Sleepy People' because they brush their teeth each morning in their underwear before putting on their uniforms, and they love to nap all day. I take pictures of them in case they do anything to us so I can go to the police station and have them arrested."

Did this strange driver just tell me how to conduct myself, and if so, where is the respect?

I won't even go into detail about the day I didn't wear makeup and expected Vinay to drive me to the Santa Cruz market to look for baskets. He wouldn't put the key in the ignition until I ran back upstairs to apply mascara and lipstick.

I can't sleep. Inevitably, I lie awake through the early morning hours and hear Vinay's lectures going through my head along with the ongoing construction next door. Stanley snores the minute his head hits the pillow.

However, the sleepless nights are taking an extreme toll on my body. I call on Dr. Shah again for guidance. His assistant delivers a small number of pills so I can actually make it to REM sleep amid the noise and the ongoing stress. Trust me, Trammell Crow Company did me no favors by moving us in October. By the time we arrived, every ASB-recommended servant and consulate-approved chef had been hired. The next day I ask Stanley if he's called Auto Riders again to inquire about Naushad.

"I've called several times, and he's still busy."

I raise my voice in frustration, "Well, if you don't get him back here, there's going to be big trouble, Boss!"

"I thought you didn't like Naushad. All you did is complain about him, remember? You were mad because he didn't know where any of the expat stores were located, and he ignored your phone calls when the cricket matches were on the radio while you shopped."

"Those are simple misunderstandings compared to what I'm dealing with now!"

But it finally dawns on me: Naushad is as new to driving an expat madam as I'm new to having a driver. The two of us had just started to get a handle on our relationship dynamics when Auto Riders nabbed Naushad away from me and sent cranky old Vinay.

How can I explain why I miss Naushad, whom I barely know? Yes, we might have started off on the wrong foot, like the two times he shut my finger in the car door, but we've shared fun times as well, I think. I enjoy our conversations about Bollywood on our daily joy rides. Instantly I felt a connection with him. Also, he stops to ask for directions, which speaks volumes about his personality. Who doesn't adore a man willing to do that?

Vinay shows up and we spend the better part of an hour trying to locate a newly-opened preschool Grant's teacher told me about for Matthew, which is three blocks over from Le Gardenia. After forty-five minutes of driving in circles, we spot the building and stop.

Vinay parks and gets out. I see him jiggle a locked gate. The school is closed. A polite delivery person headed to Crossword, the neighborhood bookshop next door to the preschool, stops to speak with Vinay. He confirms the school is out of business. After a number of journeys end on the same note, I'm starting to think "closed" and "out of business" is the norm for the city.

Once he's back in the car and before he's willing to put the key into the ignition, he announces, "I need an hour every day for lunch instead of the thirty minutes you're giving me."

At first I'm surprised to think he plans on being around that much longer, but I remind him I'm desperately trying to complete our household and fine-tune our kitchen and living spaces. I remind him we don't get much time to run errands every day, because we collect Grant from school at noon. And then afternoons are unpredictable because it's wedding season and the insane traffic is even more insane.

"Thirty minutes, tops," I say, not backing down.

He tells me how he had seven teeth knocked out in the early 1960s during a cricket match, and he needs a full hour to eat his meal because he has to gnaw his food. I look up just in time to see him withdraw the upper denture out of his mouth, smiling profusely and proudly displaying four crooked teeth several spaces apart on his lower gum.

"See, Madam. I don't have much to work with."

I stare at him. I glare at the primitive denture apparatus and then I look down at my *Namaskar Mumbai* guide. Then, I look to the left out the car window. Good Lord. Friends back home think I'm living the high life.

"No, no, no! You did NOT just show me that thing. Put it back in your mouth right now! Never, and I mean NEVER, take it out again! That's not acceptable."

I compromise and give him forty-five minutes.

I'm torn between giving him an entire hour and recalling what Cathy and Roberto told us—don't be too nice to the help or it will come back to haunt you two-fold.

Finally, after a long day running errands with Vinay, I call Stanley again when we stop for gas. I get out of the car before the pumping begins and make my way to the entrance while you-know-who lights up. I pray he doesn't blow up the petrol station while he smokes as he watches the attendant fill up the tank.

"Stan," I say. "First of all, mid-afternoon, Vinay got a traffic ticket. He ran a red light while in the midst of changing prayer tapes. So much for divine guidance. I told him he should pray much earlier in the day and pray he doesn't get tickets."

Stanley laughs. "Sounds like you're having a wonderful day, Madam."

"I was in shock when the policeman motioned for us to pull over, and Vinay begged me to pay the 100-rupee ticket fine. I politely declined and told him it was his problem to resolve."

"Good job, Madam. I have meetings to attend. I must go, and remember—be sweet."

Figures.

I'll admit I was guilty of leaning out of the car and snapping a quick photo of Vinay paying bribe money to dismiss the traffic citation. He's been talking trash about how he's such a better employee than Naushad for several days now. I've still got high hopes that I will see Naushad soon to show him the photograph for a laugh.

We're back driving on Linking Road when Vinay tells me he's Hindu. While he's weaving in and out of traffic, he also divulges he's married to a German woman from Goa and he respects the philosophies of Hinduism, Catholicism, and Buddhism. In his exact words, "I can celebrate all the holidays and have many, many days off from the service, Madam."

He swerves to miss clipping the bumper of a rickshaw, and as he turns left on Khar Danda Road, I go flying across the backseat. I didn't buckle up when we left the station.

Vinay jerks around and flashes a stern stare.

I glare back at him, irritated. He immediately turns up the volume on the prayer tape and speeds forward.

I just can't take it anymore. Between the incessant chanting blaring out of the Toyota Corolla speakers and *Madam this* and *Madam that*, I'm done!

I scream at the top of my lungs, "VINAY! PULL OVER. STOP THE DAMN CAR AND GET OUT NOW! I need a moment of privacy."

He looks scared and conforms precisely as instructed while I motion with my hand to shoo away from the car once he parks on a side street and gets out.

I hit missed call on my phone and squeal when Stanley answers, "I WANT NAUSHAD BACK, AND I WANT HIM BACK RIGHT NOW!

"I know you called several times to request Naushad again, and, obviously, you aren't getting the message across because they keep sending Vinay," I gasp. "You tell them I know where the service company is located, and if they DO NOT, I repeat, DO NOT send Naushad, I will show up and physically take him. I weigh more than he does!"

I struggle to regain my composure.

Stanley chuckles. For a minute, it crosses my mind he wants to see if I'm serious.

"If you don't get Naushad back, you will walk into the Marble Palace one day soon to find your family gone back to Texas!" I holler.

Guess who isn't laughing anymore?

"As far as you're concerned, *I* am the most important assignment in India. Whatever the service is doing with *my* Naushad, they better stop and send him back right this minute!"

I know this is a defining moment for Stan. At last, he realizes that when Madam is happy, everyone is happy.

The next morning I hear a faint knock and begin to fume, but when I open the door, it's Lolita, the building cleaning lady, speaking Hindi to me. Through a lot of pointing and waving, she lets me know someone is waiting for me in the car park. I'm positive Vinay is up to something. Stanley dropped Grant at school on his way to work. Matthew and Fiona are up and eating breakfast. I get dressed and make a to-do list of errands, hoping today might be a new lease on life in the suburbs, and take the lift down.

The doors open and I stroll through the dusty marble lobby, past the Sleepy People, and there stands Naushad with a huge smile on his face, waiting by a white Innova service car.

"Good morning, Madam."

I look him up and down. "Wait? Have we met before?"

He lets out a long sigh.

Something transpired over the course of those first few weeks between us.

I can sense our relief at having a second chance, and I know we'll be more respectful of each other's differences. I'm not sure if Naushad knows I'm going to need him more than he might ever need me, but I'm willing to go the distance. With a little tweaking on both sides, this could be the beginning of a beautiful friendship.

Also, I'm confident he will play a key role in my happiness, a central part of my life in India.

When Naushad opens the front door, this time I decline and point to the bucket seat behind the driver's seat, right where Madam *should* sit.

He nods in approval.

Once we're inside the car, Naushad sees my reflection in the rearview mirror, and I flash the pearly whites.

"Were you seriously going to stick me with Vinay?"

I can read the expression on his face and I know I've met my match.

Naushad is equally determined to be heard and stubborn enough to stand his ground—based on his own set of principles. I'm attempting to do the same but obviously under a set of rules not of my own making.

He does the Indian head wiggle and then we both explode into a fit of giggles.

This is the first time I see a glimpse of our future—and sometimes a glimpse is all you need.

12

I'd like to ask for a moment of silence in memory of the time I wasted in Citibank on Linking Road completing my portion of the paperwork to access the Erwin joint bank account.

Stanley can cash checks and use the automatic teller machine excessively, but apparently there are issues with my signatures not matching the original documentation I signed in May before the move.

Madam hasn't been able to get her fair share of rupees out of Citibank on a daily basis and there have been big arguments with Stan, and now there is major and not-so-sweet talk with the employees who are controlling my every move.

In addition, there's a disclaimer Citibank failed to mention. It's called a "limit" and apparently you're only allowed to extract $250 a day in cash from your account through the ATM.

No joke.

My inner voice chimes in. It's been a while since I've heard from her. *Is this a real limit or a Stanley-imposed limit, given that India is a man's world?*

I laugh out loud.

I made sure it was a real limit immediately—but thanks for thinking of me.

Given the situation, if I need to make a large purchase in cash, I have to go inside the bank, where the air con does not function well, and stand in the long, long line to cash a check.

I tried to do just that last week, but my signature didn't match the original because I made the misstep of writing my full name, including my middle name.

Big mistake.

Now, I'm waiting.

And waiting.

Now there's more waiting still to clear up the confusion about what my "good name" is and what I should sign moving forward to have access to my rupees.

I decline the tea and coffee for the hundredth time because I'm pissed off.

Now I understand why Citibank India is not linked with Citibank USA: because if they were linked, this would be a non-issue.

A new employee, reporting to duty, offers me tea and coffee for the umpteenth time.

I snap.

"Send someone to go get me a Diet Pepsi," I say loudly. "Or champagne?"

Then I stand up, walk to the administrative assistant's desk, and demand to speak to the manager—again. I let her know my time is valuable and I don't have all day to hang out at Citibank.

Now I sense urgency.

I don't understand what has changed, but it seems my drink request (or the fear of what I might say next) has gotten the ball rolling. It's clear they want me to go far away.

I text Stan: "I want to document, this is three hours of my life I can absolutely never get back."

His reply: "Remember to be polite and use your inside voice. And good luck."

This is incomprehensible to me. Why does each employee pretend to be busy when I'm the only customer at this moment in the branch?

Naushad waits patiently outside because there are no parking spots. He watches me from afar, wondering what in the hell is taking so long. It's unusually humid and I text him to start the engine and enjoy the air conditioning.

He refuses. He's a stubborn cat on a hot tin roof.

I'm told to "lunch" and that when I return my paperwork will be in order. "Madam, you will no longer encounter obstacles at the cash bin, nor will you experience delay when cashing checks."

I grab my handbag and exit the lobby. I strut to the car and climb in as Naushad opens the door for me. We both breathe a heavy sigh of relief when the cold air fills the interior.

Inhale. Exhale.

Never fear, I do have credit cards. Naushad drives onto Linking Road and off we go to the few stores that accept plastic to charge the weekly groceries.

Why didn't Anuj tell us India wants to be paid in cash so they can cheat the tax collector? In addition, why didn't the AWC members tell me rupees have wings?

Obviously, if you pay in cash, you get a better deal and rate. I get it, but I just didn't know it until now. Consequently, when I can't get my money out of my own account it creates a big problem, particularly when I have projects to complete. Moreover, only one in eight stores accept credit cards.

Remember Jodhpur? I need someone to hang the antique black-and-white photos and to install the toilet paper holders, glass shelving, and towel racks.

And guess what? The people who do manual labor only accept cash.

Yvette recommended her maintenance person, whom she calls Mr. Carpenter Man. He will soon be on-site drilling and installing with a vintage drill, a screwdriver, and a hammer.

Another thing no one told me about is the bizarre lingo used in conversations with low-caste individuals who do speak English.

For example, Naushad, who has a fifth-grade education, says, "Madam, they were talking, talking, too much talking."

I reply, "So they were just talking, right?"

He nods and says, "Yes, Madam."

Then he quickly adds, "But they were talking, talking, *too* much talking."

Oh dear, lots of repetition every day.

All right, another thing no one told me about is that expat life is like living in a cocoon, similar to my former Westlake bubble, where everyone sees everybody at the cleaners, the grocery store, the restaurants. You get the picture.

Consequently, we've begun to make more friends and establish expat relationships; therefore, the mobiles are ringing, the texts are flying, and the plethora of playdates are under way.

Anastasia from Russia is over for her third playdate. The teachers say Grant and Anastasia sit together at lunch every day and hold hands on the playground.

Her mother is an ice skater from Moscow, married to a shipping giant.

They'll live in the city for three years before moving on to another country.

Due to no ice rinks, she models for a jeweler in her spare time.

Ben from California invites Grant to weekly playdates at his flat several blocks away.

His mother, Roseanne, is part of the American Women's Club. I attended my first official meeting this month as a paid-in-full member, and she was the gracious host.

Through her I met two key local contacts: Sabal and Anil the Wine Guy.

Sabal is a serial expat driver whom Roseanne hired from a service similar to Auto Riders. She calls him Teddy Bear when he's not around because he's a big, burly kind of guy but a real softy. He now seems to be her lifeline. British mums say she drinks a lot of Sula (the cheap wine made in Nashik, a city in northwestern India), and one time, Teddy Bear had to pick her up and put her in the car after a late-night binge with expat girlfriends.

Hearsay, I think.

Anil, a friendly local liquor store worker, delivers on-demand 24/7. Now he might be the BFF I really need, especially when the going gets tough.

At any rate, I'm thrilled to meet new people who can help me help myself.

Earlier before my bank debacle, we attended Family Fun Day at the ASB—a carnival of sorts, and more like a United Nations picnic than anything else. Highlights of the day are pony rides and a merry-go-round that was turned by hand. (The equipment has the year "1957" emblazoned on it.)

We were in awe over the international crowd, and we got a chance to see how high-caste ASB families roll on weekends. I finally met every classroom parent and the nanny assigned to each child. Stanley laughed when the principal commented on the pink bunny costume Grant sported for the Halloween parade.

"Well, now you know what I forgot to pack in the crate—costumes!" I said. "I had no clue India celebrated Halloween, and he didn't mind the pink fluff. In fact, he loved being the only bunny at the party."

Theek hai, Grant.

Once the event is over, we head to the Grand Hyatt for lunch and air conditioning—along with many other expats who are hiding from the heat. When I call Naushad after lunch, he races out of the hotel car park and proceeds to the front of the hotel entrance to pick us up. He always opens my door first. India has strict laws requiring passengers to buckle up, so we lock the boys into car seats and off we go. Thirty miles an hour. Or less.

I sit behind Naushad so he can communicate with me in the rearview mirror without fully turning around. Trust me, I know Madams do not sit in the front seat unless they're driving their own car. I learned that lesson the hard way.

Naushad decides to take a new shortcut through Santa Cruz to avoid afternoon traffic. We later learn he always takes this route to avoid congestion, but for now, we simply think we're crossing into no-man's-land, never to be seen again. Stanley knows the city better than I do, but we don't drive and we don't know all the roads or neighborhoods. We give each other "the look" because we have no idea where we are. We should know our whereabouts. *Does it really take six months to get your bearings?*

Naushad is driving through a tunnel when he suddenly swerves to miss an older woman driving a damaged white Tata. However, he clips the back end of her car.

I hear him swear under his breath.

I hear myself mumble, "Keep going."

People are shouting as if he has done something terribly wrong, so he stops because he's trying to be honest. Suddenly, we've created the world's biggest traffic jam.

Now everyone is honking.

Everyone is staring.

Cars are honking, buses are honking, motorbikes are honking, bicycles with bells are ringing, and everyone is yelling at us for hitting this Tata car, which has obviously already had its share of accidents.

Stanley and I look at one another and pull out our wallets. Do we need to pay someone something? Naushad rolls down his window, yells in Hindi at the Indian woman, points his finger at our bumper, then gets out of the car, looks at her damage, shouts some more in Hindi, stomps his feet, gets back into the car, and we head straight to Khar West.

No bribe money exchanged, period.

We sail into the car park, and as we pile out the security people stand at attention. I notice they are very sleepy again.

I can tell Naushad is tired too, so I let him go early for the day to get some rest and give him a 300-rupee tip. He doesn't want to accept it, but I insist. I'm learning that what Madam says goes, no questions asked—and I like it.

Stanley and I catch the lift upstairs and relax for the rest of the day.

We celebrate Thanksgiving in Goa on the beach eating Indian food. Not a bit of turkey or a bite of dressing in sight.

Having said that, the Christmas season has begun. Gorgeous hand-stitched stockings, tree skirts, and artificial trees are waiting to be purchased.

Finding staff has been difficult, but finally, with the aid of Sabal, Naushad, and AWC members, we've gotten the word out and have hired a Goan cook named Luisa. I'm sad to say she cannot read or write English, but she does have a system for keeping track of what she spends on food. Of all the people who knocked at my door at unfathomable hours to display their cooking skills, she was the sole standout.

Sigh.

The gods are not looking favorably upon Madam. Remember, if we had moved in August, I could have hired a cook who worked for an expat family or better yet, a chef who worked at the consulate. Sadly, I tuck away the Junior League of Austin cookbook.

It's not meant to be.

Luisa and I discuss food and then she shops in the markets and we pay her $120 a month to prepare our meals. She wants to work 10 a.m. to 8 p.m. each weekday with the weekends off so she can rest and go to church.

We're adjusting to her style of cooking, and on the plus side, Luisa is Catholic, so she knows exactly where to take me to purchase holiday decorations.

On Monday, she tells me we're taking a rickshaw to Hill Road to get a six-foot artificial tree and other festive supplies. Sounds like a plan to me. I make a mental note to call Harry at Bhagheim Bombay to inquire about those hand-painted Christmas ornaments he sells.

But for now, we head to the fruit and vegetable market. She's good at negotiating a fair price, but I speculate they all probably charge the same fee when a "Madam" is around.

Once back in the flat, she scrubs and rinses the vegetables with filtered water and then soaks them for fifteen to twenty minutes in bleach to get rid of bacteria and pesticides. After a final filtered-water rinse, they are cut, sliced, or peeled, and stored in Ziplocs in the refrigerator for future use. Kudos to her for introducing us to a new bakery she walks past on her way to work. The boys love the fresh bread and cookies.

Luisa also helped us hire Neelam, so now we have someone to clean and do the laundry. Neelam has a passport and has worked for several high-caste Hindu families, but she has no documented recommendations. I think she's honest. She takes an instant liking to Matthew. Since Stanley is always at work, it's up to me to hire the people who will take care of my family.

I've asked Naushad to speak Hindi to her and assess the situation since I trust him more than Luisa. He seemingly approves, and since Fiona will be around most of the time over the next few months, it's not like the two new strangers can do much damage. Our passports and cash are locked up in our safe.

Neelam is in her late thirties and has never been married. She's direct, doesn't wear typical Indian clothes or makeup, and dresses in jeans and T-shirts (considered Western clothes). This woman just completed her interview and is now cleaning my dirty flat.

When they report for duty the following morning, Neelam and Luisa start us on a "recycling" program. Basically, this means they want all our plastics, glass bottles, and newspapers.

Who knew we had to move to Mumbai to go green?

They wash out every single dirty plastic bottle and Ziploc bag to take home to "resell" for extra rupees.

We'll pay Neelam $100 a month to clean, mop, wash, and iron all the laundry Monday through Friday (or just three to four days a week, depending on our schedule, for a few hours each day).

We seem to have a game plan in place now.

Inhale. Exhale.

Inhale. Exhale.

Something else I'm adding to the list of things no one told me is that mums seem to run in packs, so you can't get great deals on anything at first. Yvette told me to send Naushad into every shop to speak Hindi to the owners to let them know I'm going to be here for awhile so they should give me the best price. However, we discovered that the owners often get mad at drivers for putting employers' interests before theirs.

Furthermore—why didn't anyone tell me people talk? Like…the entire population of the city talks about your business?

It's true.

Anil the Wine Guy tells me his brother is the photographer who is printing my pictures at the Kodak store on Linking Road. Then he says, "You need DJ," and then states, "Hmm, how do you say this?"

I reply slowly in English, "Let me guess—your cousin."

"Yes, yes my cousin does DJ, and he will work at your party should you want to throw a party or just party, Madam."

I announce I just want cold wine, and we will talk DJ later. He tells me ten times, "You just call me for *anything*!"

Then he says he just made deliveries to some households whose children attend ASB with Grant.

I'm thinking, *How does he know I have a child named Grant?*

After that, he says he saw me at an expat party last week while he was making a delivery, and he wanted to say hello but didn't because it would not be proper.

As a sidenote, I took a picture with him on my digital camera and now he wants me to take it to his brother to print it. Stanley said it's probably going to end up on the *Girls Gone Wild in India* DVD sold in Crawford Market (South Mumbai's most famous household market).

We'll see. Tomorrow I'm calling Anil to ask for an elephant—the only animal I've ever wanted to see up close.

I'm really trying to get a grip on my life in Khar West, one of the many suburbs that make up Mumbai.

I feel like the main character in *Groundhog Day*. This life I'm attempting to lead is not normal. I'm straddling two worlds, not steady in either one. I feel like a child one second and then I rally and become a mature adult the next. The days are crazy and every morning I wake up and wonder what I'm going to do with my time. I try to plan things but nothing actually turns out quite the way I expect.

Grant got in the car from school yesterday and pointed to a temple. "Mummy, I think that design is quite nice." Then on the way home we stopped at an intersection when a gypsy woman and her baby approached the car window. She tapped several times to beg for rupees. I said, "Look at that sweet baby."

Grant did the head wiggle to her, turned, and said, "I don't have enough rupees to buy a sister today."

He's so used to people approaching the car to sell CDs, magazines, and other items, that he just guessed she was selling babies.

Can you imagine the thoughts racing through his head?

Riots started several streets over from our building today. It's illegal to have guns in Mumbai, so no one was shooting (a surprise for those of us from Houston), but rocks were thrown and many of the storefronts shut down for the day. ASB sent a text advising us not to use public transportation.

I was in a rickshaw over in the holiday section of the market scouting sale bits and pieces during the commotion and luckily made it home safely. Well-traveled expats react differently to this type of news, since some have lived in parts of the world where it's a daily occurrence.

I've started wearing more Indian clothing—*salwar* suits, long tunics with baggy or tight-fitting leggings, and a *dupatta* (a type of scarf). Stanley calls them buffet pants (because of the drawstring waist!), but I feel I'll garner more respect if I dress the part. In fact, I like wearing *bindis* and shiny bangles, and locals seem to treat me better because I'm embracing the culture.

Plus—how can you have a bad day when you sparkle?

Another way I've gone local: I'm addicted to rickshaws! It's really hard for me to imagine life without these black-and-yellow beetles. They provide a refreshing relief to the everyday landscape. They're toy-like and wriggle their way through the endless traffic jams. I know, because I sit in traffic every day and love to squeeze through tiny pockets of space to get home quick, quick. I love the freedom of jumping in and out and not knowing who you will see pull up right next to you at an intersection. And sometimes the drivers race each other!

I'm downstairs, but Naushad is asleep in the car. The other drivers are frantically calling his mobile, but not one speaks English so I wave them off. I don't need him right now.

Where I'm headed is to the handsome gray-haired man in front of my building who's selling *bhel puri*—deep-fried flour disks loaded with diced onion, boiled potatoes, crushed crispy chickpea noodles, coriander leaves, and a sweet tamarind chutney. Pinky, my neighbor on the floor below, told me about him, and I am determined to try his *chaat* (street food) for myself.

I pay thirty rupees for six pieces of *bhel puri*, take one bite, and gasp. It is *delish*!

The drivers and the Sleepy People are staring, watching my every move in disbelief.

I carry the plate to the car and knock hard on Naushad's window. He wakes up out of a deep sleep, freaked-out and embarrassed. He thinks I need to go somewhere.

"I want to share my new treats."

He races to the building loo, washes up, and returns. "Madam, how do you know of this?"

"Pinky told me to try the *chaat* and I love it."

He seems proud of me for stepping outside of my comfort zone. He's hesitant to eat in front of me, but I insist he take the remaining servings.

Then it dawns on me. I have a question. "Naushad, why are you tired every day? I let you go home early to get some rest so you're not always asleep and missing my calls when I need you to pick me up."

He looks down.

I repeat, "Naushad, no joking. Why are you always sleepy? You're turning into one of the Sleepy People. I need you to be alert—you're driving my boys!"

He looks straight at me. "Madam, you send me home early, but Auto Riders makes me pick up businessmen at the airport until three or four, like this, like that, in the morning because I speak your English. Then I must be here for you, Madam. But I want to be here. I do my best."

I take a moment to collect myself, take a long, deep breath, and then sigh. I thought I was giving him additional paid time off (and sleep), since we had a contract. I had no clue the agency pimped him out.

Inhale. Exhale.

Inhale. Exhale.

First, I give him the photo of Vinay receiving a ticket.

We laugh a lot.

Then we hatch a plan. "If you research expat shops among other expat drivers and help me coordinate deliveries (boxed milk, bottled water, Diet Pepsi), and speak Hindi (translating from my English) from time to time with Luisa and Neelam, I will help you!"

He has *no idea* what I'm talking about, judging by the look on his face. I remind myself to speak slowly and clearly.

My plan is keep him at the flat even if I don't need him. In other words, I won't send him back to the service.

Period.

So, every day he finishes his duty and then relaxes around the building, napping on the futon mattress I bought and placed in the laundry room until he heads home at a decent hour. Then he reports for duty the next day.

Trammell Crow Company will pay the due diligence—rightfully so.

The Erwin boys are in bed and Stanley is watching a cricket game. I pour a glass of cold Sula white wine and grab my journal. The balcony calls.

I write:

- Matthew is a rock star. Locals love the blue-eyed chunky baby. Strangers take so many photographs of him, I shout, "100 rupees!" each time someone snaps a party pic.

- Roseanne recommended a yoga instructor named Amol, and I'm finally signed up to work with him starting next week.

- The internet connection has been stabilized.

- The Indian head wiggle does not elude me anymore.

- I refer to the city as "Mumbai" or "Bombay" depending on whom I'm talking to. Older citizens use the colonial reference.

- I've thrown American terminology out the window. I'm living in a former British colony and I've adopted their holidays and their language—mums, lift, loo, and nappie, etc.

- As an American, I never discuss politics or religion, except with Naushad. (Long hours in the car make for interesting conversation.)

- I notice I've started to refer to myself in third person—"Madam needs to go shopping" or "Madam needs to order more Diet Pepsi," because servants won't address me any other way.

- I feel torn between two countries.

Next week, president/CEO of Vignette Corporation and fellow YPO member Mike Aviles will be our first guest. He's only one of four friends who rallied and said they would visit. I'm thrilled he's keeping his word.

I never told Stanley this, but before we moved, Mike and I talked at length at a charitable function. I was embarrassed by self-doubts and I think I came close to tears, because after all, here was a man who turned Foster Grant and numerous other Fortune 500 companies around. In other words, he can move mountains.

After dinner that night, Mike grabbed my hands and with these wise words, gave me the utmost reassurance: "Just because you don't know how to finish something, doesn't mean you shouldn't start it, kid. Go for it!"

So I did.

13

Dr. Babasaheb Ambedkhar, an Indian economist, politician, and social reformer who campaigned against discrimination against untouchables and, I'm told, inspired Modern Buddhism, is one hip guy.

I can vouch for his popularity, because more than 6,000 people are camped out in Shivaji Park near my building to pay homage to India's first law minister and principal architect of the constitution of India. Neelam tells me this event occurs each year on December 6, because that is the date he "expired" many years ago in Delhi.

"Neelam, this is Bollystock—like the Woodstock festival in the sixties: awesome people-watching and cool music!"

She looks puzzled. "Madam, did you go to this Woodstock?"

"No, Neelam, how old do you think I am?"

Pinky calls to let me know it's not safe to go out near the park. Many residents actually are staying away from their property. With the crowds of low-caste people camped out near them and the celebrations continuing late into the night, they can't go about their normal business. Streets and shops are closed. I tell her I'm aware of the man's celebrity status and that I pass by his statue on my way to the Fab India store at Khar Danda Junction on 18th Road.

"Oh, Rhonda. I forgot to tell you the city refused to clean the bird droppings off the statue. Young followers got a bit crazy and started rioting. Guess what? They knocked his head off by mistake," says Pinky. "Now city managers demand to know who will fix it!"

Click.

The day seems to be passing with no additional drama, so Fiona and I leave Stanley at home with the boys and head in the opposite direction—to Zenzi, a Bandra bar and restaurant that offers a tasty blend of Asian-inspired tapas to yuppies and movie industry shakers. I like Zenzi because they have free salsa lessons and live music. I would go more often, but they're always out of the reasonably-priced white wines.

After we pay the bill, we decide to visit the neighborhood Irish pub.

Naushad has the night off, although the service thinks he's working for us. We try to flag down a rickshaw, but no one wants to pick us up. This is normal, so we walk farther down the street in hopes of finding a ride.

Lo and behold, not one but two rickshaws stop in front of us—a regular dirty beetle and then one all tricked out in pink pleather interior with a black light hanging in the back. The entire interior glows purple. A cranked-up woofer blares techno music while we stand and stare.

"Are you thinking what I'm thinking, Madam?" Fiona yells.

"Yeah, baby!"

We jump in and off we go into the night, cruising the neighborhood and racing down Linking Road in style.

Once inside the pub, we meet a wild group of cargo pilots and flight attendants from the UK and we drink to India.

Mike Aviles, our first official visitor, has landed in the city for a two-day stopover. Naushad drives us south, where we meet Mike and a coworker in the lobby of their hotel, the Taj. After exchanging big hugs, we casually walk over to Indigo—still one of my favorite hotspots—for a delicious dinner and intimate conversation.

It's wonderful to see a friend from Austin in this neck of the woods.

The following day, the four of us decide to visit Shree Siddhivinayak Ganapati Temple, Big B's Hindu temple dedicated to Lord Shri Ganesh, the remover of obstacles. Big B is the legendary Bollywood actor and personality, Amitabh Bachchan, who gained his popularity in the early seventies and *is* old enough to have attended Woodstock.

We admit to Mike we've never been to temple. After a team huddle and discussion, we resolve to simply follow the locals in the procession, since we're not quite sure what one "officially" does at temple other than pray.

Naushad can't believe his eyes or what he's hearing. He understands English very well and he's listening intently—he wouldn't miss this for the world. He parks the Innova and watches our every move as we exit the car. He warns us about pickpockets and makes me leave my purse in the car.

We remove our shoes and hand them over at one of the shoe stalls outside the temple. Then we each buy a basket holding a coconut, a flower lei, and sweet treats (sugar cubes), and proceed barefoot into the queue to enter the building.

Many people waiting to give their items directly to the Elephanta god are in a larger, separate queue.

Two Hindu priests who form Team Ganesha take your basket of goodies, empty its contents onto a large counter filled with other offerings, and then fill it back up with another person's stuff (coconut, sweets, flowers) and hand it back to you. Afterward, they grace you with a powdered mark on your forehead via a finger that has touched hundreds of sweaty foreheads.

We didn't receive red dots. We figured maybe they don't give them to non-Hindus, but we're not exactly sure. With baskets full of new tributes, we walk to a large silver rat and have no clue what to do next.

A polite auntie puts her arm around my shoulder and tells me to whisper a wish into the rat's ear but cover his other ear with my hand so no one else can hear the wish. Then, I should put the lei around the rat's neck, leave my treats on a nearby tray, and pray my wish comes true.

I inquire about the coconut, and she mumbles something in Hindi and points to a "donation" stand.

Sounds good to me.

We perform as instructed.

Before I hand over the coconut, I feel a firm hand grip my arm. It's auntie again with stern advice, "Don't forget to eat a chunk of the coconut or your wish won't come true!"

I don't like coconut, but I sure did scarf down some of the pieces passed to me at the exit gate!

Namaste.

We waltz back to the *shoe wallah*, pay one rupee per person to get our shoes back, and we're gone.

Moving along on our tour trail, we visit the Dhobi Ghat, the largest open-air laundry service in the world, where 5,000 *dhobi wallahs*, all men, wash the city's laundry. Imagine 5,000 people—not standing around rioting like Dr. Ambedkhar fans, but standing in concrete tubs washing hundreds of items of clothing by pounding them clean by hand.

It's time for me to say farewell and catch a taxi back to Khar West. Stanley continues on for the remaining stops, business talk, and a guys' night out.

Laxman calls while I'm stuck in traffic. The VJ Home furniture we ordered from Jodhpur is ready for delivery, and he thinks it's best that he takes a train into the city to help us unload the truck when it arrives late tonight.

Tonight?

By the time I tuck the boys into bed, he's knocking at the door.

Within seconds, he answers a phone call from the delivery driver. He informs me they're stuck at the border and our transport is delayed by a day.

I roll my eyes.

I'm grateful he can speak Hindi and coordinate all the details, but I have to ask, "Are you kidding me? Is this for real?"

He grins and assures me things are fine.

We're starving so we take a rickshaw to Aurus, a new, more formal international restaurant with a view of Juhu Beach and a well-stocked bar.

During dinner overlooking the Arabian Sea, I text Stanley the update on delivery details. He's having a fantastic time catching up with Mike.

Good for him.

The next morning, the truck is a no-show. Stanley decides to go work out at the JW fitness center, and while I cook breakfast, the driver calls Laxman for a third time to declare our shipment will now promptly arrive on Sunday morning at 8 a.m.

Laxman sips *chai* and eats peanut butter on toast and tells me not to stress.

This time I don't roll my eyes or flinch. I scream, "This country thrives on stress! This is the load from hell!"

Shocked, he glares at me.

I clean the dishes and go hide under a long, hot shower.

It's safe to say we're on Indian time—whether we like it or not.

Bright and early Sunday morning, the truck finally shows up. Laxman barks orders.

It takes two hours to unpack and move the boxes up to the third floor. We pay the Sleepy People forty-five dollars' worth of rupees after the job is complete.

Head Sleepy Boss starts to give Laxy lip about how they want more rupees, but he snaps back, "You will take the rupees and be happy or get nothing."

Now our flat will be a *real* Marble Palace.

Neelam has the day off and Fiona is in the car park playing soccer with the boys. While I dust the tables and cabinets, Laxman goes behind me and rearranges things, like the hand-carved wooden musicians. Two in front, three in back. "Madam, this is how they sit when they perform in Jodhpur," he says.

He studies my Shiva pictures and tells me to hang the framed Elephanta portrait above the door for good luck. The rest can go on the living room walls.

"Rhonda, you have a good eye. You selected very good artwork of the Lord Ganesha, Lord Shiva, and Hanuman."

Then he goes to the loo and comes out screaming at the top of his lungs. "RHONDA, MADAM RHONDA, DO *NOT* PUT THE GODS IN THE BATH-ROOM! This is not acceptable *ever*! Put them anywhere, but not the loo!"

I yell back, "Oh, hell, Laxman, can't I pray to the porcelain god?" but he doesn't get the joke.

"No! No! Not ever! Never!" Then he gently says, "Please do not say curse words in the same sentence when you reference any god."

I feel dumb. I know better.

Quietly, I remove the statues from the loo and pray silently, *Hear me out, gods…if there are 330 million of you…I meant well, and I'm worthy of your blessings.*

It's a slow day, so I ask Lax to ride with me in a rickshaw to Kala Niketan, one of the best *sari* shops in Mumbai. I pick up my *sari* package and once we return to the flat, he drapes the *sari* over my clothes. Then he says I have to take the extra piece of fabric back to have a *choli* sewn.

A *choli* is the top that is worn under the *sari*, made from the extra piece of fabric that is part of the *sari* when you purchase it. They cut it off, stitch it into a top, then restitch the *sari* section where the cut was made. Then I have to purchase a petticoat (a cotton or satin slip worn under the skirt portion).

Why didn't the sales clerk instruct me to do this when we were in the shop?

My mobile rings and Laxman picks it up. "Who is Yoga Hottie?"

I grin. He's the young, up-and-coming instructor—Amol—who teaches yoga in my flat. I answer the call and confirm our next appointment. Then I show Laxy my list of contacts: Anil the Wine Guy, B3 (British Babe Brett), Laxy in Jody, Cathy, Roseanne, Krishna Tennis, Plumber Man, Boss, Fab Gautham, Naushadie, Mr. Diet Pepsi Man, *Egg Wallah*, and Mr. Carpenter Man.

He shakes his head in disbelief.

"I just list them by description because I can't pronounce all their names and I can't speak Hindi to them. I dial the number, hand Naushad the mobile, and he speaks to those who don't know English."

He wants to know if I'm going to learn any Hindi.

"The short answer is no."

Pursuing this further, I say, "I have learned to speak very slowly in English so people can better understand me. Plus, my expectations of what I need to get done in a day have been significantly lowered. When I want the best price in the market, I wiggle my head or walk away. The good thing is I've started to think like an Indian."

He smiles.

"Continue, Madam Rhonda."

"I sip afternoon *chai* and I scream orders at the staff."

He laughs and I'm embarrassed.

"I'm *kidding*, Laxman! Naushad is teaching me how to distinguish between Indians from the north and Indians from the south, and Hindus from Muslims. Not only am I altering my language, my senses are not as overwhelmed as they once were, smells don't knock me off my feet, and the honking doesn't seem as loud as it did when I arrived."

He seems impressed but demands to know if I trust Muslims.

I'm confused. Remember, I don't talk about religion except with Naushad.

"Absolutely. I trust Naushad. We're like Captain and Tennille, or better yet, Whitney Houston and Kevin Costner."

He laughs.

We walk to a nearby market, and he negotiates on my behalf for a pair of *jootis* and a tunic. Oh, when expat Madam who lives in the hood is in the market with the cute middle-caste Hindu man from Rajasthan, she gets the major stares. I listen while he tells everyone Madam needs the best price so she can return and buy lots of things—which is the truth, but boy, it's a big help to have him say it in Hindi to all the street vendors within a four-block radius.

I'm starting to feel like a local because the neighborhood gypsies blow me off to heckle the tourists.

I decide to lose my dignity again and go play tennis with Roseanne in my tennis outfit, tan legs in full view.

When I get home after our 1,200-rupee private lesson ($31) at Bandra Gymkhana, there's a *bang-bang-bang* at the door.

"Hello, Pinky!"

She rushes into the flat with a plumber because water is leaking in her master bathroom.

Okay.

Then, she says the plumber wants to peek down into the dark shaft in our master bathroom to see if there is a correlation. But, he hasn't brought a flashlight. I sprint down the hallway and return with Matthew's green dinosaur flashlight.

OMG.

I take a picture of the plumber using the toy flashlight, trying to fix Pinky's water leak, because Stanley will never believe me when I retell the story.

When the plumber pushes the button to turn on the flashlight, it roars and scares him.

We all laugh.

The plumber digs around in the drain and acts like he's fixing the problem. Here again, I can't speak the language, but I can understand he has no earthly idea why her bathroom ceiling continues to leak and cause problems.

Pinky tells them to bring the proper tools next time. Such is India.

Pinky's mum, Ms. Harwani, will be visiting soon from London, and I like it when she's in Khar West. I met her the day we moved into our building. She speaks Hindi really loud, yells at the Sleepy People, and loves giving sweet gifts from Denmark to the Erwin brothers.

Luisa shows up to cook and Neelam shows up to do laundry and iron. It's a full house when Mr. Carpenter Man begins drilling, drilling, drilling into my cement walls and marble bathrooms, again. Neelam explains the remaining work we want him to complete, which is great since I can only communicate with him by drawing pictures on the pad of paper I carry around.

Then Naushad appears at the door, takes off his shoes, and strolls in like he owns the place.

"Madam, Lolita, who takes all of the rubbish away from our building, wants you to pay her 200 rupees ($5) a month, Madam. It's like this...it's like that...it's just like this...she needs rupees, Madam."

What is he saying?

I don't think we pay for trash service in the city, Naushad, I'm thinking to myself. I could have sworn it's included in the rent.

I text Pinky, who just left with the plumber, and she confirms she was only asked to pay 100 rupees—the Indian price.

Naushad agrees to speak to Lolita. "Make sure you tell her we know the other families only pay 100 rupees, but we're willing to pay extra since we do create a lot of rubbish."

He says he misunderstood her and she only asked for 100, so she's thrilled we're paying the most.

Good job, Naushad.

I notice one of the glass doors leading into the living room is coming off the hinge, so I ask Naushad to stay in the flat and speak to Mr. Carpenter Man.

While we—Naushad, Madam, Luisa, Grant, and Matthew—stand around, Mr. Carpenter Man lets out a huge burp. And then he farts.

I can't contain myself. "That did not just happen!"

Matthew and Grant run down the hallway howling and waving their arms.

I turn to Naushad and even he can't keep a straight face.

I go to the loo.

I look in the mirror. Yes, this is my reality.

I return and ask Naushad to question him, because it looks to me like he's just unwinding a few screws and then twisting them back precisely where they were. They're staring at the door, speaking Hindi super fast as they turn around to face me.

"Let me guess. He doesn't know why it's coming off the hinge and he can't fix it."

Naushad snorts and grins.

I'm right, but I still can't get past the fact he openly farted.

"Madam, see—you do know a little bit of the Hindi."

"No, no, I don't know Hindi, Naushad, but I do know bullshit, which apparently is universal."

Just then, I hear yelling in the toy room at the end of the hallway.

I thought I'd seen enough uncouth behavior for the day, but now Luisa is bossing Neelam around behind my back.

She cruised down the hall during all the commotion and spoke very ugly to Neelam after she noticed new dirty dishes in the sink. I think she's telling Neelam in Hindi she will only clean the part of the kitchen she uses to prepare food. Then in English, Luisa confirms: she's decided to clean only the dishes she cooks with. Neelam is responsible for cleaning the dishes she uses during the day and the parts of the kitchen she uses for herself or the boys.

Excuse me?

I look at the two of them and raise my voice, "Who do you think is in charge?"

I motion for them to get into the kitchen, and boy, do I give them an earful.

Naushad tries to leave, but I tell him to step away from the door until I'm done ranting.

I make it clear to Luisa she will clean *all* of the dishes, and then I excuse her for the day.

Neelam slowly appears with a full laundry basket of clothes to fold once the door closes. She lets me know she's scared of Luisa, who expects a favor in return for finding her employment.

"No one tells you what to do but me! There is only one Madam in this flat and you're looking at her!"

My inner voice chimes in and is on my side for a change. *You tell 'em, Madam.*

Grant has asked to send an email to any potential visitors asking for kid-friendly food like chicken Vienna sausages and Cheetos. He heard us ask Mike for taco seasoning packets and summer sausage and is adamant to put in his request to the next guest.

Matthew is growing and picking up new habits very quickly. When Neelam arrives at the flat, he takes off, reappears with the vacuum hose, and hands it to her. When Luisa reports to cook, he sprints to the utensil drawer and grabs a wooden spoon. However, perhaps his most beloved thing to do is hang out with Naushad, pretending to drive the car.

Despite a few hiccups, we're just one big, happy Indian family.

Furthermore, something is stirring inside our hearts, and this country is beginning to feel like home.

14

There's not a single flurry falling and more palms than pines, but Khar West is bursting with Christmas spirit—specifically 15th Road, which has transformed itself into a stage for festive holiday activities.

It's colorful, crowded, and quirkier than we've ever seen it.

For example, the Khar Gymkhana marching band woke us up bright and early on Sunday morning. I thought a prankster from Austin sent the University of Texas Longhorn Marching Band to serenade us, but a neighbor on the fifth floor told me the band was practicing for a big wedding gig.

Then late in the afternoon, we watched a tall, handsome groom on a white horse pass by, with the family in tow, dancing in the street. The bride followed closely behind in a car decorated with flowers and leis. The family set off fireworks and our neighbors gathered to wish them well. Eventually, they sped off to our former homeaway, Sun-n-Sand Hotel, for the remaining festivities.

On Monday, the local college performed its holiday show from 2 p.m. to midnight—*American Idol*, Indian-style. It was shocking to see the cricket field turn into a stage with seating for 500 attendees. Young twentysomethings took turns singing songs by Elvis, U2, and Britney Spears. It's hard to believe the boys can sleep through these events that can last until 3 a.m. on weekdays.

On Wednesday, Naushad left me at Shopper's Stop, India's top retailer on Linking Road. I told him I needed twenty minutes, tops, to run into the store. When I came out, he was nowhere to be found. I tried to call him, but I got the network busy signal.

After twenty minutes, I grow tired of the staring, so I pounce into a rickshaw and bravely give directions back to Le Gardenia by means of pointing. The driver didn't speak English, but I was thrilled he helped me get home since the first two rickshaw drivers refused to pick me up.

My inner voice whispers, *Way to go, Madam. Forget six months—you've got your bearings!*

Come to find out, Naushad sat for forty-five minutes in the car waiting for me near the store on one of the side streets, and I couldn't see him from the mall entrance. I guess he thinks I like to shop.

To his credit, he did walk into Shopper's Stop to look for me but freaked when a fellow building driver, Chahel, called to inquire why Naushad's Madam had returned to the building in a rickshaw without him—a prime example of why locals need to mind their own business.

Naushad barely knocks before walking in the front door, leaving his shoes in the foyer. He is out of breath. He calls my mobile to see if there is a connection problem, but our two phones work perfectly in sync.

He shrugs.

But while he's in the flat, I decide to give him a stern talking-to.

I say very slowly, "Naushad, I'm still learning how to describe directions using landmarks, but I still don't know all the landmarks. Madam was frightened today. I depend on you to be there for me, to wait for me, and to protect me. You didn't park where you said you were going to park. I thought you were napping like the Sleepy People."

He cracks a smile, then gathers his composure, but doesn't move a muscle.

Fiona has told me he has a crush on Whitney Houston. In fact, he watches *The Bodyguard* DVD once a week in the car between cricket matches.

"Naushad, I consider *you* my bodyguard."

He stands up very straight in the white formal driving uniform the service makes him wear and seems to gain a measure of confidence.

"You must always stand outside the car and make sure I can see you. Kevin did this for Whitney."

He nods in agreement.

"Even if you must leap in front of a rickshaw to protect me, will you do this for me?"

"Yes, Madam. I will for you."

Fiona walks by and laughs on her way to the kitchen to feed Matthew.

We're interrupted by a loud knock on the door.

It's Pinky again—still attempting to fix the water leak in her bathroom. In she waltzes, followed by a plumber, followed by Luisa, and followed by Neelam.

Naushad's mobile rings in the midst of the parade: it's Mr. Carpenter Man saying he's set to work in our flat on Thursday. When the conversation ends, Naushad puts on his shoes and heads downstairs without saying goodbye.

Stanley better not ever complain about the cost of the remaining household improvements. Raj and our landlord didn't deliver on several items they promised, and it's taken me weeks to find craftsmen to do the odd jobs I need done, like making screens for our bathroom windows so the mosquitoes with dengue fever don't fly in. The glass was never installed.

Pinky picked the right plumber this time. He pulled out the bathroom fan, crawled down into the thin, concrete shaft—all sixty-five pounds of him—rattled the pipes, and finally stopped the running water.

Suddenly, Neelam is screaming bloody murder. "THERE'S A STRANGE MAN IN YOUR HOLE, MADAM!"

Seems she walked into the bathroom to clean the sink while Pinky and I were in the living room, and Mr. Plumber Man scared her to death when he popped out of the shaft.

Ms. Harwani mentioned once that Pinky attends Bollywood parties, so right after she leaves the flat, Fiona and I Google her—*score!* Turns out, our neighbor is a Bollywood actress. Actually, she's a model who's done a couple of movies, but one of them got a "B" review. I text Naushad to inquire if he's seen any of her films and he sends a quick text back: "She is bootiful, Madam, butt no goode movie heeroiine."

Pinky was born in Denmark and has a BSc (Hons) in business studies with a major in finance from City University Business School in London. She worked as a banker in top firms like Merrill Lynch and Deutsche Bank (while living in London, Hong Kong, and Singapore) before she decided to give it all up and try her luck in acting. Despite her lack of ultra success in Bollywood, she's intelligent and makes lots of rupees in the stock market.

You go, girl!

On Thursday afternoon, I send Naushad home early because he shut my finger in the car door again! I'm quickly running out of holiday spirit with him. I'm starting to wonder if he's moonlighting at the service for extra rupees against my wishes. I have no clue what he does once he leaves Le Gardenia. He seems crabby lately.

He has just left the car park in a rickshaw when a motorcycle driver crashes in front of our building. I hear all the commotion and peek over the balcony to see the poor guy sitting in the middle of the street surrounded by a large crowd of people. A cricket player runs over and offers water. Stanley takes down a towel and ice cubes in a Ziploc bag. There is blood everywhere.

While the accident isn't comical, what is funny is that it happened right in front of the Sleepy People—who saw nothing because they were asleep. Pinky sends me a text saying her driver heard the guy knocked out four teeth and bit off half his tongue. Someone put him in a taxi and the driver left him at a nearby clinic. Turns out he was drunk.

The Khar Gymkhana marching band is practicing again. I text Raj. He replies: "They're gearing up for the big New Year's celebration, an all-nighter. Beware, Erwin Family."

How does he know what an all-nighter is? Glad we're going to miss this one. We've got big plans: Singapore for New Year's!

Despite getting a reprieve from *Idol* performances, Friday morning at 2 a.m. we wake up to a poltergeist—strange beeping sounds are coming from the boys' room.

We jump up and open their door. The TV, which is turned off, is nevertheless *on*. A bunch of static is playing across the screen. Stanley doesn't know what to do, so I frantically rip the plug from the socket.

Turns out we have frequent power surges and they do weird things to electronics. Seriously. Our computer printer started smoking yesterday. We unplugged it and put it in the stairwell. As Mr. Painter Man left our flat, he said to us in perfect English, "I need this, and I will take it as payment for my work" as he handed back rupees.

I think these things explain why our building lift gets stuck. The last thing I want is to get trapped in there during a poltergeist moment. You could be in there for hours, if not days, until somebody rescued you.

Early afternoon, I run a few errands with Naushad. Then, I buy him a Santa hat from a vendor at one of the intersections—ten rupees. People are hustling around our car trying to sell holiday stuff—toys and artwork. He graciously wears the hat while we drive around the neighborhood. It's comical to see the faces of locals when they see him.

We head back to Le Gardenia. Naushad needs a lunch break, and I change clothes and flag down a rickshaw to Bandra Gymkhana for a tennis lesson.

I instantly notice Roseanne on the courts so we double up. Coach Krishna tells us we must run the courts after we finish warming up, and she kindly informs him, "The white people don't run. Get on with the lesson."

I notice he's taken aback by her abruptness. Me, too.

I played on my high school tennis team, and our coach sure did make us run the courts; heck, I need to burn Sula calories. I thought the point of tennis was to exercise and run, but she set him straight. We play several sets and pay him 1,200 rupees—the equivalent of $31 dollars—and we load up our equipment in her service car.

I ask, "Do your security guards sleep all day?"

"Hell, no. I would have them all fired."

Sabal grins at me in the rearview mirror. Then I ask another question, "How on earth did you find your incredible cook—Esther?"

She looks directly at me. "We arrived in July and I got stuck with a young cook, who was also a thief. She stole from us until I finally kicked her to the streets and reported her to the embassy in Delhi, the consulate down south, and the AWC. I had to file a police report, but she continues to stalk me because no one will hire her. I had to change my mobile number because we were getting some pretty terrifying death threats."

Hmm.

"Remember Amy on the eleventh floor of my building who is also a member of AWC?" she asks.

I nod.

"She invited us up to dinner four months ago. I watched Esther work her magic in the kitchen, and the food was exquisite. Luckily, she agreed to meet me for *chai* the next day. I offered to double her salary and to have her work fewer hours. She couldn't resist."

I roll my eyes. "Sounds like you did a little thievery yourself, Madam."

Sabal drives to Le Gardenia, drops me, and picks up Grant for a playdate with Ben.

Stanley is at the JW working out, and now that I'm home, Fiona and Matthew take a rickshaw to the hotel to play and swim.

I undress and step into the shower, load up the shampoo in my hair, and start to shave my legs. The water all but stops. Tiny drops drizzle from the spout. Then nothing.

Damn it.

I grab a towel and step out of the shower. I'm alone in the Marble Palace.

I don't know what to do so I call Naushad.

First of all, he can't stop laughing.

"Madam," he says, "Calm down. Please wait like this, like that, like fifteen minutes and you get water, Madam. The truck is here putting waters in the building tank."

Seriously?

He giggles some more.

"Madam, can I tell you something?"

I'm scared he's got a vision of me in the bathroom, naked, covered in shampoo and soap.

"Madam, you never, never take a shower this time at the day, each day, Madam."

"Why?"

He cackles, "Madam, you smart. There is no more water in the tank, Madam. You wait like Indian madams for later to take bath."

I do finally finish my shower—not bath—and a few hours pass. It's time to call Roseanne to let her know Naushad and I are ready to pick up Grant. Seems there was a poop problem on the way to their house.

I cringe.

Thankfully, Ben did the honors. When Grant and I got back into the car, he told Naushad Ben had to go number two so bad he couldn't wait until they got home. Madam Roseanne made him go in a plastic bag while Sabal wove in and out of traffic.

Smugly, Grant admitted, "Mummy, it was very stinky in the car and then Sabal threw the bag with the poop and dirty underwear in it out the window."

Ben got to ride commando all the way home.

It's time for me to get a haircut and highlights in Mumbai. I've been dreading this moment for the past two months!

One word: prayer.

I pop into Peri's Salon several streets over from the Sun-n-Sand Hotel in Juhu. Seth, an American from New York, gives me a J-Lo cut. He's a former stylist to the stars, or so he says. He's talkative, and overall the thirty-dollar experience was pleasant, but I always wonder about a bald guy cutting hair…

The good news is that I still have hair on *my* head. The bad news is that I'm now a blonde. The second I get home, Fiona tells me the layers he cut in the back of my hair are totally uneven.

Roseanne stops by unannounced. She's in disbelief when she sees my glorious living space. I've known since we met she presumes she has the better flat because she lives in Bandra, the stylish area Bollywood hipsters and wealthy expats call home.

I live closer to Dharavi (the city's largest slum) by default because our two Bandra residence options were sold out from under us.

Fiona shakes her head and reminds me, "She has no idea about the downtown view you have back in Austin."

Roseanne is drunk and goes to the kitchen and yells at Neelam to serve us Sula—now!

She yells, "*You* always have wine."

Reluctantly, we partake, and I do smirk when Neelam pours the most grape juice in Madam Roseanne's glass.

Boss arrives home from work, shocked at the spectacle: Madams and Fiona sipping Sula during broad daylight and talking, talking, too much talking.

When she leaves, Fiona and I move to the balcony to relax, but hear a piercing scream and then my mobile rings. It's Roseanne, and apparently a large, hairy rat in our lobby charged her, causing her to wet her pants. I say, "No, no, no! You did not just pee in your pants!"

"Yes, I peed in my pants in front of your security guards you call the Sleepy People and they were awake!" Then she adds, "Have you *seen* that nasty rat that lives here?"

"Well, uh, maybe…oh yeah…I think I have, but I acted like I didn't and ran into the elevator…I mean the lift…quick, quick. We're not cordial with the building rat."

The drama subsides.

Stanley puts Matthew to bed and we get ready to take Grant out for the evening, leaving Fiona on duty.

Naushad drives us to dinner and then to Roseanne and Nick's flat for a Hanukah Party—the last place I want to visit. As drinks flow, Nick explains the dreidel game to the children while Roseanne proceeds to recount the "I wet my pants today" story for all eight couples present.

Lovely.

Over dessert, I quietly whisper in Stan's ear, "The Sleepy People call her 'Crazy Madam.'"

He shakes his head.

Naushad shares on the way home that Madam Roseanne tumbled out into 15th Road traffic and our neighbors looked at her in disgust.

"Madam, she would not get in the service car, *really* Madam. Sabal picked her up. He put her in the backseat, Madam."

He makes eye contact with me in the rearview mirror.

"Seriously, Naushad?"

He glances at Stan, "Yes, seriously, Madam and Boss."

Looks like those British mums were speaking the truth.

On Saturday we sleep in until the construction noise peaks.

Knock, knock, knock on the door.

"Hello, Mr. Carpenter Man. We waited half a day for you on Thursday. Do come in and install my mosquito screens. Please."

Burp!

No, he did *not* just belch before going downstairs to build the screens in the basement. I call out, "Remember, today is a no farting day!"

I shut the door and walk across the living room. I look out over the window seat and there is a cow resting in the Khar Gymkhana driveway, causing everyone to walk around her. She doesn't seem to have a worry in the world. The Sleepy People are brushing their teeth at a snail's pace in front of the building. I open the kitchen drapes to neighboring construction workers eating breakfast in their underwear.

They wave to me.

I wave back and shut the drapes.

Fiona and I are heading to the fashion boutique, Amarson's, today for Indian attire to wear to the Christmas Eve brunch at the Taj Land's End hotel tomorrow. A salesgirl quickly adopts us and helps us try on a number of selections. At one point, she lifts up her tunic to show us how she tied the *salwar* pants properly. We pay for our outfits and—can I just say—I *will* be wearing a *salwar* suit this Christmas!

On our way back to the flat, Naushad starts snorting and slapping his leg. Out of nowhere he says, "Madam, the security guards smoke marijuana and that's why they sleep."

Fiona says she knew all along they were stoners.

I asked Naushad if they order Pizza Hut late at night and he mumbled about how they don't have enough rupees for food.

Today is Sunday. I comb the newspapers Vinay set up to be delivered to our flat and write down words I have trouble pronouncing. Then, on Monday, I show the list to Naushad and we practice speaking Hindi together while we run errands. I'm secretly maintaining a list of Hindu names I would love to be called—like Twinkle and Shiny.

How could you have a bad day if your name was Twinkle?

Stanley reads the list from time to time and just shakes his head. Honestly, my little task helps me practice saying and remembering names of local friends and teachers because I'll never be fluent in Hindi. Some of my favorites to pronounce are Ipsita, Soumi, Lla, Pune, Mukesh, and Sveta.

Stanley thinks I should change my name to Sula—after the Indian wine I drink on a regular basis.

It's midday, and we're dressed in Indian clothes, ready to visit the Taj Land's End for our Christmas brunch. By the look on Naushad's face when the Erwin family rolled out of the lift, I sensed pride.

We show up in time to see Santa make a special appearance. The Taj has a wonderful children's event with temporary tattoos, balloon artists, and games. Kids eat on special holiday dishes, and rockin' Christmas carolers complete our first holiday buffet.

Now it's time to head back to the flat.

Naushad's at the helm of our white sleigh (Auto Rider Tata Mini-Van) in his Santa hat as we coast into the car park. The security guards are at attention just waiting to see how we plan to spend the rest of the day. Everyone has to talk, stare, and then talk some more. The drivers and the construction workers are checking us out in our Indian attire—Grant and Matthew are in *kurta* pajamas and sporting brand new navy *jootis*. Stanley is wearing a *kurta* and jeans with sandals.

We steer clear of the building rat and head up when I remember we need to pay Lolita the 200 rupees plus a Christmas bonus. I take the lift back down and ask Naushad to find her. He tells her we appreciate the hard work she does for us and presents her with the rupees.

She speaks Hindi and tells Naushad I look pretty, but she wants to see her madam in a *sari*.

In due time, Lolita.

While we're changing into western clothes, there's a *knock, knock, knock* at the door. It's the Indian family from the fourth floor delivering Christmas cookies and sweets.

Then another knock on the door, and a young maid enters with a Christmas delivery from Pinky—Danish cookies and Indian candies.

Wow!

We seem to be quite popular, considering we're the only white people in the building. I bet we're good entertainment, and I'm sure the minute we returned from the hotel, word got out. Once again, every neighbor, servant, and driver is talking about our business, and making *us* his or her business.

Just as we're enjoying the stash of gifts, it's *knock, knock* again. This time, it's Mr. Carpenter Man, ready to finish installing door handles and mosquito nets.

Are you kidding me?

He's completely oblivious to our American holiday. A few nasty burps later, the screens are installed. I pay him and he's gone.

I barely sit down when we hear another knock at the door. It's Luisa, dropping by to give us fresh flowers just so she can pick up the extra glass I told her she could have from my shelf project, without guilt.

Lovely.

On the spur of the moment, and still under the influence of the buffet champagne, Fiona and I decide to go back downstairs. We put Grant's Elvis sunglasses on a sleepy guard and the Santa hat back on Naushad to take a few Christmas party pictures. I even capture Head Sleepy Boss in a Santa hat, stoned.

Before catching the lift up, I make Naushad tell them in Hindi I would tip them to brush their teeth behind the building in the mornings. They speak Hindi back to him. They will think about it; it may be too far for them to walk.

We spend the rest of Christmas Eve watching the activities on our street—mule-driven wagons passing by carrying trash or building supplies, motorcycles racing on, bingo at the Gymkhana, women in beautiful silk *saris* walking to market, young male teenagers playing cricket, the lime vendor squeezing limes for limeade, the *vegetable wallah* and *fruit wallah* trying to get a few more sales in before closing time, mangy stray dogs napping, rickshaws flying by, the ear cleaner cleaning a late-day client, the building rat sitting in front of our building holding court, and a slew of drivers just hanging out waiting to see if any Madams need to visit last-minute holiday sales.

It's Christmas morning and the boys are up, exploring under the tree.

Brrrrring! Brrrrring! Friends are calling to wish us well through Skype. We celebrate the morning with breakfast tacos—the best gift of all—made with Old El Paso flour tortillas given to us by Amy, who lost her cook to Crazy Madam. Craig—her husband, who is a DHL executive and a player in the monthly poker events Stanley coordinates—received a care package from his family in California and they were gracious enough to gift the tortillas to the Texans.

As I reflect, Christmas in Mumbai hasn't been bad after all. It's a wonderful opportunity to sit back and see the season through a different cultural lens. Hindus and Catholics celebrate and decorate, eat too much, and pay too much for presents, like we do—and stress out about pleasing family. But one of the few differences I see is that America starts the madness in July, and India starts the madness the second week of December. We are not missing the marketing blitz and the barrage of toy commercials.

I check the weather on the BBC. *Darn. No snow in the forecast.* Looks like my wish in the rat's ear was a bit much to ask for on my first temple visit.

So I turn down the single air conditioning units in the Marble Palace to fifty-five degrees. Now it feels like the North Pole, and it's worth every rupee. (I do the same thing in Austin before I light the fireplace and imagine snow-flakes falling outside.)

Tonight, as we sit on our balcony and watch the cricket field gates close and lock, the night begins to come alive. We view white Christmas lights hung sporadically on many of the neighboring buildings, and as they glow, I hear holiday carols in the distance, loud and clear.

We raise two flutes of Sula champagne in honor of new friends as well as to friends far, far away…sleeping while visions of sugarplums dance in their heads.

Namaste, Virginia.

15

We've returned from a long sabbatical in Singapore, where we brought in the New Year. What a great, clean city. It was a fantastic way to celebrate the school holidays: festive lights, nice weather, and clean air. Plus, we discovered a popular expat restaurant serving interior Mexican food and margaritas. Yum-O!

Truth be told, we slept most of the trip. *A-h-h-h*, to crawl in bed and not hear a peep of honking and sleep in till noon, then eat, shop, and tour each day.

Heaven.

I must admit, after catching up on our sleep, we began to look around and wonder...why *is* it so quiet?

Where are the cows, where are the ambassadors, and where are our people? I think India is getting into our blood and, oh gosh, have I the audacity to say—we miss the homeland?

One of our trip highlights was a two-hour visit to a large, clean grocery store.

India allows you to bring anything back into the country, so we did: $350 worth of groceries. In addition, we packed a cigarette lighter that plays the theme from *Titanic* for Naushad. While he loves Whitney Houston, he also adores Céline Dion and watches the *Titanic* DVD on a regular basis.

Climbing aboard Thai Airways, I spray Liz Claiborne perfume to dismantle the body odor, and we head off into the sunset with razors, bottles of liquor, clippers, scissors, snacks, and real silverware—all without a blip on the X-ray scanner.

Arriving back to the Chhatrapati Shivaji International Airport was the usual brouhaha. We got caught in a holding pattern, circled the airport for forty-five minutes, and then plopped onto the tarmac.

Naushad and Preytap, Stan's company driver, were waiting patiently for us. It was a wonderful trip, but it's great to be back in Khar West.

As we enter into the complex, the Sleepy People are saluting us. There's the building rat sleeping under a car; and there's Lolita waiting with the drivers—eleven people in a row just standing and staring. The next morning, Head Sleepy Boss appears with thirty-five Christmas cards looking for a tip.

Some friends put on one stamp and some put on two, but most people just slapped ten stamps on the envelope, hoping for the best. It costs eighty-four cents to send a card to Mumbai. I can't believe the cards without proper postage even made it.

All day we receive calls wishing us a Happy New Year: Neelam; Crazy Madam's driver, Sabal; Raj; Tejas, the manager of our local dive bar, D'Nosh. There are texts from Pinky, ASB teachers, and Sandy Shah, a friend Stanley works out with at the JW gym.

Unbelievable.

While we were in Singapore, Anil the Wine Guy called many times, but we never answered. I bet he wanted to make sure Madam had enough Sula white wine and champagne for 2007.

Someone is banging on the door, frantically yelling my "good name"— Rhonda. (It must be an emergency because this is rare to hear from a local.) It's Naushad warning us to stay inside because the police are swarming Le Gardenia.

Little did we know that the son of a leader of a major political group created in 1980 lives in our building. He's being tried for price-fixing petrol. Translation—he's shortchanging customers at the pumps in Khar and Bandra neighborhoods. The word on the street is that he illegally makes 150 million rupees a year.

I can't stand it. We take the lift down to stand beside Lolita. There is Madam with *all* the people looking and staring—the drivers, the building maids, and the Sleepy People. The police order the man's wife, cook, nanny, driver, son, and daughter-in-law into the police Land Cruiser and off they go to jail. No sooner do they disappear from the car park than another police Land Cruiser returns for Head Sleepy Boss.

Bye-bye, Head Sleepy Boss.

I wave to him, but he does not wave back.

I tell Naushad to come upstairs and explain what it means. I can tell he's scared. He whispers, "This big Boss and very powerful man in India."

Stanley shakes his head and goes to mix a cocktail.

"Is this like the Don in 'The Godfather'?"

Still whispering, he says, "I know this and he is the mafia of India, Madam."

I whisper back, "Naushad, this is major drama!"

He does the head wiggle.

"Madam, he pays the police off."

I'm caught up in the moment and suggest, "Naushad, should we throw a party and serve chicken curry and Kingfisher? The Don is at last going to jail."

Boss walks past us and says, "Naushad, your Madam uses any excuse to throw a shindig."

He looks uncomfortable.

My elation is short-lived.

I leave to drop off love-gifts from Singapore to Ms. Harwani and Pinky on the second floor. When I'm done, I get into the lift, but it doesn't go up to my floor—it takes me to the ground level.

In steps the Don, going up to his flat, which is barricaded.

Ruh-roh.

I don't have my mobile, so I can't text Naushad, or Boss, or the police station, or even Pinky.

It's a tense ride, but I get off at my floor, no problem.

When I get back, I tell Naushad, who stayed to visit with the boys and Fiona, that I rode up in the lift with the Don. He's surprised, but reminds me I once said hello and waved to him and he waved back.

"Madam, I hope they do not call you to the Indian jail," he says grinning.

Actually, the Don had to go to court in New Delhi the following day and pay a large fine. It was in all the papers, and a policeman is still at the entry to our building. In addition, another policeman remains in his flat answering his phone and documenting all of his calls until he goes back to court.

Later, Boss and I stand on our balcony and watch the Sleepy People speak Hindi to the police on a cigarette break. At exactly 11 p.m. all of the building security guards, including the police watchmen, are night-night.

Extra! Extra!

Pinky Harwani is engaged! When I delivered the gifts, Pinky was out and Ms. Harwani told me the American boyfriend called from New York to ask for her hand in marriage. He's what's known as an NRI, a non-resident Indian—otherwise known by catty locals as "not really Indian."

Daddy Harwani is thrilled that Pinky can get off the payroll.

Furthermore, Ms. Harwani, who will not return to Denmark until the actual engagement occurs, insists I stay for *chai* and sweets, but I politely decline.

I never overstay my welcome at the Harwani residence long, because the air conditioning units are not always in use and Pinky's hyper dog, Dior (like the one in *Something About Mary*), jumps on me and humps my leg.

Today I leave the car park on foot to explore Khar West. I want to know if anything changed while I was gone. The Sleepy People don't know what to do when Madam heads out of the complex without her driver.

I see:

- A schoolgirl sporting a purple backpack with a picture of a little gray kitten and the word PUSSY above it in big black block letters
- A man with a tumor on his neck the size of his head—I thought he had two heads
- People getting haircuts and shaves on the streets
- A man in the slums listening to an iPod
- A high-caste Hindu woman in a green silk *sari* buying cheap shoes in the market
- New Year's Day decorations hanging in intersections
- Gypsy kids yelling "hello" in English to me
- A sign saying, "If you have a weave…say, HO!" (This in the shop window of a hair salon called "Curl Up & Dye.")

I walk two streets over and then turn back toward 15th Road. I see a man pulling a dead rat out of a dirt pile. Then I look more closely. He's pulling a live rat out of the construction mess and he flings it into the air! My walk turns into a sprint to our building, but I stop in my tracks when I spot a vendor selling okra and radishes. I pick up and pay for a handful of each.

I'm close to home, but I can't resist! I jump into a rickshaw and ride down Khar Danda Road with no worries, the wind blowing my hair. Before we turn down 16th Road, we hit a red light. As I peek out of the beetle, I look at the passenger next to me at the traffic signal. I think it's a famous actor.

I'm back at the car park and Naushad takes me to the fish shop to buy more fish food for Grant's Nemo aquarium, a gift from Santa. As we're driving down Linking Road, I hear a broadcast over loudspeakers. I ask Naushad about the propaganda. He looks at me in the rearview mirror. "Madam, can I tell you something, Madam?"

"Yes. You can always ask or tell me anything."

He calmly says, "Madam, I'm Muslim. What you hear is prayer, like this, like that five times a day, thirty minutes each time, Madam. I did pray at 7:14 a.m. and 12:46 p.m. but I cannot pray now. I work."

I glance out the window.

I'm positive I knew Naushad was Muslim before Laxman pointed it out to me on his visit last year. Muslims usually wear the white *topi* with a white linen *salwar kameez* and sandals to mosque. Unfortunately, he has to wear the ridiculous white Auto Riders outfit (basically a 1970s band uniform, or think: the captain on *The Loveboat*) every day. It's hideous, including the hat.

"Madam, my wife, Nisha, is Hindu, and she prays for me."

Hmm.

Muslim driver married to Hindu girl?

What a modern match.

Then I add with a smirk, "Maybe you need to buy a prayer tape like Vinay."

Fiona and I buckle up the boys in the car and head to HyperCITY.

Grant announces, "Mummy, I love to get *HYPER!*"

The highlight of the trip is placing our cart onto an escalator that goes up and down each of the three floors.

For the record, it even makes me a little hyper. We didn't load up entirely, but we purchase tortilla chips, sodas, fruit we can't find in our neighborhood markets, chicken lunchmeat, makeup, hair products, and books written in English. On the way home, we cut through Santa Cruz, the dreaded narrow back way, with trains running above a dark tunnel.

Naushad knows I don't like this route. During monsoon last year, cars got stuck in the tunnel due to flooding and people were trapped and had to swim out through their car windows to safety. We slow down to enter the passageway when a small delivery truck cuts in front of us.

Wham!

The top of the truck hits the ceiling and stops in its tracks, flinging the driver out onto the road. Naushad slams on the brakes and we all look at each other, thinking, *that did not just happen!*

Oh, God, there is major honking behind us, traffic stopped on the other side, and people are staring at the poor man. He gets up and twelve locals try to push the car through, but it's stuck. I tell Naushad, "Drive onto the median and get out of here now!"

He does exactly as instructed.

As we cruise away, I look back. The driver is letting air out of the tires in hopes the three-wheeled vehicle can be freed.

Once home, I hear a stern knock at the door. Mr. Locksmith Man is here to *finally* install childproof locks on the windows. It's only taken him two months to surface.

Knock knock! Then there's another loud pounding on the front door. Here's Mr. Plumber Man to fix the new water leak in the servant's quarters.

Brrrrring! Brrrrring! My mobile's ringing. It's K-Value in the lobby, asking if they can take the lift up to deliver Diet Pepsi, Nestlé's milk, and bottled water.

I inhale. I exhale.

Today, Luisa announces a new dinner menu: salad, macaroni and cheese, and baked potatoes served with grilled chicken. It's a new year, and perhaps the gods have decided to intervene in my kitchen!

I want to say the Easy Bake Oven grills, but I'm not sure. I've never used the grill mode, but Luisa clearly has a newfound confidence. Maybe she woke up out of the Hindi coma and can now read the English.

Who knows?

I'm not going to rain on her cooking parade, but I am going to bust a move to find sour cream in this city. I'm on a mission to surprise the family.

Several local restaurants do serve curd or *dahi*, a yogurt made from non-pasteurized milk. ASB friends have confirmed via text that it's what expats call sour cream. After we pick up Grant from school, I feel adventurous and decide to stop by an Italian/Mexican restaurant suggested by an

AWC member to get an order of actual sour cream they officially list on the menu.

My conversation with the hostess goes like this:

"Can I get a 'takeaway' order of sour cream?"

"No."

"I just want sour cream and nothing else."

"No."

"Here is the menu and it clearly states you sell sour cream. I want to purchase sour cream to take back to my flat."

"No. It says that Mexican pasta comes with sour cream on top."

I look in the distance at Grant and Naushad in the car.

Grant waves freely.

Naushad gives me a thumbs-up.

Inhale. Exhale.

"Yes, but I only want the sour cream and not the pasta."

"No, Madam."

"I will pay the full price for the dish, but I only want the sour cream."

"No."

"Okay, *theek hai*. Please go get the manager."

Then I give a double thumbs-up to Naushad because things *will* go my way.

Period.

I can do this.

The manager appears. "You are the supervisor and you can make a powerful decision for me and sell me the sour cream separate from the pasta."

"No."

"Okay, let's try this again. Can I order the World Nachos that include sour cream for 'takeaway' but can you package the sour cream separately?"

"No."

"Can I just purchase chips in one bag and sour cream in a 'takeaway' container as well as the salsa in another container?"

"No."

I look around and I'm thinking, *Are you fucking kidding me?* But I don't drop the f-bomb and I say nothing.

Then it dawns on me!

You must always act insulted, pace yourself, and then leave, but not lose your cool—*ever!*

This is the Land of No and it's the principle, but you can defeat the system if you can remain levelheaded in the game.

I thank the supervisor and waitstaff for their time and leave.

I go to the ice cream store next door and sample ice cream while everyone in the Italian/Mexican restaurant stares at me through the glass window.

Who needs sour cream when you can have ice cream?

Grant and Naushad jump out of the car and join me in the shop, and I purchase ice cream cones for both of them.

India is many things, but on days like today, it's the *Country* of No.

Naushad studies me at length.

"Madam, do you need me to speak the Hindi for you?"

Politely I tell Naushad, "I've got it all under control. You and Grant finish up your cones and wait for me in the car."

I walk back inside the restaurant and over to a table and I pick up an empty ashtray. "This is how much sour cream I want to purchase, this size—like an ashtray full of sour cream. Can you help me?"

I swear, this is all a test to see if I can withstand India. I think she does this from time to time to weed out the weaklings. The manager (whom I called "supervisor" to make him sound more important) stands up from a table. He looks directly at me, and then he turns and looks at the waitstaff who are standing and staring at Madam.

Meanwhile, Grant is eating his ice cream in the car still waving at me, as I turn to glance out the glass door.

Naushad is making funny faces.

I'm up against all of India right now.

I inhale. I exhale.

I inhale. I exhale.

The manager doesn't say 'no' and he doesn't say 'yes' to me. He paces back and forth slowly. There are fourteen waiters standing around and no one is in the restaurant, and someone can't sell me an ashtray of crappy sour cream for my baked potatoes?

Geesh.

Finally, he says, "One hundred rupees."

Done.

I wave to Naushad, who's in shock I won.

Internally, I say a small prayer to the Lord Ganesha that I didn't strangle myself or knock someone out in the process.

We make two more short stops on the way home.

First and farthest is Sante, a delicatessen selling tons of costly imported merchandise, where I load up smoked turkey-breast lunchmeat, Manchego cheese, olive oil, and Irish butter into a shopping basket, when I spy something foreign on the shelf.

Sour cream!

Immediately, I want to run out into the streets and yell at the top of my lungs, *"India sucks! Why can't things work according to how they're supposed to work in the universe? Why? Just tell me why?"*

But I don't.

Sante betrayed me and whipped up homemade sour cream in lots of little containers bigger than my "ash-tray" container. I'm deflated. I purchase two containers and thank Milan with a smile, because I know her sour cream is much healthier than what I scored. But it will go down bittersweet.

As we pass by an unfamiliar makeshift fruit market on the way home, I jump out and cross traffic against Naushad's wishes. I grab five golden red apples. *Darn, I don't have enough rupees*—but instead of me putting one apple back, the *fruit wallah* tells me I can pay him tomorrow.

"I know you, Madam. You live here."

Ah, the juxtapositions of India.

I waltz over to the *vegetable wallah* on the same side of the street and pay no attention to Naushad and Grant, who I think are still in the service car where I left them.

I run into an AWC member and we chat for a few minutes. I see an ASB teacher and we talk while she buys tomatoes. I move to a side market and ask for an asparagus delivery to the flat.

Then I move, thinking I can make good time crossing the road, but I've lost my bearings while talking to a neighbor who is also out shopping.

I turn, and I'm face-to-face with a small lorry whose driver has lost control and who is about to hit me head on. Instantly, someone, something, some force grabs my waist, jerks my tunic, and pulls me out of harm's way.

It's not pretty. I fall hard to the ground, but I'm safe, unharmed.

I look up. It's Naushad.

He carefully picks me up and I brush off the dirt.

I turn to see the lorry driver, who, having regained control, is cruising down the street in the left lane. Hand-painted on the bumper, the words *INDIA IS MY LOVE* glare back at me.

I take a deep breath. I'm speechless.

"Madam, I'm too sorry I made you fall," Naushad says. Then his facial expression changes. He's perturbed. He is *real* mad at me.

"Madam. You were thinking, thinking too much thinking of the sour cream and you did not watch the traffic. Grant is in the car, Madam. It's locked. I had to follow you, to protect you. You could be hurt, Madam. Then Boss kill me, Madam."

I collect myself.

He says again, "Boss *really* kill me, Madam."

I'm shaken.

We cross back to the car. Grant gives us a thumbs-up.

"Naushad, I don't think the driver meant harm. I think he just lost control of the truck. Besides, perhaps the gods are gracing me with a New Year hymn forcing me to love this country, literally."

Naushad is not happy and does not respond to me. He does not want to hear my Texas twang. We drive to Le Gardenia in silence.

I can tell Grant is tired, and Naushad refuses to make eye contact with me in the rearview mirror. He parks the car in our sole parking space and helps Grant carry the shopping bags up to the flat.

Naushad does not realize we've made a key decision to buy a car, and we want to offer him a full-time job.

Maybe once he's over his anger, we can discuss the offer.

If he leaves the service and accepts the position, he won't wear the awful uniform most high-caste families make drivers wear. I will take him to purchase *kurta pajamas*, jeans, dress slacks, oxford dress shirts, belts, shoes, and sandals—even though Stanley already told me I'm not allowed to take Naushad shopping.

Who only knows what my future will hold if he accepts the proposal to be my full-time driver and bodyguard.

Naushad's mobile rings and he answers. Grant runs off to watch cartoons with Matthew. Naushad can't keep a straight face. He hangs up and says, "Madam, Vinay just got fired from Auto Riders because he wrecked three cars in two days. He was changing his prayer tape again."

We all laugh hysterically.

Fiona pours me a Diet Pepsi and Naushad a cup of *chai* while I recount the mishap story. Naushad is listening intently to every detail.

"Fiona, I saw my life flash before me. Thank God my bodyguard showed up. This is a sign. This country will do a lot of things to me, but it will not kill me. From this moment forward, *India is my love* is my mantra."

16

The days are longer, the cows are multiplying, and the daily urinators are out in full force. Moreover, I'm afraid winter may be over, and an early spring has sprung.

A text is coming in from Pinky thanking us for the pink flowers we had delivered in honor of her birthday. It says: "Take the lift down. Let's talk."

I don't need to knock—the door is open. I hear the juicy engagement scoop. Pinky is set to marry August 26, the same day as my Matthew's birthday. I introduce myself to the makeup artist while he works his magic. I admire the pink *sari* she plans to wear to the engagement party tonight, and I try on all her jewelry while the hair stylist finishes last-minute touches.

"Mummy and Daddy Harwani are happy the birth charts align," she says. "Although they wouldn't allow it to get in the way of my engagement. It's my decision to marry."

It's remarkable to witness the whole family preparing for the big dinner at Kyber, a high-end Indian restaurant, where they will meet up with the in-laws sometime before midnight.

We decline the gracious invite to the "intimate" celebration of sixty family members and friends. I have plans. Roseanne and I are set to attend a zany society party at Good Earth down south for a collection of textiles called "The Bombay Project," created to promote the city. Smart graphic designers decided to take vintage black-and-white images of everything from women in *saris* to rickshaws to the Victoria Terminus Train Station and silk-screen them on everything from matchboxes to tote bags to coffee table trays and pillows.

It's precisely the type of event I thought I might attend every weekend when I moved to the homeland. Zee Television—our version of E! Entertainment—interviewed me, as one of the few expat Madams in attendance, and boy, Crazy Madam was real jealous they didn't interview her!

The next day we continue to scan the newspaper for engagement news. Coincidentally, Pinky's NRI boyfriend mumbled the proposal on the same day Abhishek Bachchan, Big B's son and Bollywood actor, popped the question to Aishwarya Rai. No mention of Pinky on the front page, but a tiny reference on page thirty-six. I feel bad for her.

Meanwhile, Julia, Brett's lover from Austin, lands at Chhatrapati Shivaji International Airport and we sure have fun. She brought corn tortillas and M&Ms—two things we can't find. She has the privilege of meeting the Sleepy People, Luisa, Naushad, Fiona, and of course Pinky, Pinky's sister Kavita, and the NRI fiancé.

Julia's visit is short, just two days, because she has work to do in Jodhpur. Naushad takes her to the domestic airport while I pack for my trip to London—a Christmas gift from Stanley.

I leave Mumbai at midnight, and boarding the British Airways flight is pure bliss.

I sleep the entire way to Heathrow and wake up just in time to hear the pilot announce it is zero centigrade. Here I am in black leggings, a short-sleeved long *kurti*, and black ballet flats. I forgot to check the weather—something I forget to do time and time again over the course of living in Asia. In fact, it is snowing. Looks like my temple wish finally came true—just a little late.

Oh, my God. People speaking the Queen's English.

No cows, no rickshaws, no honking, no Boss, no kids, and no travel buddy.

What?

Brrrrring! Brrrrring! "Channing, darling, where are you?"

"What do you mean, where am I?" She sounds cranky.

"I just landed. Let's grab our bags and a pint. It's happy hour somewhere in the world!"

"Uh, I'm in bed. You woke me up. I don't leave until tomorrow."

"Oh, shit!" I call Boss the minute I arrive at the hotel and wake him up too. He's apologetic that he and British Airways mixed up the tickets. In addition, he's terrified Madam is in her favorite city alone.

In actuality, it makes for a relaxing first day. Other than a shopping spree at Gap to purchase winter attire, it is uneventful—except when I literally run into Naomi Watts at the Covent Garden Hotel as she tries to leave and I try to enter through the same door.

Our girls' trip rocks. We have lovely weather despite the initial snow, and one evening we drink red wine in the company of actor Clive Owen at the hotel bar. Boy, is he tall and handsome.

On our final night, we dine at Brasserie Max, the hotel's international restaurant. Then we take the lift up to the honor bar, check out a bottle of red wine, and head to the room.

We remove makeup, put on pjs, and pour two goblets of vino.

"I'm happy you're safe and sound in your new city. Friends hear bits and pieces from short emails, but we're worried about you!" she says bluntly.

"You need to communicate with everyone back home."

"It goes both ways!"

The word "home" catches me off guard. I don't dare tell Chan I don't feel like Austin is home anymore.

She takes a sip of red wine and exhales.

"Moe has a betting pool. He thinks you'll stay in Austin this summer when you return for a visit. However, my money is on you. I'd say a lot of money is riding on you, Madam."

I'm taken aback.

Friends are gambling I can't make it in India?

Seriously?

No wonder no one calls or emails.

I go to the loo and collect my thoughts.

I return. "Are you ready for the truth, the whole truth, and nothing but the truth?"

"Let's hear it, Madam!"

Ready. Okay.

"I was naïve to think I could control myself, my husband, my boys, the move, an entire country."

She cracks up when I say "the entire country."

"It's too much too soon. In due time, Madam."

"I talk about food all the time, and I'm tired of talking about food all the time. We don't have an oven. I own a microwave that cooks, defrosts, grills, bakes, and reheats."

"This is your box you call the Easy Bake Oven, right?"

I nod. "I spent the first two months trying to use it and it was awful. Every time I burned a meal it reminded me that my father once said I wouldn't find a man unless I knew how to cook."

"Well, that's baloney, and you proved him wrong."

Yes, indeed I did.

"We ate out a lot until I found Luisa. But think what it takes to cook simple dishes even if, you can find the ingredients, on a two-burner stovetop or in an Easy Bake Oven.

"The stress of all things India brings up memories from my past I thought I had buried deep."

I take a sip of wine.

"There is a lock on our refrigerator. We are told to use it when we leave the flat so the servants don't steal food. Eyes follow me everywhere unless I'm in a five-star hotel. Comically, there is a female expat tampon network, since India has low-quality feminine products, and we share the wealth.

"People walk down our street yelling—all day. Neelam finally explains to me that vendors announce their presence with a distinctive chant or call specific to the product they want to sell to neighbors."

Channing takes a large sip of wine.

"Stanley and I fight over the amount of rupees leaving the ATM on a daily basis. He thinks I'm spending our life savings away."

Channing laughs. "He hasn't changed."

"We make ice the old-fashioned way: in trays. I buy bottled water in bulk. You know Madam loves the ice. Speaking of water, Grant uses the squirter at school. Laxman said toilet paper is costly and rough and since Indian food makes you go to the loo, the squirter is 'water relief on your bum.'"

She laughs. I laugh too.

"The city's vulnerability is very human. When India is not the Land of No, I discover little things daily that I should enjoy, things I take for granted, simple pleasures in life. I have too much time on my hands—lots of time. I fill it with workouts, tennis, AWC meetings, yoga, shopping, reading, and then I shout orders. I'm tired of telling people what to do in a foreign country I know little to nothing about.

"Setting up the Marble Palace was tough, but—cough, cough—if I can continue to lean on others, it'll get easier. I haven't made any real expat friends, but I adore Pinky and her family. I've met amazing women in AWC and ASB, but Roseanne is a wolf in sheep's clothing. She has no conscience. Women judge you by the size of your flat and how you roll in the city, which is bizarre to me because we're all on borrowed time. Eventually we'll move on and no one knows the life you lived before you landed in the city or the one you'll live after."

I inhale. I exhale.

"Chan, I think some of these women embellish their former lifestyles to impress others. But then there are those people who really *did* do cool things—like Yvette, who was a film and TV costumer/designer who worked with Charlie Sheen, Burt Reynolds, and Jim Carrey. She also performed stylist miracles on *In Living Color* in Hollywood—like dressing the Wayans brothers.

"She sounds like a bad ass," Chan chirps.

"You got that right!"

I inhale. I exhale.

I inhale. I exhale.

"It feels good to fly under the radar. Back in Austin, Stanley pressures me to care what people think, but here I don't give a hoot. It's liberating."

She nods.

"I'm beginning to listen to what I *feel* and *know* instead of what I *fear.*"

"Wow, Madam, that's deep."

"I don't feel like a tourist, Channing, I feel like a local, but the only Hindi I speak is *kya hal he* (how are you) and *ab ja sakte ho* (now you can go)."

"Oh dear!"

"Stanley wants Fiona to stay another three months for *his* peace of mind. In other words, I can't complain about his absence if she's around helping with the boys. I'm not sure it's a smart idea, but she has been accommodating and I've stopped researching preschools."

I pause and take a sip of wine.

I add, "Naushad is like my doula co-pilot."

Channing chokes, "Are you his muse?"

Now I gag on my vino.

We giggle.

"Okay, cut me some slack. Maybe doula isn't the right word…more like Eagle Scout. I couldn't have made it this far without him. We're going to offer him a full-time job, and I pray he accepts."

We finish the bottle and begin to pack.

Channing says, "Let me guess: you're going to buy him a new wardrobe if he takes the job?"

"Correct. He's a reflection of me."

Meanwhile, 9-1-1, 9-1-1!

Turns out that while I was in London, the Sleepy People were smoking pot in the basement and caught a bunch of rubbish and two cars on fire. Luckily, the Don's family, with their windows open, smelled smoke, and called the fire department. They instructed their drivers and maids to knock on every stairwell door and yell *fire!*

Pinky called, but my mobile was switched off.

Stan, the boys, and Fiona were asleep and they didn't hear any mobiles ringing or any banging at the doors.

Naushad arrived exceedingly early to the Auto Rider's office and heard about a fire at Le Gardenia. He jumped in the service car and raced to our building.

He couldn't find Boss in the car park so he took the lift up and frantically knocked on our front door. By the time Fiona woke up and heard the commotion, the fire was out.

As usual, British Airways must circle the airport for an hour due to air traffic before the plane can land.

Naushad picks me up, but he's unusually quiet.

"Did you miss your Madam?"

He grins but remains steady.

I don't see Lolita as usual in the car park when we pull in. On the other hand, I notice the building is dark and none of the lights are working in the lobby.

Stanley breaks down and confesses the whole story after Grant tells me about firemen visiting the flat.

The next morning, I explore the basement to inspect the damage and then go up to the fourth floor to talk to Mr. Kohli, our neighbor who wears a *sabat soorat* (turban) and sports a beard. He moves his furniture at all hours of the day. (I swear he was an interior decorator in a former life.)

He tells me the security team—or as I refer to them, the Sleepy People—will be replaced, but it may take some time. In the interim, they can no longer cook, smoke, or beg for tips. Their days of being useless are over.

I want to believe him, but I know India, and this will not go according to plan. But I'm optimistic. Then he tells me the builder will send workers next week to install fire safety equipment. I laugh out loud. "It will happen, but it could be days, weeks, maybe even months before we see improvements."

Meanwhile, I switch gears and send a nasty text to Mr. Sanjay, the man who owns a temp agency that supplies workers to high-caste families who need domestic support. He's the thief who took my rupees as well as Pinky's money and sent all the wrong people to our flats despite the list of qualifications for domestic help we provided. Per the contract, since he was unable to fulfill my worker obligations, he must refund the seventy-five dollars. Stanley tells me to let it go, but now it's the principle.

Battles are fought in India over principles and this is my own private war with Mr. Sanjay. I'm still searching for a culinary expert star, but so far, I have no new candidates. Just when I want to can Luisa, I think of all the shady locals that appeared wanting an interview.

Fiona told me to lower my expectations, but yesterday afternoon Neelam was cleaning the kitchen and found a large jar containing used oil.

I asked her to throw it away.

Now I know why we're ill from Luisa's cooking. It's common for low-caste families to reuse oil, but I told Luisa when I hired her, "We never re-use cooking oil. Not today. Not tomorrow. Not ever."

The day is dragging by when there's a *knock, knock, knock* at the door. The Harwani girls are escaping wedding drama. Boss has a client dinner, thankfully, and will be out late.

"We're so glad you're home. My flat is full of family and my future in-laws talking wedding talk," says Pinky. "We told everyone Dior needed to go out and tiptoed up."

Ms. Harwani says, "Rhonda, we're not sure about this union."

I nod.

"He's engaged and his mum still does his laundry!" Pinky complains, "He's really conservative, which I don't get—because he's a New Yorker!

"I don't want to live in his one-bedroom flat, but he's done nothing to resolve the dilemma. Also, he doesn't want me to model or act in Bollywood movies anymore. We seem to argue constantly—even the smallest things get blown out of proportion."

I say, "Pinkster, it sounds like a high-caste Sindhi marriage made in hell."

They both agree.

We drink two bottles of Sula and by 10 p.m. we're saying goodnight.

Despite their reservations, they plan to leave late tomorrow to tour Bali, Thailand, and Singapore to investigate wedding locations.

We've permitted Neelam to watch Matthew during the day or the boys when date night happens, since Fiona may be leaving soon.

However, the other day, she took Matthew downstairs for a walk around the building. I gave instructions to remain in the car park. After kicking the soccer ball, she placed him inside the service car and let him play with the steering wheel while Naushad and the other drivers supervised his playtime.

When Fiona called Naushad to pick them up from a playdate, Neelam took Matthew along for the ride without asking permission. Imagine my surprise, after thirty minutes pass, and they don't return up to the Marble Palace.

The lift is stuck so when I get to the car park through the stairwell, I can't find Naushad or Neelam or Matthew. Chahel speaks Hindi to me and then points to the street.

Panic attack!

After a very long talk with Naushad and Neelam together and then separately, we got things worked out, but for a few minutes that seemed like eternity—my worst nightmare came true: someone stole my baby.

Friends think servants are a luxury. I swear, life is more stressful managing a staff.

Brrrrring! Brrrrring! It's Seth. He saw me on TV talking crapola (actually I was saying positive things) about Mumbai. He's drinking whiskey at a friend's flat, not cutting hair. I hang up and then he sends a text. It says he's still turning expat hair different colors—such the comedian. I message him from time to time: *I'm not letting him forget he turned my hair orange when I went in for blonde highlights last month.*

Brrrrring! Pinky's calling to say her new driver is coming to drop off the keys to her Mercedes while she's out of town. She says I can use it while she's gone because she doesn't want him driving it. I tell her I'm in the car park and to have him take the lift down. I tell Naushad my former car in America was a Mercedes bigger than Pinky's. He laughs. He doesn't believe me.

"Madam, you had a driver," he says. "You can't drive a Mercedes, Madam."

Brrrrring! Hello, Mr. Clifford the Painter Man. You're coming next week to paint the door leading to the stairwell that the owner of our flat never re-painted after the fire...

We buy a new car, a Toyota Innova, and we officially hire Naushad away from Auto Riders as our personal driver. I won't go into detail about the amount of paperwork it takes to purchase a car in a foreign country, but the deal is done.

Shobhit negotiates the sticker price in Hindi, but once Boss and I sign the carbon copies and the dealership hand-stamps all the documents, it becomes official.

To our surprise, the Toyota employees dish out coconuts, flowers, and red powder for a *puja*: the ceremony to bless the new car and keep it safe from evil influences. Preytap is up first, marking the engine with a right-hand swastika; then he puts a red *bindi* on Boss's forehead. (I didn't plan on him participating in the *puja*, but Boss told me it was the right thing to do.)

A *bindi* or a *tilaka* is applied low in the center of the forehead, close to the eyebrows. The area is said to be the sixth chakra, *agni*, the seat of concealed wisdom. The *bindi* is said to retain energy and strengthen concentration. It is also said to protect against demons or bad luck.

Naushad, the only official driver of the car, scribbles a Muslim symbol in powder on the engine and then gently places a small *tilaka* on my forehead.

I break the coconut in half and we share several pieces, and then the dealership gives us chocolates. Next up, we wave a beautiful brass plate of incense around in circles an odd number of times over the engine. I'm instructed to do five circles, but an employee is snapping photographs with my camera and distracts me. I circle the engine six times and now I must go another round; even numbers are not auspicious.

Once the *puja* is complete, the salesperson hands the keys to Boss, who hands the keys to me; I turn and give them to Naushad.

"Thank you, Madam!" he says.

Boss climbs into the company car with Preytap to head back to the office.

Naushad studies the car and immediately notices a small scratch on the front bumper and points it out to the dealership employee. They send a repairman to buff it out before we leave the premises.

I send a text to Boss: "See—Naushad and I didn't even put the first scratch on the car!"

We get home late Monday and share the coconut and chocolates with drivers drinking *chai* and servants in the car park on break. Naushad speaks Hindi to the Sleepy People and shares only the coconut pieces, since Madam is still mad about the fire.

The staff and neighbors are thrilled about our new car. Naushad acts like he's showing off a first-born son.

The next morning, when I take the lift down to run errands, Naushad looks gloomy.

He has bad news.

Head Sleepy Boss keyed the car.

He was jealous he didn't get chocolates, and he was mad Naushad had paid the lone Non-Sleepy Night Watchman (who ran into the burning base-ment to try and put out the fire) to wash our car out of his own money.

I want to run into the street again and yell, *"India, I don't love you any-more! Why on earth does Head Sleepy Boss remain at Le Gardenia?"*

But I stay put.

I call Stanley at the office.

"I'm furious the high-caste Punjabis in our building did not follow through on the promise to fire the Sleepy People. If they had, this wouldn't have happened. Where are the Texas Rangers when you need to kick butt?"

Naushad listens intently.

"Rhonda, calm down," Stanley tells me.

"No, oh hell no. The fact that this jerk is still working at our building is unfathomable. I'm going to the Khar West Police Station."

"Settle down, Madam. I will call the builder and Raveev, the landlord. Then, I will call Mr. Kohli and tell them Head Sleepy Boss is gone today or you're going to the consulate."

I scream, "Raveev is an idiot. He's never followed through on any of his promises. Enough is enough. I have a few errands to run before I pick up Grant at noon. Make your phone calls and report back to me in an hour."

On our way home from picking up Grant, Naushad turns the corner and slams on the brakes. There in front of the car is a one-armed man—drunk and standing in the middle of the road. Immediately, he hits the hood of our car with his fist and tears off our flower lei from the *puja*. He drapes the garland around his neck and stumbles down the street.

Naushad looks at me in the rearview mirror.

We're stunned.

Grant says, "Mum, he's wearing our lei as a necklace."

As we drive into the car park, who do we see but Head Sleepy Boss drinking *chai*. All the drivers are staring and smoking cigarettes because the word is out: Madam is furious.

Naushad parks the Innova in the back of the lot and tells me he needs *chai* too.

A young servant comes up and in perfect English tells me to visit Ms. Kohli on the fourth floor, where I reiterate the entire story to her son and the builder who has been summoned to Le Gardenia. Mr. Kohli is at temple. Then, Raveev calls and I hand my phone to the builder and then to her son, who is being my "man" since Boss is still at the office.

He tells my story in Hindi to Raveev, taking my side, of course. The funny thing is Ms. Kohli's son mixes up my naming of "Head Sleepy Boss" during the conversation in Hindi and calls him, "Head Fat Security Man." I want to laugh, but don't.

We all go downstairs to view the damage. Head Sleepy Boss tells the builder my driver must have scraped the car at the traffic signal—he's done nothing wrong.

For the first time, I see Naushad lose his temper and go to the dark side. He rakes Head Sleepy Boss over the coals. I don't know this side of him, but I'm wondering why it took so long to appear.

I hold up my hand and yell, "STOP!"

"He goes now. Make him get his things and leave."

The men stare at me, in shock.

The builder calls the supervisor of the Sleepy People over and asks in Hindi why he has tolerated this behavior.

Naushad translates for me, but I know by his body language he's professing innocence. I turn to everyone and say loudly in English, "Ludicrous! He's saying he knows nothing about these scratches on my car?"

Naushad turns to me. "See, Madam, you do know a little bit of the Hindi."

Inhale. Exhale.

Inhale. Exhale.

"He knows he's guilty. In fact, he and the supervisor are both guilty."

The builder speaks Hindi to the supervisor again and then English to me, "No, they know nothing about the scratch marks."

"I'm telling you one if not both are responsible."

"No, Madam, he says they know nothing."

"He's at fault."

"No, he says he knows nothing."

I look around. Everyone is standing and staring at me. Doing nothing. *You have got to be fucking kidding me, because even the construction workers and our neighbors know he keyed the car.*

I say it one more time slowly, but now I'm shaking, "I'm telling you, he is very, very guilty."

"No, Madam, he says he knows nothing."

Suddenly, I remember one very special Christmas brunch with complimentary champagne. "I've had enough of this gibberish. He's guilty and I have photographs of every Sleepy Guard smoking marijuana and drinking alcohol, with Santa hats on. They drink and smoke on duty every day and we all know he did this to my car."

Silence.

I look around again and seven drivers are grinning at me. Ms. Kohli, her son, and the builder are all smiling at me, too. The construction workers next door have stopped making noise. Lolita hums a tune from *Fanaa*, my favorite Bollywood movie starring Aamir Khan. She's been listening as she sweeps around us.

Wanna know who's not grinning?

Head Sleepy Boss is not grinning.

I look over at Naushad and he winks at me for the first time.

The builder goes off on the supervisor in Hindi and then they escort Head Sleepy Boss out of the complex along with his brother and brother-in-law, whom he lets sleep on the tenth floor for free while our building construction continues.

The builder gives me his mobile number in case I see anything else happen with the Sleepy People. He will be the first to respond and the rest of the group will be fired upon my request.

Back in the Marble Palace, I text Pinky the good news and call Stanley.

Fiona appears from the kitchen and hands me a glass of Sula.

"Well done, Madam," she says. "What will you do for an encore?"

The very next day, I am met with many firm handshakes from the building drivers. No one misses Head Sleepy Boss.

And guess what? The Sleepy People aren't sleeping anymore. Of course, they can't smoke marijuana or cigarettes, drink alcohol, or cook, but they're doing their jobs—service with a smile. They get the lift for us, they lock the gates, and they carry our bags. They don't even brush their teeth in front of the building in their underwear anymore.

Just now, I saw Ms. Kohli going for her daily walk in her *salwar kameez* and white Nikes. She told me how much better the building aura is now that the vagrants are gone.

I smile and think to myself, *Why did it take a girl from Texas to raise Cain to get rid of someone who set our building on fire and keyed my car?*

Ah, India is my love again.

Knock, knock, knock at the door. It's Naushad and Mr. Tailor Man. Time to try on my *sari choli* to make sure it fits. I go into the bedroom and appear with the top on. I feel awkward showing my stomach to a complete stranger and my driver. Mr. Tailor Man measures me and takes a "correction." I return to the bathroom to change and hear Naushad speak Hindi, stating the sleeves need to be tighter or it won't look good.

Mr. Tailor Man leaves to walk two streets over to fix the top—all for three dollars.

Valentine's Day is here.

I stop on the way home from my tennis lesson with Krishna and pick up forty roses for six dollars.

Once home, I hand out chocolates to the drivers and the Alert Security Team (formerly known as the Sleepy People). I ask Neelam to deliver flowers to all the building madams. When Boss arrives home, I give him a bicycle I had tricked out by a painter who decorates rickshaws.

OLD MONK is painted on the front fender and I LOVE MY INDIA is painted on the back fender. Stanley drinks an Indian rum called Old Monk with Diet Coke and we always say we "love" India even on "no" days. I just hope the lock will protect the bike from thieves when he rides it to Subway on the weekends.

Knock, knock, knock at the door. It's Ms. Harwani. Welcome home! I hand her Pinky's spare Mercedes key and accept the chocolates and wallet she bought me in Singapore. Bad news—the wedding may be off. The plump NRI was a no-show on the scouting trip and Pinky is livid. Ms. Harwani is headed to Denmark later in the month to help with the delivery of a new Harwani grandbaby, and the Pinkster must make a decision about her future.

I head to a small temple off Khar Danda Road to make an offering to the

Lord Ganesha in honor of my upcoming birthday.

Halfway home, Naushad meets me and asks if he can walk along beside me, and tell me something. I stop, sigh, and say, "Of course, Naushad. You can tell me anything. Nothing fazes me anymore."

He says, "Madam, it's like this, like that, I'm sorry Head Sleepy Boss keyed my car, your car, Madam." He adds, "I'm too happy, Madam, to drive this car. Thank you, Madam. Thank you so much, Madam, for letting me drive our car."

I know Naushad is very proud of the new purchase. Expat friends utilize services like Auto Riders, and no one we actually know has bought a car. Naushad was pole-vaulted instantly to the highest status among the drivers because of the new Innova. They know Boss and I bought the car without driving it. I adore Naushad and I'm pleased he outranks and outperforms all the others.

I stop and buy bananas for the gypsy children. I inhale a large breath of polluted air and jump out of the way as an ambassador passes too close for comfort.

We continue walking and see a woman in a stunning beaded *kurti* waiting for her decorative sandal to be fixed by the *shoe wallah*. We see three men walking side by side, all holding hands. An old man riding a bicycle with a fake plastic Gucci seat pedals down the road. The Egg Man shouts Hindi to Naushad, and I understand he just told him we don't need eggs today, maybe in three days.

Boss and I celebrate Valentine's Day over dinner at Aurus, and I wear a sassy red *sari* and a silver *bindi*.

I seriously thought I was hot stuff in Indian attire enjoying the evening and the three-course meal, only to get home and discover two large burn holes in the folds of my hem. I show Stanley and he laughs. *The Devil Wears a Burning Sari!*

Unfortunately, the restaurant placed mosquito coils under all the tables to help with dengue fever control, although there isn't a problem due to a strong breeze off the beach.

The next day I take the *sari* to Kala Niketan and after deliberation, a decision to cut an entire inch off the bottom is handed down.

Valentine's Day will always have a special place in Naushad's heart too.

As a surprise, we bought him a 14-inch color TV—a huge no-no in the world of having servants. I wanted to get him something for his hard work—something practical. Fiona told us he mentioned his TV was broken, and I couldn't stand the thought of his wife and daughter staying at home with no entertainment while he's working.

When we return from the restaurant, he parks the Innova and we insist he take the lift up with us. We give him the wrapped TV and he's speechless. I think I see tears, but he chokes them back. When Boss excuses himself to check on the boys, I give Naushad 1,000 rupees and tell him to take a taxi home, not the train.

I wink at him. "Keep the extra rupees for *chai*."

"Madam, I thank you so much." he says. "Boss too, Madam."

We load him up with the champagne flutes, Sula champagne, cologne, perfume, chocolates, and flowers we scored in the Aurus gift bags. It felt good to pass them along to Naushad, who apparently had worked on Valentine's Day for the past five years. For once, he was going home to celebrate.

Namaste, bodyguard.

Of course, he is late the next morning and feels awful, but I don't care. I eat a muffin for breakfast and take a rickshaw to my tennis lesson with Krishna.

When he picks me up two hours later, he tells me he stayed up until five o'clock in the morning watching TV with Nisha and Firoza, his six-year-old daughter.

"Naushad, that's one special night you will remember long after Madam leaves your country."

He smirks.

Personally, I think he pulled an all-night rompfest by the look on his face and his swagger.

Way to go, Romeo!

17

It's hot, really hot. The Mumbai heat is killing our senses. It's not even the hottest it's ever been in the city, yet we're sweating even as we go from air conditioning to air conditioning.

I'm tired of the spit, the urine, the heat, and the smelly sweat next to me, in front of me, blowing on me, and dripping on me when I'm in the market.

The minute I enter the Marble Palace, I walk toward the ductless multi-split wall-mounted unit in the living room and crank down the temperature—now it's working overtime.

Brrrrring! Brrrrring! It's Ms. Harwani calling to invite me to participate in the Mahashivratri festival at the end of the month. Married women observe a fast and perform a *puja* to appease the Goddess Parvati, who bestows marital bliss and a long and prosperous married life.

"We will take sweets and milk to temple," she says.

I accept her courteous invitation. What a treat!

Then she informs me that next year, the festival will be held on February 16th—my big day (now considered auspicious) that I share with Brett—and she will see me later tonight at my party.

Okay.

Knock, knock, knock on the door and three birthday cards from girlfriends in Austin are delivered. Then, *knock, knock, knock* on the door and it's suddenly delivery central: purple orchids from Raj, a bottle of Sula from Anil, white orchids from Laxman.

Fiona shuts the door but there's more knocking and, lo and behold, more gifts: six dozen red roses from Stan, pink gerbera daisies from Naushad, yellow chrysanthemums from Neelam, purple roses from the Harwani family, and a large chocolate cake from Pinky and her fiancé.

Flower power!

I'm in awe. My mobile rings and Naushad appears to be in charge today.

"Madam, we need to move now to your birthday lunch at Hard Rock Cafe. Preytap is driving Boss."

I collect the boys and the diaper bag and head down to the car park.

Wait—more flowers?

Naushad has four flower leis strategically draped and secured on the Innova.

What a surprise!

Grant says, "Mummy, you are styling today."

I'm thrilled the TCM office is near the Hard Rock Cafe because Stanley can join us. The waitstaff recognizes our family and seats us in the same booth we always sit in and they place the usual order: chicken nachos, macaroni and cheese, beef burgers, and potato skins. But this time, with extra sour cream.

Lunch is spectacular, but before the check arrives, Stan the Man hands me a small wrapped box.

Looks like my first birthday temple wish is coming true—jewelry!

Theek hai, Boss.

Later in the evening, it's *knock, knock, knock* on the door and Ms. Harwani has vegetarian starters she's had her cook prepare.

Knock, knock, knock on the door and in walks Neelam, in tight dark denim jeans and a new tunic. She wants to help cook more starters and bartend.

She says timidly. "I left early today, but I want to help you celebrate your special day, Madam."

I'm taken aback because I've never seen Neelam sporting lip gloss or mascara.

The United Nations—the name our spouses call the group of ASB and AWC women representing India, Trinidad—Germany, England, Scotland, USA, Canada, Thailand, and Taiwan, gather along with Fiona to devour starters and drink Sula.

When the Harwani ladies leave, we move the party to the Boat Club, a local bar where the DJ booth moves up and down three floors, and we dance until 2 a.m.

I feel like hell the next day. Boss takes Grant to morning drop-off at ASB and Fiona takes care of school pickup with Naushad. Once Grant arrives home, I declare an official "pajama day." Matthew and I haven't moved from the sectional. The rest of the troops get ready to join in.

Grant and Fiona change clothes and we watch two Bollywood movies back-to-back and order Domino's pizza for lunch and dinner. Luisa and Neelam have the day off—thank goodness. Naushad is happy lounging in the car park with the other drivers, drinking *chai* and smoking *bidis*, just in case his older Madam needs anything.

Turning thirty-eight, despite the maharani treatment, made me think back to college days—staying out too late and drinking one too many. This time around, without a single ounce of guilt, I feel older and wiser. In other words, I will not have fun this way again.

In spite of scarves, bangles, and earrings from friends, Lolita surprises me with the greatest gift of all. She greets me when I go downstairs

Saturday, and speaks Hindi to Naushad. She says she's sorry she missed my birthday while she was outside the city visiting her daughter.

At first, I think she's asking me for rupees; however, when Naushad explains their conversation to me in English, I understand the shock on his face. We are equally stunned when Lolita walks up to me, and in front of all the drivers, hands me a wad of rupees.

I count the stash. Five hundred rupees—a hefty sum.

"Naushad, what do I do? I don't want to insult her," I say.

Lolita is so proud. Luckily, she does not understand English.

"Madam, you take."

All right.

I accept the wad of rupees and thank Lolita graciously. I bow to her. She bows to me and I give her a thumbs-up instead of the usual hug. Pinky told me at the party not to hug her anymore; it's not proper Madam behavior. Then, Naushad drives me to the makeshift florist stand on the sidewalk up near Pali Hill, and I select different colored roses from each of the nine white plastic buckets, forty in all, for a total of 240 rupees, the equivalent of $6.15 US.

When we return to the building within a matter of minutes, Lolita is sweeping the car park. We jump out of the Innova and Naushad waves her over.

"Naushad, please speak Hindi and tell Lolita thanks to her kind gift, I was able to purchase forty roses. Please also tell her that I understand she is willing to go without for me. I'm deeply touched."

He turns around and stares at me, "Seriously, Madam."

"Yes, seriously, Naushad."

I'm positive he didn't tell her precisely what I told him to say, but I return 400 crumpled rupees to Lolita.

Then, Lolita does what any smart woman would do—takes the change, stuffs it into her bra, and leaves to go finish sweeping.

Naushad carries the flowers to the lift. I press the third floor button to go up—still in disbelief.

"Madam, you not good in adding, you gave her too many rupees, but you a good Madam, very, very good Madam," he says. "You don't need more flowers, but flowers are not too many rupees, good choice, Madam."

I do the head wiggle and he laughs.

Inside the flat, Naushad reiterates the story to Neelam in Hindi, and then tells Fiona in English while they drink *chai* standing barefoot in the kitchen.

"Madam, I can't believe this story. You are the only Madam in the building she would do this for because you are the best Madam. Indian Madams not nice to Lolita. She is the low-caste, Madam. I will tell my mother and auntie. They will never believe this story," Neelam says. "Never."

Turning thirty-eight did take a community here in Mumbai, and it's too bad Luisa is no longer a part of it. Four days after my birthday, Luisa was late and acted like she forgot my special day among the sea of floral arrangements. To top it off, she served grilled cheese sandwiches with the plastic wrappers still on the processed cheese.

"Fiona, is she stupid? Does she think I won't notice she left the wrappers on the cheese *and* I won't notice she's oblivious to the fact I had a birthday?"

"Stupid is as stupid does."

Seriously, I can pardon her lack of reading skills, I can ignore the fact she can't make chicken salad, but when you feed my family plastic, I draw the line.

I send Luisa packing immediately.

The second she is out the door, I call Naushad up to the flat. I describe what happened, march down the hall, and take 6,000 rupees ($154 US) from the safe and hand it to my bodyguard.

"Go give this to Luisa and tell her she's fired."

He glares at me.

"But Madam, you are the Madam and you—" he says before I cut him off.

"You are correct. I'm the Madam. Go do it for me now, bodyguard. Tell her she has the rest of the month to find another job or pray for one."

Knock, knock, knock on the door and it's the Exterminator Men, who arrive to spray for roaches recently making appearances. Neelam follows them so they don't steal anything.

Seth sends me a text: he's stuck in Delhi. I text back: "Are you turning hair orange in Delhi now?" No, his visa is expired and he's trying to get out of India to attend his father's funeral. I offer condolences while he goes off on some poor guy in the American Embassy while he's got me on the phone. I guess now I need to find a new hairdresser to fix my hair—which is still two colors—before the upcoming ASB gala.

While India can be the Land of No on most days, this month it's the Land of Poop. Never in a million years did I think I would talk about going to the bathroom so much until I moved to this side of the globe, especially during my special month.

Thank God we brought an entire year's supply of Charmin double-ply, because no matter what we eat, the traveler's diarrhea comes knocking at our back door. We've been here since early October and we're still talking about bowel movements. We go shopping and people are taking way too much time in the stalls. We walk down the hall at ASB and parents are racing to the loo before picking up Paris or Makoto.

There are only two Western-style public bathrooms in our neighborhood, and expats fight each other constantly over the ability to cram ourselves into them, sometimes with children, and do our business. You learn to avoid eating certain foods, or you simply learn to just hold it—although your stomach does weird things, and we're not talking gas. We're talking extreme discomfort, as in "Houston, we've got a problem!" I have lost my dignity many times over, and I'm afraid Mumbai has not seen the best of me yet.

Recently, Grant and I were in the car and he had to go number two, and we were stuck in traffic. I was not going to have a feces-in-the-car moment like Crazy Madam and Ben had, so we jump out and race to the Boat Club, which appears to be closed. I knock desperately and someone opens the door.

I'm in shock!

I scream out, "I need the loo for my son! Help me, please!"

Swiftly, we're escorted straight to the employee bathroom. I hand Grant my packet of Kleenex and he goes about his business.

Whew!

Back in the car and heading down to Linking Road, I realize I can now use my boys as an excuse in case I have to go number two while we're running errands and no five-star hotels are in sight.

A-h-h-h!

Madam has finally found a little comfort in this wild city.

Yesterday Naushad said, "Madam, can I ask you something? Why do you call my India the homeland? I do not know this word."

I replied, "Naushad, I started calling India the homeland because I'm home here. In fact, my house is rented in Austin. Texas is a place Madam can visit, but Madam lives here now."

You should have seen the smile on his face.

We cruise by Lilavati Hospital in Bandra and it's swarming with media trucks and reporters.

"Madam, it's Saif Ali Khan's driver there," Naushad says as he points to a secured area like I know which car he's talking about. Due to the hectic amount of traffic, he has to slow down and stop, then roll down his window. Speaking Hindi with the young crowd, Naushad is told sexy Bollywood star Saif suffered a mild stroke; the smoker had a blocked artery. It's bizarre to be right in the middle of all the action. From the society pages, I recognize his Italian girlfriend and his mother entering the hospital.

Then, three days later, Naushad and I are at a stoplight—one of the few in the neighborhood—when I look over and notice the leading male actor from *Fanaa*. Naushad tells me he knows the car plates do indeed belong to Aamir Khan, and we follow his orange car down several streets before losing him.

Darn!

"Naushad, next time you see Aamir Khan, you crash the Innova into his car so I can get a photograph with him," I say, grinning.

He stares at me in the rearview mirror.

"Boss will approve, I promise, Naushad."

Now he's totally confused as to why Boss would ever think it would be okay to wreck the car.

"This is how we roll in Bollywood."

He shrugs.

"I like it, Madam."

The boys are settled into a routine. Grant hops into the car every day after school and instructs Naushad to drive to McDonald's.

We laugh, but I don't think so, Little Boss.

Happy Meals from McDonald's don't make you burst with joy. They consist of a large masala chicken patty on two pieces of Wonder Bread, a Sprite, and a toy. Fries cost extra. Consequently, in addition to playdates and visits to the parks, Grant loves to play soccer with the drivers during their spare time.

Matthew is teething. He shakes his head from side to side (the Indian wiggle), and loves to watch Hindi cartoons.

One thing you may never understand until you live in a developing country is that you need to depend on the kindness of strangers and new acquaintances. Seriously. You meet someone one day, and the next day, you're putting your life in their hands. Forget "Help me, Obi-Wan Kenobi!" It's "Help me, Raj, Cathy, Pinky, Kavita, Anuj, Shobhit, Sandy, and Laxman."

We call or text at the drop of a hat, and they respond—no matter the time of day:

- "Can you call a plumber at midnight?"
- "Can you talk Hindi to this person and tell them I need my dryer fixed?"
- "The internet is down—any idea who to call who can actually fix it?"
- "Dr. Shah doesn't answer. Is there another hotel doctor I can call?"
- "Did Toyota speak the truth about the car?"
- "What should I pay a new cook if I find one?"
- "Where do I buy a charcoal grill?"
- "How do I get to Aamby Valley?"
- "How do you get a package out of customs?"

Our need for assistance is dwindling with time and knowledge under our belts, but these new friends are lifesavers.

No kidding, India lives and dies by mobiles. I get messages from Naushad, Pravin (my JW trainer), Jenny Bhatt (the local artist I met at a party down south at the Bombay Project event), Pinky, Krishna, Boss, Seth, Grant's teachers, the Chicken Delivery Man, Anil the Wine Guy, local restaurant owners, K-Value grocery store, AWC members, Yoga Hottie, ASB mums, and the American consulate; the list is endless and messages happen twenty-four hours a day, seven days a week.

We don't own a landline and voicemail doesn't exist. Naushad told me if I want a person to return my call, I call them, let it ring once, and then hang up—a missed call.

Got it.

Also, he tells me I need to send a text or call to have items delivered to save time and rupees. I thought he was joking, but it's the truth. Recently I had an elephant delivered to Le Gardenia.

A sixteen-year-old boy, Yash Gholap, rents an elephant for 500 rupees from an elder neighbor near Dharavi. He rides it around the city earning 1,500-2,000 rupees a day. Locals provide its food.

Boss, on his way to the office, passes the elephant on Linking Road and calls. "Madam, February is turning out to be a banner month for you. I found Ganesha!"

I race down to the car park and yell to Naushad to bring the car around. We drive through the neighborhood, skip the traffic signal, and cruise onto Linking Road. Ten minutes into traffic, we spy the young elephant in all its glory.

Naushad pulls over to the curb and waves frantically to the young man. Yash steers the elephant over to the side of the road near our Innova. After an exchange of Hindi, Naushad looks at me, "Madam, how much rupees will you pay?"

I shrug.

He speaks Hindi back and gives my mobile number to Yash.

I pinch myself.

India is totally my love.

Naushad jumps in the car and we make our way back to Le Gardenia.

Caught at the traffic signal, Naushad looks at me in the rearview mirror, "Madam, I told the boy you will pay 500 rupees ($12.82) if he delivers the elephant." Then he adds, "Elephants move very slow. He said one hour. I gave him your address and the Khar Gymkhana landmark."

I burst into a fit of giggles.

Back inside the flat, I text the United Nations and give details.

Crazy Madam instantly replies, "Sula Sister, you must be drunk. No one has an elephant delivered anywhere in India unless you're royalty."

Precisely one hour later, I receive a text: "Madam, your elephant has arrived."

For the most part, Matthew was terrified when I handed him off to Yash, who held him atop the elephant while I took several photographs, but I didn't care.

Fiona says, "You have certainly lowered your standards, Madam."

I think I took pictures of every driver, security guard, child, and Khar West resident posing with my Ganesha.

In the end, neighbors contributed an enormous amount of fruit, and I paid Yash an extra 500 rupees. Looks like the second birthday temple wish came true; I met an elephant face to face—an omen—and so did my boys.

It's Sunday, and finally a day for relaxation.

My favorite Indian names today in the Sunday *Hindustan Times*: Chunky Pandey, Poonam Joshi, Riva Bubber, and Pooja Bedi.

There's an article on Arun Nayar and Liz Hurley's wedding set for March in Jodhpur.

I send an email to Cathy inquiring about the scoop and ask to be included on the invite list.

Then I text Anil the Wine Guy: "I had an elephant delivered yesterday!"

After breakfast, the power goes out. I can't reach any neighbors, and none of the drivers in the car park speak English, so we jump into a rickshaw and take the boys to swim and eat lunch at the JW.

The five-star hotel, famous at the moment for hosting a prostitution ring last week, runs off generators, so all the expats head to Juhu for the air conditioning and free wireless services.

On the way home I receive a text from Anil: "*Namaste,* Madam."

When we moved to India, no one but Mike spoke of visiting; now, three groups of friends are going to arrive in the same month!

Fantastic!

Grant Gottesman is passing through from Africa on his way back to Austin the first week of March. Then Rex and Debra Gore will be in town for several days to sightsee with us after a stint in Delhi. Liz and Spencer Williams will stay three days en route from Bangkok on their way back home to Dallas after a one-year work spell abroad.

English will be spoken and they, too, will get to see just how hot it is in the city. Later in the afternoon, Cathy returns my inquiry with a short email. It reads:

Roberto and I are fortunate to be working with the official wedding planner, but confidentiality agreements are thicker than the Holy Bible.

Monday rolls around and Neelam arrives to work in tears. Apparently, I have caused a snag in our recycling program. I had no idea Lolita supplements her income by selling our tin and aluminum cans, glass bottles, and plastic empty water bottles. She also sells the newspaper and magazines and just about anything else that looks good for the taking, a common practice for her caste.

In addition, I had no idea I put a wrench in the system when I hired Neelam and told her she could keep the plastic bottles and newspapers to repurpose; undoubtedly, she knows caste boundaries and took advantage of the situation.

We go through cases of bottled water and Diet Pepsi, not to mention we drink a lot of alcohol and continue to receive five newspapers a day—a small goldmine of potential extra rupees to be had. Lolita has endured long enough and is yelling at Neelam. She wants her trash back—today!

Neelam is upset.

Lolita is upset.

The Alert Security Team is upset and is also yelling at the girls yelling about my trash. Naushad sends me a text: "Madam, big trouble, you come to car park, please, now, Madam."

Naushad greets me shaking his head. I can hear the screaming before I leave the lobby.

Good grief.

I see Neelam and Lolita pointing fingers, circling around pieces of trash Lolita uses as examples of what she demands to be returned. There is much more to the trash debacle than I imagined.

All the drivers watch me walk over to collect a stack of newspapers and seven glass bottles and instruct Neelam to pick up the pile of plastic bags near the driver's loo.

Silence.

Faintly Neelam says, "M-m-m-madam, what are you doing?"

Nonchalantly I say, "Oh, I'm taking all the plastics, glass bottles, and papers back to sell myself. I do not approve of this behavior. I was trying to help you and Lolita, but you both are too greedy."

Naushad is holding back a huge smile.

More silence.

Inhale. Exhale.

Inhale. Exhale.

Lolita speaks nice Hindi to Neelam and then to Naushad, who informs me with a smirk, "Madam, they will divide the trash by two."

Oh, really? Good. "Don't push your luck, girls."

With the drama over, I head to an AWC luncheon at the Grand Hyatt. When I return home, I find our holiday cards and magazine cutouts of Beyoncé, Heidi, and Gisele from my fashion magazines taped up on a wall in the building lobby.

Unbelievable.

Naushad speaks Hindi to Lolita, who is very proud of her work. She's been saving up to make a large collage; the cards seem too pricey to send to the slums. (I let her leave it up until Boss gets home to view it, and then I quietly tip her to take it all down and return it so we can shred it.)

Lolita speaks Hindi to Naushad and he tells me she is happy the recycle ordeal is over, but of course not in those exact words. I make my way through the lobby to the lift and feel peace, for once. I see Naushad smoking one of those cheap Indian *bidis* and give him a sinful stare, but he doesn't care.

"Madam, you too much. You never gonna sell your trash."

I step into the lift and spin around, "That's for me to know and you to find out!"

Thank goodness we brought a shredder. I should start using it on any photos or receipts—for fear India might see and read more than they need to know about Madam and Boss.

Naushad takes the train home early and with no new chef prospects, I order Chinese food from China Gate for dinner. Free delivery.

Fiona helps me clean the kitchen and the boys turn in early for the night. My fortune reads: *Mistakes show us what we need to learn.*

A-h-h-h…a cold front is here. No more unbearable heat. A-h-h-h…I feel coolness on my cheek. Wait—something's wrong. I sit up. I've been dreaming. My hair and forehead are damp.

The air conditioning unit above my head is leaking.

Argh!

The pillows are wet. I turn the unit off.

Boss left at the crack of dawn for a business trip to Chennai and won't be back until late tonight.

I head for the kitchen to make a cup of Twinings English Breakfast tea and retire to the window seat while Fiona and the boys sleep.

I don't know how long I'd been dreaming of cool weather, but I do know I'll be waiting for Ice Cool Services all morning to show up to fix the leak.

I glance across the road. My neighbor, a cute bald gentleman, is on his balcony finishing his yoga routine. He waves. I wave back.

Then we both sit, watching the cows go by.

18

I read a quote in a travel magazine about experiencing Bombay: "I was startled by the intensity of color, sounds, smells, and tastes. It was as if all my life I viewed the world in black and white, and when brought face-to-face with India, experienced its entirety re-rendered in brilliant Technicolor."

"That's spot on," I tell Stan. "Color is inextricably tied to the beauty of this country—the flowers and vegetables are more vibrant. Seriously, I mean, if you aren't a rainbow junkie, you better pack up and get the heck out of Dodge."

He looks up from *The Times of India*. "Do you ever think about things before you say them?"

"Yeah, I do. I think: *That's marvelous. I should say that out loud.* Then I do say it out loud—*real* loud, and it exceeds my expectations."

Friends are arriving this month, and I can't wait to hear about their impression of the homeland.

Speaking of first impressions, we celebrated International Women's Day on March 8. Out of nowhere came a barrage of texts—from my mobile representative, Sabal, Laxman, Pinky, Yoga Hottie, Pravin, and Raj—with messages like "You're sweet," "You've got everything," "Take the world in your stride," and "May your sunny and enthusiastic spirit be with you always."

There you have it.

I head downstairs to run errands with Naushad and once I reach the car, I ask, "Do you know anything about this odd holiday?"

He does the head wiggle.

"Madam, I wished Nisha sweet thoughts like this, like that, to avoid her complaints all morning," he says.

"Is this day comparable to Valentine's Day or Mother's Day?"

He does the Indian head wiggle again.

Whatever.

Exactly six days after we ring in Women's Day, we welcome Holi, one of the most important two-day Hindu festivals. Holi embodies all the liveliness and exuberance of spring. As the sunshine warms the landscape, India cuts loose with dancing, drumbeats, bonfires, and the random spraying of powdered colors—it's hog heaven for rainbow junkies!

Holi is also the festival of letting go of what has passed, awakening new hopes, and strengthening ties with friends and loved ones. It's also the festival of pranks and the theme of the day is, *"Bura na mano Holi hai!"* (Don't be angry, it's Holi!) Cathy emails action shots from Umaid Bhawan Palace in Jodhpur, and I notice the Rajasthani Sula Sisters are sporting headscarves to protect their hair (particularly Cathy, who is a real blonde) from the powdered multihued clouds and showers. Naushad and Neelam have the day off.

Fiona and I are partying at the Marble Palace by throwing water balloons off our third-floor balcony onto innocent locals walking along 15th Road. Boss and Grant are celebrating with expat friends on Juhu Beach.

I'm back on the interview circuit, thanks to Sabal, Neelam, and the Le Gardenia drivers. Word is I need to hire a cook—in a jiffy.

First up is Menoksee, a petite girl who will prepare a quiche for me, but before she starts, she asks Neelam in Hindi to crack the eggs for the recipe she wants to bake. Then, she asks me in English to crack the remaining two eggs as if I didn't understand what she said the first time in Hindi to Neelam.

"Wait a minute? You're interviewing for a cooking position but you can't crack eggs for a recipe you want to cook?" Perplexed, I inquire, "Does this have something to do with a religious belief?"

"No."

Then she turns to Neelam and tells her in Hindi a guru told her not to crack eggs because it will bring misfortune to her two-year-old daughter.

Neelam shows Menoksee to the door, quick, quick.

Second up is a no-show.

Third up is polite and speaks English, but she's a vegetarian and won't touch meat. I lie, telling her we've filled the position, and thank her for her time.

Neelam locks the flat door and goes into the kitchen to make *chai*. Fiona and the Erwin brothers are swimming at the JW. Naushad is down in the car park smoking *bidis*.

I walk into the kitchen and pour a large Diet Pepsi into a plastic cup. "Neelam, looks like we dodged a few bullets," I say.

She smiles, "No worry, Madam, I will keep cooking."

I send an email to Boss:

You know this is why high-caste individuals hire consulate-approved candidates who pass police background checks AND CAN CRACK EGGS!

It's the night of the ASB Oscar gala, a formal evening at The Leela Palace—a five-star luxury business hotel down south. Stanley and I dress up. Neelam and her girlfriend wrap me in six yards of fancy teal fabric and arrange the matching bangles I bought from Shrinath Art Jewellery on each arm in just the right order. I notice they take lots of pride in making sure Madam rolls in style. I channel my inner maharani by wearing Pinky's Bollywood heels again and the same handbag she let me borrow on Valentine's Day.

Boss, wearing his custom American tuxedo, escorts me down in the lift to the car park. When I step out of the lobby, kicking my feet forward just like Pinky showed me how to do when wearing a *sari*, I get the nod of approval from the Alert Security Team, Lolita, and the other drivers just staring and looking—everyone looking at Madam in her *sari* and shiny silver *bindi*.

Naushad whispers when he opens my door, "Your carriage is here, Madam."

Boss climbs into Rocket—the name Grant calls our car, since it's one of the few red automobiles in the city. He's a fan of *Little Einsteins*, the American animated preschool television series where four main characters explore the globe in their favorite red rocket ship.

The route to the Leela takes one hour, during which Stanley nurses an Old Monk cocktail. I'm wondering how Naushad knows about Cinderella. Perhaps he's watching pirated Disney movies from Chor Bazaar—otherwise known as Thieves Market—with his daughter?

I'm also thinking about the United Nations (otherwise known as the Mumbai Mafia). We roll via yoga sessions, lunches, shopping trips, tennis lessons, child playdates, carpool, brunches, dinners, and what will soon be our first official gala. I adore these women, but sometimes the togetherness is strenuous, especially the ongoing element of being judged.

Suddenly, there's a break in traffic. Naushad speeds up and Boss sips on. I send a text to Channing and Annika. I'm missing them tonight. They should be up for breakfast and work. My inside voice says, *When are you going to learn? Your girlfriends are busy.*

The gala turns out to be loads of fun despite my apprehension. I'm particularly pleased to visit with Caron Kobos, mom to Skye, whose husband, Jiri, is the general manager of the Hyatt Regency Mumbai. I met her at a charity event at the home of Aloise Price, an ASB mum whose husband, Dominic, works for JP Morgan. Come to find out, we discover mutual friends and professional contacts—six degrees of separation at its best.

Unfortunately, I don't see them much because our children are different ages, and Caron and Aloise aren't members of AWC, but I admire them. Combined, they've been in the city more than eleven years. Two words: class acts.

To avoid the long valet line, Stanley and I skip out early. I text Naushad and he pulls up in Rocket.

I check email but there's no reaction from Channing or Annika. I send a text to Moe too.

Then I compose a text to John, a buddy from my Student Council State Convention days, and avid pen pal:

"Bartender calls out,
'Last drinks, bar closing at twelve.'
Sadness engulfs me."

Then I hit SEND.

I wait patiently during the drive through Khar West but hear nothing from anyone. Why don't friends in Texas connect with me... ever?

We make it home in a record time of seventeen minutes—much less than the two hours it took us to get there.

Naushad parks the car and Stanley takes the lift up, but I'm concerned about my bodyguard's situation. We had too much fun and time slipped away.

"Madam, the last train left like this, like that, it's fine. I will sleep in the laundry room," he says.

Feeling guilty, I oblige. We take the lift up and I hand over bottled water and say goodnight.

Upstairs, I unwrap the yards of fabric, slip into pajamas, and lower myself onto the window seat when I hear a bing.

It's a text from John:

"Regal Elegance.
Her Sauvignon Blanc in hand.
My Mumbai barfly."

I have never loved this friend more than in this moment. I'm not forgotten—at least for tonight.

On Sunday, we set clocks forward an hour. Daylight savings time is here.

We've got back-to-back guests this month, so the Marble Palace needs to be in tip-top shape. Manu, now captain of the Alert Security Team (because he called the fire department), is washing our car. Lolita is busy cleaning the mud out of the lobby the construction workers on the tenth floor track in and out every day. Neelam shows up early, collects the empty water bottles from the counter, and tells me how she attended a wedding Saturday night.

Before she begins to iron and clean the flat, she announces she's proud of herself for helping her friends with the reception. I casually ask how she "helped" at the party. Perhaps she set up the flowers? She replies in an arrogant tone, "Madam, I furnished the plastic water bottles. Each guest at the reception had filtered drinking water."

I'm staring at her with a blank face.

"You mean you took all our empty plastic water bottles and gave them to your friends for the wedding reception? They filled them with water to serve to the guests?

"Yes, Madam," she says. "Seven hundred guests got filtered water."

I did the math and that's fifty-eight cases of drinking water.

Glad to know our recycling program makes a dent in the city's "Go Green" campaign.

Neelam—holding her own maid position but cooking and babysitting when Fiona has date night—is a rock star. But when Pinky finds out, she tells me the servant who cooks usually refuses to clean the bathrooms. She also tells me I need to hire one person to do each job. Well, Pinky, if you can find a proper cook for me, then Neelam can do her original job. In the interim she continues to multi-task and loves the extra rupees.

Every payday, Neelam hands me back 3,500 rupees and asks me to put them in our safe for her because she has no bank account. Stanley and I do this out of kindness, but it scares us to death. I take the rupees, put them into an envelope, seal it, make her sign it, and then date it. Then I make sure she, as well as Naushad, watches me put it in the safe.

It's Tuesday. I race to the JW to work out with Pravin, the personal trainer Stanley hired for me. He's a young mini-me Hindu Schwarzenegger, and he drives me nuts. He stalks me on my mobile with texts until I show up for the pre-paid appointments. For the record, I don't really like working out at the JW because the gym is in the basement. I would rather smack the ball with Krishna and run on the courts like I did yesterday, or sprint on the sidewalks seaside across from Café Coffee Day along Carter Road, than be a gym rat with no view.

Today is the perfect example of drama: four personal Marriott trainers standing and staring at me running on the treadmill along with one gentleman who's lifting weights.

I have a water break during my session and Pravin asks me if I've been to Aurus, the new restaurant in Juhu.

"Yes, but it's not considered new anymore, Pravin. I will be there with friends on Friday."

He tells me he can't get a table, and I wonder if it's because of his unibrow.

"I always get a reservation, because I call and tell them my 'good name' is Priyanka," I say. "People have trouble pronouncing my name. It has something to do with the *Rh* I think, so I just give them an Indian name instead, and I get better service."

Right then, in walk three Indian women and a tall, dark, and dashing six-foot man.

Pravin leans over and whispers in my ear, "Do you know who you're in the company of now?"

"Do tell."

He glances over to the first girl on the StairMaster. She's an up-and-coming Bollywood actress working on two films. Then girl number two, she's a singer, he says, like Christina Aguilera. Girl number three on the treadmill is a much older actress who left the industry to have kids and now is back to play "aunties" in lieu of Bollywood vixens, he explains.

She has to be my age, but I don't dare tell him. The tall man is the guy who plans the National Awards and the other two top events, the Filmfare Awards and Mirchi Music Awards. He tells me they're all rich and famous. They seem like average citizens to me.

Then, he looks at me with a conceited grin and says, "...and then there is you, Ms. Priyanka...what do you do?"

I look at him sternly, "Mind your own business."

Naushad heads to the flower market, then circles back to collect me before we drive to the domestic airport. I spot Neelam eyeing the leis on the car as she arrives for work.

"I see Pussycat (a pet name she recently started calling Naushad) remembered the *nimbu-mirchi*," she says before entering the lobby.

She's talking about the lemon and chilis hanging from the front bumper of the Innova. Naushad purchases them throughout the month with his own rupees, to ward off the evil eye.

It's highly unusual she didn't give the usual dissenting position, since she regularly offers her opinion on everything from my makeup to my clothing to my dishes. She turns, does one final glance over, and says, "Those leis are for gods and weddings, Madam. Pussycat doesn't know what he's doing, because he's Muslim."

"Neelam, these friends *are* gods. They're flying all the way from America *and* they're bringing Velveeta, beef jerky, Taco Bell seasoning packets, and El Milagro tortilla chips. In addition, two large suitcases filled with groceries, including fifteen cans of chicken Vienna sausages for Matthew."

She rolls her eyes.

Bottom line, the Gore Family has set the visitation bar very high and it's a fantastic start to the weekend.

After Rex, Debra, and their son Matthew are introduced to the Alert Security Team, we visit the Gateway to India, the Taj Mahal Palace Hotel, the Dhobi Ghat, Crawford Market, Chhatrapati Terminus, and Haji Ali Dargah. We finish the first day with a tranquil dinner at Aurus.

Krishna Pujari, part owner of Reality Tours and part-time tour guide, suggests we meet at Leopold Café—an institution in Colaba since 1871—to take a tour of the slum of Dharavi. Just when I think *my* recycling program is producing income, we're told its annual income is $500 million. Everything is recycled in a system of buying and selling that has been followed for generations. We're getting to see firsthand where our trash goes and how it's reborn into new products.

Debra and I can't believe the sight of emaciated men cleaning out poisonous barrels with their bare hands and rags, readying them for transport to the shipyards in Bangladesh. Name-brand computers are torn apart and their plastic components are separated into containers. Painted pottery is left to dry in the sun. People are happy to talk to us, but cameras are not allowed.

We visit the local school, where children are reading books in Hindi. Inside the carefully planned-out maze of the slum, the nucleus is lined with narrow corridors and is a showcase of life: a loud rooster, a litter of puppies, a snotty-nosed young girl, a mother with four-year-old twin girls, an albino woman cooking samosas in a skillet over a makeshift fire, and two teenagers playing Space Invaders on an actual video machine from the eighties. Open sewage drains run along each side of the main walkway that is covered in boards where children squat to urinate.

When the tour concluded, we paid and tipped Krishna for his services. His transparent company pledges eighty percent of its profits after tax to NGOs and discloses all revenue and costs. I was humbled by the warmth of the people and shocked by the infrastructure and the types of activities. It's a world unknown to most Westerners.

On Saturday, Rex and Stanley sneak off to Aamby Valley, a nearby resort, with the Mumbai Mafia husbands to play a makeshift game of golf—Ryder Cup style, America vs. Europe.

Back on 15th Road, Debra and I wave down a rickshaw and head to Fab India for retail therapy. Then we grab the boys (Grant and the two Matthews) and head to the JW for lunch and pool time.

A day later, Rex and Stanley meet us back at the Marble Palace in time to clean up; dinner will be at Vie Sunset Lounge & Deck, another Juhu restaurant with superb outdoor seating overlooking the beach.

After arriving home and much talking, laughing, and watching cricket from our balcony, the Gores leave the Marble Palace for the airport to fly back to Texas. When Naushad returns to Le Gardenia, he takes the lift up to show me the 1,000-rupee bill ($25.50) the Gores gave him. That tip will help him move into a new place down in Colaba.

I've tricked out the servants' bathroom so when Naushad spends the night again, he can see to shave in the morning instead of borrowing a piece of broken glass from one of the Alert Security Team Members. On another note, Pinky told me the servants are supposed to use the bathroom in the laundry room. Naushad has always abided by this rule, but Neelam uses the indoor loo, and I'm not about to tell her otherwise.

Stanley and I are relaxing, eating *migas* (a Tex-Mex dish) and reading the dailies. The boys are finishing their breakfast and watching cartoons. Neelam has the day off and Fiona is at a doctor's appointment. At last, we have a bit of privacy. We're exhausted from our wonderful company and spend most of the day in our pajamas lounging, around the flat and watching Zee TV.

Hours fly by and we decide to get in bed at a decent hour to catch up on some sleep. The minute our heads hit the pillows, the construction workers begin loud banging next door. It's 9 p.m. We bolt upright, turn on the light, and look at one another like, *This is so not happening.* It's grueling enough just living in Mumbai. What the hell are workers doing making this much noise on a Sunday? The boys have school tomorrow!

Stanley doesn't give it ten minutes and he's down the hall, ripping open the sliding glass door in his underwear, screaming, *"Be quiet! The workday is over! Give it a fucking rest!"*

You could have heard a pin drop—dead silence.

Boss returns to bed, and I smile. "You know, you should really ask Shobhit or Raj how to say those words in Hindi. The only reason we're not hearing anything right now is because the crew is in shock you flashed your tighty whities."

He turns the lamp off.

I whisper, "India is your love."

The minute Stan's head hits the pillow the snoring begins.

Inhale. Exhale.

Inhale. Exhale.

I can't sleep.

Inhale. Exhale.

Inhale. Exhale.

The noise continues.

Inhale. Exhale.

Inhale. Exhale.

I get out of bed and walk to the living room and climb onto the window seat. Up above in the dark sky is a crescent moon. I say quietly, "Hello, old friend," and lie down. I set the alarm on my mobile and dwell on how alone I continue to feel, even while I'm surrounded by hundreds of people each day. Then I remember: everywhere I go, the moon goes with me.

The next morning, Naushad hands me the receipt he just received after opening his very first bank account. He's twenty-eight-years old, and it's the only time in his life he's saved rupees.

Liz and Spencer are here. We scoop them up from their hotel lobby and head south to see our usual tourist spots and have a late boozy lunch at Indigo Deli.

On our way home, Naushad points to a black Mercedes riding alongside our Rocket. "Madam—Aftab Shivdasani," he says to me.

Liz and Spencer say, "Who is that?"

Naushad announces, "Pinky's hero!"

Oh my God! This is Pinky's co-star from a Bollywood movie, *Life Mein Kabhie Kabhiee*.

Naushad points to the license plate number. "His birthday, Madam—June 25."

I shout, "Follow that Mercedes, Naushad!" and he speeds up. We race and screech to a stop side by side at the traffic signal.

Naushad rolls down Liz's window and Aftab rolls down his window.

I yell across the car from the front seat, "Hi, Aftab!"

"Do I know you?"

"I'm Pinky's neighbor. These are friends from Texas."

Liz adds, "We're fans from Bangkok and Austin. Can we take your picture?"

Aftab laughs. "Of course!"

He smiles for several photographs while we wait at the traffic signal, and says, "Pinks is an awesome gal."

Yes, indeed.

As soon as the light changes, we head to temple. After living in Thailand for a year, Liz and Spencer know temples, but they've never visited Big B's temple. Naushad parks and warns Spencer about pickpockets. Liz urges him to leave his wallet in the car, but he refuses.

"I like this temple because my wishes always come true," I announce.

We purchase offerings, leave our shoes at a stall, and stand in the entry queue. After much pushing and shoving into the mosh pit to exchange offerings with the two large priests, we move along intact. I say my blessings, eat the coconut, and whisper my wishes into the rat's ear; Liz does the same.

Upon arriving back at the car, Spencer's wallet is missing. Thankfully, it had fallen out on the floorboard of our car, and Naushad found it. Spencer thought it had been lifted in the commotion inside the temple. On a grander scale, Liz's temple wish came true: Spencer finally decides to keep his wallet in his front pocket when he travels, or leave it in the car as instructed by locals.

The highlight of the next evening is introducing Jakhussain, a dwarf doorman, to Liz and Spencer on the way to Aurus. Naushad stops for party pics, and lo and behold, the guys discover that Love Birds Bar and Restaurant is the kind of place to find girls in compromising positions with customers.

Ouch.

Seated at a table overlooking Juhu beach, Stanley and Liz talk shop and Spencer and I compare traveling spouse tips and stories. Life is superb living in another country, not having to physically go to an office, although it does take a considerable amount of work to manage the household and the people.

Liz inquires about Fiona, whom she met in Austin when I hired her through a service to babysit Grant.

I do the head wiggle.

"Stanley extended her contract since his travel schedule is busy. It makes life easy for me, but Neelam holds her own. Fiona seems to ditch most of her duties when I'm not around. She's scheduled for breast reduction surgery in a few weeks when her mother plans to visit. We told her she could stay until the end of May. Then we'll use her to babysit over the summer in Texas before we return in August to attend Pinky's wedding."

After dinner and two final rounds of cocktails at D'Nosh, Stanley and I walk the two blocks home, and Naushad delivers our guests to the airport.

Liz emails the next day to tell us they landed safely with all six pieces of luggage—a record on British Airways. Furthermore, Shilpa Shetty was in the business class line behind them. Shilpa is a Bollywood actor and model who attended Liz Hurley's wedding in Jodhpur and was the winner of the reality show franchise *Celebrity Big Brother 5*.

Liz said all the passport control guys were drooling over her. Poor Indian worker in booth number one got the Jewish couple from Austin, and lucky Indian worker in booth number six got the Bollywood Diva from Mangalore.

The alarm rings loudly. I grab breakfast and a rickshaw to Bandra Gymkhana for a tennis lesson with Krishna.

When Naushad picks me up, he tells me Spencer tipped him 500 rupees; he'll add it to his savings account.

"Madam, your friends are too nice. I never have many people like this—nice to me and give Naushad tips. Just one time a Bollywood actress give me big tip when I worked for the Auto Riders Service, Madam," he says.

Glad to know.

"Madam, can I tell you something?"

I glare back at him and sigh.

"Madam," he says, "You and Boss too good, Madam and Boss. Your friends too nice, too."

On Thursday, we finalize plans for spring break. Naushad takes me to Yvette's tailor on Linking Road to order a custom shirt and then to my tailor to alter two tunics. I get out of the car and walk over to the sewing machine where Mr. Tailor Man holds court one street over from Le Gardenia. He smiles at me.

I speak English and ask him how he's doing. I present two tunics and show him how I need the sides taken in to fit more closely. Naushad shows up beside me to speak Hindi to Mr. Tailor Man to make sure he understands what I want. (I'm doing just fine on my own, Naushad, but thank you for your assistance.) This is the tailor who came to the flat and sewed my *choli* and saw my stomach. He speaks Hindi back to Naushad and does the head wiggle.

"Did he just tell you he won't take them in because he knows my measurements, and says I'm not as small in the waist as I think I am?" I ask cautiously.

Naushad replies, "Yes, Madam," and he walks back to the car with the tunics, laughing.

Neelam arrives with her usual greeting and heads into the laundry room. Almost instantly, I hear ear-splitting screams, then the sound of running footsteps.

She throws open the front door, yelling, "Madam, Madam, he's Muslim, and they do this, Madam! Muslims throw kerosene on Hindus and light them on fire, Madam. I know this. He's trying to kill me!"

Naushad casually walks into the living room from the foyer shaking his head with a bottle of fuel, a treatment for a powder post beetle issue we discovered in one of the furniture pieces from an obscure warehouse in Jodhpur.

"Neelam, I think you said Muslims are lazy, so therefore, he would be too lazy to kill you, right?"

She mumbles in Hindi, "*Mujhe sir dard hai. Mujhe espirin kee aavashyakata hai,*" and walks down the hall to begin cleaning the bathrooms.

Naushad slaps his thigh and laughs.

"Did she just say we need aspirin?"

He can't stop laughing.

I hand him a large plate of scrambled eggs, a bowl of white rice, and a stack of *chapati* to share with the Alert Security Team for breakfast.

"Madam, I'm going down. *Dhanyavaad* for the food."

Growing up in Houston, I know what it's like to go without lunch money and supper. My father got two paychecks a month, and the few days before payday were low days. We were lucky to have bread and peanut butter on the pantry shelves. If I can make a small difference here at Le Gardenia, I'm happy to do it. Who can do any type of work on an empty stomach?

Dubai, located on the southeast edge of the Persian Gulf, is the most populous city in the United Arab Emirates. Spring break there is magnificent.

We spend most of our time at the Hyatt pool, the Mall of the Emirates, the indoor Ski Dubai resort, and the restaurant Al Muntaha within the seven-star hotel Tiger Woods tees off from in the Nike commercial.

Two of my favorite things in Dubai are Barry's Bench Mexican

Restaurant and the small brass plaque in the hotel room displaying an arrow in the direction of Mecca. I snap a photo to give to Naushad.

During our holiday, we sleep like babies. No noise, no pollution, and the onslaught of burkas and sheiks have no impact on us.

Our drivers are waiting patiently at the Chhatrapati Shivaji International Airport upon our return. Preytap takes the luggage, gift bags, and stroller, and puts it all in the company car. Naushad takes Matthew and puts him in the car seat in Rocket. I jump in with Grant and Boss.

"Did you miss your Madam?"

Naushad says, "Too much."

Normally, British Airways or Jet Airways literally drops the plane from the sky onto the tarmac, but United Arab Emirates lands smoothly.

However, no sooner have we paid the parking attendant than the honking and yelling begin. Matthew and Grant cover their ears, and it takes an hour and thirty minutes to get home—typically a twenty-minute ride. The kids go to sleep after dinner. Once again, at 9 p.m. we hear the construction noise start up.

The following morning, Amol shows up for an hour yoga session.

He turns on a CD to place me into a peaceful state of mind, but in my head, I can hear the cricket players at Khar Gymkhana, a band playing one street over from Le Gardenia, and the continuation of construction noise.

I had an amazing eight-day holiday, but less than twenty-four hours back in the homeland I'm on edge from all the clatter and stress.

The Land of No can't get the best of me. In two months I'll be back in America for eight weeks and none of this will matter.

Yoga Hottie refuses to understand my frustration. He stops twenty minutes into the session. He's irritated I'm not breathing. I stretch out onto the floor.

"I'm sorry. I can't focus with all the racket around me. I can't even hear myself think."

"You must learn to defeat the noise in your head. Silence and meditation will help clear your mind of distractions to gain perspective." Then he adds, "Sometimes answers appear in silence."

I sit up.

"Look, I hear what you're saying, I really do. But I can't go there today. I will try my hardest next week, promise," I say softly. "For now, can we talk, not yoga talk, but normal talk for a minute?"

He does the head wiggle.

"Amol, am I doing a decent job?"

With a blank look on his face, he says, "Yoga?"

I laugh. "What I mean is from your viewpoint, am I doing an okay job here in the city? Part of my stress is because I have to learn as I go, but I'm not sure I know what I'm doing half the time. I mean, we all seem to be surviving, so obviously I'm doing something right?"

He does the head wiggle again. "We are not perfect human beings, and letting go isn't the end; it's the beginning of a new, best version of yourself. I have faith in you. Have faith in yourself." Then he asks, "Can I tell you something?"

OMG! Don't ask me—just tell me!

"Let me give you small advice. Write shorter texts to Naushad. He calls my mobile to make sure he understands what you're asking in English."

I don't know what to say.

"Naushad confides in you?"

He smiles. "Yes, *jaan*." Then he laughs. "Did you really take him shopping?"

"I sure did."

Neelam arrives for work and we wrap up our conversation while I pay him rupees. I like Amol and maybe there's truth in what he says—let's see.

Pinky sends a text. She's fighting with Mr. Sanjay again because she wants her deposit back. She threatened to go to the police but he says the former cook he provided to the Harwani residence for a forty-eight-hour trial period said Ms. Harwani slapped her with a stick.

Manu told Naushad, who told me he saw them return to Le Gardenia after a meeting with Mr. Sanjay and they looked upset. I personally know Ms. Harwani could not harm a flea. Her only fault is telling it like it is; she's a straight shooter—something I'm guilty of myself.

My parents send an Easter package for the boys, and along with Channing's Easter gifts the Erwin brothers will have a sugar high well into May. Quickly I write a grocery list and check email. The Gore family and Liz and Spencer both wrote to us about their mind-boggling trip:

> *Many things about the homeland were beyond words: the honking, the poverty, drinking chai made with unknown water sources, the traffic, the cows, the beautiful saris, the curry, the Marble Palace. We enjoyed meeting your friends and we saw things we will never see again.*

They arrived from a black-and-white world and experienced India in brilliant Technicolor—with humility and with grace.

19

I'm reading an article in the newspaper:

> *Reaching the end of a job interview, the human resources executive speaks to a young engineer fresh out of the Indian Institute of Technology (IIT), "What starting salary are you thinking?"*
>
> *He replies, "135,000 rupees a month, depending on the compensation package."*
>
> *The interviewer responds, "We'll also include five weeks of holiday entitlement, a furnished flat, full medical and dental, a company matching pension fund to fifty percent of salary, and a company car—a Skoda, leased every two years."*
>
> *The engineer sits up straight. "Are you joking?"*
>
> *"Yeah, but you started it."*

"Stan, remember when Trammell Crow Company offered a proposition including a new base salary and job description?" I ask. "First-class travel twice a year, a new car, healthy deal bonuses, full medical and dental, a furnished flat, and six weeks' paid vacation, not to mention reimbursement for a cook, a driver, a maid, a nanny, and to top it off, private school tuition?"

He's reading *The Times of India* but stops and imitates Bob Sulentic, his boss, "We started it, Erwin, but you gotta move to India to get it!"

My mobile is ringing. Naushad's calling from downstairs to wake me up. It's the start of the week, the temperature is rising, and I've overslept. Naushad asks if we can give the Don's daughter a ride to school.

No problem.

I race out the door and then realize it's a water day. Swim lessons are offered within the curriculum this semester.

Grant says, "Madam, we don't have time for mistakes this morning."

Back to the closet, off come the clothes, and the uniform and underwear are stowed in his backpack. On swim days children wear swimsuits, sunblock, and Crocs to ASB. We're finally out the door and down in the lobby. Naushad grabs the backpack and I plead, "Next time I oversleep, please walk up to the flat and bang on the door instead of calling me."

In the car park, Lolita says good morning in Hindi while Manu and the other four Alert Security Team Members file rapidly into formation like Radio City Rockettes and wave farewell to us in unison.

The Don's daughter is sitting in the backseat. A young boy is upfront with Naushad. I make them both buckle up. The little girl informs me she's never worn a seatbelt. I tell her it's something we like to do in Texas and it's the law, and she follows my orders.

"Who is this boy?" I ask.

Politely she answers, "He's my servant."

She does not call me Madam or even Ms. Erwin.

I can identify with her. When I was her age and my parents had issues, I too had to comp a free ride to school wherever I could get it.

Naushad hauls butt out of Le Gardenia like a Nascar professional, skids while making a lefthand turn, and skips the light onto Linking Road. If he doesn't kill us, ETA is eight minutes.

The ASB parking attendant sees our approach, looking like General Lee on *The Dukes of Hazzard.* When Naushad slams on the brakes, I jump out with Grant and we sprint inside. I glance back just in time to see Rocket fishtail off to deliver the Don's daughter to the DAIS.

Relieved to be living, I stop to chat with Anne, Caron, Aloise, and the principal before stepping out of the secured area back into the parking lot.

Naushad returns to pick me up, but the young boy is still in the car.

I'm perplexed.

Climbing back into Rocket, I ask Naushad, "Does he understand English?"

"A little, Madam."

"Naushad, he doesn't go to school with her?"

The young boy speaks Hindi and says he rides to school with Tanu each day. He carries her backpack and water bottle to her locker and then returns for afternoon dismissal to carry the items back to the flat.

I inhale. I exhale.

We pass a policeman directing traffic as we cruise down the highway. Naushad announces the servant's name means "just around the house" in case I didn't know.

Quite simply put, the boy whose name means "around the house" was hired to be around as a servant, and that is how Tanu rolls in Mumbai.

Driving back to the Marble Palace, I get a text from Boss. At last, he's landed in Dallas. He misses India.

I hit DELETE.

Wishful thinking.

What he doesn't make out is the texts flying across my mobile—dinner and a girls' night out at Wasabi, playdates, Mr. Embroidery Man from Calcutta's trunk show, pre-monsoon vendor night at the German School with proceeds benefiting worthy charities, and a scheduled visit to view Harry at the Grand Hyatt's new gemstones.

Man, it's hot. Sweat trickles down my back.

I step into the lift, relieved to be back home. Neelam is ironing. I eat a small breakfast and turn on the computer. An email from Boss reminds me to submit Naushad's timesheets for reimbursement. I call him up to the flat and ask him to sign his John Hancock on each one.

"Madam, I don't know this man?"

I have a flashback. I remember questioning Stanley about the Alamo when we dated years ago during a weekend trip to San Antonio after we toured the tiny mission. "Are you telling me you didn't learn anything about Davy Crockett or James Bowie while you were in school?"

Stanley gives me the once-over and says, "In California we studied the Gold Rush, sweetheart! Not every person on the planet knows or cares about Texas history!"

I snap back to reality.

"Naushad, just sign your name on each timesheet, please."

He slowly prints "NAUSHAD" and nothing more.

I can tell he's embarrassed. He does not print his middle name or his last name.

"Madam, my parents took me out of school after fifth grade. You know this. I'm sorry, Madam, but this is how I write my name."

My heart breaks.

I look at him. "Naushad, you sign like Madonna, Cher, and Sting."

He snaps back, "Shakira."

Naushad's mobile rings. It's Sabal calling. He tells Naushad he's fed up with Crazy Madam and as soon as she leaves during monsoon, he's going to ask to be reassigned to a new client, since he drives for an agency. He wants us to know the facts in case we need assistance in the future. I feel his pain. I've been the target of her jokes many times. She's a mean person.

Crazy Madam paid for Sabal's dental surgery and now she holds it over him to make him work additional hours on the weekends without pay. I guess she doesn't grasp that anything you do for any servant is a gift.

Naushad hangs up and we take the lift down to the lobby. Rather than stay in the air conditioning, I decide to visit a new toy store and bookshop. Grant's birthday is next month and maybe I'll find something new to add with the gifts I brought from Austin.

Once Naushad starts the engine, he looks at me in the rearview mirror and says, "Madam, I would die before I would ever drive for Crazy Madam."

I smile. "I catch your drift, Pussycat, and I'm with you—can't reason with crazy."

We cruise out of the car park. We have loads of time. Grant is on his class field trip to a paper factory, Fiona is at a doctor's appointment, and Matthew stayed with Neelam while she cleans and finishes the laundry.

We turn onto Khar Danda Road, and out of nowhere a Skoda crashes into the back of a rickshaw. Naushad slams on the brakes, preventing us from crashing into the bumper of the car. The Skoda doesn't have a scratch on it, but the rickshaw has a flat tire and a damaged side panel.

"Oh, shit!" he says and then, "Sorry, Madam."

"Oh shit is right! Let's get the heck out of here before the traffic backs up and the police arrive to issue tickets."

As we maneuver around the accident, I look back and see the two drivers arguing over the fender-bender.

Pussycat and I laugh about how we escaped a catastrophe. I lean forward and tell him slowly, "These two clowns will pump fists in the air, speak loudly, walk around, and stomp feet. They will block hundreds of drivers and passengers as the honking continues to blare and bystanders stare. Then, the lone clever person in the crowd will give the rickshaw driver 100 rupees. Quietly everyone will get back into their vehicles and go about their merry way."

He nods, "Madam, you know India."

Just as we calmly steer clear, a man on a motorbike wrecks on the street in front of us and we miss killing him by a hair.

For the love of Shiva!

With errands complete, we head straight home. Inside the car park, I notice a strange woman I've never seen standing in the lobby while the Alert Security Team is on a break sipping *chai*.

"Naushad, is this a new resident?" I ask.

"No, Madam. It's the daughter of the Boss Samir drives for, the one who lives on the eighth floor and parties all the time when his wife goes to London."

I roll my eyes.

Naushad snorts and slaps his thigh. He tells me the entire family is the Fat Family.

"This daughter," pointing to the woman, "is too fat, the second daughter is too much fatty, the Mama is short and way, way too much fatty, and the Papa is just short with one leg longer than the other, Madam."

I'm not sure how to respond.

Indians are so blunt when they talk about each other or about other people. They simply call it like they see it. I know, because I've been on the receiving end of this tell-it-like-it-is. Not long after arriving in India, I was told I looked too white and skinny. Also, I was too frail.

Last week, Pinky's maid said I was fresh. You mean I've never looked or smelled fresh the other times I've visited the flat?

I no longer take it personally. Neelam tells me weekly I seem tired or puffy, and now I'm accustomed to it. It's just part of the culture.

While we sit in the car waiting for the various drivers to park in the assigned spaces, I ask Naushad how Indians get fat, since it seems to be a recurring topic of discussion.

"Madam, Indians eat too many sweets."

He tells me a year ago he weighed eighty pounds more than his current weight.

"I smoke more now, Madam, but I stopped the sweets and lost a lot of weight. Now I'm forty-five kilos (100 pounds)."

For some reason, I can't picture a fat Naushad.

He parks the car and we walk into the lobby.

I glance over at the new Alert Security Team Member and he's sleeping on the job—not a good sign. I ask Naushad, "Why is he lazy?"

"Ninety-nine out of 100 Hindus are lazy."

I laugh. I ask if Muslims are lazy, too, and he doesn't respond. I say, "White people are lazy. It takes all kinds of lazy types to make the world go round."

Naushad looks irritated.

"No, white people aren't lazy, Madam. Americans are good and not lazy."

"Naushad, don't kid yourself. I know plenty of lazy citizens."

Then as I step into the lift, I hear him mumble, "Fine, Madam. Five out of every 100 white people are lazy."

I turn the tunes off when Yoga Hottie, Phoebe, and Grayson—one of Grant's classmates—arrive late to the flat. The boys head to the playroom.

ASB mum Phoebe is on a roll talking about how dreadful expat life is in the city. Amol looks disinterested and talks Hindi to Neelam in the kitchen and graciously accepts *chai*.

After yoga, McDonald's delivers food for the boys. Neelam serves pasta salad and sliced tomatoes for lunch.

"Our friends think we're living like royalty, but here we sit savoring chicken ham for lunch because it hasn't been available at Sante for three weeks," Phoebe says.

Ah, the joys of living the high life.

Later in the evening, the Mumbai Mafia meets at Penne. There's a good turnout—around eight countries are represented. I'm having a lovely time until Naushad calls me during the main course.

"Madam, please come out front, there is a problem," he says sternly.

The girls carry on and I excuse myself and step outside. The Penne security guard stands at attention, watching me in case I need assistance. It's pitch black and there is only one streetlight. Naushad walks up to me, sulking.

A rickshaw driver crashed into our bumper, but luckily, the only damage is a slight crack in the taillight.

I'm real mad, though. "Who is going to pay for the damage?"

The rickshaw driver looks at Naushad and says nothing.

I smell liquor on the driver's breath, but there isn't much I can do. "How many rupees do you have in your pocket?"

The driver glares at Naushad for help.

Then, I raise my voice, "How many rupees do you have? Show me, now."

The driver hands over ninety rupees, which is about two dollars and thirty cents.

I tell Naushad to check his pockets. There's nothing more.

I hand over the rupees to Naushad and tell him to keep them to pay for the light cover. We know this is not enough, but it's a matter of principle once again.

The rickshaw driver climbs into his beetle and cries.

Oh, stop the drama!

Back inside the restaurant, I finish dinner and we order more Sula and dessert.

Unbeknownst to me, the restaurant guard, a few Mumbai Mafia drivers, and a shop owner have been discussing the damage. The rickshaw driver continued his pity-party and after much talking, talking, everyone talking about the crack in the light cover, the men, including Naushad, decided to return the rupees.

The Mumbai Mafia wraps up the evening and as I leave Penne, the security guard salutes me.

Naushad opens my door and as I slide into the seat, I notice the rickshaw is gone. We head home and upon our arrival I let myself out of the car. Naushad doesn't like when I do this because it's usually an indication I'm upset with him. Then I ask for the ninety rupees. Naushad steps out of the car and coughs and acts like he doesn't hear me.

I stare at him and say, "I want my rupees and let's call it a night. I'm tired."

He looks away.

Then, I get back into the car and demand he get back into the car so none of the Alert But Tired Security Team Night Guards can hear what's about to go down.

"No, no, no. You did not give the rupees back to the rickshaw driver, Naushad."

He actually starts the engine and backs the car out of our parking space. Then re-parks it like he's adjusting it to save face in front of the guards and the other drivers standing around smoking *bidis* and chewing *paan*.

He turns the engine off, takes the key out, and turns around to me and says, "Madam, he was crying. He needs the money for food. You have plenty of rupees."

I yell, "He should have thought of that before he started drinking and driving. He could have done more damage to the car or hurt you, or worse, hurt himself, and then where would we be?"

I lean back and then Naushad gives me a stern look in the rearview mirror because he knows I've been drinking and I just ate a high-priced meal at Penne.

"You're giving me ninety rupees because I asked you to hold the money for me and you didn't do what I asked you to do. If you wanted to give the rupees back, then you should have given him some of your rupees."

Then I scream in my drunken stupor like Crazy Madam, "Boss will be furious at me, not you, Naushad."

I inhale. I exhale.

There we sit in silence, not saying a word to each other. Construction workers and drivers are staring at Madam and Naushad sitting in the car doing nothing.

I'm not pleased with him and he's not happy with me. I do feel a little guilty, considering I just spent 2,000 rupees ($51) on dinner and imported wine, but again, it's a matter of principle.

I don't say another word, but I open my door, get out, and walk swiftly to the lift.

Suddenly, Naushad steps in front of me, sticks his arms out and pulls the doors back from closing.

"Madam," he says slowly, "I did get his drivers' license number and I wrote down his plate number. We can go to the police and make him pay for the damages."

I know this will never happen, and I would rather walk barefoot on hot coals than deal with the bureaucracy in this country, but his efforts are greatly appreciated.

I underestimated my bodyguard. (Shame on me.)

He lowers his head and releases the doors.

Boss calls the next day and I'm quite the informer. "Well, this week proved to be stellar. Let's see, Boss, you left town and we ran into a concrete pillar on Monday and now Rocket has scratches on the front grill. On Tuesday, Naushad tried to kill us by racing to ASB with Tanu in the car because I overslept. On Wednesday, we dodged a three-car pile-up but almost ran over a pedestrian. A rickshaw driver ran into the back of Rocket while I dined at Penne with the Mumbai Mafia last night... and Lord knows what today will bring?"

"You guys are on a roll!"

Yvette drops Grant from ASB and I'm not in the mood to run errands with Naushad. I sit with Matthew watching a DVD. I pick up one of the monthly fashion magazines and love the new tunic styles for summer. I flip to the horoscope page and under Aquarius for the month of April, it says:

Someone questioning financial or factual matters has no doubt caused you headaches lately, but this month you'll be more inclined

to respond in a clear and positive manner. Remember, even the right
answers can raise new questions.

Interesting.

I'm hungry and need a snack. I take the lift down with empty plates. Somnat, the gray-haired older man who sells *chaat* in front of the construction site next door five days a week, is open for business at exactly six o'clock.

Months ago, Pinky suggested I try his treats so I watched him bop down 15th Road sporting a pressed white tunic and *lungi* and then setting up his wicker table. I was impressed by the glances he received from the neighborhood aunties and I'm awed by his perfectly coiffed hair. Somnat is the Tom Selleck of India!

It's 5:30 a.m. on Friday. I'm up before the construction workers. Matthew is teething and fussy. Fiona's door is locked and she's snoring, oblivious to his cries. I notice it's completely quiet outside and I could have slept in much later this morning, but mummy duty is calling.

I pour a Diet Pepsi and fix a bottle for Matthew. I want nothing more than to take a large skillet or pot out onto the balcony and bang on it sporadically to wake up the construction workers and the Alert Security Team, who are peacefully sleeping, but I don't.

Instead I sit with Matthew and watch *Tom and Jerry* on the Cartoon Network for the next two hours until Neelam shows up to work.

Today is Friday the 13th; nevertheless, I'm confident luck, a fickle ally, will be on our side today.

Naushad and I head out of the car park, with two *nimbu-mirchis* on the front bumper, when I discover I've forgotten a receipt to take to the cleaners. Naushad makes the block and we drive back to the building. I jump out of Rocket and race up the stairwell and grab the receipt and two *saris* I left on the dining table. Then I race back down the stairwell and through the lobby.

Damn it! A large piece of white marble from the building next door is smack-dab in the middle of the windshield on the passenger side of Rocket. A crack, roughly nine inches long, has formed. Undoubtedly it will run. I also know it will be a pain in the butt to fix.

Boss is going to kill Madam and Naushad when he returns.

While Naushad mopes, I march next door and there in front of the construction site are thirteen skinny guys cutting white marble. Naushad and Vihaan, member of the Alert Security Team, are speaking Hindi to the workers and they go up to the second floor to locate an authority figure. A young manager and two building owners materialize from the ninth floor and we all walk over to review the damage.

The entire group is standing in front of Rocket, staring at the windshield and speaking Hindi.

Finally, I say, "Please speak the English."

Grinning, the two building owners speak slow-as-molasses English to me like I'm stupid.

"Madam, you simply need to file a proper insurance claim and we will pay the deductible," they say in unison.

"No, I'm not filing a claim. I refuse to deal with bureaucracy at any level since one of your workers decided to throw marble down on my windshield."

The men are not pleased with my answer.

I take my camera out of my purse and proceed to take pictures of the damage and aim the lens at the young manager, rapidly snapping five headshots.

Instantly, the construction noise halts and all eyes are on me.

"I need to get your company business cards."

"We don't have cards."

"No one has business cards?"

"No."

I find this impossible, considering Naushad has business cards, I have business cards, and even the *fruit wallah* has business cards.

One of the building owners says to me, "Lady, just get the proper estimate and give it to the manager, and if we see it's our fault, we will pay it."

I may look stupid, but I'm not.

"Excuse me? It is your fault. I have three witnesses and you will pay for the damages, or I will go to the Khar West Police Station and file a complaint."

"No need to be upset. Just get the estimate and we will go from there."

We stand around for what seems like forever.

"I need the construction manager's mobile number and name, please," I say and hand Naushad my mobile so he can add the information into my contact list.

No one speaks. I stand still for another five minutes, and again, no one has moved a muscle.

The manager and owners begin speaking Hindi again. No one is making headway—not even for a pen and paper to fulfill my request. Not one person will make eye contact with me aside from Naushad.

There are a number of ways to get your voice to project across a gymnasium, football field, or car park. I know this.

Years ago, in seventh grade at Stovall Junior High, I learned how to project my voice. I own a cheerleader's voice, and my diaphragm—still a sheet of muscle—is always ready. I dig deep and shout, "*How many men does it take to write down a 'good name' and a mobile number? Give me a name and number, right now!*"

Utter silence.

The three men are standing and staring at me, but no one moves an inch. Naushad attempts to grab a notepad from the glove compartment when I call out, "*Get back here!*"

Two of the three men holding papers all have pens in their shirt pockets. I look at the older building owner—the one who is terribly annoyed with me—and jerk the pen out of his pocket.

He's flabbergasted. He doesn't know what to do.

Then, I turn toward the young manager, low man on the totem pole, and snatch a piece of paper out of his hand.

I ask Naushad to speak Hindi and get the proper information for me. Naushad instructs him in Hindi to write and print his name, mobile number, and the date of the accident. Then, as we walk away, Naushad calls to double-check the number.

I think we're done, but one of the owners notices ongoing construction in our building on the top three floors. I look at Naushad and we're both thinking, thinking, too much thinking the same thing.

Now, the men are speaking Hindi fast to the Alert Security Team—it's a brawl. I'm feeling pride because my people are standing up for me. I know exactly what they're saying by their tone and body language.

Before the conversation finishes, I interrupt them and say in English, "This marble came from your building. Furthermore, I have three witnesses to the accident and you will pay for a new windshield."

It's not enough.

I'm a small woman in a big man's world.

Sure enough, up we must go with the manager and owners to the tenth floor of Le Gardenia to inspect the construction zone. I'm crammed in the tiny lift with six men. I laugh when the young manager reaches over and turns on the fan.

As soon as the door opens, it's a mad scavenger hunt. I see five workers mixing cement. These workers aren't anywhere near an opening where marble could have slipped off the floor. Better yet, there's no marble in sight. Nonetheless, the manager sees a fleck of limestone and grabs it from a far corner.

This might be the last straw.

I'm agitated that he thinks they've won the battle.

I take the lift down with the rest of the motley crew, and the two pieces of stone are compared. The Alert Security Team Witnesses speak Hindi announcing our construction crew hasn't worked with marble for seven days. I think about this and it's true. I remind the manager this is the third accident in the past two weeks his workers have created with materials from the various floors. Two weeks ago, a hammer landed on the roof of Ms. Kholi's Maruti Suzuki.

I don't know if it's malicious or if it's accidental.

What I pray is that it isn't revenge for Boss yelling at the workers in his underwear.

"I will provide an estimate, and the windshield will be replaced without a doubt," I say and turn to walk away. Entering the lobby, I hear the word "manners" in English.

I stop dead in my tracks.

I spin around, walk briskly up to one of the owners, and stick my index finger in his face. "You want manners? You really want nice manners? Do not *ever* talk to my people with disrespect again. And—" Out of nowhere, my inner voice cuts me off, talks me off the cliff: *Do not embrace the drama. Use the force and walk away.*

I shut up and gather myself.

Naushad and I make eye contact.

He winks.

I wink back.

I inhale and reel myself in. *Always leave them wanting more.* While the group disperses, I graciously hand rupees to my witnesses for a job well done. I will need them next week when I receive the estimate for the broken windshield. I will need to name names and I want them to stay confident we will win the fight. They're thankful for 200 rupees ($5.12). I know it took massive bravery to speak up.

I check my watch. I desperately need to get to my hair appointment with Natasha at Nalini & Yasmin, a popular traditional salon on Waterfield Road.

"Hey, you're going into the salon with me after you park."

He gives me a harsh glare. "No way, Madam."

I give him an unyielding glare back. "I promise it will make you feel better. Remember—if you look good, you will feel good."

I forgot to mention Seth cut his hair after he clipped my mullet and then Nisha put red dye in his bangs while he was asleep. He tried to cut out that particular section, but it now needs reshaping.

He's irritated but feels guilty about all the car trouble, so we race to Nalini & Yasmin.

Side by side we sit, Madam (in foils) and Naushad (pretending he's invisible), getting our hair coiffed. We're bringing sexy back to Khar West—and this is how Madam and her bodyguard roll in Mumbai.

Returning to the Marble Palace, I send Naushad home early. I think the salon visit might have pushed him over the edge.

Fiona is out on a date.

I give Neelam 200 rupees, plus an additional fifteen for the rickshaw ride home. I know she will pocket the change and walk.

I read bedtime stories to the boys and tuck them into bed.

I'm fed up with the homeland and send a nasty email to friends titled, "Savin' Up for Therapy—Life in India SUCKS!"

I climb into bed and open a recent issue of *Hello* magazine. Reviewing the short cut-offs I won't be sporting this summer, I turn to the horoscope section as usual and under Aquarius, it says:

There are days when you love to be alone—the freedom revitalizes

you. But right now you have the company of those who both need and
challenge you, so your precious solitude will have to wait.

I get up and grab bottled water out of the fridge and check the computer.
One of Channing's sisters has instantly emailed:

Dear Rhonda,

Svyateysheye der'mo! Girl, it is time for you to leave Mumbai. Did
Chan ever tell you about her visit to Russia to see me? I used to get
asked for my documents at the door of my Moscow hotel every night
when I came home from work. (Usually exhausted from fighting to
get the smallest things done, and from biting my tongue when deal-
ing with the sexist Russians). That's what the guards ask from
women who look like prostitutes coming to service foreign business-
men. And, since they knew me, it was just done to hassle me. Now,
mind you, I spent $250K in their little hotel by the time Chan and
Dad came for their visit. So when they asked Chan (clearly my guest)
for her documents, giving her the once-over, and calling her
devushka, I totally lost it. I threatened and yelled until the hotel
manager came down to see us. From that day forward, when I
checked into the hotel, I was greeted in the lobby with champagne.
To this day, my father warns me not to go 'Russian' on some poor soul
when I get angry. But often life in a Third World country just gets to
you. Sometimes you just need to push back.

All my best,
Blair

I'm thankful for the camaraderie.
The Land of No is closing in—perhaps the honeymoon is over.
I cry myself to sleep.
Around midnight, I wake up drenched in sweat. I dreamt the two con-
struction owners shot me for talking back.

It's Saturday night, and I'm already in my pajamas after a fun day with
the boys, including a lunch with Amy at the Hard Rock Cafe—one of our
favorite places.

I tuck the boys in bed when Pinky sends a text. She's bored and wants to
visit. I swear, this is the sixth time I've been dressed for bed. She's a night
owl. I only stay up late because I can't sleep through the construction.

The wedding is still on. Ms. Harwani is back in town and has a personal
trainer at Gold's Gym helping her get into shape for the big day. I tell Pinky
we met Aftab, who apparently has a big crush on her. She's ecstatic about the

news.

I ask why she didn't marry him.

She's aloof and says, "He never proposed to me, because if he had, I would have said yes!"

I make a note to self: strangle Naushad for feeding me driver gossip.

Pinky says, "Let's call Aftab. He needs to come over."

OMG! I don't want Aftab to see me in pajamas!

Pinky gives me his mobile number and I send him a text: "I'm the girl who took photographs with you and friends weeks ago in Colaba."

Guess what? He's at the Taj Land's End for a premiere and wants us to join him. I can't believe it. I change and tell Fiona I'm headed out for the evening. Pinky grabs her purse and keys from her flat. We climb in the Mercedes and off we go.

I can tell Aftab is smitten with Pinky, and then he remembers I said Texans love him. He gives me a gigantic hug.

Help! I forgot my camera. I've taken so many pictures with riffraff in this city, the one time I want to capture a genuine Kodak moment I'm empty-handed.

Casually we hang out and talk to actors and industry professionals. An hour later, back at Le Gardenia, Pinky parks, and she speaks to the building drivers who are freaking out that Madam rolls with the in-crowd. Thirty minutes later, we take the lift up.

Sweet dreams, Pinks. Thanks for making me feel like a star.

I get up Sunday morning and check my phone. Sure enough, I have Aftab's mobile number and text. I wasn't dreaming. The minute I pour a Diet Pepsi, Pinky sends a text about last night.

"Big fun, Sula Sister!"

I text back, "Stanley will be mad about the car and now he's going to be jealous I saw Aftab again."

Pinky's text reads: "He won't be mad about the car or Aftab, but he'll be mad you took Naushad to the salon."

Naushad spent the night in the laundry room so he could drive Fiona and me to the brunch at Mezzo Mezzo, even though Sundays are usually his day off. We turn up fairly quickly and once we're seated, much to our surprise, big-time Bollywood actor Hrithik Roshan is seated nearby. It's funny to see the high-caste Indians act like he's no big deal while all the high-caste non-Indians gush. We watch a German tourist ask for a photograph and we decide to do the same for Grant.

After we're done, I text Naushad and he pulls Rocket up to the lobby. We climb in and Grant asks Naushad to turn on the soundtrack from *Fanaa*. Instantly, he and Matthew start singing, "Fanannnaaa, Fannnaaaa, Fannaaana." Then, they make motions with their hands appearing to screw in lightblubs while flapping their arms up and down recklessly. Grant says, "Mummy, we're Bollywood dancing!"

On the other side of the world, Stan the Man—coming off a major high after playing golf with Rex and Ben Crenshaw in the Austin Golf Club tournament—is getting dropped at Austin-Bergstrom International Airport with three bags: one eighty-pounder, one sixty-pounder, and a thirty-pound computer bag.

Once up to the counter, the American Airlines employee tells him he has to pay $110 for extra baggage weight. Okay. (Little does he know, this is the going rate for 500 grams of chicken ham we generally devour in a week.) Then she takes the e-ticket from Boss, leans out from around the counter, and looks him up and down. "How strong are you?" she says. More important, "Do you have superhuman powers?"

He asks, "Why?"

She informs him that according to his reservation, he must land at Gatwick Airport, pick up all three bags from baggage claim, catch the Gatwick Express to London Heathrow Airport, re-check all three bags at the AA counter, clear security, and board the aircraft for the flight to Mumbai.

"Even if you were really strong, I don't think you could physically carry the bags through two airports and make the connection."

So, after discussing various options, the AA employee changes his itinerary and re-routes Boss on a plane to Chicago; then Chicago to Delhi; and then Air India to Mumbai. He is assured the new flight is behind schedule, so there's no problem with the change.

His luggage is scanned and checked in. With a new boarding pass, he glides through the security checkpoint and arrives as the plane departs from the gate.

Unbelievable.

Boss sprints to the Admiral's Club and is told he must pay $150 to get on any plane and business class is sold out on the next flight to Chicago. He's assigned a middle seat in coach and handed a new boarding pass.

American Airlines is no longer his love.

He finally lands in Delhi, only to learn one of the large bags holding all his work-related items did not arrive. Stuck in customs completing paperwork, he misses the connecting flight.

Welcome back, Boss.

He checks in at the Air India counter for the 1:30 a.m. flight to Mumbai, but is told by the ticket agent he can only bring the thirty-pound computer bag onboard because the seventy-pound bag is too heavy for the plane. It might have to stay in Delhi to be placed on a larger plane the following day.

After he screams at the agents, they reluctantly allow him to pay the additional rupees to check it.

Normally, the Delhi to Mumbai flight would be categorized as international to domestic since he arrived from Chicago, but because he missed his connecting flight, now it's categorized as domestic to domestic—hence the major weight restrictions.

Meanwhile, Naushad, bombarded with texts from Boss, is waiting patiently in the car park trying to keep up with all the loony changes. Finally ,he drives to the airport at 3:30 a.m.

Stanley calls Naushad. "Where are you?"

"Boss, I'm here, sir."

Stanley looks around, "I don't see you. In fact, I don't see the Johnny Walker billboard."

Naushad is startled.

"Boss, I'm looking at the billboard. It's at terminal two, sir, at the international airport," he says nervously. "Where are you?"

Stan the Man has been flying more than thirty hours and he's dog-tired—at the *domestic* airport.

In the end, they arrive to Le Gardenia at 6 a.m.

On Wednesday, Naushad is nowhere to be found in the car park, so Manu is frantically directing us toward Tanu's driver when we step out of the lift. Jolly Driver is back from a funeral, and I'm hoping Grant doesn't say anything about his shaved head and small "tail" hanging off the back of his scalp. This is a normal way of respecting the dead, and different castes practice different customs when a close relative expires.

When Jolly Driver waits for me in front of ASB after I return from walking Grant to class, we drive back in silence because he can't speak English and I can't speak Hindi. He's very sweet, and he always drops us first each time we've had to bum a ride.

We're just one big happy family! But it's exasperating owning a car I can't drive.

When we return to the car park, I spot Naushad. He tells me the train ran over a man on the tracks. The conductor delayed the route while a cleaning crew cleared the body.

"Madam, I really saw it. I was hanging out the train door, Madam," he says.

It's too much.

India is closing in.

Stanley receives a call from Air India, which assures us we can send our nanny to pick up the suitcase. Preytap drives Fiona, the paperwork, and baggage claim ticket to the airport.

Several hours later she returns—bag-less. Not one security guard would let her enter the airport without a passport.

Stanley is furious again and decides after a late lunch he will go to the airport with his passport and get the bag. However, he returns bag-less too, because the lost-and-found office was closed.

Neelam finishes cleaning the dishes, puts away the laundry, and leaves. Fiona has another date.

We put the kids to bed, turn on *American Idol,* and watch Sanjaya belt out another pitiful performance.

After watching CNN, Stan the Man decides to make one more trip to the airport with Naushad and returns empty-handed after two hours of fighting with Air India because they can't find the bag.

For grins, I call the number and no one answers. We shake our heads in astonishment.

"I had to tip the security guard 100 rupees to enter the airport with my passport. He couldn't comprehend why I needed to go inside without a ticket."

We check on the boys and climb into bed.

Stanley looks over at me. "I hate India."

I, too, dislike India tonight. I've reached my limit. It's really, really too much with all the talking, honking, lack of common sense, "your signature doesn't match," staring, grabbing, nothing getting done, "come-back-tomorrow" bullshit.

I want things to be done right in a timely manner because that is how *my* universe works.

It's Thursday and Stanley calls the number again and ends up speaking to an employee at Lufthansa. They have the bag, not Air India. They tell him they don't trust Air India and they keep the luggage when they receive it from American Airlines until an owner picks it up. We don't understand how Lufthansa Airlines got the suitcase, but now we're finally going to get it.

Once again, Stanley arrives to the domestic airport and there's trouble. Not one employee can tell him when the office will reopen because it should be open now. No one has a key to unlock the locked door.

My mobile rings and Stanley is fuming. All I can hear is heavy breathing on the receiving end.

"I *fucking* hate India," he slowly says and hangs up.

I'm terrified he's either going to purchase a one-way, first-class ticket and leave me in this shithole, or he's going postal and I'll see him on the BBC news.

Quickly he calls again. "I've been walking up and down the hallway in front of the office for the past thirty minutes. A worker appeared, discreetly unlocked the door, spoke to me, and went inside quickly. I'm watching him drink *chai* through a side window. When he's done, he will unlock the door and give me the suitcase."

Margaret Mitchell wrote *Gone with the Wind* in less time than it took us to get the suitcase.

May is around the corner.

Let the countdown begin.

20

I'm leaving Siddhivinayak Ganapati Temple, on my way to meet Naushad (who has parked on a side street), when a monk waves to get my attention and ushers me to come closer. He's sitting crisscross applesauce under a tree.

"I believe this is not your first visit," he says politely.

I grin.

He makes direct eye contact with me and takes a deep breath.

Flashback to 1975: I'm six years old, watching a TV program with my father.

> *Master Po: Close your eyes. What do you hear?*
> *Young Caine: I hear the water. I hear the birds.*
> *Master Po: Do you hear your own heartbeat?*
> *Young Caine: No.*
> *Master Po: Do you hear the grasshopper at your feet?*
> *Young Caine: Old man, how is it you hear these things?*
> *Master Po: Young man, how is it that you do not?*

I focus.

I inhale and exhale and look into the monk's eyes, startled by this unusual positive memory of time spent with my father.

This chance meeting is a rarity that makes India stand alone amid a billion tourist destinations.

I pinch myself.

I watch as he takes a piece of red string, a *kalava*, out of the folds of his saffron-colored toga. Leaning forward, he ties it around my left wrist. The wearing of this red thread, typically given by a priest during a *puja*, is a common practice among Hindus. It symbolizes allegiance to the Hindu faith, and it's worn for good fortune. Raj and Laxman wear the red thread—along with eighty percent of the population. Neelam told me she wears her *kalava* until it naturally falls off.

What I'd rather wear are the vintage beads he's sporting. I make a mental note to ask Yoga Hottie where one buys sassy monk beads.

I ask him if placing this string around my wrist can actually change my luck.

He smiles.

"Madam, I tied this on because you received a blessing today. You believe, that is enough," he says. "Its presence will remind you of our encounter for days to come."

I place my hands at my chest and bow.

When I approach the car, Naushad says, "Wow, Madam. Look at you!" pointing to the *kalava*.

I sit quietly in Rocket during the ride back home.

Then, it hits me. I've got six weeks left before we head to Paris, and then to Texas. I plan to make the most of it. I will not return with a bad attitude. The monk said I believe, and I do believe India is still my love. I twist the *kalava*. I wonder if he knows I intend to pig out on Tex-Mex for two months.

I text Stanley the minute we enter the car park, and he exits the lobby with the boys. We head to the JW. Naushad drops us and heads home for the day.

We check the boys into the Kid's Club and take the lift down to the work-out facility to run on the treadmill and lift weights. I'm grateful Pravin (and Fiona) have the day off. After a two-hour workout, we shower and grab the boys for lunch at Mezzo Mezzo. I scan the restaurant, but I don't see Hrithik Roshan. However, I see the talented Irrfan Khan, director and actor in *The Namesake*, a movie friends and I saw last Thursday. Khan is charmed when I exclaim, "We all cried when you died!" The sweet Mezzo Mezzo manager asks for my camera and takes our photograph.

After dessert, Boss takes the boys and joins other fathers and children for an afternoon pool playdate.

As I'm walking down to the street level (the hotel won't allow rickshaws up by the front lobby entrance), an elephant appears to my left, casually walking in the direction I need to go. I do a double take and think, *This is how Madam rolls to her Marble Palace!*

Two hours later, I arrive at Le Gardenia. The looks on the faces of the Alert Security Team and the construction workers are humorous.

When the elephant lowers his right shoulder, I scale down his leg and land softly in front of the car park. In exchange, I put 600 rupees in his trunk, which he lifts up to the owner sitting in the howdah, and then my LV tote bag is delivered curbside. I attempt to step away but the elephant wraps his massive trunk around my waist and draws me back. I lightly embrace my Ganesha.

Having the bravery to take the slow way home, it occurred to me: an intense desire to live is a powerful survival instinct.

Fiona's mother is here from Austin for twelve days. Despite the jet lag, she seems shocked by how her daughter rolls in the Marble Palace. "Fiona is living like a princess," she says. "We had no idea." (She'll stay in the guest bedroom and play nurse after Fiona's breast reduction surgery on April 28th.)

Stanley and I are set to meet up with friends in Jaipur who are on a World President's Organization (WPO) trip. I make a call to Caron, who has agreed to check in on the boys during our absence. Skye, her daughter, will also check in with Grant during school hours.

I spend the afternoon coordinating deliveries of bottled water and Diet Pepsi. Naushad takes me to Sante to purchase yogurt and cheese. I give him Caron's contact information and once again go over his duties in my absence.

Fiona and her mother are down in the car park smoking, waiting for my return. I glare at Fiona because the doctor said to quit smoking two weeks before the procedure. They're headed out to shop and eat an early dinner at Aurus. We've decided to allow Naushad to drive them for the evening.

Back up in the flat, I have a stern talk with Neelam.

"I'm not sure what happens when I'm not here, but Boss and I are trusting you to take care of Grant and Matthew. Ms. Caron and Ms. Yvette are available to help. Promise me you will call them if you need anything."

She agrees.

"Also, be nice to Naushad, because the two of you will need to work together."

"Of course, Madam. I will be nice to Pussycat only while you are gone," she says.

The big day is here! We board Kingfisher Airlines and are welcomed like royals at the Jaipur International Airport. Then it's into the private air-conditioned bus with Bob and Sheri to go play elephant polo at the Rambagh Palace Hotel, a former residence of the Maharaja of Jaipur, located five miles outside the walls of the city. After a long day, we retire to our rooms, shower, and meet up with them in the Polo Bar. Later in the evening we join Maharaja Jai Singh, who grew up in the palace, for a British Raj dinner.

We're thrilled to overhear a nearby tourist ask if I'm the young daughter of the Maharaja and if Stanley is my husband. We're the only two people in Indian attire except for Maharaja Singh. Madam's in a black-and-gold *sari*, and Boss is in a black *sherwani*.

We sleep in late the next morning, but after breakfast we're ready to get on the road. We have to travel separately, since there isn't any room for extra passengers on the private 747 the group leased. I didn't want to bother Cathy about a rental car, so I contacted Laxman, who assured me he would hire a respectable driver who could transport us safely to Agra from Jaipur—a four-and-a-half-hour trip.

Bob and Sheri walk us to the lobby to bid farewell until later, when a very teeny tiny white Tata Indigo sedan driven by a skinny toothless driver pulls up. The driver speaks Hindi to the doorman. Then the doorman speaks

English to me. He confirms we are his passengers and places our luggage in the miniature trunk.

Apprehensively, we climb into the backseat. There are no seat belts, but there is a plastic Ganesha affixed to the dashboard. Our co-pilot.

The car stalls twice. Then the driver turns off the air conditioning, turns the key for a third time, and the engine roars. Bob and Sheri wave goodbye and we head out onto a dirt road leading to the main highway.

"We look like the Mumbai Hillbillies, Stan. I'm positive real royals do not roll this way." I'm embarrassed. "I should have told Laxman precisely the vehicle we wanted to rent."

The roads are harsh in Rajasthan, and the comfort you feel correlates with the size of the automobile you're riding in.

Stanley adds, "Laxman should know better. We'd never survive a crash in this tuna can."

I have to call Naushad several times to speak Hindi to the driver when we need a snack break or a loo stop. Undoubtedly, Laxman has more confidence in my Hindi-speaking ability than he should, because he hired a driver who can't speak English.

We peak at sixty-five miles per hour and pass lots of fields, cows, and religious sites. For the record, you *can* fit twelve people in a rickshaw. Another record: three cars, one lorry, and two motorbikes can drive side by side down a two-way road. We never went over seventy, and twice the driver turned off the air conditioning in order for the car to be able to continue to sputter down the Highway of Death.

Two hours into the trip, I relax my white-knuckle grip on the seat. I smile and ask Stan, "Do you grasp the fact that we have no clue where we are and no way to find out, now that our mobiles are dead?"

Stanley smirks. "Yes, I do, Madam!"

Agra is in the state of Uttar Pradesh. It's the most popular tourist city in the country because it's the home of the Taj Mahal. However, there is no commercial airport. Bottom line is if you want to see the Taj, you catch a fast train, hire a suitable driver in a proper car, or simply purchase *The Complete Taj Mahal and the Riverfront Gardens of Agra* by Ebba Koch—a coffee table book—and call it a day.

Arriving into the city, my pulse slows, although the traffic congestion is overpowering. Downing a bottle of Himalaya water, I wonder if the Taj Mahal is worth the physical therapy we'll need to adjust our spines back to health.

As we hit the roundabout, we spot the WPO buses and follow them straight to our hotel: the Oberoi Amarvilas, just 600 meters from the iconic white marble mausoleum.

Laxman calls the driver's mobile to confirm we're safe.

"Yes, Laxy, we're here! We survived driving on the Highway of Death in the hunk of junk you rented for us."

Silence. Then laughter. "Madam Rhonda," he says. "I've never heard this term "Highway of Death" before, but you are correct."

He tells me he's lived in India his whole life, and he's never seen the Taj. He's pleased we made the journey and wishes us well. I'm stunned that with the amount of travel he does all over the country, he hasn't made a point to see this famous UNESCO World Heritage treasure.

The Oberoi Amarvilas is a sight in itself. It's ornamented with cascading fountains and gold leaf frescoes—unlike my Marble Palace.

We check into our Mughal suite (with a view of the Taj from our bedroom), drop our bags, and join the WPO group for an official tour. The weather is perfect—not a cloud in the sky—but it's boiling hot. Sweat is dripping down my back. Stanley is fanning himself with a brochure he picked up at the entrance.

A picture is worth a thousand words.

I'm in awe of this magnificent structure on the southern bank of the Yamuna River. Never in my life did I imagine I would visit this wonder, nor will I ever be fully able to describe the way in which I arrived to it today— lucky to be alive. The Taj is grand, and whoever said you should go at the crack of dawn was a genius. We're rolling in at 2:30 p.m. on a Thursday along with hundreds of buses from villages all over Rajasthan.

Walking back to the hotel, Sheri tells me some of the guests have a view of the Taj from their bathroom. A loo with a view!

After charging my mobile, I call to check in with Naushad. Then I call Neelam and she's busy feeding Matthew a snack and Grant is watching cartoons. Stanley calls Fiona, but she doesn't pick up. I text Caron, who made a surprise visit to the flat. The servants are working and the boys are well.

I inhale. I exhale.

I inhale. I exhale.

We've got spare time to shower and relax before meeting the group poolside for cocktails. It's been an incredible day.

Sporting Indian chic attire, we take our place at the dining table.

A waiter approaches and discusses menu selections.

When he takes our drink order, I sweetly say, "I'll have a Bombay Sapphire and tonic with four cubes of ice, please."

Our friends look on in amazement.

Sheri says, "Obviously, you know something we don't know. We've been fighting to get ice, lots of it, in our cocktails."

"Well, now you know the secret!"

Stanley squeezes my thigh when every guest orders steak. We pass on the beef and order pasta. Cows are sacred to us now. Once the candlelit four-course dinner with Bob, Sheri, and new WPO friends Paula and Wayne is complete, we retire early and enjoy some private time—one luxury we never seem to acquire.

We sleep peacefully under the spell of the Taj.

The next morning, it's time to hop nervously back into the teeny tiny Tata Indigo for the five-and-a-half-hour drive to the Delhi airport for the two-hour flight back to Mumbai. Oh how I miss the boys, my driver, and my luxury Rocket. I have a whole new admiration for Naushad's ability to speak English and drive without making me carsick. Boarding the plane, I wonder just how many of our friends back home would go through hellfire and brimstone to see us? My inner voice says, *Not many, Madam.*

The fifteen-minute drive home from the Chhatrapati Shivaji International Airport takes us one hour because it's Friday, when locals head to mosque or home early to start the weekend. The honking is louder than any other day of the week, and the hubbub reminds me of a symphony fine-tuning its instruments before the curtain rises. However, no more complaints. I'm in high spirits to be back.

May first rolls around and we're celebrating May Day, known here as Maharashtra Day. It commemorates the attainment of Maharashtra's statehood in 1960, when then-named Bombay was divided into two states, Maharashtra and Gujarat, on the basis of different languages. Besides that, May 1 is also Buddha Poornima, the holiest time in the Buddhist calendar, commemorating the birthday of Buddha.

Anil the Wine Guy sent a text to remind me to stock up on alcohol because May 1 is a dry day, per government orders, whether you're Hindu or Buddhist.

The month of May, come to find out, is when flowers and trees start to blossom. Well, warmer weather made an early entrance. Plants are bursting with color. With luck, monsoon will get here before we all die—or should I say *expire*—from the heat.

I actually thought the monsoon had arrived early when I woke up, but the air conditioning unit was leaking on my head and the bed once more.

It's Sunday and Naushad has the day off.

Brrrrring. Brrrrring.

The air conditioning people are calling me back to say in broken English they'll arrive after lunch. I shut off the unit and wait for the water to stop dripping.

Knock, knock, knock..

Manu wants the keys to the stairwell to unlock and wash Boss's bike.

Knock, knock, knock. The Ice Cold Air Conditioning People are early with a toothbrush to clean the units.

Knock, knock, and knock.

In comes Ms. Harwani, bringing the Erwin boys Haribo gummy bears from Denmark.

We visit for an hour before she drops the bomb: Pinky's wedding is now set for December because she's still not 100 percent sure about her decision.

Stanley and I walk her out. We're off to Juhu with the boys for a late lunch.

Penne restaurant is one of our favorite spots because the hostess carries Matthew around once he's done with his entrée, and Grant is allowed to serve patrons at the gelato bar on slow days.

In a rickshaw on our drive home, I ask Stanley how he's going to answer friends when they inquire about what we do.

"I'll them we spend 10 percent of our time loving our expat life and 90 percent of the time bitching about it."

On Wednesday, when Naushad arrives to take Grant to school, I swear he's wearing black eyeliner. I say nothing but keep looking at his reflection in the rearview mirror all the way down Linking Road.

Bollywood heroines and maharanis line their eyes with black kohl, and now Naushad seems to be doing the same. I'm distracted and amused for a minute near the traffic signal by a man selling *My Big Fat Coloring Book* to tourists.

Thursday night is Sula Fest. The United Nations gathers for a girl's-only night out at Laura Entwistle's bungalow. Laura's husband is chairman of South East Asia for Goldman Sachs and her children attend ASB.

I'm delighted to receive a much-coveted invitation to spend time with remarkable women from all over the world: Spain, Germany, America, Scotland, Poland, England, Russia, Sweden, Canada, and Denmark. Laura's longtime cook serves yummy starters and delicious California wine—an imported treat from a friend's winery in Napa.

The best part of the evening is participating in a makeshift game:

- State where you went to high school
- Declare if you were a cheerleader
- Give a thumbs-up or down to your overall high school experience
- Finish with one special thing you remember

OMG!

Not one of us would repeat high school, nor would we send our children to our previous educational institutions. The former cheerleader from Minnesota made us laugh describing how she "cheered" on ice, and so did the salsa dancer who quit school at seventeen to marry an older man. My favorite is the woman who got kicked out of so many boarding schools her parents sent her off to a finishing school, where the only reason she stayed was because a flasher appeared every day at lunchtime! High school has an odd way of shaping us, no matter where we're born.

Naushad reports to duty on Friday and I can't take it any longer. I have to ask about the eyeliner.

He cracks up and tells me Muslims apply special opium eye drops before mosque to feel good during prayers.

"Madam, my eyes look good, like this, like that."

Seriously?

I ask if a doctor has approved these drops and he says yes.

Hmm.

"Madam, do you want to try the drops yourself?" He pulls a bottle out of the glove compartment.

"No. No thank you, Naushad. I like to see all of India—and my boys. *Theek hai.*"

I inhale. I exhale.

"Please don't use those drops before you drive us. When I fly back from Austin, I'll bring you black Lancôme eyeliner as a souvenir. Safer for all of us."

It's a hot Saturday night and we head to The Dome Bar. We know it's going to be a long evening when Nick wants to buy a round of Sex on the Beach shots. The bartender doesn't understand the order, nor does he understand how to make the concoction. I forget what country we're in and yell, "Let's all have sex on the beach!"

Open mouth. Insert foot.

Colin and Archie (both bartenders while attending university) go behind the large counter bar and mix twenty-five shots. The next thing you know, all the patrons in the lounge are pointing in our direction. "We want what they're having!"

Nick says, "Maybe we're too old for shots," but we do them anyway and head out to DJ Paul Oakenfold's rave party.

Stanley and I roll into the Marble Palace at 3 a.m.

OMG! It's Mother's Day.

Seriously.

Happy Mother's Day to the brilliant mums who decided to stay out late and rage with themselves!

We celebrate five calendars: Hindu, Islamic, Christian, British, and American. It's exhausting keeping up with all of the revelry.

Later that afternoon, I waltz into the shower. The minute I put shampoo in my hair, the water stops. No, no, no. Why didn't I check the time? I know better than to take a shower in the afternoon. I *know* the building water tank is empty. I grab a towel, step out of the shower, and call Naushad.

He answers immediately. "Madam, the truck is here to fill the tank. Like this, like that, ten minutes, then you have the running water. Don't stress."

Then he adds, "Happy Mother's Day, Madam."

There I sit on the toilet lid, wrapped in a towel. Happy Mother's Day to me.

Well, I'm no longer counting the days until I leave the homeland.

I'm merely counting remaining inventory: two rolls of double-ply toilet paper, three boxes of SpongeBob Mac & Cheese, one Taco Bell seasoning packet, one small bottle of Liz Claiborne perfume, three cans of fat-free refried beans, one box of Tampax tampons, six AA batteries.

Preytap returns Boss from a client meeting up north.

"Rhonda, I'm going to give you two Mother's Day presents," Stanley says.

First up, he's going to clean out his side of our small closet and purge the clothes he can no longer wear. He's lost weight and he needs room for skinny jeans and *kurtas*.

Then, he leads me to the computer and shows me the Hot or Not website, where he's posted a photo of me wearing the teal *sari* from the ASB gala. Strangers rate you on a scale of 1 to 10. My average is 9.4.

I am mortified!

I know India is having an identity crisis, but now I'm concerned Boss is having a mid-life crisis or going AWOL. Who has time to go online and judge strangers on their appearance?

Monday rolls around and I call Naushad to bring Manu up to the flat.

"Naushad, Boss is giving all these clothes to Manu and the Alert Security Team. Please speak Hindi and tell them it's a gift," I say politely.

They leave with the two large laundry baskets.

Thirty minutes pass.

Naushad calls my mobile saying, "Madam, you won't believe. Please come now."

Exiting the lift, I'm astonished. The Alert Security Team is sporting the new and gently used clothes, and they're all looking very smart.

Mr. Tailor Man is marking measurements, thrilled with the new business. He races over and touches my feet. I laugh at the Alert Foreman, Jolly Driver, and Imam, the newest Alert Security Team Member, who are all sporting the clothes from Boss too. They're very spiffy in the Ralph Lauren polo shirts, Docker khakis, Nordstrom jeans, and Austin Golf Club shirts.

Naushad and I take the lift up. I grab my purse and the grocery list and we head out. We take the lift down, but it stops on the second floor. The doors open and Ms. Harwani and her mother step in. They're going to Santa Cruz to purchase mangos. We're laughing, laughing, all too much laughing. Mango season is in full force and an article in the *DNA* newspaper states Indians are being "duped" and cheated whenever they purchase mangos in the local market.

Naushad keeps quiet. He looks uncomfortable amid the talking, talking, too much talking.

"Really? You think people in India would cheat?" I ask.

Ms. Harwani sternly tells me the article says people are selling immature mangos on the streets and I should only buy from authorized dealers.

"Are you kidding me?"

Then Ms. Harwani says, "Who is really authorized to sell anything?" She looks around, shrugs, and exits the lift to go buy mangos on her own terms.

Mango season reminds me of peach season in Fredericksburg, Texas, and I will never look at mangos the same again. The funny thing is if you didn't fancy mangos before you lived in India, you would now. Local five-star hotels offer mango teas, coffees, milkshakes, mimosas, and the Mumbai Mafia's favorite—shots!

Naushad knocks on the door, walks in, and hands me a letter.

As I look closer, it's a letter from Toyota explaining a proper vocabulary list for detailing car issues when calling the dealership to schedule maintenance appointments.

Fiona, fully recovered from her surgery, informs me Stanley has taken a rickshaw to the corner store to purchase Diet Cokes and snacks.

He returns and takes the lift up and I show him the list. "I can't believe a dealership sends this crap out," he says.

"Maybe the employees at the dealership need to find ways to entertain themselves when there's absolutely nothing else to do."

Naushad calls me down to the car park for the second time. When he approaches, I know we have to go next door and yell at you-know-who about the new windshield.

I'm fuming.

Mr. Construction Manager Who Broke My Windshield called Naushad several days ago and said he needed two more days. We gave him two more days and now time is up. I don't care if the two owners are out of the country. Madam is pissed. I want my broken windshield fixed.

We walk over to the construction site and climb the stairs up to the second floor among the debris and find Mr. Construction Manager Who Broke My Windshield. He understands English but speaks Hindi in front of me to Naushad, who nods at every word. I can't fully comprehend the conversation.

I'm mad—real mad.

In fact, I'm enraged.

I scream, "I know you understand English. I've given you two weeks and it's over. Sadly, I only have your photograph. I suggest you find the rupees. I will get my windshield replaced, whether you like it or not."

He looks at me unsympathetically. He can't believe he's fighting with a foreigner. It's unheard of and I'm wishing Aftab, Irrfan, or the Don was around to kick some hiney for me.

I wave my finger at him. "You have forty-eight hours to solve the problem. Then *Fanaa*."

Then, I throw my water bottle down to the ground and abruptly walk away. I sneak a look back to see his face and he's staring at me.

Re-entering the building complex, Naushad begins to laugh uncontrollably under his breath, "Madam, Neelam could have used the water bottle for her wedding collection."

The morning newspaper reports that all the airports in India have been put on alert to arrest Shilpa Shetty, the Bollywood actress who was at the British Airways counter with Liz and Spencer. She's the actress who won *Big Brother* in the UK and was noted for being kissed by Richard Gere in a much-publicized episode. The moral police are out in full force this month and want her in court to settle an obscenity case brought by a religious fanatic in Jaipur against both actors.

I shake my head in disbelief.

What this means is Gere, a staunch Buddhist, won't be allowed back in the country to do humanitarian work unless he pays a bribe, and she won't be allowed back to make films or model unless she pays an even bigger bribe.

India is no longer their love.

Stanley and I open the front door to check the lifts. The power is off again. I go out onto the balcony and look down. Ms. Harwani is walking Dior on 15th Road. I find a flashlight, head down the stairwell, and literally run into her as she makes her way back up to the second floor in the dark.

She starts speaking Hindi and forgets I can't understand most of what she's saying. I've found the longer I live in Mumbai, the more people do this to me, just assuming at this point I've picked up the language. I wish I could go back to Texas and return fluent in Hindi. I want to understand precisely what is said to me and about me.

She invites me into her flat and shouts to Pinky, who is working by candlelight in her office. As suddenly as it went off, the power returns. Ms. Harwani blows out all the candles and turns on the air conditioning. She knows I need the cool air during the hottest month. She yells at Pinky to bring chocolate, mangos, and red wine. They're in a frenzy to be gracious hostesses.

I tell them there's no need to dirty the platters, given the late hour, and that in Texas, for the most part, we eat chips straight out of the bag. She laughs and says they do the same in Denmark, but in the homeland you serve your guests the Indian way. Within minutes, trays of Danish cookies, gummy bears, chips, imported cheese, and wine are on the coffee table.

As soon as we sit down, Pinky begins to rake her fiancé over the coals—hot coals, I might add. However, she slips off to her office and returns with none other than the official wedding invitation for my review. It's beautiful and all six hundred invitations are ready to mail, but it's been four days and she can't pull the trigger to take them to the post office.

I look at Mummy. She is tired of Pinky and her wedding-on-wedding-off-planning self. "Pinks, this is a sign from Lord Ganesha. Perhaps this wedding is not meant to be. Have you re-checked your astrological signs?"

"I want you to marry Aftab," I say, and she says she found out he has three girlfriends.

I laugh. "Typical Indian man. But he has no wife—you could be the one."

Even Ms. Harwani laughs out loud.

Finally, Mummy speaks up and tells her not to marry the NRI because she is tired of his family. She goes on and on and on. I like this feisty attitude. The kicker is Pinky's in-laws refuse to allow her to select the wedding attire. They've purchased it for her and don't want her to see it yet.

"How can you not pick your own bridal outfits?"

Ms. Harwani adds, "This is not a suitable way to start the relationship."

Forget a wedding in Mumbai. Pinky is thinking on a far grander scale: a big wedding in Bali reset for August 22–26. My mind wanders and I contemplate. Maybe Stanley and I need a big fat Indian celebration for our fifteen-year wedding anniversary. I might be able to rake in a ring upgrade, not to mention a party for 400 of our closest friends.

Pinky refills the Sula and Mr. Harwani walks through the front door. Pinky debriefs Daddy Harwani about my windshield problem and he says straight up, "Don't file papers with the police."

"It takes years before complaints are heard and you never know when your number is up," he says. "You could be traveling through India in seven years and you're arrested at immigration because you didn't show up in court. It's three strikes and you're out. Last week we were *harassed* for missing a hearing date and ended up paying an exorbitant amount of fees to an attorney to get a case we filed revoked. I'm surprised the drivers haven't spread the news throughout the neighborhood."

After two hours, I say goodbye and give Pinky a hug, Ms. Harwani packs mangos for me to take home, and Dior runs over to hump my leg before trotting off to the indoor Ganesha Temple.

"I'll support you no matter what happens with the NRI fiancé. You have lots of choices, loving parents, more opportunities than most women, and life is too short. Be happy, Pinks, and goodnight."

I take the lift up, honored by the kinship Pinky and her family consistently and wholeheartedly give to me.

Friday is finally here, and I can't believe where the week has gone. I drop Grant at ASB and visit Harry the Grand Hyatt Jeweler to purchase presents for family members.

I've included Harry on my "Tour of India" when friends visit. He has a wonderful selection of genuine stones and silver jewelry, and he can make anything from a photograph. I'm a favored client, as are the rest of the Mumbai Mafia.

Returning to the flat, Amol arrives for yoga. It's just the two of us.

He puts a CD on and I ask, "Must we practice yoga today?"

He quietly says, "*Ruko*. Please breathe." (Laxman told me *ruko* means "stop" in Hindi.) Then Amol adds, "Gandhi said the human voice can never reach the distance that is covered by the still, small voice of conscience."

I close my eyes and lie down on my mat.

"Why are you always serious?" I ask. But he doesn't answer.

From the beginning, I've had a comfort level with Amol—the young married twentysomething yogi with one male child the same age as Matthew. I suspect it's because we're both trying to find our footing.

Plus, I'm curious about the lives of the locals I meet, including him. I know he attended a military academy in northern India, and was, perhaps, a rebel in his former life. He told me one day he wants to own a yoga studio, but for now he studies yoga training under an instructor named Preykash, who is popular among the expats and ASB parents.

I lie still.

"Yoga is an effort to explore ones divinity personally. Stop worrying about the future; seek a journey of enlightenment now."

I take one last breath, flex, and bend my body. I dig deep and focus. I'm determined to start my journey of enlightenment sooner rather than later. I listen to the sound of the air conditioning unit humming over the music and feel my pulse slow. I'm content. All the stress melts away, despite the honking and traffic sounds outside my Marble Palace walls. I feel renewed and my head is clear after the hour-long session when I rest my stomach comfortably on the top of my thighs and my forehead on the mat in child's pose.

I decide I need Amol and I need clarification in my life. He will be the one to help me stay centered amid the ongoing chaos.

Later, I take a rickshaw to a hair appointment, and on the way home pick up food from China Gate.

The boys squeal with delight, wielding their chopsticks, and the entrées are delicious.

Just my luck—I have *two* fortunes: *It is much wiser to take advice than to give it,* and *Love conquers all.*

It's six o'clock in the morning on Saturday, and the construction workers are at it in full force. Boss races down the hallway and yells out the window again.

"How many times do I need to say this to you? The workers cannot comprehend what you're saying in English. You need to ask Naushad or Shobhit how to curse in Hindi. Besides, no one cares anymore about being quiet or polite. They know the expats are all leaving early ahead of monsoon season."

After breakfast, Naushad and I run to the cleaners and Sante. I see him wipe his brow at the traffic signal with a handkerchief. Man, it's humid. I take a tissue out of my tote bag and wipe the back of my neck. Despite the air conditioning, I'm sweating to death in short-sleeved T-shirts and capri pants.

Speaking of short-sleeves, Naushad refuses to wear short-sleeved Oxford dress shirts because he doesn't think short-sleeved shirts look professional. I try to sway him, but he draws the line and won't budge. I remind him he wore a short-sleeved uniform, but he starts mumbling in Hindi, often the reaction I get when I'm right and he doesn't want to argue with me. He knows it shuts me up because I can't speak Hindi to argue back.

Whatever.

I'm looking for paper plates and party favors for Grant's class birthday party on Tuesday. The only Hallmark store in the city has closed, so we drive to a shop on Hill Road to buy poor-quality paper products. As we move along in relatively little traffic listening to Bollywood tunes on the radio, I tell Naushad about Pinky's police station adventure and he says, "I know this, Madam."

He describes how, when he picked me up from the JW after my workout last week (and when I was sitting in the front seat—where I'm not supposed to be sitting—and we were talking and laughing about our India, while driving down Linking Road), he spotted the Harwani family as we passed the Khar West Police Station.

He says he thinks and thinks and decides it's better not to tell Madam, because Madam might want to go to the station to help Pinky. And, if Madam gets arrested helping Pinky, Boss is not going to be happy with Naushad.

He says slowly, "Boss kill Naushad, Madam, if you get into trouble at India police station."

I'm looking, looking, too much looking at my Muslim driver and thinking back to that day. I remember seeing a look of shock on his face after I turned around to get my handbag out of the backseat. Naushad assured me nothing was wrong. I assumed we passed a daily urinator, *not* Pinky running to her Mercedes!

I insist he should have told me.

After he dropped me in the car park that day, he quizzed some of the building drivers, but no one knew anything. Not even the Alert Security Team, which is unimaginable, given how everyone knows everyone else's business in this country.

"Madam, when Pinky's driver drove into the car park, I spoke to him."

Pinky's driver was surprised Naushad saw the scenario. He confirmed the shakedown and said he was getting clothes for Pinky. He left the complex and returned around 6 p.m. Naushad, who was in the car park smoking, saw the whole family return with a consular aide and go quietly up to the flat.

"I could have at least tried to help her or make a phone call on her behalf."

Then, Naushad says sternly, "No, Madam, you are one of Pinky's best friends, Madam, and it is better you stay out of her problems. I mean it. This is a good thing for her and her family.

"Something is not right in her flat. Too many workers come and go, Madam, and she says too many people steal things. This needed to happen to stop the crazy like this, like that. Now nothing more happens."

I can't believe what I'm hearing. However, maybe he's right, and I would have created more problems. Although, deep down, I know he's a pussycat and he was too scared to go to the jail. Having said that, I appreciate my bodyguard was doing exactly what Kevin Costner would have done in the same situation—protecting.

Naushad and I return to Le Gardenia and Mr. Construction Manager Who Broke My Windshield appears in the lobby to tell me he can't pay me rupees but he can get "his friend" to fix my windshield. I'm floored. I tell him to bring me something official such as "his friend's business card" and we'll talk. He disappears. I'm about to take the lift up when I run into Ms. Kholi's son, and now he's real mad.

He tells me when he walked out of the lobby last night, construction workers threw a stove of hot oil and empty beer bottles down into the car park from the eighth floor, barely missing him. In addition, he's irritated that the men have begun harassing his parents' maid when she's down taking *chai* breaks in the evenings.

Isn't that special?

After much talking, talking, too much talking about the construction workers, I text Boss and we all go up to the fourth floor to personally speak with Ms. Kholi again. Come to find out, her son went to school and played cricket with the developer who owns the land and is building the apartments.

I don't tell Ms. Kholi and her son or even Stanley that Mr. Construction Manager Who Broke My Windshield has spoken to me. Ms. Kholi places a call to the developer and he's meeting us next Sunday. She says he'll pay cash for the windshield and will fix all the construction problems our building is having due to his workers.

"We're just one big happy Indian family again," I say to Stanley on the way back down to our flat.

Surprise! Surprise! The developer doesn't show his face on Sunday.

But on Monday, much to my amazement, Mr. Construction Manager Who Broke My Windshield does.

Naushad calls my mobile and hangs up before I pick up.

It's a missed call; his way of letting me know I need to get downstairs without him wasting precious minutes on his mobile—which I pay for, I might add.

I throw on a *kurti* and jeans and sprint down the stairwell. I have no time to waste on the slow lift. Naushad and Mr. Construction Manager Who Broke My Windshield are speaking Hindi back and forth, and now both want to get the deal done so I don't go to the police.

Five minutes later, I give Naushad the authority to drive to the shop listed on the business card I'm holding and get the windshield replaced. Naushad assures me I have nothing to worry about, and I reluctantly agree.

I don't tell Stanley anything when I return to the flat. I just pray he doesn't need to go anywhere.

An hour passes.

I give Naushad a missed call but he does not call back. I look down and twist the *kalava* on my wrist.

Another hour passes.

Once again, I give Naushad a missed call, and he still does not call back.

Unexpectedly, Naushad returns in less than three hours, and I have a brand new windshield.

He tells me they drove straight to a shop not too far from HyperCITY and two men in official Toyota dealership uniforms went to work quick, quick.

"Seriously?"

"Yes, Madam. Seriously. Like you say this all the time to me, seriously."

I look at the windshield, "This really happened?"

"Yes, Madam. Seriously. I saw it happen."

I'm impressed and forever grateful it's over! Then Naushad kindly walks next door and locates Mr. Construction Manager Who Just Fixed My Windshield to let him know the job is done. Madam is happy, and Madam is not going to the Khar West Police Station.

I win!

I waste no time and mark the windshield off my to-do list. I'm energized, and now I need to revamp the recycling program—there's no stopping me now.

Grant's birthday is May 22. It's hard to believe I have a five-year-old who sings cartoon theme songs in Hindi, points out interesting antiques in hotels, and argues in the market for a better price on toys made in China. Almost every day on the way home from ASB, Grant gracefully gives his leftover snacks (or the spare granola bars we keep on hand) to the gypsy children at the traffic signal.

Good golly, we're down to our final week.

Knock, knock, knock. It's a courier with the wedding invitation. It's finally official. Stan, working hard to wrap things up at the office, will be in shock Pinky pulled the trigger.

On Wednesday the same courier delivers an official document requiring a signature.

I do a double take.

It's a damn eviction notice saying we must vacate the Marble Palace by August fifteenth!

There must be some mistake.

I'm leaving on June fourth and I don't intend to return until the end of August.

At this very moment, Stanley walks in the door from a doctor's appointment. He's been sick with Delhi belly for the past few days.

I tell him he needs to call Raveer this instant and find out what the hell is going on. Raveer shows up at the door within minutes.

He tells us *his* family must move in—precisely what two other expat couples heard from their landlord. The fact of the matter is the landlords found Canadians who desperately needed a flat and offered to pay more rupees.

We offer to increase our rent, but he rebuffs; therefore, we refuse to sign the paperwork and simply say we'll do our best to move out by August 15.

Stanley is blindsided.

I inhale and I exhale.

I say, "If we have faith in the Lord Ganesha, he will guide us to find a new palace." Then add, "Look at the endless opportunities we've had. We can do this!"

He acknowledges I'm calm because I see this as a new venture to strengthen the economy.

"No, we have the power to say 'this is not how our story will end.' All I know is my expat adventure will not stop here," I tell him.

Before I crawl into bed, I send a text to Gautham at Fab India and to Laxman letting them know I will need their help on a new project. I text Amol: "Yoga 24/7 in August."

The next day, Fiona is watching the boys and I'm out the door with Raj and Sunita to find a new home.

Raj, who spent four months last year searching to find us a flat, is very optimistic we can find a new palace in one day. I tell him I have remarkable faith we will—if not, we might end up back at the Sun-n-Sand Hotel or the JW.

After a series of looking, looking, re-looking, we pull up to Oberoi Crest, a building on 16th Road. It's the last listing of the afternoon. I'm disgruntled because I know India, and I'm afraid I may end up having to pick something out of what we've seen, period, if I want to remain abroad.

Sweat is dripping down Naushad's cheek, and he grabs his handkerchief for the second time. He's lost all hope, despite my optimism.

He opens my door and I get out. Sitting in front of the building is a middle-aged Hindu man with his pet monkey; and they're playing music for rupees. I twist the *kalava* again. Then I look at Naushad, who has a huge grin on his face.

"Raj, this is the flat. I don't even have to see the interior. Hanuman, the monkey god, is the deity you pray to, and he's here in person."

I glance back at Naushad, who gives me a thumbs-up.

"Once the deal is done we must go to Hanuman's temple and make an offering."

I can tell Raj is nervous.

Naushad parks Rocket and I invite him to accompany me.

"*It's perfect*," I yell the minute we walk into the foyer.

"I want it *now*. Make it happen, Raj. I'll take it." But of course, I'm a female, and Raj does not take my word.

So we call Stan, and only after he says to run with it does Raj push forward with negotiations.

Starving, we head straight for China Gate, where I'm on a first-name basis with the staff. The lunch crowd is long gone. I remember Raj and Sunita are vegetarians and we share three vegetable dishes. This time, when the waiter arrives with my Diet Pepsi, I confidently say, "I want three ice cubes."

I look out the window and see Naushad eating *chaat* at a stall on Waterfield Road.

Raj pays the tab and Sunita distributes the fortune cookies.

My fortune reads: *Life is never more fun than when you're the underdog competing against the giants.*

I can't help myself. I holler, "You can say that again!"

I text Naushad, "Ready." He drives Rocket up to the side street to pick me up.

I show him my fortune. Then I slowly read it to him in English and explain it just to make sure he comprehends the message. He looks at me in the rearview mirror. "Seriously, Madam."

Unbeknownst to me, at the urgent request of Raj, Stanley is waiting back at the Marble Palace. He and Raj need to drive over to the new flat for a quick look-see. Raj should have taken my word, but now I know how he rolls.

The day is over, and it's time to celebrate.

Fiona is on a date and Neelam arrives to babysit the boys.

We shower and freshen up, then load into Rocket. We pick up Wendy, an AWC board member who literally lives a block down from my new palace on 16th Road. Stanley and I sat next to her and her husband, Robin, at Aurus on Valentine's Day when I was the Devil Wearing a Burning Sari.

We drop off Boss at the BBB building (short for Blond Brit Babes, because of the women who live in it) for poker night and see Roseanne, who lives across the street, waiting in the middle of the road for us to pick her up. It appears Roseanne's thrown back a few glasses of Sula already because she's talking to the TV crews in front of the building where Sanjay Dutt lives.

She's demanding to know why they don't interview her about expat life instead of the Bollywood actor. Sanjay Dutt was sentenced to jail last year for owning guns, but has yet to be arrested. His current sentencing drama is buzzing in the media. Local stations are staking out his residence.

Naushad is driving us to Olive for an AWC night out with drink specials compliments of Chef Max. I whisper to Wendy, "You've just met Crazy Madam. You'll see her tonight in all her glory. Just hold your horses. I'm positive a performance will unfold."

She does the head wiggle and we laugh.

A mix of ASB mums and AWC girlfriends are seated at a large table in a tight corner of the restaurant, and we proceed to order cocktails and starters. We spot Saif Ali Khan's ex-girlfriend, Rosa, sitting seven tables away.

I get up to do a look-see for stray guests when I spot a group of expat friends outside on date night, fresh from a karaoke dance party. I also spot a male client from Harry the Grand Hyatt Jeweler's store. I say nothing to his wife but notice she's wearing the gorgeous tanzanite ring I helped her husband select as an anniversary gift.

Yikes! I hear thunder! I see lightning flash across the sky.

In an instant, large drops of water hit my Bollywood top. Then, instantly, we witness the first sign of monsoon.

A-h-h-h. Here comes the rain.

I dash inside and we all sit and admire the view of hysterical patrons running for cover. The wind blows, the trees sway, and the candles have burned out. Staff is racing to grab the outdoor silk cushions and place settings.

It's quite the production.

Crazy Madam suggests we continue drinking and eating and play two truths and one lie.

She wants to start and it goes like this:

> *I once blew an Italian sailor for twenty minutes; I was a cheerleader in high school; and I had a one-night stand with a sexy male stripper in Barcelona.*

No one says a word.

I glance at Wendy. She glances back, hoping Roseanne is so tipsy she forgot the rules and those are all lies. Looks like this is the X-rated version of the game.

Wendy makes eye contact again with me and mouths, "She *is* crazy!"

Immediately, Lindsay, Sarika, and Parvati say in unison, "You were never a high school cheerleader!"

Our roars of laughter cause nearby guests to stare.

We continue around the table and each person is taking a shot at the game when Wendy gets serious.

"Uh, a little hairy thing just touched my foot."

She's looking, looking, too much looking scared at the moment.

I shout, "It's Crazy Madam's leg. She hasn't shaved all week!" and the roar of laughter continues, but Wendy and I both realize I've said "Crazy Madam" in front of the entire table. Thankfully no one seems to notice.

We go another round and now we're really talking trash when Crazy Madam shrieks, "Oh my, something hairy just touched *my* toes."

And remember, Crazy Madam knows rats.

Now I'm horrified.

In a matter of seconds, I scream, *"A little hairy thing is under the table sitting on my feet!"*

Instantly, I jump up onto the bench and a nasty, plump rat runs out from underneath our table, down the hallway past two four-tops, and toward Rosa. People are yelling and jumping up on their chairs too.

Crazy Madam shouts, "It's a *rat*, people!"

Right away, Stefa from Poland marches over to the manager and demands an explanation.

He looks very calm in the midst of the commotion. "The neighborhood has rats, and when it rains, they often come inside."

Perhaps you might want to hire an exterminator who can bring in several traps. Don't announce to the dinner crowd you know the establishment has rodents and you're cool with it.

We sigh and reach for our cocktails.

When the bill is placed on the table, Stefa demands a huge discount along with free dessert, and the staff delivers.

Friday is Grant's last day of school, and as I walk into the classroom to pick him up, I'm the only mum who made it to ASB. All the other ladies sent a nanny or maid to the school for pickup.

We head home, and after I finish yoga, Boss calls to tell me they're working on the lease. I stay worried because anything can happen.

Speaking of which, at the moment I'm not pleased with Fiona. She's checked out since her surgery, and the thought of her spending a week in Paris with our family is exasperating. She continues to dodge responsibilities and Neelam simply picks up the slack.

Inhale. Exhale.

I send an email to the owner of the Parisian flat and I confirm departure plans in June with Sheri. I'm updating our social calendar with the new activities when I notice an email from John:

> *Lawyer, leaving firm.*
> *Sent goodbye haiku around;*
> *Made me think of you!*

Aww!

It's good to hear from friends who we'll see in a matter of weeks.

On Saturday, I run errands and we all pack, pack, pack like there's no tomorrow. Raj calls to confirm the lease agreement and we prepare to meet on Monday to sign the final paperwork.

Relief.

We find out Raveer did indeed lie, and his broker had brought him another family willing to pay double what we pay in rent.

Good riddance.

Stan, Grant, and I head over to Roseanne and Nick's flat for brunch on Sunday. It's our last outing because most of us leave this week. We joke about what it will be like to return to our various countries and former lives in the interim.

Afterward, we head back to the Marble Palace. Stanley calls to finalize our salsa lessons in August and I call and sign up for rickshaw driving school in September. I go to temple one last time and ask for a big piece of good fortune from the Lord Ganesha: I will need all the help I can get to cram my bangles and tunics into my suitcase.

We watch two Bollywood movies back-to-back and turn in. The boys are snug in bed. Fiona is out on a date again. I snuggle up in bed with Stan. He's reading work documents, and I'm reading one of my fashion magazines. Before he turns out the light, I turn to the horoscope page.

> *Aquarius (January 20–February 18): Don't overreact to others' prov-ocations as June rolls in, because on the 7th, Mars is finally moving out of your relationships angle, and peace and harmony will be restored. You're going to have a whole new outlook this month, and the dark clouds lurking overhead since as long ago as last October will finally disperse. What you should be focusing on is putting your creative talents to use and getting involved in projects you truly enjoy. For the most part, June will be an uplifting month, but no matter what occurs, remember that your most important consider-ation should be to decide what is right for you.*

We sign the lease for the fourth-floor accommodation at Oberoi Crest on Monday and open a bottle of Sula champagne to celebrate. Thank goodness Hanuman, the symbol of strength and energy, was looking down on us. We can move into the new flat August 1st.

Sitting on my beloved window seat, I glance around the Marble Palace I created for my boys and savor the memories. I feel like a kung fu master.

But, actually, I'm still a young grasshopper.

What I know is this: our heads shake an unusual way, our vocabulary has altered, our taste buds have endured outrageous spices, and we see the world through rose-colored glasses.

Will our friends recognize us?

I hope so.

21

Summer is when Paris melts, we're told. Fortunately we had our official meltdown before boarding the nine-hour-and-fourteen-minute flight to the Charles de Gaulle Airport after the eviction notice was delivered to the Marble Palace.

With our new lease on life in hand, we were welcomed by the City of Lights with open arms and cool temperatures despite a reputation for heat waves during the month of June.

From a two-bedroom apartment in the 6th Arrondissement (home to the Saint-Germain-des-Prés district and the Latin Quarter), we spend seven days absorbing boutiques, galleries, and restaurants at a snail's pace. We spend mornings in markets shopping for fresh fruit and cheese, and afternoons on pony rides, watching marionettes, or pushing little vintage sailboats around the Grand Bassin duck pond in Les Jardins du Luxembourg.

Matthew slept through the Eiffel Tower tour twice, but made up for lost time on every charming carousel we found within a twenty-mile radius of the neighborhood. The days were longer, leaving us with more hours of sunlight to enjoy the city. We peeked in on Mona Lisa with relatively no lines, walked along the Seine River, and rode on a double-decker bus past the Arc de Triomphe and down the traffic-free Champs-Élysées with squeals of delight.

Despite a rocky weather forecast, we endured only one tiny afternoon shower, which allowed us to linger after a late lunch at La Maison de Verlaine. Grant made sure I took a photograph of the large glass of water and ice he ordered. He plans to take it to ASB and show his classmates, who told him ice doesn't exist in gay Paree.

"The last time we were in Paris together was 1999," Stanley says. "It wasn't this easy. Why are the French nice this time around?"

"This time we're coming from an Indian perspective and not an American one. We don't expect urgency. And remember what my friend Elizabeth said: "The Parisian set of standards for every single thing are so high that they cannot even meet their own expectations.""

Stanley does the head wiggle and we raise our glasses of rosé to staying power.

I'm packing and checking emails while Fiona takes the boys to a toy shop several blocks away.

Note one is from Madam Wendy back in Khar West, who is using Naushad as her driver for a week before heading to Seattle for a month. It reads:

> *Naushad asked me to remind you, Madam, to buy eyeliner for him.*
> *I'm positive he said eyeliner. Do we need to talk, Madam Rhonda?*

Note two is from Channing:

> *Where are you? When do you get home? We're waiting.*

Note three is from John, and it's his answer to the email I sent him when I started sipping grape juice in business class before I landed:

> *Dear John:*
> *Flying to Paris*
> *A bit disoriented*
> *Not bad for plane wine!*

His comeback:

> *Warum bist du im Paris, meine fruendin?*

Then a haiku:

> *Hope all's good with you*
> *You world traveler you babe*
> *Palais-Royal rules!*

Over the years, we've sent correspondence via postcards and now via the internet.

The last line makes me laugh out loud because he knows I adore palace tours. In high school and college, I worked at a department store called Palais Royal in north Houston at Greenspoint Mall.

Very funny, John Boy.

Stanley and I compare calendars and shut down the computer. Fiona returns, we load the luggage into the taxi, and head straight to the train station.

Approximately an hour later, we disembark into Disney Paris via Eurostar. Remember when I said the City of Lights welcomed us with open arms? I guess it only occurs once in a lifetime.

What greets us at the welcome desk is a group of thirty-six large Germans dressed in soccer jerseys, wearing dark knee socks with sandals and sporting black fanny packs. Oh—did I mention they were smoking? Actually, every single guest is smoking, smoking, too much smoking because smoking is not banned at the happiest place on earth.

Gross.

I roll my eyes.

We've traveled to Tanzania and crossed a flooded river on foot at dusk. In the Seychelles, we swam with whale sharks and manta rays. Consequently, we were kidnapped during a vacation in Greece.

And then there is Disney Paris.

We survive the long check-in process at the Hotel New York despite the smoke inhalation. We endure the comforts of a newly-decorated nonsmoking room that was previously a smoking room, and are reduced to silence by people-watching. Who needs Disney Fast Pass when you've got hordes of Europeans dressed like RuPaul and Mariah Carey, acting like Courtney Love on the red carpet?

Drama with a capital "D."

Eating dinner at King Ludwig's Castle with Stanley and the boys later in the evening, I ask, "Is this what the preacher refers to when he says, 'for better or for worse?'"

Day Two outdoes Day One.

We eat our way through the park, visiting McDonald's and the Rainforest Café. We ride Dumbo the Flying Elephant more times than we care to remember and get stuck on It's a Small World when the track jams for twenty minutes (during which Matthew has a blow out in his diaper).

I would have blown a gasket, too, if I hadn't seen the technician sprint behind the scenes with a set of keys and a screwdriver.

On the train back to the Charles de Gaulle Airport several days later, Stanley and the boys are dog-tired, but I still have spirit.

"Boss, thank you for this trip," I say grinning.

He's grumpy and nods.

"If the boys need therapy in high school or college, I'm at peace knowing it didn't stem from living in the homeland," I claim. "It'll be from witnessing the fist fight between Mickey and Goofy at the café our last night. Can you believe Goofy picked up a fork and stabbed Mickey in the arm? Definitely the best action in the park, by far."

Change is constant and life does not—and should not—stop on a dime at any given moment. But returning to Texas, I anticipated my birthplace would cut me some slack.

Not!

Austin greets me like I'm Miss Mona from the Chicken Ranch, wanting my business the minute I land in the River City. When I left I was a law-abiding citizen, Junior League mover and shaker on the Leadership Austin scene. Now, I'm an expatriate aiding the Mumbai Mafia, a secretary for the American Women's Club, and a stalker on the Bollywood circuit.

I spring into action unpacking, washing clothes, emailing, and making phone calls; but stepping into the guesthouse at Barton Creek Lakeside is surreal. It seems like ages ago since I was last here. I am not that same person.

One of the first things I do is call Naushad to wish him a happy birthday. Then I send a birthday haiku to John. The next three days are filled with pool time, seafood dinners, and BBQ. One evening, Rex and Debra join us for apertivos and the six of us share our India stories late into the night while the boys ride bikes on the tennis court.

On Father's Day, we drive our rental car to the Erwin Ranch. It's been a long time since I've seen Jim and Carole, Stan's uncle and aunt, but Grant remembers attending the big hoedown last summer. Aunt Carole serves a fabulous salad with avocado dressing, grilled portabella mushrooms, and twice-baked potatoes—delicacies we haven't eaten in nine months.

I squeeze Stan's thigh under the table when she places a large tray of chateaubriand front and center. We're grateful and hungry, but we gave up red meat months ago. Consuming Texas beef now means we are going to pay full price. Our stomachs begin to revolt in the form of heartburn and gas— or is it the fluoridated water?

Dinner conversation ends and we say goodnight. Once Grant and Matthew are in bed, I'm throwing back Tums like I down Sula—at warp speed.

We lie awake until mid-morning, bloated and belching in discomfort.

At one point, I roll over on my side, clutching my stomach, "We've come full circle. I thought traveler's diarrhea would be the kiss of death. Now the Lord Ganesha is punishing us on Texas turf."

Stanley races to the bathroom—or should I say "loo."

He double flushes and returns to bed.

We pull up the covers and instead of me reminding him to learn how to curse in Hindi, I kiss him on the cheek and whisper, "Karma is energy... what you take, you get, Boss!"

We return to the guesthouse on Thursday, and for the first time since we've been back, Fiona shows up to babysit for Stan's birthday.

Dick, who instigated the celebration at Fonda San Miguel, and friends Debbie and David, Channing, Moe, Lisa, Karen and Lance, Aileen and Mike, Debra and Rex, Becky and Fel, Sally and Steve, Christa and Patrick, and Kathryn are in attendance. We laugh and drink and share our adventures. Then I dispense textiles, tunics, Bollywood DVDs, earrings, and wooden elephants.

Goodness gracious, great balls of fire, we have fun!

I don't know how to express the incredible gratitude for this night filled with friendship, Mexican regional dishes, and tequila.

Namaste, Amigos.

Stanley and I grab a taxi to the Hotel San José on South Congress for a much-needed sexy sleepover. We check in and are led to one of the front rooms—facing South Congress Avenue, a major thoroughfare full of locals and tourists.

"There must be some mistake. We're visiting from India and requested a Grand Standard room located away from the street, in the central courtyard building."

However, we're told this is it. Hmm. I'm really disappointed. Seriously.

Not willing to let the room location deter our mission, we do succeed in having a grand time, but then lie awake, listening to the multitude of people ramble and chatter down the sidewalk outside our window—not to mention, live music blaring in the background.

We can't help but visualize ourselves back in our bedroom on 15th Road, listening to the construction workers next door. We want to open the door and yell obscenities, but we don't want to give up the loud comforts of the hotel for the Travis County Jail.

I jump up off the bed, grab water, and mumble, "Karma Part II—what you send out, comes back twofold."

Stanley does the head wiggle and turns on the iPod staring from the nightstand in hopes of drowning out the nightlife raging behind our headboard. "Now I lay me down to sleep," he says, before his head hits the pillow.

I walk to the bathroom, dig into my monogrammed rickshaw makeup bag from Vividha, and pop a sleeping pill from Dr. Shah.

Good Morning, Austin!

We waste no time checking out and heading straight to Katz's Deli on Sixth Street—a local favorite of ours since we began dating in 1994.

Seated in the bar area, I pinch myself. This is another kind of place you miss living outside the country. Marc Katz, a displaced Jewish New Yorker and former neighbor of ours from the Towers of Town Lake off IH-35, is a kingpin of fried pickles, pastrami and Rueben sandwiches, and mimosas and bloody Mary cocktails.

We chow down.

As we return to the guesthouse, Bob and Stanley disappear to play a round of golf and I relieve Fiona and decide to take the boys to the pool. I'm putting on their sunscreen when I have a flashback.

I'm at the JW with the boys and Matthew is throwing a temper tantrum, even though Grant and I are having fun. I take him out of the pool, change his clothes, and text Naushad.

He responds from the driver car park literally 150 yards from my lounge chair. Dressed in my bikini, I do a look-see, but Pussycat is standing in a sea of drivers talking. Some are smoking. I refuse to go inside the hotel, change clothes in the bathroom, and then walk through a long corridor to deliver my baby like a proper Madam would do. Besides, I can't leave Grant alone in the pool.

Instead, I call Naushad, and when he arrives at the small fence hidden by shrubs, I hand Matthew over and ask him to turn on a DVD in the car while I close out the tab, collect Grant, and we change.

He does as instructed.

I see the other drivers viewing our interaction, and Naushad gives me the thumbs-up once Matthew is in Rocket, happily watching a movie. Suddenly, I hear a commotion and turn around just in time to witness Pussycat slap a driver's face.

On the way home, the boys are asleep, worn out from the sun. I ask Naushad what happened.

He says nothing.

"Naushad, why did you hit the driver at the JW?"

He looks at me in the rearview mirror. "It's fine, Madam."

Then he looks away.

"Naushad, Madam has told you many times you can tell me anything. I'm serious. We can talk about anything."

"I don't want to tell you," he snaps.

Fine.

He stops at the traffic signal on Juhu Tara Road, and looks at me in the rearview mirror—then, takes a deep breath. "Madam, the driver called you a whore because you did not cover up."

I snap back to reality.

I hug Matthew, then Grant, and we spend the day splashing in the sunlight, just the three of us, with no one staring at or judging us.

We're on day ten post-Paris, and Stanley is spending his afternoon at the Trammell Crow office working on a few projects and memos. He and I plan to meet for dinner at Mars, a local restaurant serving Pacific Rim cuisine, while Sheri watches the boys (since out of nowhere, Fiona canceled on us).

One of my best friends, Amy-Beth, happens to be in town from Amarillo, staying at the Four Seasons to attend a wedding with her husband. It's been two years since I've seen her. Grateful Channing drove forty-five minutes one-way to pick me up, we stroll into the lobby lounge for happy hour, and spot AB holding court. The last time the three of us were together, we called London home for twelve days. Now we've got precisely eighty minutes together.

The conversation goes like this:

"Hello, Madam!"

"*Aap kaise ho?*"

"No. You are not trying to speak the Hinglish! STOP!"

They crack up.

AB says, "First, we need alcohol and snacks."

We place our order and get comfortable on the brown leather sofas.

"How are the foster kids?" AB asks Channing.

"They're adjusting."

I pause. "Channing, I saw you two days ago and you didn't mention foster kids. What foster what?"

"Well, I'm officially sponsoring two foster children: an infant and a five-year-old. I'm testing the waters to see whether I want to adopt, being a single woman."

I'm blown away.

"AB, how is Amarillo treating you?"

"Same ole hot summers and cold winters, but after three years I'm used to it. Besides that, life is different with a baby."

We chime in unison, "You can say that again."

Our cocktails arrive and we make a toast to sisterhood.

I get a little emotional and they reel me in.

"I can't help it. I miss you. With the time change and the internet working or not working in the Marble Palace, you always seem so far away."

AB snorts, "We are far away!"

"Tell us about India. We don't get that many emails from you, but when you do write us, we immediately call each other and discuss the craziness that happens to you."

"Yeah, and that struggle *is* real!"

Channing says, "Give AB the lowdown you gave to me in London on our girls' trip—you know, the truth, the whole truth, and nothing but the truth talk!"

More laughter.

I take a sip of wine.

Ready. Okay.

"If you're looking for an escape into the exotic and the unexpected, it's the place to be. One day you're in love with the city, the next day you're fighting, on the verge of a breakup. This is one of the things India does to you—it gets under your skin. The extremes are tough to process. Bollywood coexists side by side with the world's second-largest slum. The poverty is unimaginable. It would keep me awake at night, if I could get any sleep.

"Starting out, I didn't have a clue how to survive, and this is why I was adamant about taking Fiona for three months. When I visited last May, I knew it would take time to set up a flat, hire people, and get my life in order, and I needed a person I could trust to watch the boys."

Stopping me, AB says, "You don't ever have to prove anything to us. And what is that red string on your wrist?"

"It's called a *kalava*. It's a gift from a spiritual healer."

"Oh...good to know."

Tell us about Naushad.

I smile.

"I adore my Muslim driver."

Channing giggles, "I can promise he probably adores you too, Madam."

"Naushad worked for an agency and we hired him to drive our family. He's about 5'4", medium-colored brown skin, and weighs roughly 100 pounds. Remember? I emailed photographs. He has a fifth-grade education, is married to a Hindu girl named Nisha, and they have a daughter the same age as Grant.

"He's got a totally wicked sense of humor! Out of all the drivers I've met and seen, I'm thrilled he's part of our family. We're lucky. The boys trust him, and that's the most important thing about our relationship."

AB says, "Channing told me you took him clothes shopping."

"I sure did!"

They're screeching loudly. "He's a reflection of you!"

Heads turn in our direction.

Then they pipe down.

AB says, "What's Naushad doing while you're gone?"

I laugh nervously.

"Your guess is as good as mine," I say. "He's had more than thirty-five days off. He told me he had plans to take the train to Hyderabad to visit his mother, who lives in the family home. We paid him to check on the car to make sure it's safe and to start the engine from time to time. I know he's joy riding, but no one is around—not even Pinky—to check up on him. I just pray he doesn't wreck Rocket or run over a pedestrian."

"Tell us about Yoga Hottie," says Channing.

I smile again.

"Well, he's a cute Hindu instructor who teaches yoga, core training, and weight training to expats and high-level executives in local corporations. He has long, wavy shoulder-length hair and shows up in jeans on his motorbike. He's friendly, and I ask him a lot of questions about India and about his life."

"How are things with Fiona?"

"Initially, things were okay. Some stuff happened before we left Austin that raised yellow flags, but we took her along anyway. I regret not sending her home after the contract was up, but Stanley wanted her around since he travels all the time. Once I hired Neelam, Fiona's done little to help anyone but herself.

"Pinky told me she's seen her smoking in the car park while Matthew sits in Rocket pretending to drive. If that isn't enough, when she goes on dates, she wants Naushad to drive her. Naushad is *our* driver and whether we're using him or not, we're paying him to remain at the flat should we want to go out or just in case there's an emergency. The date needs to pick her up or she needs to take a taxi to meet the date—which is exactly what we had to do one night when we wanted to go out and she had Naushad driving her around.

"We feel responsible for her, but she's taken advantage of us. We pay her a certain amount of money per month along with all her expenses. In other words, we've been too nice, and I told you before what Cathy says happens when you're too nice to the help.

"Another example: I give her my credit card to buy groceries, and then I noticed men's cologne was on the bill. At first it was little things, but the point is she's traveled with us via first-class and business-class to Nevis, Goa, Jodhpur, Singapore, Dubai, and most recently, Paris. Not one time has she ever come across as grateful or appreciative."

Channing says, "You paid for food, alcohol, and clothes, if I'm not mistaken."

I give a thumbs-up.

"Another example: a group of us partied late one night and I woke up the next morning and realized it was Mother's Day. I crawled out of bed, made Grant's lunch, and handed him off to Naushad to go to school. Matthew was crying in his crib, but when I tried to open her bedroom door, it was locked.

"So I made his bottle and sat in the window seat, hoping he would go back to sleep. An hour or two later, Fiona woke up and made her way into the living room. She says, 'I can't believe Stanley didn't get up and take care of the boys. It's Mother's Day.'

"In shock, I responded, 'Actually, that's your job, Fiona. You should have set your alarm and taken care of the boys.'"

Channing asks, "What's the 411 on her summer babysitting?"

"Here, again, we have a major problem, and I've fought Stanley on this. She sucked up to him, and he paid her two thousand dollars to be on call for me while we're in town. She gave him a lame story about how it would take her time to get another job and she needs cash to survive in the interim."

"Oh, please!"

"What about the money she made living high on the hog in the Marble Palace?"

"Breast reduction surgery," I answer. "All I know is she better babysit a few more times, because she's holding a business-class, round-trip ticket to Mumbai."

AB runs to the loo and back.

"Pinky is getting married in Bali in late August. Stanley booked a ticket for Fiona to fly to Mumbai the beginning of August to help while we move, then to Bali to take care of the boys during the three-day festivities, and then back to Austin."

"Why in the hell does she need to fly business class?"

"She doesn't. Stanley is nice and used miles, and you'd think she would be a little more willing to deliver on her promise to work. I mean, she's on a retainer!"

"I'll go!" Channing volunteers.

Amy-Beth asks, "Why are you always running errands in Mumbai?"

"Locals don't buy up everything like Americans. You buy what you need for the day and perhaps the following day. I have to go to four to six stores or markets to get what we need to cook and eat. The food is seasonal. One area of the city has chicken and another has fish, for example.

"It's the same for clothes and shoes, makeup and hair products. Then, you need to factor in the traffic. You can't even begin to understand the traffic unless you visit."

AB adds, "What's a typical day like?"

I inhale. I exhale.

"Those don't exist.

"Mondays are low days, very, very low days, because you have a marvelous weekend, and then you wake up and remember it's the start of the week and you'll need to survive five days until another weekend.

"Let me think.

"Okay. One afternoon, while the boys are napping, a random guy appears at my door and demands 3,000 rupees for the water bill. I ask Neelam to speak Hindi to him and find out what company he's with and show me an actual bill. He knows nothing. He plays around on his mobile. I instruct Neelam to tell him to call his people and let us talk to them.

"When he doesn't, we escort him out and lock the door. Furious, I call Stanley at the office and he tells me we don't pay for water. Who was this person and why was he allowed up in the lift and into our foyer? What were his intentions?"

"What did you do next?" they ask.

"I walked downstairs with Neelam and asked her to yell at the Sleepy People. I told her to tell them what just happened and not to let it happen again. The landlord promised to install a peephole and an intercom system, but it's never materialized. On the other hand...we've been evicted and have to move, so it doesn't matter anymore anyway!"

We burst into laughter and order one more round of cocktails.

"Look, we love to go places and it's all about reaching the destination with savoir-faire, as the French would say. When I entered this hotel lobby I looked around for the staff with clasping hands to greet me with a cup of rose tea."

"OMG! You're never moving back."

"Listen, Naushad and I drove to the Dadar flower market one morning. There among the mounds of marigolds, roses, and gladiolus, I met his friend who sells him the flowers he uses to decorate my *urlis*, which are brass pots from Rajasthan that I have in our narthex and on our balcony.

"Naushad spoke Hindi and made the introduction. I spoke English back. Neither one of us understood the other, but he gave me a handful of pink orchids and told Naushad to tell me he's blessed by my business. In return, I'm filled with gratitude by kind gestures like this each day."

"Are you going to survive the next four years, Cheer Spice?"

I think for a minute. "Change is nerve-wracking. Just when I solve one crisis, another one takes center stage, but luckily I do have a small but strong support system—namely, Pinky and Cathy. Besides, I won't let a bad moment equal a bad day. I just need to focus on what can go right and forget about what can go wrong. If the pendulum continues to swing my way, then yes; if not, then help me, Jesus!"

Amy-Beth's husband walks up. I give him a hug. Our gossip girl session is finished.

"You and AB should visit us in Mumbai," I say.

"Fuck India. Who wants to hang out with liars and eat curry? We'll see you when you move back to Texas," he says.

On Sunday, I take the rental car to shop for everything I'll need to fit in multiple suitcases. I'm real mad at Stanley again. He hasn't been too helpful. He has a full plate and that's why he paid Fiona to be accommodating. He had a stern talk with her today and she's babysitting tonight—our last night out together before he returns to Khar West.

When she arrives at the guesthouse, I sense tension in the air.

We leave with Bob and Sheri for dinner at Rocco's Grill off Ranch Road 620. I scarf down chicken fried steak and mashed potatoes. After cobbler for dessert, I hand Sheri photographs from the WPO trip Anil the Wine Guy's brother printed for me.

The guys are talking business and Sheri reads my mind. "You're missing India, aren't you, honey?"

I do the head wiggle.

She laughs.

"I am missing my India a lot. I thought our visit would be different, but I don't know in what way. I've loved visiting with friends, but I drove by the house today and cried. Sheri, I'm a visitor. I don't live here and that house won't be mine until we move back.

"Besides, I feel childlike in my colorful tunics, Mughal earrings, and beaded *jootis*, but I was stopped three times yesterday by women wanting to know whether I bought my top at Nordstrom or at Tory Burch. Stanley leaves tomorrow to attend a conference in Montreal then onward to Mumbai. A big part of me wishes we could go with him."

On Monday, I drop Stanley at the airport and then we move to Channing's house for three nights. On Tuesday, Fiona babysits, and I meet Moe for happy hour at Uchi. I haven't seen him since the Bombay or Bust going-away party, and over a shag roll and the hama chili appetizer, he promises to visit in the fall.

On Thursday, we're all up for breakfast when Fiona calls to tell me she can only watch the boys for three hours today. I make a few rude comments and hang up.

"What was that all about?" says Channing.

The boys join the foster kids in front of the TV watching cartoons.

In the kitchen clearing the table, I go ballistic.

"Stanley paid Fiona money to be on call *and* I'm expected to pay her an hourly fee each time she works. I have a full day of errands and doctor appointments to fulfill—and she needs to go walk on the trail? She's insane."

Channing says, "Are you joking?"

"This is bullshit. I'm not sure what she's up to, but I've had enough."

Channing races out the door to drop the kids at preschool and then is off to work when Fiona arrives before lunch. She snakes into the house and sits on the sofa to watch a movie with the boys.

My inner voice says, *Are you positive you can survive without your American nanny?*

On the third of July I load up the rental car and head to Houston for couch surfing and guest-bedroom hopping at my mom and stepdad's house in Splendora, a suburb outside of Houston.

There isn't much to do there, but I managed to pick up all the packages I ordered online in Paris—pajamas, shorts, shirts, underwear. You name it, the boys needed it. We shopped at the local mall, and I loaded up on shoes— for myself included. And I remember to buy the black Lancôme eyeliner for Naushad.

Stanley calls and I'm not in any mood to talk to him. I let it go to voicemail.

An hour later Laxman calls and I answer. He's in Austin on business with Four Hands Home.

"Madam Rhonda, where are you?" he asks.

"I've been in Houston six days and now we're headed to Galveston in an hour."

"What is Galveston?"

"It's our version of Goa, but on a smaller scale."

"When are you coming back to India?"

Getting a little choked up, I say, "Not soon enough."

Galveston embodies summers of my youth spent at my aunt's beach house on the island. It's not crystal-clear water, but I've got nothing but fond memories of the coastal city. My mother and I set up our lounge chairs and reminisce about those days, which are happy memories for her as well, I think.

My brother, my stepsister, along with my stepbrother and his fiancée, arrive and join us. It's been years since we've been together, but within a few hours we're all caught up. We grill and watch the sunset. Then the conversation turns to my homeland.

My brother says, "You couldn't pay me to live in India. How on earth are you surviving?"

I look around and all eyes are on me.

"I have a driver who helps me find stuff and speaks Hindi for me."

My stepsister says, "How long are you going to live there?"

"We signed a five-year employment contract with the option to renew for another five years."

"How are the boys adjusting?"

I do the head wiggle.

My brother looks at me. "Do you know you just moved your head funny?"

I ignore him. "What's not to like? Grant and Matthew are rockstars. They're treated like celebrities because it's a male-dominated society. Their brown hair, fair skin, and blue eyes get them tons of attention. They love India."

My mother says, "Rhonda loves India because she has servants—a nanny, a housekeeper, and a driver."

My brother takes a sip of cheap beer.

I add, "Labor isn't out of the roof, and I have luxuries I wouldn't necessarily have in the States."

"Rhonda asked me to iron her shirt yesterday before we left," my mom informs the group. They burst into laughter.

My brother says, "You can't iron your own clothes now?"

"I was taking care of Matthew's breakfast and I asked nicely if she wouldn't mind helping me out."

"How long has it been since you used an iron?" he asks.

"Nine months."

My stepsister asks one final question. "What do you like about India?"

"The color, the festivals, my American Women's Club friends, the American School, my driver, yoga, tennis lessons, cooking lessons, rickshaws, markets, flowers, temples, and the food stalls."

Each of them announces, "I *hate* Indian food."

When Stanley calls two days later he lets me know he won an iPhone, a new invention from Apple, at the conference, and I let him know my mind is made up: I'm going back with the boys sooner than we planned.

He's totally shocked.

"Why *should* you be shocked? My friends work full-time jobs. Their kids are at camp or I'm babysitting them while I stay in their homes, since it's the least I can do in lieu of paying rent. I'm a homeless person at the mercy of others. I'm tired of living like this; it's grueling.

"I've bought what I need, and I've seen everyone I wanted to see. I miss my Marble Palace. I miss Naushad. Hell, I miss the cows. If you don't change the tickets, I will. I'm ready to go home."

"What do you want to do about Fiona and her ticket?"

"Fiona's ride on the gravy train is over, dude! There's no work for her in

Mumbai. I can manage without her. Neelam already works full-time for us, cleaning and taking care of the boys."

"What about her ticket?"

"I've got it under control and I'll get it back. Change our tickets to the first available flight and have TCC FedEx them to me at Channing's house."

Click.

For the remaining time, we fall into a routine, and hours are filled with beach time, BBQs, and trips to the seawall, Moody Gardens, and the Strand, with no further mention of my India.

I call Fiona on my mobile during a pit stop at Buc-ees—a popular chain of highway gas and convenience stores in the Central and Gulf Coast region of Texas—headed to Austin.

"It's me. Stanley emailed and Pinky's wedding date has changed again. I need you to put your ticket in an envelope and drop it into Channing's mailbox. We'll get you another one for the new dates. Can you drop it off this afternoon?"

She agrees.

We roll into downtown before the five o'clock traffic begins, and I unload all the suitcases and shopping bags. I got this.

Channing's agreed to babysit Grant and Matthew for two hours so I can meet Debbie at Zoot for dinner and drinks. Her husband's high school best friend was Stan's college roommate at CU. While I'm waiting at the bar, Stanley calls to say our tickets are booked and should arrive tomorrow. We leave in three days on July 18—a month ahead of schedule.

He says, "I hope you're sure about this. I don't want to hear any complaints about monsoon. It's been raining every day."

"Don't tell me how to act," I say. "I can handle India better than you can."

"Did you get the ticket from Fiona?"

"No, I did not."

"You better get it. She can take it to any American Airlines counter and do a trade to fly business-class anywhere in the world."

"Sounds like your problem, not mine."

Debbie, dynamic and beautiful, struts in. "You've got a twinkle in your eye, Madam," she says, giving me the once-over.

We order martinis and get down to business and girl talk—she's well-traveled and has endured things most people have only read about in travel guides.

"I feel like a foreigner in my own country," I say. "I can't shake it. What's wrong with me?"

"You've got reverse culture shock, girlfriend," she says.

I'm taken aback.

"I've been looking forward to this visit for months, but after the first week, it's not what I expected. Friends don't get it. No one likes my India, and if I do talk about my life in Mumbai, all I get are blank stares. No one can or wants to relate.

"I think my perception of normalcy has permanently changed, along with the way I perceive people, even though I can't pinpoint a specific incident that changed me. The silence I've craved since last October is unsettling. I can't sleep in the suburbs! It's too quiet, it's too clean, and I feel like I'm speaking a foreign language because my vocabulary has changed. I end up sounding elitist. And no one does the head wiggle."

She smiles because she understands.

"What gets me is tons of friends in our area have housekeepers and nannies, but because I live in a developing country, I'm perceived as 'superficial.'"

Debbie says, "It's totally natural to return with preconceived notions about coming home based on how things were when you left. The same thing happened to us after the big trip we did after David finished his MBA and I graduated from Baylor. But in reality, your situation and the circumstances of friends and family *have* changed," she says. "Embrace it. Be in awe you have this remarkable chance to see the world in an unordinary way."

"On a positive note, I love waking up each day with the traveler's high!"

"I bet you do. From what I take from your monthly emails, you guys have been through the ringer, but I admire your spunk!"

"Living in India is like a drug, because it tweaks the senses. When we first landed, I was lonely because I didn't know anyone, but after meeting women through AWC and ASB, I understood I could be either extremely happy or extremely miserable. I chose happiness—and immersed myself into the culture. My loneliness has been replaced by solitude. I'm the master of myself and my Marble Palace." I laugh nervously. "I love the freedom to be me on numerous levels every single day."

"I know India. It does many things to you, Madam."

We giggle uncontrollably.

She leans in and says, "Let me guess. You're going back early."

I take a sip of my martini. "Debbie, this adventure has afforded me an opportunity to greater understanding—and the world certainly needs more of it. My horoscope this month stated I need to decide what is right for me."

"Well?"

"I need the homeland and it needs me."

"This envelope from Fiona was in the mailbox yesterday after you left," Channing says. "And most important, here are your tickets, Madam. I got a late start this morning and FedEx delivered it while I made a second pot of coffee."

"Thank you, Lord Shiva!" I say clasping my hands at my chest.

As I lace up my running shoes I say to Chan, "My whole life, everyone except my grandmother and a few teachers told me I couldn't do things. I tried to be the perfect daughter and it never mattered to my parents. Think about the amount of time I wasted internalizing their stage show. Seriously."

I kiss the boys, set the timer on my watch, and leave.

I do a few stretches and warm up, select my "Hydrate" playlist, and walk to the corner stop sign and turn left. I walk slowly, then pick up the pace and begin to jog. "Clocks" by Coldplay blares through my ear buds. Steadily, I increase my speed and the wind picks up.

I run fast, then faster, and I kick the non-supportive voice inside my head out and replace it with nothing except clarity.

22

There's a theme of rain in my life. I blame my zodiac sign: Aquarius.

When I boarded the American Airlines flight to move to India, the large cumulonimbus cloud above Austin Bergstrom International Airport launched our plane across the Atlantic Ocean. On cruise control at 33,000 feet, we leveled out over the Indian Ocean and then landed in Mumbai, where sporadic thundershowers gave us a proper welcome.

Drizzle and high winds followed me back across the pond this summer and were my companions for the first fourteen days. I thought I was avoiding the monsoon downpours, but instead, I brought them with me as baggage.

Truly, Lord Ganesha is determined to get Madam wet!

Visiting Texas was splendid, but living out of suitcases with two small boys was traumatic. And, what? Madam has to cook? Madam has to do laundry? Madam has to drive? That's loco talk!

The night before the flight home, I lay in bed staring at the ceiling. I was longing for that blast of polluted, humid Mumbai air that slapped my face whenever I descended from the plane, which both energized and terrified me.

I had loved reconnecting with friends, but after a few weeks, I felt removed from Austin. I missed my expat luxuries, but what I missed most was the constant presence of the people who invaded my privacy.

I no longer liked being alone. Each day, as the sun faded over the River City, I craved the evening walks around Khar Gymkhana with hundreds of others. I missed the taste of Somnat's fresh *chaat* and weekly gossip sessions with Pinky. I wanted Amol's wisdom and yoga sessions. Most notably, I wanted my trusted driver. And I wanted the color back: dark; shadows loomed in my former Westlake bubble.

I wanted to feel vibrant again.

When the departure day arrived, I was ready. As a result, all the probable issues that could arise did.

We left two hours early so I could check eleven pieces of luggage, only to be informed of a two-hour delay due to bad weather in Chicago.

After reaching the Windy City, inhaling McNuggets (the boys, at least), and boarding the next plane, an announcement from one of the pilots confirmed yet another delay. This time, it was due to a severe electrical storm so intense we sat in our seats for another ninety minutes without power until the staff gave way to anarchy and began to serve drinks.

I'll never forget overhearing Grant, rolling back home maharaja-style, speaking to the flight attendant as I returned from the loo, "My mommy really needs an ice cold Chardonnay, my baby brother needs a large cold milk, and may I have warm trail mix and a big glass of ice with water, please."

Finally, landing at London Heathrow and being told by British Airways, "Actually, there's no room on the 9:50 p.m. flight tonight (nine hours later), and the three of you might need to stay overnight and fly tomorrow," was the last straw. I didn't balk.

In fact, I cackled like a witch while the entire lounge full of uptight passengers glared at me. For a split second, I channeled Crazy Madam.

"We're not staying overnight in London. I suggest you rethink your strategy," I said sternly.

Forty-five minutes later over the lounge speaker I hear my "good name."

"We can put you and your boys on the flight, but you'll be in the back of the plane. It's the best we can do."

I sit my tote bag down and breathe multiple times like Yoga Hottie instructs me to do when I'm stressing out.

I look around. No one is paying attention to me now. I've left the boys in the kid's area watching a Mr. Bean video.

I want to scream—no, yell, like when I was the eighth-grade head cheerleader at Stovall Junior High. British Airways does not g-e-t my game plan.

Action, action, I want action!

A-C-T-I-O-N!

But instead of making a complete ass out of myself, I calmly say, "My husband's company paid $24,000 for our three business-class tickets. These are not mileage reward tickets. Not to mention, I'm an AA Advantage Platinum Member and my boys are AA Advantage Gold Members.

Earth to British Airways!

"We're not sitting in coach. You'll need to upgrade us to first class or call Richard Branson to see if he has empty business-class seats on Virgin Airways you can purchase on our behalf.

"I don't know who you need to talk to, but figure it out."

Then it dawns on me: British Airways is like my India—who is really in charge?

No sooner do I return to the lounge after stocking up on magazines and snacks, than my "good name" is again called.

"Ms. Erwin, we found three business-class seats for you. Here are your boarding passes. Safe travels back to Bombay."

I look down at Grant. "Seriously? Did this just happen?"

"Yes, Mom, it did."

I call Stanley, but he doesn't answer, as usual. I send an email instead detailing my hellish reality.

The following morning we circle the airport for an hour, then hold tight for the customary drop onto the tarmac.

However, before we land, a flight attendant kneels down beside me. He's just received an important electronic notice from Heathrow.

Oh joy!

"Did you really check eleven bags?" he asks slowly.

I blink, and all the color drains from my face. I've been up for the better part of the long flight with anxiety.

"Our sincere apologies, but we just got word none of the bags were loaded onto our flight in London. Actually, British Airways will load them on the next direct route to Mumbai—you should see them in two or three days."

I freeze.

"We killed nine hours in the airport and not a single person could load any of our bags on the plane?"

I want to scream, "This is how British Airways rolls to India!" but I don't want to wake up the boys.

I get up and step into the loo. I lock the door as crocodile-size tears roll down my cheeks.

However, something comes over me as the pilot announces our descent.

I look into the mirror and have a moment with myself.

It sounds silly, but in this split second of despair, I'm back at Southwest Texas State University, in the bathroom, applying red lipstick, ready to collect a diploma, an education gifted in the form of scholarships, financial aid, and a ton of bank loans, feeling nervous. But as I cross the stage, a spark ignites. I know the happiest people don't necessarily have the best of everything; they just make the most of everything that comes along.

I complete the necessary paperwork, skip baggage claim, and bop out of the exit in record time, with nothing but a cross-shoulder bag, two backpacks, a tote bag, and a Walmart umbrella stroller with two plastic bags full of chocolates, crackers, and wine—consolation gifts, compliments of the flight attendants.

Stanley is in utter disbelief when we're the first passengers out the door.

I walk past him and his goofy driver.

Preytap speaks, "B-b-b-b-u-t, b-b-b-b-u-t, we drive two cars for new crap, Madam, you bought in America."

I shake my head.

Immediately, Naushad takes Grant's hand and walks to the car. I push Matthew in the stroller behind him.

"See you at the Marble Palace, Boss." We leave them standing and staring with hundreds of other locals.

Naushad makes eye contact with me once we're near Rocket, "Really, Madam, no crap?"

Quietly I respond, "Seriously."

For the first time in more than twenty-four hours, I smile.

"Yes, Naushadie…BA forgot to put all of Madam's crap on the plane."

I'm seated behind him, and he stares at me in the rearview mirror. "Seriously, Madam? Like this, like that?"

I do the head wiggle.

He drives out of the airport parking lot, points to the shiny new plastic Ganesha superglued to the leather dashboard, and opens the glove compartment to reveal a series of stickers he's placed inside the door. "Madam, these are my lucky numbers."

Then he turns to me before heading into the honking traffic. "Welcome home, Madam. A little puffy, not too much, but looking good."

The minute I open the front door to the flat, translucent geckos scatter across the dusty floor. It's grand to be home!

I notice the curtains are pulled back and a light rain dances on the Khar Gymkhana cricket field. Monsoon is all around us.

Stanley stops by the flat to visit with the boys before heading back to the office, and Naushad calls Neelam, who arrives within fifteen minutes to babysit and clean.

I feel a bit lost since there are no suitcases to unpack. Neelam does a quick inventory. The pantry shelves are bare except for cereal.

Naushad speaks first, "Boss has been eating out a lot, Madam." Then, Neelam hands me a sheet of paper and a pen and tells me what food items and staples I need to buy. I do as instructed and make a list.

On our way to stock the kitchen, Naushad describes the flooding situation around the neighborhood. I'm perplexed as we make our way slowly down 15th Road. Now it's raining heavily. I look to my right at one of the traffic signals, and the street is completely flooded. Locals walk knee-deep in dirty water into a grocery store. I see dark, low-level clouds.

I look to my left and women wearing *saris* hoist the yards of fabric up around their knees, children kick water, and rickshaw drivers race by, spraying innocent victims waiting at the bus stop. Umbrellas are useless.

"Madam, K-Value is closed, but Boss discovered a new store by the JW. I take you there," he says, driving slowly, weaving in and out of traffic.

There are no normal activities: no goods being sold on sidewalks, no professional ear cleaners working on clients, no bullock carts filled with vegetables, no sleeping bodies on cardboard mats.

The light turns red and we stop.

I look at Naushad's reflection in the rearview mirror. "What did you do with the car while we were gone?"

He smiles. "I looked at car two to three times a week, Madam. I also drove a little bit to make sure the battery didn't die," he says.

"I bet you did!" I say grinning.

He lowers his voice, "Maybe more, Madam."

"Three people know what you did this summer."

He looks baffled.

"Me, myself, and I!"

He grins.

"Madam, can I tell you something?"

I roll my eyes.

"Madam, Boss was too much hungry for chicken while you were in America. He asked me where we get chicken, and I drove him to the shop where you buy the chicken, but he would not go inside, Madam. He did not believe Naushad. He thought it was a trick."

I laugh and can't stop.

Boy, I wish I could have seen the look on Stanley's face when Naushad pointed to the shop full of live chickens!

The rain stops.

Shopping done, we return to the car park.

Before Naushad opens my door he says, "Madam, Boss also asked me how we got the windshield fixed."

"Really?"

"Yes, Madam."

We share a moment of connection reliving the production.

"What did you tell him?"

"I said, 'Boss, the window was broken and talking, talking too much talking, Boss. No one help Madam, no one help get the window fixed like this, like that. My madam got it fixed *herself*, Boss.'

"Then Boss said to me you like to take a bull by these horns but I don't know this talk, Madam."

"It's an expression that means to confront a problem head-on."

He nods, and I know he hasn't a clue as to what I just said.

"Madam, are you bringing Fiona back?"

"No. There is no work here for her."

He seems content with my answer, but I find it odd he asked.

I launch into extreme move mode.

Sixteen men descend upon the Marble Palace and possessions fly off shelves. They're wrapped carefully and placed into cardboard boxes.

The following day, rain and thunder hold fast over the neighborhood again. Lights flicker when lightning slashes through the sky. Workers pack diligently as Grant and Matthew emerge from the playroom with life jackets on. Grant holds up a sheet of paper. Written in red marker, words on the sheet state: "My hourly rate is 200 rupees!!!"

On the third day of packing, Mr. Carpenter Man appears to patch all 114 holes he's drilled in the walls to ensure we reclaim the security deposit. I'm checking email before the internet connection is disabled, and Channing has sent words of wisdom from the River City—my daily horoscope from the *Austin American-Statesman*. It reads:

Aquarius (January 20–February 18): You've already proved that you could turn your vaguest longing into a concrete plan. You're at that place again. Can you articulate this desire yet?

I reply, "HELL YES," and hit SEND.

I walk among the maze of stuff and spray Liz Claiborne throughout the flat while the workers sweat profusely to Bollywood oldies blaring on my iPod Touch. The air conditioning units are working overtime, but nothing but my precious perfume can mask the foul smell of body odor.

When Naushad returns from a delivery to Oberoi Crest, he looks like death warmed over. He promised to see a doctor down south yesterday but forgot.

I grab a thermometer from the bathroom drawer and take his temperature—103 degrees! Against his wishes, I call Dr. Shah at the JW, who sends an employee to draw blood and collect a urine sample. When the medical technician arrives, Naushad, who has never had blood drawn except when I hired him and made him get an HIV test, is mad at me.

"Madam, I don't like needles." He pouts. "I maybe have a little cold."

"Whatever you have, I'm going to fix. I can't afford to lose you and none of us want to get what you've got."

Naushad, who has an audience, puts on a brave front.

The employee draws blood from his left arm, and then speaks Hindi, giving instructions for the urine test.

Neelam spills *chai* on the table while she listens. She can't control her laughter and chimes in with a little Hindi too, but Pussycat still doesn't understand the concept "to capture pee" in the small plastic cup. When one of the packers stops working and joins in the debate, I grab the cup, walk out of our flat, through the foyer, and into our servant's loo as Naushad follows me.

Then, I turn to Naushad, "Imagine Madam is a maharaja. This is how you capture pee." I stand tall. I unzip my pants and he gasps. I pretend to pull a penis out and urinate in the plastic cup I'm holding in my left hand. Then, I hand the cup to Naushad. I shake and put the penis back in my pants and zip up. I adjust. I take the cup, screw the cap on, and set it down. Finally, I wash my hands.

After that, I turn and smile. "That's how it's done. Now you go do it."

"Seriously, Madam?" he says.

"I'm not kidding, Naushad. Seriously!"

After the workers finish up for the day, a courier delivers two prescriptions for Naushad. I call him up to the flat and give him the diagnosis—a urinary tract infection—and hand over rupees for him to go and purchase the medicine.

"Lay off the *chai* and feel better, please! I'll see you tomorrow, Naushad."

"*Theek hai*, Madam."

The flat is quiet and I begin to think how a move allows you to blend the old with the new. When we moved into Le Gardenia, I was not allowed to paint the walls; therefore, I filled every nook and cranny with color. In the new space, I get to hire painters and craftsmen to install shelving and a bathtub. In general, I'm happy to start fresh, because I like to roll up my sleeves and reinvent a space.

Neelam interrupts my train of thought when she enters the living room, talking about how disrespectful it is that my driver is ill on a very important day in his madam's life. I remind her he has a fever, but her odd behavior surprises me. Is she trying to make herself seem indispensable?

The truth is I need them both, but what I don't need is competition for my time.

The final move day is here!

While I put the boys in the car with Sabal, Neelam speaks Hindi to Archie's driver, who is taking refrigerated goods and clothes I didn't want packed over to the new flat.

My mobile rings and when I answer it, I hand it to Neelam. It's not Naushad, but Nisha, who can't speak English. Naushad is not reporting for duty today. He's sick in bed. Sabal sees the look on my face and assures me he will take charge and fill Naushad's shoes, since Crazy Madam has not returned from California.

The caravan emerges from the car park onto 15th Road. The Alert Security Team, standing at attention, watches two cars and a lorry full of my belongings and movers ease into traffic. Literally, we drive six blocks and pull into the new compound, one street over.

The Oberoi Building Society Manager and the Professional Security Team greet me with firm handshakes. In addition, Mr. Carpenter Man and Gautham the Tailor from Fab India are ready to get to work. When the last load of the goods is placed inside the fourth floor foyer, I tip all of the workers, security guards, and drivers. I shut the door and collapse onto the rug.

I cannot believe I moved during monsoon, and the gods cooperated— truly a sign we're right where we should be. I take a moment and brood over the fact that India gave me a second chance to continue my journey, which is happy disarray. With the help of a window cleaner, an electrician, a plumber, a contractor, and four internet geeks, we unpack, rewire, clean, organize, and christen the flat as the "Mini Marble Palace," which makes me want to cheer!

Knock, knock. Neelam is reporting for work. In the midst of the move, I forgot to give her a new key. I increased her salary again, now that she works full-time as housekeeper and nanny.

Naushad calls and he's downstairs. I ask him to coordinate a Himalaya and Diet Pepsi delivery.

I call Amol and schedule back-to-back yoga sessions. "How much weight did you gain in Texas, *jaan*?" he says. I still don't know what *jaan* means, but when I tell him six pounds, he howls.

Then, I call Pravin and schedule my remaining training sessions at the JW. Mr. Unibrow is ecstatic I'm taking charge of my health again. Little does he know, the minute I hang up I'm calling Anil the Wine Guy to restock the bar.

Brrrrring. Brrrrring. It's Pinky calling and she wants to see the new flat this week and talk Bollywood. We pencil in a girls' night.

I order Domino's pizza for lunch before Naushad drives me to Le Gardenia for a final walk-through with Raj. The Alert Security Team, drivers, and Lolita wave and salute. They ask Naushad in Hindi how we're doing and tell him the building is not fun anymore now that we're gone.

We return to Oberoi Crest. No sooner do I take my shoes off than there's a knock at the door. Neelam races down the hall and looks through the peephole. Unmistakenly, a Professional Security Guard has escorted none other than Crazy Madam up to our foyer. Neelam speaks Hindi, confirming we know her; she's allowed inside the flat.

My, my, my, how fancy we roll in our new digs.

"I've been in town two days, and I need California wine," she demands. "School can't start soon enough. Nick is traveling next week to Chennai and I'm ready to fire Sabal once and for all."

Phoebe calls. She just landed. The boys are with the nanny and Archie is stuck at work. She needs grape juice and is headed our way, too. "I just spent more than two months taking care of my kids with no help from anyone while in the UK," she says. "I don't care about jet lag, I just want adult time!"

Neelam springs into high gear and out comes the Cakebread Chardonnay. When Stanley walks into the flat at six o'clock, we're tipsy. "Looks like the Sula Sisters are back on tour."

It's great to catch up, but I wonder if this is how we're going to roll each time a member of the Mumbai Mafia returns to the city.

While we down our third bottle of wine along with dip and chips—contraband from Whole Foods—Channing sends an unexpected text: "Late night dinner and drinks! Miss you!"

I text back: "At the Sula Welcome Reception on 16th Road. Thank God for Indian nannies."

On Wednesday, I accidentally interviewed Crazy Madam's former psycho cook. Sabal set up the meeting, and what a disservice he did to me. How dare he try to lead me astray with a thief! Fortunately, Roseanne calls to coordinate carpool and overhears Neelam speaking in English to Sakina in the background.

"Did I just hear Neelam say Sakina?" she says.

I'm nervous. "Yes."

She says sternly, "Rhonda, Sakina is the stalker who threatened to kill me after I fired her. She stole from us. I know you've been interviewing cooks, but she's psychotic."

Ruh-roh!

"Get her out of your kitchen now and don't tell her you know me," she says.

Click.

Luckily the cooking demonstration is over, and I escort her directly to the foyer and lock the door.

My bad.

I was present a few times Sakina sent evil texts to Roseanne and it wasn't pretty. It was downright scary. I explain the situation to Neelam and call Naushad to speak Hindi to the security team. I want to ensure she's not allowed back on the property ever again.

It's Thursday, and I wake up rejoicing. I've officially hired Mary, a cook, and the Junior League cookbook reappears in my life. Plus, she knows how to prepare chicken thirty-one ways.

Friday rolls around and after school, the boys stay in and watch a movie. The weather is awful and the flat feels damp.

Later in the afternoon, I head over to Roseanne's flat for group yoga. It's great to see Amol. He gives me the once-over, perhaps confirming I did indeed gain weight.

I smirk. "It looks like you have your work cut out for you."

After the one-hour session, I call Naushad but there is no answer. Hmm. I wait while Roseanne pays Amol the group fee she collected. I call Naushad once more, but again, no response. I take the lift down, but still there is no Naushad. The Lapsara Security Guard tells Yoga Hottie in Hindi that Naushad left me.

Unfortunately, rickshaws don't drive up to this section of Bandra.

But I'm in luck! It's not raining, and Amol offers me a ride home on his motorbike before his next session. I haven't ridden a motorbike in Mumbai, but I see thousands of locals weaving in and out of traffic every day. They get to go places trucks and cars can't go—more so than rickshaws.

Amol shows me how to perch behind him so I don't straddle the seat, which is unsuitable for proper Indian women. But it forces me to hold onto him with only one arm, which makes me very unstable. I don't like sitting sideways.

By the time we reach the end of the street, I ask him to stop. I get off, readjust my yoga bag across my shoulder, throw my leg over the bike, and straddle the seat.

"We're just going five blocks—who will we see to disapprove?"

He drives past Le Gardenia and Khar Gymkhana. I give him directions to the new building before we're caught at a traffic signal on Khar Danda Road. As he moves into the turn lane, a small white-haired man wearing a *lungi* and carrying a tall, thin wooden stick walks up. Before the light changes, he turns and shouts, "Whore!" directly at me and continues on.

Seriously?

Amol drops me outside Oberoi Crest and takes off. I look around the car park, but still no Naushad.

Up in the flat, I discuss the situation with Mary and Neelam, but they haven't heard from or seen Naushad. Two hours later, he appears in the foyer mumbling about some business he had to do. I give him a stern talk and send him home.

Lightning and thunder wake me up in the wee morning hours. The boys are sleeping peacefully and Stanley is snoring like a freight train. I walk to the living room and turn on a lamp. I grab the monthly AWC newsletter and scan the monsoon health tips article.

According to Dr. Kalpana Rao, one of the in-house doctors at the JW, warm, humid conditions and stagnant water can cause a variety of unpleasant and potentially dangerous diseases including malaria, jaundice, typhoid, gastroenteritis, leptospirosis, viral and fungal infections, and conjunctivitis. Perhaps returning early wasn't such a grand idea. I pray Grant and Matthew stay healthy.

I scan the list of do's and don'ts. We are strongly urged to stay home if the rain is heavy and continuous, or at the very least, we should avoid going long distances within the city. We're warned: "If you must leave home, carry at least two bottles of water and snacks in case you get stranded."

The most frightening *don't* is this one: "If you must go on foot, tread slowly, particularly when water levels are higher. Manholes are kept open during monsoon and you could easily fall into drains or other large holes. If at all possible, carry a walking stick (like the man who called me a whore) and probe the ground ahead of you."

The author closes with this: "Monsoon season need not be a fearful time (well, the list of potentially deadly funk we could all catch sure made me wish for sunshine) but one of great fun. Follow doctor's orders, use common sense, and curl up with a good book or go dancing in the rain."

That's my kind of spirit.

Speaking of spirit, Saturday evening our expat group (with husbands in tow) meets at Vie Sunset Lounge and Deck for people-watching and yummy food. The bill is paid and drivers are called—with Enigma as the next stop.

But when Naushad steps out of the car to open my door, someone shuts his door while the car is running. He pulls on my door, but it's locked. Stanley tries to open his door, but it's locked too. Now every door is locked and a crowd has gathered behind the car to watch the *Mission Impossible III* DVD playing inside.

Naushad looks at me in distress.

Boss is furious. What in the heck did Naushad do to enable the auto-lock feature on the car?

"Madam, I'm sorry. I need the spare key to the car."

Stanley walks over to where we're standing.

"The spare key is in the safe back in the Mini Marble Palace. Neelam is babysitting, but I'm not about to call and give her the code to the safe," I say.

The other drivers are talking smack about Naushad in Hindi; I can tell by their body language.

"Maybe you need new lucky numbers, Naushad," I say sarcastically.

Stanley says, "You go with Roseanne and Nick. I'll take a rickshaw back to the flat and get the spare key. I'll meet you on the dance floor. No worries, Madam."

The three of us climb in the service car. I look back at Naushad. He shrugs his shoulders and jumps into a rickshaw with Boss.

It's 3 a.m. and Naushad doesn't answer our call to pick us up at the JW. I try repeatedly, but his phone is switched off.

We bum a ride home with Yvette and Steve. Our car is parked in our building car park, but once more, there is no sign of Naushad. We can't ask anyone who is awake any questions, because we don't speak Hindi. We enter the flat quietly. The boys are sleeping. Neelam is sound asleep in the guest room.

It's mind-boggling. We hired Naushad away from an agency who treated him like a slave, gave him keys to a car we never drove, and paid him two months' salary for six weeks of vacation when we left in May. Plus, I bought him a new phone and all-new clothes and shoes.

He hasn't been calling me when he arrives for duty.

When I confront him, he snaps at me.

I did not see this coming.

The next day after breakfast, the boys need a ride several streets over to attend a birthday party, and at this quarter in the game, I'm on defense. I'm nobody's fool. The lift is taking too long so we walk down and Neelam speaks to a Professional Security Guard, who flags down a rickshaw. I hand Neelam some rupees and off they go.

Out of nowhere, Naushad pulls the car around.

"It's too late," I say. "Go put it back in the space and meet me upstairs."

I'm unable to think on the way up to the fourth floor. Remember, I have trust issues?

I call Stanley in Delhi to ask him what to do.

"I think you should fire him and hire a new driver, but it's completely up to you. Just be willing to live with the consequences."

I want to yell, "Jesus, take the wheel!" But I'm so hurt I can't say a word.

There's a knock, and in walks Naushad.

"I need to see your phone for a minute, and I need to borrow the car keys. Boss wants me to switch out a key on the keychain," I say. Without thinking, he hands over both.

I, in turn, give him an envelope with a month's salary in rupees, "You're fired. I don't know how we got to this point, but it's over."

He doesn't move a muscle.

"Go. We're done."

He still doesn't move. "Madam, I want my phone," he says.

I shrug my shoulders. "I bought the phone and it stays with me," I say, clenching my teeth. I motion for him to move into the foyer and I shut the door behind him.

When I hear the lift take him down, I burst into tears.

Two hours later, Neelam drops off the boys and heads home.

I walk down through the stairwell to get a bag out of Rocket when I see Naushad lurking in the car park. A light rain begins to fall and I hear thunder overhead. He approaches.

"Madam, please, I'm begging for my job back," he says. "I'm too sorry."

I don't know what to do. The thought of calling Auto Riders gives me a headache.

"Things need to change, Naushad. You're not treating Madam with respect. I don't know you anymore. Show up tomorrow, and we'll talk after the smoke clears. I need to think through my decision and get some rest. Madam is heartbroken."

He begins to cry uncontrollably, and I walk away.

Stanley won't be home until late tomorrow.

Of course, I get no sleep—not because I'm totally hysterical, but because Naushad's phone beeps constantly throughout the night. It's a foreign number. At six o'clock in the morning the phone finally rings, and when I answer it, I hear a familiar voice.

"Naushad. It's Fiona. Are you there?"

It's Monday morning, the first day of kindergarten for Grant, who will attend ASB from 8 a.m. to 3 p.m. I pack a lunchbox and gather his backpack and water bottle, and we ride the lift down. Swami—the new service driver who replaced Sabal—and Roseanne have graciously agreed to give him a ride to school.

I glance over in the car park and Naushad, in a white *kurta* and skinny jeans, is lurking near Rocket. He's in shock he isn't driving Grant to school.

I take the lift back up and get dressed for the day.

Roseanne returns to our building with Swami thirty minutes later to collect Matthew to drop at Little Butterflies, a local Montessori school up near Carter Road.

Matthew, sporting a new backpack, water bottle, and lunchbox, runs to Naushad when the lift doors open.

Oh my God! I can't believe this is happening.

Swami puts the car in park, opens his door, and jerks Matthew out of Naushad's arms. Crazy Madam then takes Matthew, straps him in a car seat, and yells, "You're done driving the Erwin brothers!"

Matthew starts screaming, "Naushad! Naushad! Mummy, Naushad!"

As we leave the car park, I look out the back window. Naushad is crying in front of the other drivers.

Breaking up is so damn hard to do.

After school, Neelam picks up Matthew in a taxi while I run errands with Roseanne to fill my time until ASB carpool; eventually, we all make it back to the Mini Marble Palace.

The boys bathe to wash off monsoon germs, and Neelam folds laundry. After a shower, I blow-dry my hair and put on pajamas. Sitting at the dining table sipping English tea, I think about the advice from Cathy about the help.

Already I feel a void, but I press on with the boys, read my Bollywood magazine, and send emails to friends back in Austin.

I don't have a plan to hire a new driver.

Stanley calls to say he's stuck in Delhi because his flight is canceled due to bad weather. I give Neelam rupees to take a rickshaw home in the rain. After dinner and cartoons, I tuck the boys in bed. I'm sad. I don't know what to think.

I go into the kitchen and pour a large glass of Sula. I hear noise outside our front door. It's nine o'clock. I peer through the peephole. It's Naushad. He's distraught. Thinking I'll probably live to regret this moment, I let him in.

"Madam, I need you and Boss. I need Grant and Matthew," he says, trembling.

He breaks down, crying uncontrollably.

I reach out and give him a hug. I let loose a few tears as well.

"No one cares about Naushad but you. I make big mistake," he says. "Biggest mistake of my life, Madam."

I lead him to the sofa and we sit.

He can't stop crying.

I say calmly, "If you want your job back, I need the truth."

Stanley calls, but I don't pick up. I have a gnawing fear I will be forced to confess to him the three most difficult words in any marriage: "You were right."

The floodgates open.

"Madam, I'm really sorry. I tell you the truth," Naushad says. "Fiona told me she was going to move here and marry me."

I can't do anything but stare.

He nods. "Yes, Madam. She said this to me too much times. She's calling, calling, too much calling me. She's mad you didn't bring her back. She told me she loves me, Madam. She wants to be with me."

I inhale. I can barely breathe.

I get up and grab a box of Kleenex from the bathroom.

"Naushad, you're married to Nisha. Fiona was playing you. She is not moving to India to marry you. She lied to you. She lied to us about many things too."

He wipes tears away.

"Madam, can I tell you something else?" he says.

I take a sip of cheap Indian wine.

"Remember when I don't work three or four days for you? Vinay driving you, Madam? I did this because you signed his timesheet and put he did a good job. He told my boss you like him more than me. I'm sorry, Madam," he says slowly. "I'm so, so sorry, Madam."

"Naushad, he asked me to write a compliment on the invoice because it helps him get a higher bonus during Diwali. At least that's what he told me. Maybe he tricked me, but there's no way I will ever like Vinay more than I like you."

I exhale.

"Madam, Sabal stole Crazy Madam's crackberry."

"You mean her BlackBerry?"

He says, "Yes, Madam. He took it and sold it."

I take another sip of Sula.

"Anything else you need to share?"

He wipes his eyes again.

"Madam, when I pick you and Boss up at JW first time, I thought you were the nanny. Fiona fat and I thought she was the madam," he says smiling for the first time. "Most Madams too much fatty but not you, Madam. You run like this, like that too much. You great shape."

"One more thing, Madam. I need something from you."

For the love of Shiva, I'm not sure how much more of this I can take. What else is going to come out of his mouth?

"Madam, you Indian now but you don't know our plate number. If network is busy and my mobile don't work, you need to tell guards our number, then they get Naushad for you," he says. "You can't be best Madam if you don't know plate numbers."

I take a deep breath and slowly say, "Do you mean I need to memorize our license plate number?"

He does the head wiggle.

Man, this is powerful stuff.

We hear Matthew stir in the back of the flat.

"Madam, I go now. I'm really, really sorry, Madam. Naushad make big mistake. I make you cry and Boss is going to kill me. He's really, really going to kill me this time," he says and walks to the door. "No more crying you."

We give each other solid stares.

"From this point forward, you must be honest with me. The boys love you, Naushad, but I want to be clear. This talk is a final warning. I need to discuss your phone situation with Boss when he gets back, but I'll see you tomorrow."

"Yes, Madam. You need me and I need you."

He adds, "Seriously."

I close the door and once again collapse on the rug.

I guess I needed to travel a long distance to find my way back home.

23

Culture shock is the way we describe the confusing and nervous feelings a person has after leaving a familiar way of life. When we moved to Mumbai, we faced a lot of changes, both challenging and stimulating. But after some time, the frustration and anger subsided.

Pursuing this further, we cruised into what is known as the adjustment phase. Call me cuckoo, but we've developed routines, and our negative Western responses have given way to normal reactions when things don't always go our way.

In lay terms, life is totally awesome.

With the first week of school in progress, I attend Yvette's Wine and Women party at her flat on 15th Road. I walk the four blocks from 16th Road, take the lift up, and remove my shoes at the door.

Yvette, member of the Mumbai Mafia, is boisterous, full of life, and lives in a stylish marble flat larger than my two flats combined. The atmosphere is relaxed, and I set down my artichoke dip and chips on the kitchen counter. A bartender gives me a large pour of imported Chardonnay.

I scan the living room. Ladies from ASB and AWC mingle freely, and conversations are full of gossip and tips on how to work a corrupt system.

New foreigners look nervous. I make introductions and take a seat by the coffee table when I feel a light tap on my right shoulder.

"You're busted! I finally figured out what perfume you wear! My college roommate wore the same fragrance."

As I take a sip of wine. I turn to see none other than Wendy.

"I've been waiting for you to call me since we had the rat ordeal at Olive in May. I've seen you at Bandra coffee events, but we haven't had a chance to reconnect over monsoon."

I smile.

"Promise me you won't tell a soul I wear the same perfume I've worn since seventh grade—"

She cuts me off. "Don't worry, Liz, your secret is safe with me!"

Theek hai.

Wendy gives me an update on her expat status: Robin continues to work for the same software company. They returned to Boston this summer to visit friends. Her mother, a doctor, and her father, a rocket scientist, retired in Idaho. She spent several weeks solo with them in July and August. Plus, they plan to visit this fall.

"Do you still drink Diet Pepsi like water?" I ask.

"Sure do. I just switched to plastic bottles instead of the cans. It tastes better."

I add, "Been there, done that."

Like many transplants, we bond instantly.

Roseanne walks by. "How are Grant and Matthew?" she asks.

I give her a thumbs-up.

Wendy says, "I forgot you had children, but I think it's amazing your boys can rely on each other as playmates and get to share in the thrill of discovering things in India."

"Yes it's splendid, but I've got two words: spoiled rotten. I don't think Matthew's feet have touched the ground since we got back from Texas this summer."

The bartender refills glasses, Bollywood tunes play leisurely in the background, and raindrops tap lightly on the windows.

"I'm glad to be back in Mumbai, and I never thought those words would come out of my mouth," I say. "I emailed Brett, my British friend who lived in Rajasthan for three years who knows India, and he told me cream rises to the top—remain calm during monsoon."

"What rises to the top here is not the crème de la crème in reality," Wendy exclaims.

Changing the subject she adds, "I'm so happy we now live on the same street."

"Me too neighbor. Thank the Lord I live in a quieter section of Khar West now. The first three months I had to take sleeping pills. The insomnia was unbearable."

"Don't you love how few Indian pharmacists require a prescription before handing over meds?" Wendy asks.

"Yes, I do!"

"How do you like your new building?"

"We like that it's built out, but all the Indian owners get two parking spaces; as renters, we get one and a half."

She does the head wiggle. "And you're shocked by this? Did you just get here yesterday?"

We laugh.

"Last week a courier delivered a letter from the Building Society Manager stating I must remove the table and chairs I placed in the half space. I appreciate the monitoring, but I need a place to sit while the boys ride their scooters in the car park. I know we live in a country where the rules can change at a moment's notice, but it's the principle, and we were cheated."

Wendy waves the bartender over for more Chardonnay refills.

"Well, Madam Rhonda, it isn't the first time, and it won't be the last!"

"Two days later, after I had a stern chat with the Building Society Manager with Naushad helping to translate, I was told I didn't have to write a letter and I could park what I needed to in the tiny space. I'm not sure he translated word for word, but it's good to flex my muscles again and find out I'm still good at it."

This time I do the head wiggle and we giggle like schoolgirls.

"Who is Naushad?"

"My Muslim driver we hired from Auto Riders. He's the one who drove us to pick up Crazy Madam from the Lapsara Building."

She nods. "Robin uses a company driver and I use a Hindu service driver named Rajesh part-time to run errands."

"Recently, I fired Naushad then hired him back. It's a long story for another day."

"How do you manage when he has time off?"

"I jump into rickshaws, which I love, point to landmarks, and wave frantically from the backseat. By the way, I just hired a full-time cook. Game changer!"

"I have a part-time cook because we eat out a lot," Wendy says.

Roseanne plops down beside us.

She's buzzing. "My friend's servants smell foul. She wants advice."

Wendy looks annoyed. "I don't have that problem."

Roseanne looks at me. "Do you have this problem?"

"No. I bought Naushad and Neelam gift baskets full of deodorant, toothpaste, toothbrushes, razors, soap, shampoo, and conditioner. Then I installed a mirror above the sink in the servant's bathroom and filled a bin with washcloths and towels. They use the sprayer and an empty bucket for showers."

"It must work, because Naushad told me he's low on Axe Deodorant Body Spray and Neelam is out of dental floss."

Yvette yells for Roseanne. She's wanted in the kitchen to discuss political views.

Wendy smiles with a word of advice, "Madam, never discuss politics in this country."

Got it.

"Hey, let's run errands this week."

"Sounds like a plan."

"Let me ask you this," she says, "Do you like Indian food?"

"Kinda."

"How can you live in India and not love Indian food?"

"It happens."

"Well, I'll take you to Elco and Swati Snacks while we're out running the streets with Naushad. Remember—I'm a vegetarian and you won't be disappointed, Madam Rhonda."

"Just so you know, I don't have many Indian friends."

She looks me up and down. "You seem to be doing just fine, right?"

I nod.

"Robin and I have Indian friends from college. A few live here in the city, and it definitely made the transition easier for us. One of the cool things about being an expat, whether you have local friends or not, is the chance to change directions—not to mention the freedom you get," she says.

Damn straight!

"Wendy, now that I'm no longer defined by friends, children, volunteer activities, or parents, there are no limits. I can be the person I've always wanted to be."

Wendy laughs. "I might be up for a reinvention myself, and this is the perfect place to do it."

We collect our handbags and thank Yvette for her gracious hospitality.

"Wendy, I'm thrilled we bumped into each other again," I tell her.

"I sincerely agree, Liz." And we step into the lift.

Naushad is in the car park waiting for me.

He opens my door, and I wave goodbye to Wendy.

Naushad starts the engine. "Madam, you see this madam again, long time. She good Madam, I know this."

A streetlamp shines near the car and casts a shadow on Naushad's face. He's confident about his proclamation.

This immediate bond with Wendy is a turning point—an indication she will be a genuine friend amidst the Sula Sisters.

24

When the western wind gusts belligerently off the sea (which is several streets over from our flat), I often worry Oberoi Crest will lift off its foundation and end up in Muscat.

Right now, dark clouds loom overhead on 16th Road. If the natural forces of wind and rain don't do us in, the absurd amount of water dominating our lives day and night might do the trick. (My OCD kicks in and I immediately chart an exit strategy for emergency purposes.)

Rain is seeping through the ceiling of my bathroom and dripping through the kitchen faucet, generating a rhythmic jam session while thunder and lightning rip through the sky—a constant reminder there's no escaping the wrath of Mother Nature.

I take the lift down to collect shopping bags from the lobby when I spot my trusty driver.

Our conversation goes like this:

"Naushad, when will monsoon stop?" I ask.

He takes a long drag off a *bidi* and blows the smoke away from me.

"Madam, only Allah knows this. Last year thirty-nine inches in two days, like this, like that. Days no matter, Madam. Only waters."

"Madam, you yoga, no stress. I park car up top, not in basement. Rain is here for two, three weeks more, Madam. Seriously."

I hope he's not right.

When he took me to the cleaners yesterday, I witnessed an affluent Indian woman walking under an umbrella her driver held over her head during a light shower.

"Naushad, do drivers do this so Madams don't get wet?"

He smirks. "Yes, you right, Madam."

"No way! You've been cheating! No more soaked clothes for me at AWC and ASB meetings."

"Madam, Naushad try to help you, you too much do yourself," he answers.

Back in the Mini Marble Palace, Yoga Hottie knocks on the door. He's early for weight training down in the gym. He takes his shoes off and heads to the kitchen for *chai* and yogurt.

His presence puts me at ease.

"Pinky is in the newspaper today, *jaan*, on page three," he says in passing.

I grab the daily and find the article. She and her father have joined forces to produce a Sindhi musical in Copenhagen and Dubai based on an inter-caste marriage. Interesting.

I send a text to Pinky: "Pretty in pink—extra, extra, need 2B an extra."

I happen to notice Seth in the DNA Brick & Mortar section. I show the photo to Amol, who is speaking Hindi to Mary and Neelam. He reminds me the B&M section is paid advertising. The article says he owned salons in New York and was a stylist for Tom Cruise and Jennifer Lopez.

Liar, liar, pants on fire!

Wendy knocks and walks in.

"It took forever to find a rickshaw," she says. "Sorry I'm late."

I show her the article.

"Is that the weirdo who gave you a mullet?" she says, grinning.

"Notice he uses his first and middle name. We can't Google him to find out his real identity."

Lolita's here to clean the bathrooms and floors. (I offered her part-time work twice weekly, and she gladly accepted.)

Amol hands Mary his *chai* cup and I'm lacing up my running shoes when Neelam walks into the living room to tell me about a particular food item Matthew is out of.

"Madam, Little Boss is out of the white meat he loves."

"You mean chicken?"

Yoga Hottie and Wendy laugh.

She shakes her head no. She says, "Madam, it's not the little bird, it's the bigger bird, that big bird the white people like to eat in November time, Madam...you know, Madam, you want big thanks for the fat white bird."

I'm wracking my brain while Wendy and Amol leave for the gym.

Then it dawns on me, she's talking turkey—the imported smoked turkey I buy from Milan at Sante.

Downstairs, Amol starts weight-training class.

I'm warming up on the treadmill when Wendy asks, "What happened to your American nanny? Is she still in Mumbai?"

Amol says, "I was going to ask the same thing."

Sternly, I say, "Fiona is in Austin and we never had concrete plans to bring her back. To make a long story short, she and Naushad had 'relations,' then she stalked him on his mobile, and we had to buy him a new SIM card. I don't know the full extent of what went down between the two of them, but it's over."

Amol does the head wiggle.

Wendy says, "Fiona and Naushad had a *relationship*—like what *kind* of relationship?"

I'm running and increasing the speed. "I don't want to know or think about it!" I change the subject. "I saw a group of tourists yesterday taking photos of our neighborhood cows. The women had on shorts and skirts above their knees with tank tops and no bras. Do tourists not study guidebooks before they take a trip? Why would they visit this country and show lots of flesh in public? It made me cringe."

"I hope they don't run into a skinny old man with a stick," Amol adds.

I crack up, jump off the treadmill, and hit the stop button.

Amol sets up leg weights for rotations.

Wendy says, "All right you two, what's the inside joke?"

I do the head wiggle.

"Amol gave me a ride home from yoga on his motorbike last month and a man called me a whore at the traffic signal. Do I look like a whore?"

"Were you dressed in shorts or a tank top?"

"No, but I straddled the motorbike seat," I explain, demonstrating in front of the mirror.

"I've lost all respect for you, Madam!" Wendy says. "She knows the unwritten rules, right Amol?"

He shakes his head, "Y-e-s, s-h-e d-o-e-s!"

The city is gearing up for Ganesh Chaturthi, an incredible ten-day festival we missed last year. In community halls and surrounding areas, hundreds of *karigars* (artisans) are busy making brightly-colored plaster elephant deities—a skill passed down through family members for generations.

Two days ago Naushad drove me to the best *pandal*, according to Neelam and Matkar, and from hundreds of various sizes and colors, I purchased a chunky Ganesha for twenty dollars. (Naushad has promised to submerse it for me per tradition after I move back to Texas.)

Resting on a pedestal outside our front door ever since, he's been kissed and blessed by seventeen people in our building, including the entire Professional Security Team, the window cleaners, the building society manager, several drivers, Grant, Matthew, Neelam, and Mary (who was originally Hindu, but her husband's mother-in-law forced her to convert to Catholicism).

Neelam is upset I didn't pick a white Ganesha, but I overheard Naushad telling her, "Madam loves hot pink and it has to be matchy, matchy with the other stuff in the foyer."

Last month, when the Mumbai Mafia Dads were alone during monsoon, they flew to Thailand for a four-day golf weekend.

Now the Desperate Housewives deserve a pow-wow!

When the big day arrives, Naushad drops Wendy and me at the airport and we're set to join the rest of the gang at the Four Hands house.

The rain has stopped and clear skies make the two-hour flight seem short.

In no time, we're off the plane and walking past the guards with AK-47s.

Much to our surprise, Kareena Kapoor, Dino Morea, and Koffee with Karan are at the teeny baggage claim carousel. Wendy winks at me. I want to pinch myself. Today is my lucky day!

The luggage conveyor belt beeps loudly and begins to spit out bags.

We spring into action like locals, pushing and shoving each other as we grab checked bags.

Sarika is boisterous and comes right out to ask if we can take a group photo with the stars. They oblige, but when Kareena steps forward next to me, due to the lack of security, the small crowd of Rajasthani admirers rushes forward.

Miss Bollywood has on sunglasses and doesn't seem to find the public display of affection amusing. Soldiers with AK-47s separate the crowd from the passengers, and what could have been an idiotic situation is peacefully resolved.

Thankfully, Laxman and Ushpal are waiting curbside. We make introductions and they load the two vehicles.

Out of nowhere, Koffee with Karan sprints over to inquire about a Louis Vuitton bag on one of our luggage carts.

He insists the LV bag is his bag, but Yvette, who also owns a LV bag, insists it's hers.

Ushpal digs through the packed luggage in the jeep and pulls out a second LV bag.

Oops! Sorry Karan.

We pull up to the Four Hands house and Laxman performs a small *puja*.

He honors us with flower leis and *bindi*s. But no sooner do the suitcases hit the ground than we drink a round of cocktails and head out the door and into the markets to shop.

Later in the evening after showers, we visit Cathy and Roberto's house for a chance to catch our breath and catch up on local gossip.

We have a fantastic dinner and meet the handsome, well-groomed handlebar-mustache-wearing guest of honor, the grandson of the Maharaja Hanwant Singh of Jodhpur, Rao Raja Parikshit Singh—Bozzo for short—accompanied by an avid professional polo player friend.

Saturday is sunny and hot, and after breakfast and mimosas, we're out the door again—this time, headed to a warehouse to shop for antiques and furniture.

Wendy and I are dressed in cotton tops and capri pants and sweating profusely.

"I didn't put on enough Liz Claiborne today," I tell her.

"I guess monsoon is over in this part of the woods. Do you see anything you need, Madam?"

I scan the garden section. "I spot two large wooden elephants and a tall Italian."

She laughs. "What did you say?"

I squeeze her right forearm.

The sun is blistering hot, but this is no mirage. Mr. Bollywood, Dino Morea, is walking in our direction while sweat drips between my boobs.

I whisper to Wendy, "We look like and smell like Mumbai Hillbillies."

It's hot and getting hotter and I have no lipstick on. I turn to see other Mumbai Mafia members drenched in sweat with their hair up in tacky rubber bands. Crazy Madam is sweating so fiercely it looks like she wet her pants again.

Dino walks right up to me, and without shame, I ask, "May I get a picture with you?"

He chuckles, "Yes, of course you can."

Crazy Madam says, "Do you know this person?"

I proudly retort, "Oh, I know this man and I need a photograph for my nightstand."

Wendy snorts. "You're too much, Sula Sister."

Then Crazy Madam realizes this is no ordinary worker bee and apologizes to him. "I had no idea who you are—sorry."

I whip out my camera and Wendy snaps a few shots.

The Mumbai Mafia is shocked. Those who know of him are in awe.

We conclude the photo session, and he and I begin to walk away from the group.

"Where are you ladies from?"

"Mumbai—Khar and Bandra."

"Really?"

"Yes, we're here for a girl's weekend."

"Oh, wow. I live on Pali Hill near the ocean. What are you doing tonight?"

My heart is racing.

Nonchalantly I say, "Well, we're meeting a friend (Bozzo) at Umaid Bhawan Palace for cocktails at seven o'clock in the Polo Bar."

He nods.

"Well, I'm filming a commercial at the Palace—why don't you meet me and we'll have a few drinks?"

OMG!

"So you're the reason we couldn't get dinner reservations at Risala—you're hogging the whole place!"

He throws his head back and chuckles loudly.

I don't think twice. "I would love to join you, but can I bring my girlfriends? There are eight of us."

"There are *eight* of you?"

"Yes, we run in packs."

"Perfect," he says. "Tell the staff you're my friend and they'll let you in."

I return to the garden section and the girls are hyperventilating big time.

I look at Wendy, "Did you overhear him tell me to tell the staff we're friends?"

"Yes, I did, Madam Rhonda."

Crazy Madam butts in. "I can't believe he shops for his own garden furniture—he must be gay."

At once, I call Pinky and she answers on the first ring. "He's one of my sweet co-actors in the film *Life Mein Kabhie Kabhiee* and no, he's not gay," she declares. "He's hot and loves the ladies. Bipasha Basu, the Bollywood actress and former Miss India, is his ex-girlfriend."

Thanks, Pinks!

Click.

Wendy and I leave the group and walk to the loo. As we turn the corner, I spot Mr. Bollywood, although I thought he left.

"Hello," he says. "It's me again."

"By chance, did you have dinner plans last night at Cathy and Roberto's house?"

He looks surprised. "Yes, but filming ran late."

At seven o'clock we're at the Trophy Bar where Bozzo and Dino are holding court. Wow, he's a man of his word. I walk up, hug Boz, and point to Dino. "He's stalking me."

Laughter fills the room.

The evening is full of banter and we discuss Bollywood, Pinky's career, Dino's career, living in India, and royal family history.

After two rounds of cocktails, the former winner of Mr. Gladrags Manhunt excuses himself to go work.

Bozzo says, "After Dino saw you ladies at the factory, he called me."

"What exactly did you tell him?" Sarika says.

He takes a sip of his scotch, waving his arm in the air to create drama, and replies with a hint of a British accent, "I see you've met the Desperate Housewives of Mumbai. They're harmless and loads of fun."

Namaste, Boz!

We forgot the Trophy Bar doesn't serve starters, and after a few more rounds of spirits, we're famished.

Our host makes one call and the chef opens the kitchen, prepares a lovely late dinner on the terrace overlooking the royal grounds, and we raise a toast in his honor. Cheers to new friendships.

I almost spit chicken tikka across the table when Dino walks into the room to personally escort us down the hallway after we pay the bill. I mouth to Wendy, "Have we died and gone to heaven?"

She does the head wiggle.

Dino leads us into the Grand Ballroom and from the moment we enter, the look on Kareena's face says, "What are *they* doing here?"

We watch the film crew work while Crazy Madam gives creative input. Dino is a gracious, charming gentleman and discusses his idea to promote the paint brand and explains varying stills on the computer.

Without taking up more time than we need to, we politely thank him and say goodbye.

The weather holds the next day for the usual drop from the sky onto the tarmac. We're home. I push an auntie out of the way to pick up my suitcase and notice Dino waving to us as he heads out the exit door.

I turn to Wendy. "What a humble guy."

She adds, "A *cute*, humble guy!"

I spot Kareena on the other side of the carousel with a frown on her face.

Then my mobile rings. It's Stanley calling from The Club. The Mumbai Mafia husbands and sixteen kids, to be exact, are bowling in honor of Matthew's second birthday.

I tell Wendy before Naushad drops her off, "OMG! I forgot the day my son was born."

Crazy Madam calls and we're on for rickshaw school in October. Apparently, you have to attend the school for twenty days straight without an absence or you don't get a license. Mirabella calls—salsa lessons won't start until November because she's too busy to teach. Fine. This means more yoga sessions with Amol and more workouts with Mr. Pravin.

It's Raksha Bandhan Tuesday, I tell everyone over breakfast! Stanley rolls his eyes and heads to work. Matthew is not impressed.

I start to sit down when Neelam comes out of the laundry room with a fancy twisted string bracelet to put on my wrist to replace the *kavala* that fell off during the move. It's red—my favorite color. *Raksha bandhan* means "the bond of protection" in Hindi.

The festival, marked by the tying of a *rakhi* (holy thread) by a sister on the wrist of her brother, celebrates the relationship between siblings. The brother in return offers a gift and vows to look after his sister.

"Madam, brothers and sisters can borrow brothers and sisters," says Neelam.

"You mean adopt?"

She nods.

"Matthew's celebrating at school today. He'll receive his own *rakhi* from a female classmate."

"People travel distances for this honor, Madam. Many people take long train rides for sisters."

What I know is high-caste brothers spend serious cash for this festival and you wear the bracelet until it falls off on its own. Naushad wouldn't tie one on me because I'm his madam and it's not proper. Neelam put one on me because she said she wants us to protect each other. Later when I run errands, locals notice I'm celebrating and greet me with more respect. I feel like a celebrity by just wearing a piece of decorated, inexpensive silk string.

Raindrops tiptoe on the balcony, and the sun disappears behind clouds.

Monsoon can be soothing. Lots of rain means less traffic and less traffic means less honking.

Wedding season is around the corner, and Neelam is busy collecting water bottles again. Our attempt at boiling the filtered water and drinking it out of a pitcher in the refrigerator lasted less than seventy-two hours. The water simply tasted awful, and we couldn't stick to our guns.

Knock, knock, knock on the door and Tanu delivers imported chocolates and our internet bill that got sent to the Marble Palace by accident. I start to ask about her dad, but Naushad, who escorted her up, gives me a look that says, "Don't go there, Madam, it's not good."

I bet he's in jail.

I give her a hug and tell her we miss our friends at Le Gardenia. She takes the lift down and I say to Naushad, "I forgot to ask you earlier why you're wearing *kurta* pajamas."

"Madam, I've been praying all night. I'm too tired. I took break at 3:30 a.m. and got food but my friends keep me up so long, then work for you, Madam."

"Did you bring your carpet in case I take too long in the shops?"

He smirks. "Maybe, Madam."

He's using the opium drops again, and his eyes look dark and mysterious. I hope he doesn't wreck the car. I'm wondering how he's keeping it all together with no sleep.

It's Friday and I'm driving south with Madam Wendy for shopping and talking, talking, too much talking and laughing. Suddenly HR, her driver, stops short of a head-on collision and a sideswipe. I feel carsick. I like his twisted sense of humor, but he lacks proper driving skills.

For grins, Wendy says to HR, "How did Robin look in his purple *kurta* pajamas the other day going to work?"

Rajesh hits the steering wheel with his palm and giggles uncontrollably.

I glance over at Wendy and she shrugs her shoulders.

She calls him HR for "Here's Rajesh," because that's what he would shout out, while jumping up and down and waving his arms frantically, every time Wendy came out of a store. He was afraid she wouldn't recognize his face in the sea of Indian drivers.

Wendy also tells me Robin accidentally sent HR a text meant for her. Apparently, HR got caught up in the moment on the road with another driver and decided to race while driving to the office last week. It was pouring sheets of rain and the car flew through a few intersections, but HR won against the other driver. However, Robin wasn't amused.

Wendy says Robin sent a text: "Mr. Competitive decided to race another driver this morning, and as I saw my life flash before me, we hydroplaned the last two kilometers to my office—not putting up with this shit."

Robin called Wendy and she confirmed she heard HR receive a text on his mobile. HR never mentioned the incident. Nor has he raced again.

Note to self, Robin: pay more attention to your contact list. It could have been one of those sexy texts you like to send Wendolyn when you're out of town.

We're gearing up for a big weekend. Cathy and Bianca will attend Roseanne's big Indian bash in two weeks. Moreover, Uncle Jim and Aunt Carole will visit before we board the Palace on Wheels train trip in Rajasthan.

I fish around in my purse for my mobile and I pull out a fortune from lunch at Vong Wong, a Thai and Chinese restaurant in the former offices of the Indian Express. It reads: *What at first seemed impossible now seems inevitable. That speaks to your personal will. Apply your focus and energy over time; it's all doable.*

"Stanley," I say, "We have our people in place—Naushad, Mary, Neelam, Lolita, the window cleaner, the car washer, Anil...the list goes on and on. I dig this gig—and I will not go quietly when my visa expires."

He does the head wiggle and laughs.

I exhale.

I see a flicker of lightning through a slit in the bedroom drapes and the kitchen faucet drips to a soothing tempo tonight. At the end of enduring a solid month of monsoon, I no longer panic when the wind rips off mango tree branches destined for a rough landing near our former building.

This, too, shall pass—and that is music to my ears.

25

Travel tastes and preferences are as different and diverse as people themselves. Avid explorers find enlightenment in ashrams, but we locals begin the journey each day in the spice shop, or the market, or simply on the street—nothing is what's expected.

For example, the AWC newsletter lands in my foyer and I scan an article on page eight inviting members to join the Writer Expat Club (WEC) to assist with settling and enjoying the fascinating life Mumbai has to offer.

I call Wendy. "Are you kidding me? You mean to tell me Trammell Crow Company could have hired WEC?"

She says, "They provide training in local languages and customs and information on everything from social and business etiquette to contacts for a network of resident expats. Robin's company could have done the same. My favorite is the Host City Cultural Helpline."

I laugh. "Can you picture me on hold waiting for help?"

"Totally unpredictable and useless," she adds. "Don't be upset. Look at the character-building opportunities we've had without them."

Darn right.

Tuesday is the festival of *Janmashtami*, the celebration of Lord Krishna's birth, considered a pious day by Hindus. We watch men build human pyramids to reach and break curd pots (filled with milk, butter, honey, and fruit) suspended from a height of twenty to forty feet from rooftops and intersections. We're told wealthy communities offer cash prizes for the most pots broken, thus imitating a popular game that, according to myths, Krishna and his friends played.

Matthew, in his pajamas, is home today. Little Butterflies is closed so families can honor the popular deity. Pinky tells me devotees queue at the major temples to seek his blessings. They also maintain a daylong fast. We skip the pomp and honor the ceramic Krishna I bought in Jodhpur last year with flower leis and double-stuffed Oreos imported from Canada.

I take the lift down and ask Naushad for help.

"I want you to map out eight kilometers in the car from Oberoi Crest to the Taj Lands End."

He looks puzzled.

"I want to run in the neighborhood. I'm tired of running at the JW."

He shrugs and opens my door. We climb in the car and buckle up.

Turning left out of the car park he says, "Madam, you run in cool air at JW. Why you want to be hot?"

"In Texas I ran on trails and I miss it. I don't like running indoors."

He shrugs.

"Madam, you wear your black leggings because Muslims live here. I don't want Muslims look down on you for showing skin."

"I won't wear shorts, but my arms will be visible."

He snorts and slaps his thigh. He adds, "Better you cover up, Madam, like Vinay told you."

Traffic seaside is relatively smooth. We turn around at the Taj Lands End and drive past Shah Rukh Khan's house. Naushad points, "Muslim like Naushad, Madam."

I spill water on my tunic. In disbelief I say, "Quit talking about yourself in third person like me and Madam Wendy."

Stanley calls and he's stuck in traffic. He's leaving tonight to attend a business conference in Toronto for six days. After dinner, I help him pack.

The boys are in bed and with the bulk of monsoon season over, it seems we have our own storm brewing. Crabby since my return, Stanley's had no patience for moving expenses, and he's tired of India. I think being alone this summer took its toll on him. Yes, we've had disagreements, because living abroad brings small things to a big head, but this disagreement feels more personal.

"You've done nothing but spend rupees all summer since you got home," he says. "If you're not spending rupees, you're at yoga or working out."

I'm taken aback by his comments, but it's not the first time in our marriage he has complained about finances.

"What else should I do with my time? We had to move and I had to spend money. You told me to set up the new flat and I did. I'm also managing staff expansion and the boys."

"I'm the one who has to go to the office every day and deal with the bureaucracy. It's on my shoulders to earn money for the family. You're the one who gets to live the good life."

I correct him. "You mean high life."

Stanley is not an unpleasant person. He's a keeper because he's very generous, but we all contribute to relationships in various ways, and no contribution should be trivialized.

"Don't take your work out on me; it's not fair."

He throws his hands up in the air.

"It's not my fault Trammell Crow Company sent us here. You wanted me to make this move. I've done my best under the circumstances, and if it's not up to your standards...after you go to Canada—go to hell!"

I grab my pillow and a blanket and go sleep on the couch.

The following morning, Neelam ushers Wendy into the flat. She removes her shoes and joins me at the dining table to drink Diet Pepsi.

"The boys are at school. Amol will be here at ten o'clock."

She's winded from taking the stairwell up. The lift is under maintenance. "I like your haircut and highlights. Natasha did a great job."

Dhanyavaad.

"When you look good, you feel good, but I feel blah this morning. Stanley and I got into a big fight last night before he left."

"Let me guess, you're spending all of the rupees, practically breaking the bank!"

"How did you know?"

"Robin says the same thing. Rupees have wings."

"I know Stanley is under tremendous stress, but who isn't, at one time or another?

"He was sent to here to co-manage Trammell Crow's investment in Meghraj with Anuj and pursue development opportunities. While I was gone this summer, unbeknownst to me, CBRE bought Trammell Crow Company. Then, last night, he told me the value of Meghraj is such that it's more lucrative to sell their interest to Jones LaSalle, which is now pursuing Meghraj to purchase as well as buy out the local CBRE franchise."

Wendy asks, "Where's Stanley?"

"Toronto."

"Does he still have a job?"

"Yes. Although the dynamics are changing as we speak. I'm scared our India tour will be over sooner than later."

"Regardless of our roles, the difference between us and Stanley and Robin is we like India. Who knew we would move to Mumbai and fall in love?"

"No, the real difference is we're expected to be a cheerleader for their hard work and accomplishments and manage a successful home life at all costs."

Wendy corrects me, "You mean on a budget."

We giggle.

"Actually, we both gave up our careers several years ago, and therein lies the bona fide problem. We no longer have our own professional identity or finances."

My grandmother would be furious if she were alive today. She always told me, "No matter what, earn your own money."

"Money is not the issue," Wendy says, "It's respect."

"I know we both have plenty of money. I'm tired of the condescending attitude that I'm indebted to him because he works. India's male-dominated culture invaded Stanley's body. Last night reminded me of a boxing match. We sparred several rounds and then threw in the towel. I'm mentally exhausted."

Wendy says, "Even if it's a small fight, since our senses are locked in fiery overload mode, ordinary thoughts become life-or-death opinions in this country."

"You can say that again."

There's a knock on the door and in walks Amol. He greets us, takes his shoes off, and says hello to Neelam in Hindi.

Yoga begins and over the course of forty-five minutes we explore postures and breathing techniques.

Then for fifteen minutes, we switch it up and meditate.

"Have you done meditation before, Wendy?"

She smirks.

"For me to know and you to find out, Liz."

Yoga Hottie interrupts, "Silence."

He calls me out, "Focus, Rhonda."

I squeeze my thigh to keep from bursting into a fit of laughter because he never calls me by my "good name." Man, he takes meditation seriously.

I do not like the silence, a reminder of how powerless it makes me feel, but I try to do as he instructs.

Om, Mani, Padme, Hum

Om, Mani, Padme, Hum

Om, Mani, Padme, Hum

Then we repeat it again. Again. Again. Again.

I last thirty seconds.

My mind wanders. I open one eye and Amol is staring at me.

Uh-oh!

I focus.

Om, Mani, Padme, Hum

Om, Mani, Padme, Hum

Om, Mani, Padme, Hum

Then we repeat it again. Again. Again. Again.

I unfold into *savasana* (corpse pose) for relaxation. I inhale and peek at Wendy—perfection. On a scale of one to ten, she's on cloud nine.

Yoga Hottie looks in my direction again. "If you would stop worrying about the future, you will seek a place of internal presence," he says slowly. "We've discussed this topic many times, *jaan*."

I nod. I understand completely. Which is why today I do not worry about the future. I worry about today. Maybe I worry about last night, too.

I can purr *Om, Mani, Padme, Hum; Om, Mani, Padme, Hum* a billion times, but thoughts continue to race through my mind.

Wendy unfolds and opens her eyes.

Both she and Amol shout, "What?"

"Well, now that you've asked, my major obstacle is releasing the guilt I feel over putting my needs first. It's been a long time coming, but I want to do it. I need to do it."

Wendy shakes her head.

"It's official: I've outgrown my old life."

Wendy shouts out in her cheer voice, "Thanks for sharing, Liz!"

Yoga Hottie says, "Let's end our session in *balasana*."

Wendy and I drop into child's pose—we relax, breathe into our backs, stretch our thighs, hips, ankles—we feel no pain.

I am present in the moment.

Then my mind wanders again. I'm present with Wendy, too. Then I think about Neelam, who is in the laundry room washing clothes, and I don't forget Yoga Hottie who is also present in the room with us.

I like Amol because he does not need to analyze each thought, sentence, or comment. He is totally present in the moment every day.

Our session ends. We collect our mats and pay the class fee. Wendy says, "*Dhanyavaad* for a wonderful session."

I add, "I think this is the best class yet, and by the way, expats can be a needy bunch—you should charge more for your services."

Stanley returns home just in time to attend a fundraising event for Room to Read (RTR) hosted by the CEO of Goldman Sachs India, Brooks Entwistle, and his wife, Laura. Surprise! John Wood, founder and CEO of RTR, went to the University of Colorado with Stanley, where they were both in Delta Sigma Phi, a business fraternity.

While on a soul-searching three-week trek around the Annapurna Circuit in Nepal in 1998, John met a teacher who invited him to visit the local school. It had more than 200 children, yet the library had fewer than twenty books. Even worse, those books were locked in a cabinet because they were considered a scarce resource.

The headmaster and teachers asked John to help change the situation so children could learn English to interact with trekkers and maybe study overseas. John returned one year later with three thousand books, and the idea for Room to Read was born.

John answers questions from guests and closes his presentation with this unbelievable factoid: if you combined the populations of the United States, Canada, and Mexico, all without the ability to read or write, then you have an idea of the size of the work Room to Read has cut out for it in India.

We join John for a toast and hand him a $10,000 check to build a library in honor of our upcoming eleventh wedding anniversary. Then, we mingle with fellow expats.

Hours later, we say goodbye to Laura and Brooks and I text Naushad: "Ready."

He pulls Rocket up from the car park and opens my door. I climb in behind the driver's seat and then Boss, feeling charitable, tells Naushad on the way home, "We want to sell you this car before we leave."

Naushad does a double take in the rearview mirror.

I do the head wiggle and grin. Naushad holds back tears while Boss checks his mobile. Then he points to the fuel gauge and the light is on. "Madam, we need petrol, like this, like that. I'm too sorry but petrol too much low," he says. "I forgot to tell you."

I dig two thousand rupees out of my wallet and hand it forward.

"Naushad, point Rocket in the direction of Mecca! Pray we make it to the petrol station," I say, laughing. "Or Boss might change his mind about selling you this car."

He replies, "Seriously."

On Saturday we celebrate Ganpati, the celebration of the Lord Ganesha.

We watch many elephanta gods on floats, and ox-driven carts head to Juhu while locals chant and pray.

Naushad drives me to Anil the Wine Guy's home across from the Kolis' land, although thankfully, this isn't drying season.

"Madam, I don't think this good idea," he says. "What if they give you Indian food and juice?"

I roll my eyes.

Naushad parks the car and walks beside me down a long hallway within a concrete housing complex and into a small room where I'm greeted by Anil. Instantly, I'm escorted front and center to a Ganesha the size of a sumo wrestler on a large pedestal. A priest in an orange *lungi* is chanting prayers, performing a *puja*.

I circle my hands above the fire, light incense, make a wish, and make an offering of flower leis and sweets just as Anil does before me. Then I lean in, and the priest places red powder on my forehead. Lastly, Anil patiently introduces me to eight Hindu family members sitting on the floor talking in Hindi. His wife and son, wearing one of Grant's gently used shirts, pose for photos with me.

I feel a tap on my shoulder. It's my bodyguard.

He leans over and whispers in my ear, "Madam, *puja* over, you go now."

I whisper back, "Relax."

Much to our surprise, a full glass of what looks like orange Fanta appears. *I inhale. I exhale.*

I don't know the source. I have an instant flashback to Situation 8 and pray silently to the patron saint of hepatitis, cholera, and dysentery.

Naushad is hyperventilating.

Anil the Wine Guy's extended family stares me down as if to say, how can you talk the talk if you don't walk the walk, Madam? I graciously accept the Ganpati cocktail, slurp it down, and hand back the empty glass to Anil. I fold my hands and bow in honor of the generosity this family has bestowed upon me.

The group's smiles radiate sunbeams. Naushad picks up my purse and escorts me out of the compound and back to Rocket. Once we're in the car and buckled up, he looks at me in the rearview mirror. "Madam, you okay?"

With lips pressed tightly shut, I wiggle my head.

"Madam, you such good Madam. No Madam do this *puja* and Fanta drink," he says. "Sorry, Madam. I just now think, like this, like that, Madam Wendy might do this Hindu *puja* too."

I don't want to tell Naushad I could projectile vomit any second, so I don't.

I text Yoga Hottie: "Help me."

Instantly he responds: "Breathe, *jaan. Ruko* and breathe."

Karma comes full circle when the Sleepy People call Naushad with important news the day after Anil's *puja.*

"Madam, Raveer you call liar hired workers to paint your Marble Palace but workers turned on water, too much water, and flooded the flat," he says.

No way.

"Madam, Dior barking, barking, too much barking and water off our old balcony into Madam Pinky's plants. Her maid call police for help."

Hmmm. "Seriously?"

"Madam," he says, "Raveer lied and forced us to move. He deserves bad juju, like you talk like this."

The rain stops for a few days. *Is monsoon over?*

Krishna calls to book lessons at Bandra Gymkhana and I decide to skip rickshaw school because we find out it's illegal to give a foreigner a course certificate.

"Naushad, if I can't learn to drive a rickshaw, you will teach me to drive Rocket."

He says rather sternly, "Never, Madam. Boss kill me. Remember Boss said you like this bull by horns? You gone to Texas and after Boss scared to buy chicken he told Naushad never teach Madam to drive in India—ever."

"Naushad, Boss is not the boss of me, but I am the boss of this car. I know how to drive a stick car in Texas and I can learn how to drive one here. You will teach me and Boss will never know."

He does the head wiggle. "Seriously, Madam?"

"I've never been more serious, Naushad."

We spend the next two hours in the ASB parking lot working on driving techniques and logistics.

The AWC board met at the American Consulate last week. Over lunch, we found out that due to budget cuts for all consulates, turkey and pumpkin pie would not be provided for the annual Thanksgiving dinner held at a hotel down south in November.

The US government thinks it's a good public relations move to send the food and California wine to our troops in the Middle East, who are actually doing extraordinary things for the country.

Point well taken.

My mobile beeps. Caron's in the car park. She finished a PTO meeting at ASB and wants to stop by for a visit. I'm fortunate she's in the neighborhood and I'm home. The minute she steps off the lift, I greet her at the door. We exchange hugs and plant it on the sofa to discuss the success of the Room to Read function and to catch up.

"I can't get over that Stanley and John Wood attended CU together," she says.

"The last time the two of them saw each other, Stanley was pushing John in a grocery cart full of beer in the stadium parking lot." We laugh, but after twenty minutes of discussion about raising children in an expat environment the conversation turns somber.

"With the latest move and Stanley's job description changing, we're at each other's throats. Is there any marital advice you can give me?"

She smiles and flips back her long camel-colored hair. "Darling, a marriage is a series of relationships over the years and you must be stubborn and lucky and both want it to work.

"It comes down to falling in and out of love with the same person, again and again—and again. It sounds simple, but it's a hell of a job. This lifestyle, this freedom, is terribly seductive, and you and Stanley need to learn how to balance it. You'll reap the benefits if you do."

I explain that before we left, friends told us, "This move will make your relationship stronger or you'll return to Austin and get a divorce."

She smiles. "I've been a witness to both."

Caron is a great listener, and she brings more than twenty years of expat knowledge to life coaching.

"Honestly—Stanley loathes India. But I decided a long time ago I could either be miserable or I could embrace the culture. After I quit working, I put his happiness above my own, because I thought that's what marriage was about and he had more tangible successes. What was I doing to be proud of? As far as my friends could see, I was volunteering, planning parties, and globetrotting.

"When I had the boys, once again, I put their happiness to the forefront. Eventually, it all took its toll on me and those two duties overshadowed my positive inner voice. I don't have many role models in the marriage department. Plus, motherhood is the hardest thing I've ever done. Mothering does not come naturally to me. I'm too much of a control freak."

She stops me. "There is no controlling this country," she says. "Only yourself and your behavior." I nod. "Please keep going."

"Stanley doesn't understand the sacrifices I've made throughout our marriage. There have been times I didn't recognize myself, and that doesn't make me feel good. It's only been since I started taking care of myself here that I've felt like the old me—except it's not the old me. It's a new improved version of me."

"But Rhonda, we don't live in a world anymore where you only get one chance. If it's time to grow, you have to grow. Stanley is a smart man who loves you. It might be tough for him to navigate your liberation, but he won't leave your side. He's in this until the end. I feel it, and more important, I see it."

I sigh. "I'm here for a reason. All signs from fortunes to horoscopes to decisions from day one have led me to this place."

"Rhonda, you've done an outstanding job of fitting into daily life. You see the world in a different way than you did before. This alone should give you a tremendous amount of confidence to face anything, sweetness. Stepping outside your comfort zone forces humility. It's this vulnerability that allows us to break our own stereotypes of ourselves on foreign soil—a rare gift."

Yesterday Naushad took a pile of clothes to Mr. Tailor Man for mending that inadvertently contained a pink bra. When Mr. Tailor Man held it up in front of the lunch crowd to assess what needed to be fixed, Naushad was mortified.

Back at the flat, he throws the pink bra at me when I open the door.

"Madam, next time, like this, like that, you take yourself!"

Uncle Jim and Aunt Carole, visiting India from Dallas, step into the Mini Marble Palace and greet us with open arms.

"Thank God we're out of Varanasi and back in a real city," says Carole.

Mary stays late to babysit the boys and we head to a casual dinner at Aurus. It's wonderful to visit with family. The following morning we fly to Delhi and jump on board the Palace on Wheels for a seven-day trip of Rajasthan—maharaja-style.

Trip Summary:

> *It's a fantastic way to see Delhi (the mayhem city), Jaipur (the pink capital city), Jaisalmer (the golden city), Jodhpur (my favorite city), Sawai Madhopur (the Tiger National Park city), Chittorgarh (the citadel city), Udaipur (the lake city), Bharatpur (the bird watcher's seventh heaven city), and Agra (the Taj Mahal city).*

Back home, our city is in an uproar about advancing to the ICC T20 Championship. Twenty20 is a shortened form of cricket in which only 20-overs are played per innings, making it a 40-over match in total, if played until the end by both teams. In fact, while we were gone, Naushad, Neelam, and Mary watched India cream Pakistan to become the number one Test team in the world, while the boys slept. And that is how our people roll when Madam and Boss are out of town.

Stanley and I celebrate our anniversary on Friday, September 28. Mary bakes a cake, Neelam designs pink floating flowers in the brass *urlis*, and Naushad presents me with three dozen red roses and two engraved wooden pens.

"Madam, you and Boss all the time looking for pen in the car," he says. "No excuse for no pen now."

The next day I scan *The Times of India* and list new names to practice pronouncing—Khushnooma Kapadia, Hem Hariramani, and Najina Lanja-nanani. I check my mobile. I've missed a call from Naushad. I send a text: "Call me."

Instead he comes up to the flat. His eyes are red.

"Madam, I went to mosque again last night for Ramadan. The Father let no one leave until three o'clock this morning," he says. "I never go to this mosque again in my life."

"What did the Father talk about the entire time?"

"Do not be cheating Muslims, Madam, and America needs to go into Pakistan and get Bin Laden."

"Seriously?" I say. "This father talks about good and bad Muslims?"

"Yes. Madam, I think Saddam dead now. But America has to wipe out Osama bin Laden like this, like that."

"If America bombs Pakistan, then we do harm to the good Muslims, too."

Naushad does the head wiggle and takes the lift down to the car park.

I brush my teeth and pick up my LV tote bag. My mobile beeps. There's a joke from Mary, who has the day off:

> "A foreigner had a very spicy Indian dinner, and the next morn-
> ing he comes out of the loo and says, 'Now I know why Indians
> use the funny water sprayer. Toilet paper can catch fire.'"

And, on that note, I'm out the door.

26

Trick or treat. Smell our feet. Give us more than *naan* to eat!

While the rest of the world gears up to celebrate Oktoberfest and Halloween, we're stuck in an abnormal dry heat weather pattern. Hotels rejoice by offering kebabs from Punjab, dozens of hookah specials, and hissing sizzlers.

Tommy Hilfiger and Benetton billboards show models in wool sweaters and corduroy pants. We're dragging out the *kurta* pajamas and long tunics because, after all, we're supposed to be dressing for the fall season. Sadly, the only cool breezes we encounter are from the rickshaws that race by us on our evening walks around Khar Gymkhana.

This is the hottest month of the year, and we've had three major power outages in two days. Earth to Boss! Please buy flashlights and batteries during your twelve-day business trip to Texas in two weeks. Madam doesn't light candles anymore after the Sleepy People caught Le Gardenia on fire.

I return from dropping Matthew at Little Butterflies, and there is a knock on the front door. One of the Professional Security Guards has escorted Mr. Plumber Man up to the foyer. In he struts to find out why Grant's bathtub is leaking water again. Inside the bathroom, he looks around, borrows Grant's green dinosaur flashlight to look under the damp ceiling light tiles, and decides to return tomorrow with his tool kit and his manager.

Speaking of disasters, we're dumbfounded why bad luck seems to loom around us. On Sunday a Professional Security Guard arrives at our door and in broken English says, "Crack glass. Come." We race downstairs to see that a coconut has fallen seven stories onto Rocket and shattered the windshield.

Luckily Naushad takes a train into Khar West and we spend the afternoon with Rocket at the glass replacement shop. Returning to Oberoi Crest, Naushad, looking down, says, "Madam, I am responsible. I'm too sorry for this mistake."

Stop! "Listen. The Building Society Manager is responsible for this accident. Besides, we live on what used to be an island and the palm trees surrounding us are full of coconuts." Speak of the devil—he appears to file an official report.

I ask Naushad to translate. "Why haven't you called Mr. Coconut Man on 14th Road to climb up in the building palms and cut down all the coconuts for 100 rupees?"

The Building Society Manager turns to me, does the head wiggle, and in perfect English says, "I never thought of this but very, very good idea. The society will pay for this to happen."

Wait...I thought he didn't speak the English.

Neelam is distraught about the windshield. She insists we contact a sadhu to perform a *puja* immediately on the flat because too much broken glass is a forewarning of worse to come. She's spooked and thinks there is bad luck on Oberoi Crest.

I ask, "What is the likelihood a *puja* will work?"

Naushad shrugs. "Madam, Allah never hurt you, Madam, only protect you or take bad and make better for you."

Matthew has a rash and continues to run a fever. Dr. M, the pediatrician genius among expats, and Dr. L, the young single doctor, are escorted up to examine him. These are the doctors who took care of Matthew when he ran a fever while Stanley and I were on the Palace on Wheels train trip. A lab technician collects blood and the doctors stay for two hours sipping tea and eating homemade sugar cookies. Total cost for services—285 rupees.

I direct the conversation to advice about hiring a monk or a priest to perform a *puja*.

They say in unison, "Indians love *pujas!*"

Dr. M says, "Rhonda, you should host a *puja*. Serve wine and cheese, invite expat and local friends to your home."

Pursuing this further, he warns me, "Rhonda, you're not Hindu. You can only be Indian by birth. *Pujas* might not work for you but it sure would be a fun party!"

I feel Indian, yet time after time I'm put in my place. I'll always be a foreigner, no matter how hard I try to fit in.

We talk about everything under the sun. Now I know why it often takes so long for them to show up.

"Rhonda, Beyoncé was born in Texas just like you." Dr. M says, "I've visited Austin and Galveston. I went to medical school in Detroit and I know for a fact Al Gore did not create the internet."

I giggle.

He adds, "Gore roomed with a famous Texan at Harvard, Tommy Lee Jones."

I nod.

He continues, "The only reason George W. Bush won the presidential election is because Al Gore is an ass." (He really says the word "ass" to me.)

Then, Dr. M hands Naushad the prescription to take to Asian Chemists Medical and General Store.

"Rhonda, please collect a urine sample from Matthew. I want to test for malaria and dengue fever," says Dr. L.

"He's two years old and wears diapers," I say politely.

Dr. M tells me, "Make him drink lots of water and follow him around the flat with a cup while he's commando." (They really say the word "commando.") "Or the other option is to tape a plastic bag onto his waist. It will catch the urine when it streams out of his penis."

We hear a roar of laughter from the kitchen. The doctors laugh too and hand over a urine sample cup and bag. Seriously—follow him around the flat with a bag taped to his belly? Are you crazy? The doctors assure me this can be done with patience and they wrap up the visit.

Naushad and I head to Sante after we pick up the medicine. Later on the ride home, Naushad tells me the Building Society Manager said many other windshields in the car park have been broken by falling coconuts.

"Madam, can I tell you something? I don't trust this Hindu *puja*. I'm Muslim and Allah take care of Naushad."

I stare at his reflection in the rearview mirror.

"You go to mosque and pray for us, so why would Allah allow bad luck to enter our home?"

"It is the will of Allah and maybe it was a bad piece of glass and this happened so no more bad happen, Madam, like when the glass shower door fell off on your friend Madam Amy, who is pregnant, Madam."

Well...I guess he overhead me telling Wendy about Craig taking Amy to the emergency room.

"Naushad, it's Ramadan, the holiest month of all the months. Allah isn't protecting Madam Amy or me."

He looks away. "Madam, I promise I will pray for you, Madam, like this, like that. I will pray for Madam Amy, too. It will get better and Allah is watching over you. Seriously."

We return to the flat and I take the lift up. Mary is busy preparing an early supper but she's heard about the broken windshield and is visibly upset. She wants to offer assistance. Neelam rolls her eyes when I disappear into the bedroom for the private consultation.

"Madam, this is not good. We have bad luck with things falling and breaking. Something needs to be done now to change destiny. While you were on the train trip, Matthew got sick, and we had to replace Grant's broken window (a six by twelve foot sheet of glass). Madam, thirty-three people had to raise the glass by hand with rope to fix it.

"Now the windshield is broken again and the geyser is still not working in Matthew's bathroom. The tub leaked over the weekend, all your plants died on the balcony, and one of the kitchen cabinets fell off. (I paid Mr. Carpenter Man to fix it with my own rupees.) Madam, now Matthew is sick again and you look ghastly. Madam, there is no stopping this bad luck. We need an intervention."

I look *ghastly*? Besides that, is "intervention" a word in the Hindi language? "Mary, just the other day we spent over an hour at Siddhivinayak Ganapati Temple and prayed to Lord Ganesha. Why are we having these problems?"

She fixes me with a serious scowl. "Madam, please do not be insulted. You're in a home that prays to Lord Ganesha but you still serve beef during certain holidays. You have a driver who honors Allah, but you cook bacon and serve it to the boys. This is all wrong and the gods know it and this is why you have troubles. No one is happy with you."

Shocker.

"Well, you're a respectable Catholic girl. What should I do?"

"Madam, we need holy water."

Holy *what*?

"Yes, Madam. You need holy water or the family needs to become vegetarian."

I excuse myself and go into the bathroom. I grab the hand towel and scream into it. Then I open the door and casually walk back into the kitchen.

Mary approaches. "The Church of the Holy Mary on Bandstand has sacred water, Madam. It will cure the ailments. If you give me rupees and permission to buy it, then I will go to market and get a large cross. Also, I need the rosary your friend John gave to you from the Vatican so we can hang it above the front door after the Catholic priest blesses the flat."

What have I got to lose?

"Mary, give me twenty-four hours to think about the holy water."

She nods.

What I really want is to ask her to say a tiny prayer for my college football picks in the betting pool this week, too, but I don't go there. I'm not sure God would appreciate my humor during a time of crisis.

Out of nowhere, Stanley calls to say a double-decker bus just swiped the side of company car he's riding in. He's on his way to Subway to grab a sandwich.

Finally Friday is here, and I'm running a fever, too. I call Dr. M and the lab tech is on his way to gather blood samples. Wendy calls and she and Robin just returned from a wedding in New York. His brother made fiancé number five, wife number one.

However, she's got bad news: Delta lost her luggage on the outbound trip. I remind Wendy about the time I checked eleven pieces of luggage and British Airways forgot to put them all on the plane despite a nine-hour layover in Heathrow.

"Once I got over the initial shock of returning empty-handed, what I loved was paying the customs janitor, who appeared out of nowhere, 500 rupees so he and his two co-workers could walk my bags full of wine and food past the customs officer and the CT scanner when I picked them up two days later."

Wendy says, "Do you have his number?"

"Lucky for you, he took my mobile and entered his 'good name' into my contact list and told me to call him next time for assistance."

Naushad calls from downstairs and one of the drivers accidentally slammed his finger in the door after he returned from dropping Grant at ASB. He thinks it's broken and he wants to drive to Asian Chemists. The pharmacist can wrap his finger in a splint for 100 rupees.

I hear Hindi in the background, "Madam, the guard told me Mr. Coconut Man not coming for two weeks."

Figures. Neelam makes *chai* for me in the kitchen and says she just finished furnishing plastic bottles for another wedding. Now she's going to start selling the bottles if I approve. Go for it!

She opens all the windows to let fresh air in while she cleans.

"Madam, this will help you feel better. Matthew, too."

Fresh air?

India is one of the world's most polluted countries. In fact, *The Times of India* reported breathing air in Mumbai is equivalent to smoking two packs of cigarettes a day.

Mary calls and I instruct her to stop and get the holy water on her way to work this afternoon. I tell her we must purge the bad juju when Boss leaves to go to America. I also ask her to find out when the Catholic priest can perform the exorcism and how many rupees the church charges for its services. She happily agrees. A Professional Security Guard escorts Lolita up to sweep and mop.

I desperately check email in the guest bedroom. I'm in luck—there's a note from Channing. It reads:

Aquarius (January 20–February 18): Life dreams are similar to the dreams you have at night in that they have a way of fading, changing, transitioning into different scenes. You'll be letting go of an old dream and embarking on a new one.

I reply back:

Om Shanti! Interesting horoscope so I'll put it in perspective for you: FADING...
Navratri, the Hindu festival of nine nights of worship and dance, took place on the Khar Gymkhana field—colorful, an auspicious time for starting new ventures. (This is the one event Neelam participates in—she showed up for work late the next day!)

Grant no longer uses British terms such as "Mummy" or "loo." He told me he was teased over the summer by friends and he's back to talking with a twang—yee-haw!

Monsoon (over and out). No more rain in the forecast until next year!

Feelings of living in a romance novel might be over—we've got broken glass again!

CHANGING…

Trammell Crow Company sold to Jones Lang LaSalle who bought Meghraj. Stanley's job description is up in the air.

My aptitude on how to write a check properly! I bounced two checks again because I wrote the date incorrectly and I didn't sign my "good name."

I finished the book Eat, Pray, Love that you gave me. I started it when we arrived and put it down, thinking I couldn't relate to Gilbert. After the second move, I picked it back up and a lightbulb went off! I couldn't put it down. Of course, she had a tell-it-like-it-is friend from Texas!

TRANSITIONING…

Stanley talks about a move at the end of the school year. No way. I don't want to live without the rituals of Indian high-class hospitality.

Guess what? I'm learning how to drive! Naushad and I practice in the ASB parking lot. Whenever Stanley leaves on business, I hit the open road.

Last month we took the Palace on Wheels trip. While in Jodhpur, Laxman graciously picked us up and served as an off-the-itinerary guide at the fort, and took me to visit Mr. Sharma, a palmist and astrologer who's honed his science for more than fifty years, and whom Cathy recommended. Quote-unquote: Too many people want some action from you. You are pulled in different directions. Focus only on yourself, find personal happiness, and your life will align and the rest of the universe will fall into place.

I hit SEND.

Instantaneously, an email from Moe comes in—he's on track to visit in a few weeks. I reply to Cathy's email about plans to visit with him in Jodhpur and I remind her I must visit Mr. Sharma again.

Knock, knock, knock on the door. It's the Diet Pepsi and bottled water delivery guy. While I tip him, my mobile beeps: Naushad is taking the lift up.

"Madam, remember I celebrate Eid tomorrow, Saturday, and Sunday," he says. "I will pray long time but not all night."

Eid-u-Fitr is a festival observed by the Muslim community to celebrate the conclusion of the month of fasting.

I know he's delighted to visit family and share food with friends, not to mention two days off, but he's grouchy. He's had to fast and abstain from indulging in any evil practices. Islamic religion defines these as anger, greed, envy, lust, malice, and gossiping—basically what most Muslims are known to do every day, according to Neelam. Sex is prohibited, too.

I peer into his eyes and do not see a trace of opium drops. "Are you ready to be rewarded for fasting, bodyguard?"

He cracks a smile.

"Cheer up! I won't even think about driving the car until you get back!"

While I wait for Dr. L to call with lab results, I pick up the Bombay Times.

The headline reads: "They Forgot the Battery!"

Seems there was a horrific blackout in Mumbai's air-traffic control tower yesterday because careless officials forgot to replace the batteries in the crucial UPS which runs the entire system. For several minutes the air traffic control staff had over a dozen aircraft hovering the airport without support.

It sounds like they need holy water, too.

27

Out for a jog one morning, I'm caught at the traffic signal waiting for the light to turn green when I spot a kindred spirit. I swear Ben Kingsley's twin is across the street in a shirt that reads: ASK ME! I'M FAMOUS. He grins at me with a colossal, poorly-cared-for smile reminiscent of Mohandas Karam-chand Gandhi's. Having just celebrated his birthday earlier in the month, I'm feeling festive but pensive.

I'm reminded Mr. Famous and fellow low-castes can't afford the rupees to pay for simple dental maintenance and I feel shallow that I complained about Vinay's teeth, especially since I had to wear braces. The light turns green, and he waves me onward as if to lessen the shame. I crank the volume up on my Apple Nano, run past SRK's house—fully aware of the hundreds of eyes on me—and make the loop back to Oberoi Crest in record time.

The weather is crisp. Perhaps fall is here at last.

Neelam greets me at the door and quickly ushers me to the kitchen. The food in the refrigerator is spoiled. I'm sick to my stomach. Newly purchased prawns and salmon from the Grand Hyatt are warm. Apparently the refrig-erator had a serious failure during the wee hours of the morning.

Neelam begins the lengthy process of purging food, and Naushad and I drop the boys at school and head straight to Vijay Sales on Linking Road. The refrigerator is under warranty but the repairman can't show up for two days.

We pull back into the car park and the new electrician is waiting outside in the foyer with a Professional Security Guard. When he pulls down a ceil-ing tile to replace the dead bulbs, water comes crashing down on his head and on Naushad's, who is holding the ladder. Neelam and I giggle hysteri-cally. Why is there water in the ceiling?

The electrician isn't amused and says in the Queen's English, "Madam, the fifth floor has a big leak and I cannot replace the bulbs or sockets until this problem is solved." Before he leaves, he changes one lightbulb in Matthew's bedroom—cost: forty rupees.

And so the day progresses until it's quitting time. Mary and Neelam leave for the day. I send Naushad home on the early train. For dinner, I order the usual entrées from China Gate. We eat and clean up and I give the boys a bath. We read *Harold and the Purple Crayon*, and I put them to bed.

Cleaning up the kitchen, I open my fortune cookie and read: *Never depend on others to make you happy. You can do it yourself.* I crumble it up and toss it in the trash bin.

At three o'clock in the morning I wake up in a deep sweat. My dream isn't about Harold; it's about Kevin Costner. In the dream, Kevin leaves me stranded. I'm alone to fend for myself.

After drop-off, I meet Laura for tea. They hosted the Room to Read event in their beautiful bungalow near the Lapsara Building. We spend the better part of the morning conversing about travel and kids—she has three girls at ASB.

After lunch Caron stops by before she has to pick up Skye. Jiri's exhibition was a success and they will stay in Mumbai during the Diwali break. Currently, she's busy with the PTO board and teaching nutrition classes.

I spring on my news. Stanley's position has changed.

"It looks like we're headed back to Austin at the end of the school year. I envision heated debates about our departure date because our house is rented until mid-July. I'm devastated, but I'm going to be upfront and tell the staff this week."

She hugs me. "Hang in there and remember: we are strengthened by adversity—and even enriched by sadness—during difficult situations. I'm here for you."

We discuss my upcoming trip to Phuket and the ASB Halloween parade at the end of the month. Before we leave to pick up the kids, she gives me another hug, and this time I cry. "Sweetness, it's going to be fine," she says.

Wiping my eyes, I say, "I finally got my shit together and now I have to go!"

She laughs. "If we could all be so lucky!"

Thursday is here. The rupee is strong at thirty-nine to the dollar, the holy water worked, and the bad juju is gone, so I begin to make preparations for Sula Sister Night this evening at the Mini Marble Palace. I've sent invites to Wendy, Hannah, Kate, and Annette asking them to join me for wine and starters. I call Anil the Wine Guy and he delivers the filtered ice, cans of soda, tonic, and Indian wine. He reassures me, like he does every time he makes a delivery, he can get *anything* Madam wants—*anything*.

Mary and I work diligently on a list of vegetables to purchase in the market and groceries to get at Foodland. She's happy the repairman showed up yesterday to install the new compressor for the refrigerator.

In the middle of preparations, Boss calls to check in and speak to the boys. "You must have jet lag. The boys are in school."

"I forgot."

He rattles on about work plans then asks, "Aren't you hosting Sula Sisters?

"Yes, I am!"

"You and the sisters will have a great time since you have three things in common—the AWC board, humor, and wine."

Certainly, we have more in common than that, Boss, and you are jet-lagged indeed. He'll be back home in nine days.

The boys are in bed and it's time for the party to begin; but Kate sends a text that her son Ian is running a high fever. She's calling the pediatrician and will be over as soon as her husband gets home. I put another bottle of Sula on ice just as Hannah arrives. As I begin to pour her a glass of wine, my mobile rings. I rush to answer, thinking it's Kate calling about Ian.

"Rhonda. It's Dr. L," he says. "I'm across the street from your flat attending to a client and I can see you and Hannah through the living room window. Can my group join you after we're done?"

Hannah and I look at each other and walk toward the large window overlooking 16th Road. Sure enough, there are the doctors waving genially to us.

Whoa, Nellie!

Before I know it, they're in my flat with their shoes off, making themselves right at home. When Wendy and Annette march in, they're stunned—who are these jokers? They die laughing when I introduce them. Then, Kate shows up and she's in stitches too, since Dr. L was just at her flat.

Dr. M happily accepts the plentiful Sula red wine I have on hand. However, Dr. L demands cola and when I tell him I don't have any in stock, he tells me to call my driver and get him to get one from the local corner store. I'm reluctant to call Naushad, but I do, because he's just down in the car park smoking cigarettes and hanging out with the other drivers.

Two hours later, the doctors leave to deliver a baby at Lilavati Hospital—Dr. L, the Coca-Cola drinker, does the honors.

Daylight is just starting to color the sky and I carry a Diet Pepsi out to the balcony and settle into one of our patio chairs. Mumbai is stirring and so are the wild monkeys and birds in the large mango trees facing the street.

My mobile beeps with a text: "Call me."

Wendy is up early too.

"What's up, Sula?"

"Nada."

"Last night was big fun."

"I drank too much."

"What?"

"I drank too much. Stressed, I didn't want to tell the group we're leaving in June. Stanley's company was acquired. We're making out like bandits in stock options, but I'm not ready to leave India. I don't want to think about moving back." I take a sip of Diet Pepsi.

"I drank a lot too, but that's how we roll together as members of the Sula frequent flyer program."

We laugh.

"Hey, I want to tell you, Crazy Madam is talking smack about you. She's trying to go around you to get to Jodhpur to shop. She also told members at the AWC coffee you take Naushad to the salon to get his hair cut on a monthly basis."

Really? "I've been nothing but nice to her since day one. What's funny is Fiona told me the day we met Crazy Madam, 'Stay far, far away from her.' I brushed it off but as the weeks and months have passed, I should have heeded to the warning. She exerts a ton of energy to make others look smaller so she can feel bigger."

"I agree, Madam."

"She's setting the stage for her own doom. Plus, I don't allow others to undermine me."

My favorite Madam reaffirms our bond.

"I've got your back, Liz!"

She adds, "Hey, I want to hire the florist you use to design floating flowers in your *urlis*. I have a Buddha on a wooden pedestal and one brass *urlis* that I want decorated each week."

"My flower designs *are* fancy—but you have no idea who I pay to do the work," I say.

"Who?"

"Naushad."

"Are you kidding me?"

"No. I'll ask if he wants to earn extra rupees each week."

Before we hang up, I say, "Do you feel India has a way of unfolding you to allow you to become the person you were always meant to be in the first place?"

Wendy says, "I can't agree more. Seriously—like you say all the time."

Click.

I call Naushad and he's thrilled to help Wendy. "Madam, I will decorate too much, like this, like that, because blondes have more fun."

It's Sunday and Ms. Harwani is calling. We chat briefly and then she drops the bomb. Her daughter-in-law is coming from Dubai with the seven-month-old grandbaby and she needs a big car for the airport pickup. I tell her Naushad is off because it's his daughter's birthday.

She is upset. "You should call him into work because he is your driver and it is his job. Indian Madams would call him to work."

I'm not sure whom she's referring to. Maybe she talks about herself in the third person like Madam Wendy and I like to do, but I remind her I don't have Indian DNA. I will not call Naushad.

I make a suggestion—I offer her our car for free. I tell her she can have Pinky's driver leave her small car with us at the Mini Marble Palace and take Rocket to the airport. She'll double-check with Pinky and get back to me.

The boys and I spend the afternoon piecing together puzzles, building Lego creations, and watching cartoons. They're singing the jingles in Hindi and when I ask if they want me to change the channel, they shout, "No, Momma!"

Ms. Harwani calls back. She's decided to take me up on my offer. She needs Rocket—pronto. She's pulling into the car park.

I dash downstairs and leave the car keys with the new English-speaking driver the Indian family on the sixth floor has hired. I grab the newspapers and walk back into the flat.

My pal Kareena Kapoor is now in the *Bombay Times* news again. She's dating Saif Ali Khan, who dated Rosa (who dined at Olive when the rat ran across my shoes and headed her way), and now they're an official item. Her sister, Karishma, is the actor who owns the flat on the fifth floor and took pictures with Matthew down in the lobby. Karishma is beautiful, talented, and down-to-earth. Her daughter is enrolled in Matthew's Little Butterflies Montessori school.

Saif and Kareena are the "It-Couple-of-Bollywood."

Neelam arrives for a late shift and calls from downstairs. "Hello, Madam, sorry to bother you, but a security guard, the wild one, caught a snake that crawled out of Ms. Harwani's car when she dropped it off in the car park. Can you come down and see it, and should he keep it?"

"What type of snake?"

"No, Madam, just a small snake like a child would have as a pet."

"I don't like snakes. Let me call Ms. Harwani and ask if Tanu has a pet snake that's missing from Le Gardenia."

"Ms. Harwani, did you and Pinky's driver pick up Rocket and are you headed to the airport?"

"Yes."

"*Namaste*, but by chance did you leave something behind in the Toyota?"

"What do you mean?"

"Well, a snake crawled out of the car as you were leaving our building and one of our security guards caught it and he's holding it for you until you return. Do you want this snake? We need to know or we're turning it loose on 16th Road after the servants leave the building tonight."

Silence.

Ms. H. belts something out in Hindi and then rapidly reverts back to English, "How can this be possible?"

Within seconds, Pinky calls. "Who put the snake in Mum's car?"

"Hey Pinks! I have no idea how a snake crawled out of your mom's Toyota!"

"I'm freaking out! Your building must have snakes."

"Pinky, we don't have snakes at Oberoi Crest, but we do trap rats. I lived at Le Gardenia and I know the building has rats, but I know nothing about snakes. If it doesn't belong to you, then we'll set it free."

She quickly changes the subject and we speak briefly about a new movie she's filming in south India. I start laughing and say, "Pinky, when you need to get away, you *Goa!*"

We laugh and agree to get together for dinner at China House after the film wraps up.

As much as I don't want to interrupt Naushad, I can't stand it. I call him. I want to share the craziness of the day because it just can't wait until Monday.

He answers my call on the first ring. When I relay the entire story to him very slowly in plain English, he calmly says, "Madam, there is a big snake at Le Gardenia. It had babies. Many drivers hear the big snake eating rats at night, Madam. The drivers and your Sleepy People, Madam, have seen small baby snakes around the car park like the one you said crawled out of Ms. Harwani's car."

Neelam races from the kitchen to answer the front door. It's Ms. Harwani returning the keys. She wants to borrow the baby stroller she saw in the back of Rocket. I remind her I need the stroller for my own use.

As I'm trying to get her out the door, she says she has no crib for the baby. Her daughter-in-law forgot to bring a stroller or small bassinet with her. Ms. Harwani tells me she would rather not purchase these items from Mothercare because they are only here for a few days. I can simply loan her Matthew's play yard. I say I'm more than happy to lend her the play yard, but I want it back in a week because we're traveling to Thailand for Diwali.

I pull the play yard out from under the bed in the guest bedroom and launch into a tutorial. By the look on her face, I lost her at "Step 1: Remove the cover." But off she goes downstairs with my play yard in tow.

The boys and I are missing Boss. Mary is cooking breakfast and cleaning the kitchen before Naushad arrives to collect us for drop-off. Much to my surprise, she prepares fruit salad and an omelet with toast. My Diet Pepsi is served in a large wine glass filled with ice made from bottled water. The boys are eating pancakes. I'm speechless, stunned by her behavior. I can only ponder what it means. Frankly, this is how we should be treated every morning.

Over breakfast, I scan the *Bombay Times* front page:

HOT JOBS IN MUMBAI

Jain Manuscript Transcriber
Many Jain manuscripts were destroyed in battles and wars years ago and the ones left are crumbling, so a trust has been set up to copy the scripts, some as old as 3,000 years. When

Mohan, a local Hindi transcriber, makes a mistake, he gets out his little pot of butterscotch correction fluid, which is the same shade as his handmade paper. (I love it that the transcriber uses Liquid Paper because I do, too.)

Change Giver
Change is the only constant thing in life—it's even more true for Mahavir, a local Jain, who goes around providing change to shop owners by charging three percent to five percent commission per transaction, as well as purchasing old and torn notes for less than face value. He then cashes them in at the Reserve Bank of India, thus pocketing the margins because people don't want to wait in line to do so.

Dog Mater
Rumor has it that canines living in Mumbai are stupid because there are only three people in the city who claim to know how to "help" dogs mate correctly. The mater experts are called in to "ensure" the female and male dog do the deed, including lubrication if needed.

After dropping the boys at school, Naushad and I are heading down south to an AWC event at Good Earth. He reminds me to call and order flowers for Wendy and Caron's shared birthdays on October 26. He points out the Muslim neighborhoods and the building the Don owns. I say, "The Don, as in the man who lived in our former building and was in jail?"

"Yes, Madam. He now lives in Pakistan."

"Naushad, what is the Don doing there?"

"Up to no good, Madam."

When I inquire about Tanu, he says her family is still living at Le Gardenia and the Don remains outside India until he can work out legal details with his attorney.

When we return home, I find Lolita in the flat finishing her work. She speaks Hindi to me like I can completely comprehend. Neelam is boiling *chai*. Lolita starts waving her arms and shaking her head at me until I understand I'm being summoned to join them in my own kitchen. Laxman would be proud of Madam drinking *chai*, but in the end he would criticize me for lowering myself to these people.

There's a knock at the door and in comes Naushad. Apparently Mary summoned him to join us. This is a special treat for me. I announced earlier in the day that our family would be in India until June 2008. They're elated we've got eight more months together—and they want to celebrate with cookies and *chai* from the Santa Cruz market. (For celebration, I was thinking more along the lines of imported wine and cheese from Sante, but *chai* will do.)

I'm sitting on the kitchen floor between Naushad and Lolita. I'm to the left of Lolita—the side with her functioning eye. I'm admiring her gold jewelry, which is more than I own. The four of us are sitting on the marble floor barefoot—laughing, laughing, too much laughing about the snake drama. We change the subject and giggle and discuss how the remaining Sleepy People at Le Gardenia got fired because they were stealing and selling construction materials from the tenth floor.

At one point, the boys walk in and sit down between Naushad and Mary. Matthew is chowing down on double-stuffed Oreos and Grant is eating Cheetos. They offer their snacks to Lolita and Naushad, who graciously accept.

Mary breaks the harmony. "Madam, what did you do before you lived in India?"

All eyes are on me. "I had a career. I was a professional public relations director for a non-profit, and then I changed jobs and worked at an advertising and marketing agency."

They are full of wonder. Neelam says, "Madam, you have this life no anymore."

"Madam, you need to get a new life," Naushad tells me. "Long time you have no life. You yoga and drink and talk like this, like that."

"Madam, you shop and run too much," Mary agrees.

Lolita speaks Hindi and laughter fills the kitchen.

"Lolita thinks you should not hold onto old ways," Mary is gracious enough to translate.

Hilarious. My horoscope during my first visit to India instructed me to do the same.

This is a treat my expat friends would never allow to happen in their flats—except for Madam Wendy.

Servants are servants, period. But, this is how we roll when Boss is out of town. I'm struck by their honesty and their willingness to share personal stories. Humor and kindness are high on my list of important qualities in a person, regardless of caste.

At six o'clock, I receive an email from Boss. His flight is delayed and he's been stuck on the JFK tarmac for three hours. He'll miss his connecting flight to London.

Inhale. Exhale.

I immediately text Naushad, who is downstairs waiting patiently to find out whether he will need to go to the airport tonight: "No."

Before the sun completely sets, I decide to head over to 15th Road. A slight breeze is blowing. I catch the drivers smoking cigarettes in the front of the car park.

"Naushad, finish up and then we can go together. I want the laundry man at Le Gardenia to iron a tunic for me, and I want to buy *sev puri* from Somnat." I'm tired, so I ask for the keys and tell Naushad I'll wait in the car.

What he doesn't realize is that the coast is clear. I've peeked out through the gates and there's not a car in sight. I want to drive myself one street over to get my snacks. He will *never* allow me to drive solo in the car unless it's an emergency. He gladly gives me the keys and is boastful his madam needs to wait on him to finish up and then he will go. He has no clue I just understood Hindi.

No one is standing in my way but if I backtrack slowly and sprint around the corner of the building to the right, I can make it to Rocket.

However, I forget to remove my shiny gold sandals before I start running. As I take off, one of the Professional Security Guards leans back out of his plastic chair because he hears the noise from the soles of my shoes clicking on the tile.

"Naushad," he yells, and some other words in Hindi I can't translate.

The next thing you know, three drivers and a window washer are chasing after me shouting, "No, Madam! No, Madam!"

I shout back, "Catch me if you can!"

Most of them aren't very smart because they follow me. Only Naushad and one guard race in the opposite direction to head me off, but I make it to the car in record time, jump in, and lock all the doors.

Every male in the car park is laughing, laughing, too much laughing at me, but when I start the car they stop. I want to practice driving and Naushad doesn't need to act cocky.

I start the engine, put the car in drive, and pull out of the space and up to the gate. Naushad is pleading for me to stop the car and get out immediately. "Boss is going to kill me and then Boss going to kill you. Please get out of the car, Madam!"

Just as I motion to the drivers and guards to move, they form a line in front of the gate and refuse to budge. Unbelievable. India is a man's world... although I proved my point.

I get out, hand the keys to Naushad, and climb into the backseat of the car. He slams my door shut, climbs into the driver's seat, and exits the driveway.

We return to the Mini Marble Palace twenty minutes later with *sev puri* for Naushad and the building staff as a commiseration prize. I carry some upstairs on several old *National Geographic* pages—now everybody has something to talk about.

Mary and Lolita finishing their duties and leave. Neelam stays behind to finish laundry and put the boys to bed. The flat is quiet. I check email.

There's one from Stan. It reads:

Dear Rhon,
Indeed the Jones Lang LaSalle merger is well under way, and they
will purchase the CBRE franchise at all costs while I remain in a
consulting position. It will make for interesting days at the office
during the merger, sleeping with the enemy.
Love,
Boss

Before Neelam leaves, she says, "Madam, I thought you in India five years."

"Neelam, I want to be in India, but it's not meant to be. I'm devastated."

She says slowly, "Madam, you see my life. I too always what you say this devastated. You get to leave, but I know you are not like other expat Madams. You love India. You will come back." She does the head wiggle. "Boss never coming back to India, Madam, maybe never in this life. I know this."

I give her a big hug.

"Madam, India is part of you."

On Saturday, we're getting ready for swim lessons. Mary and Neelam report for duty, and they both say they need to talk to me despite the fact we're running late.

Mary tells me her sister works with a cook who just got fired for dividing deliveries between her madam's flat and her own flat. The Scottish Madam figured out the accounting scheme. It dawns on me she's talking about Lindsay, Sophie's mum.

Ruh-roh!

Naushad calls wanting to know what's taking me so long to get down to the car park.

"I'm coming as fast as I can."

Then, Neelam tells me she worked for a Punjabi family for thirteen years. When they left Hong Kong they didn't provide her with her final month's pay or a return ticket home.

"How did you get back to India?"

"Madam, I pretended I could only speak my Hindi and a pastor from a nearby church took me to the Indian Embassy. They paid for me to get to Mumbai." She breaks down in tears rehashing the story. "Madam, Pinky is from this caste and this is why Ms. Harwani wants to borrow things— because she is cheap. She knows Punjabis won't let other Punjabis use their things, but you are too nice, Madam.

"I was kicking the soccer ball with Matthew yesterday and the Madam (confirmed Punjabi according to the second floor resident) walked into the lobby and told one of the security guards I was pathetic. He should send me up to her floor and she would hire me to clean."

I don't think Neelam, in a pair of Banana Republic white capri pants and a Paul Frank T-shirt of mine she shrank, looked pathetic.

"Madam, I told my mother and auntie when I got home. Then today, I told the guards and the drivers this woman wants me to work like a dog. My madam not only pays me well, but she buys me coffee from Café Coffee Day each month."

She wipes the tears away.

Here is another example of the servants talking, talking, too much talking about a case of mistaken identity: the Harwanis are not Punjabi. They are Sindhis!

I finally get down to the car park and Naushad is furious. We're totally late and he knows I expect him to make up time on the road. He skids into the parking lot at ASB and I jump out with Grant and race him into the pool area. The lifeguard gives me a thumbs-up. Whew! Quickly I return to the car and wave Naushad off before he gets out of the driver's seat to open my door. I climb into the backseat.

"Naushad," I ask, "Can I tell you something?"

He laughs.

I look at him for what seems a long time. Regardless of what he's told me about his family and life, he knows me far better than I'll ever know him. He speaks Hindi, and therefore all the retail owners and building employees tell him what I do. He could trace my footsteps across the city—it's the nature of this country. We've shared situations and circumstances one can only imagine.

Stanley told me before he left for Canada, "I travel at least two weeks out of each month, if not more. Naushad is like your day husband and I'm your night husband. Thank God, I don't have to listen to you talk all day in the car."

It's an odd feeling that this person, who started out as a stranger, would end up knowing me more than my own sibling. In truth, he really is my bodyguard. Moreover, it isn't without surprise that I tell him with total honesty, "Naushad, Madam is too sad to move back to Texas, but I will get you a job and we will sell you the car with a discount, I promise."

"Do you really have to go, Madam? Boss and you and the boys, really, Madam?"

I do the head wiggle.

He takes a deep breath and checks the watch we gave him for Christmas last year, and tells me we have nine more minutes until Grant is done. Then he looks off into the distance.

I burst into tears. I grab Kleenex out of my tote bag and can't stop crying.

We sit in Rocket for what seems an eternity and then he starts the engine, spins out of the ASB car park like Bo Duke, and swerves into the petrol station. He disappears into the store and returns with an ice-cold plastic bottle of Diet Pepsi. "Here, Madam, this will make you feel better."

After swim lessons, we drive down Linking Road. I've pulled myself together, but I'm hungry and ask him to stop at Elco on Hill Road. I've craving Indian *chaat* again. "Park the car and we can order food and eat at a table with Grant."

He says promptly, "Never, Madam. Thank you, but it is never right for Naushad to eat at a table with you and Little Boss anytime. I will wait. This is my job."

He leaves us on the sidewalk and we enter the small café and enjoy our lunch. I text him when we're done and he pulls the car around and delivers us to Oberoi Crest. I notice he's lost some spirit with news of our move.

I take the lift up and Matthew and Grant want to watch a movie, so I send Naushad and Neelam to pick up the play yard from Le Gardenia. They're back within thirty minutes.

"Madam, Ms. Harwani gave me and Naushad 1,000 rupees each for a Diwali bonus," Neelam says.

I glance at Naushad, who can't keep a straight face. He laughs, "No, Madam, only 500 rupees each."

I look back at Neelam.

Then she carefully hands over a large woven decorative bag full of Danish chocolates, pistachios, and three tins of cookies—a generous thank-you gift from Ms. Harwani.

Naushad rolls his eyes at Neelam.

"Madam, Muslims don't think like this, like that about Pinky's family."

I give my Hindu nanny a hard stare. "Neelam," I say, "Never speak another negative word about the Harwani family again."

She lowers her head.

My mobile rings. Boss is calling.

"I'm waiting for luggage and praying all the bags made it back. What do we have to do for the rest of the month?"

"Brunch on Sunday with friends. Diwali assembly on Tuesday, and the boys have a Halloween parade on Wednesday."

"Do we have Halloween costumes this year?"

"It's the first thing I bought in Austin this summer."

My mobile beeps. It's a text from Rohit, Stan's new company driver: "All bags + Boss." I show it to Grant, who is eager for Daddy to get home.

"Momma, when do we get to fly?" Grant asks.

"Soon. We're going to Phuket in five days."

Stanley calls back saying, "I just saw a guy in the airport wearing a funny Tantra T-shirt. I want to buy one for Moe at the Bombay Store as a souvenir—you know—it's the one that says: INDIA: I'll Never Do It Again."

28

Upon landing at the Phuket International Airport, the first things I observe are tourists decked out in Burberry, Chanel, and Ralph Lauren. Feeling 100 percent underdressed, I spot the culprit on the way to our hotel—knock-off stores and stalls galore.

Why, oh why, haven't we visited sooner?

Thailand, a country known for ancient ruins, ornate temples, and tropical beaches, is paradise. My only complaint is we find ourselves here in the latter part of monsoon. Despite a little precipitation and having to translate the menus for Neelam, who can't read, it's grand. The only other notable hiccup is convincing her she doesn't have to make the beds every day like she does at the Mini Marble Palace. *H-e-l-l-o!* It's called housekeeping, and that's how Neelam learns to roll at the Le Méridien beach resort.

We have spa treatments, daily interactions with a baby elephant on the beach, and return with duffels stuffed with 200 pounds of food, discounted clothes, Crocs in three sizes, watches, DVDs, CDs, and jewelry—gifts for friends and staff.

Back over Mumbai, we've been circling the airport for an hour and thirty minutes—I hope an employee remembered to change the batteries in the UPS system and we aren't caught in a blackout. The pilot, speaking Hindi, has just announced we're number eighteen to land. We recline our seats.

Grant spots millions of Diwali lights below—simply magical; an image that will forever be ingrained in my memory. (Last year, we moved smack-dab in the middle of this notable holiday and were completely unaware of its importance.)

A-h-h-h. The next morning, I hear honking and rickshaws buzzing down 16th Road. Brightly-colored lanterns are hanging up in trees and boutiques. Locals are cheery and the neighborhood has a festive vibe. Diwali signifies the triumph of good over evil, justice over deceit, and truth over falsehood. It's a holy time when prayers are offered to the Hindu deity, Lakshmi—the god of wealth and prosperity.

Families gather to celebrate and line tables inside their homes with small pots of oil that are lit. Children play with sparklers and fireworks explode sporadically all over the city. On the day of Diwali, everyone wears new clothes and shares sweets and snacks, but the true meaning of the festival is dispelling the darkness of ignorance; it is a festival of light, inspiring us to shine brighter. To expats, it feels a little like Christmas because not only do we decorate, we give bonuses to employees for dedicated service.

We've barely begun to unpack when the doorbell rings. It's our mailman, whom we've seen four times since moving into the building. Normally a Professional Security Guard brings up the scarce card or letter along with the Great Big Book of Everything for the required signature. But of course, here is the official mailman wanting his bonus.

He has an important letter for us, and as he hands it to Stanley, he realizes it's for the previous expat family. He looks at me and shrugs. Stanley calls out to Neelam who is unloading her suitcase and washing laundry.

"This letter isn't for us."

Neelam rattles off Hindi to the man and giggles when he confesses to the mixed identities. "Boss, it's Diwali. He should get like fifty rupees." So Stanley hands back the envelope and rupees, and shuts the door as the satisfied courier turns and leaves.

"Neelam, do not answer the door again. I'm terrified the bonus floodgates just opened."

She keeps laughing. "Boss, if you didn't pay today, he will keep coming back again and again. Better you pay now."

We gave bonuses to Naushad, Neelam, Mary, Lolita, Rohit, Anil, Amol, the Professional Security Guard Team, two window washers, one supervisor (who doesn't tell the society manager we've hired building employees as personal employees), one car washer, and the trash man before leaving the city, but who knew the mailman would also appear wanting $1.35? It's still hard to swallow that we have a staff on payroll.

The boys are sleeping in, and I head to the supermarket on foot. I score fruit, vegetables, and cheddar cheese, but no tortilla chips. The seafood is paltry. Shop owners recognize expats have been away during the break and no one is around to purchase the costly imports.

I walk briskly past Khar Gymkhana and instantly notice five *goras* (white people) dressed in tacky tank tops and flowy silk skirts, posing aimlessly with our cows. Disgraceful.

I wave to my neighborhood ear cleaner, avoid a pack of wild, nasty strays, and spot Anil the Wine Guy making a delivery on his motorbike. I hear a cricket match in motion and do a look-see into the gated, packed field. Players wave me in but I decline the offer. I waltz home in time to see Neelam organizing plastic bags and empty Diet Pepsi bottles, not to mention a plethora of hotel toiletries she brought back from Phuket.

"Madam, I can't help it. The whole holiday we threw away nice things I can sell in the recycling market."

"It was also very difficult for me to throw plastic bottles and cans away." I don't mention I loaded up on toiletries, too—to give to Naushad. Nor do I mention I've been known to pilfer a sewing kit or two. She gathers her clothes and takes the lift down. She looks very feisty walking out of the car park and down 16th Road with her fancy Thailand gift bags full of goodies.

My mobile beeps with Diwali wishes from Laxman, Pinky, Chef Max from Olive, and Raj. Naushad and Mary have the day off and we decide to take the boys to Out of the Blue. Stanley sends a text to Rohit, who pulls the car up to the lobby, and we zip down Union Park. Once inside, I request a four top and the hostess escorts us to a table for two.

In hindsight, this should have been a sign.

We decline the seat assignment and move outside under the covered patio in the smoking section. We hop into the booth while the waiter stands at attention. I politely ask for menus when he reaches over, takes a lamented page from the table centerpiece, and hands it to me. It's the drink menu.

"Do you have a children's menu?" I say.

"Yes, I handed you one."

"No, that's the drink menu."

"Do you want the kids to drink or eat?" he says.

"Um, both."

"What do you want the kids to drink?"

"Ah, all right. Let me see. How about cold milk, two glasses of cold milk."

"Juice."

"No, no juice, just two cold milks."

"Coke."

"No, no soda, just two cold milks."

I'm antsy. In a flash, I take out my notepad geared up to draw a picture of a hand so he knows what I'm about to strangle him with when Boss interrupts and says, "Room temperature bottled Himalayan water."

"Fizzy or still?"

I growl.

He knows the Americans don't drink fizzy water.

Eventually, he returns, standing before me and staring at Matthew.

I blurt out, "I now want two bowls of fusilli pasta with nothing but butter."

"You want two bowls of Fusilli pasta with butter and garlic and parsley?"

"No."

Right then, Stanley springs up from his chair. "We want two bowls of fusilli pasta—no green stuff, no garlic, no tomatoes, no cream sauce, no mystery sauce, no pepper, no cheese—nothing but pasta and melted butter."

"Okay, sir."

This is not the fun family brunch I envisioned.

At some point, a Caesar salad lands on the table, along with Grant's and

Matthew's noodles. Then a new waiter plops down Stanley's hot soup and his Cajun chicken entrée. Remember Luisa, who tried to poison me? She can cook better than the chefs at Out of the Blue. Suddenly, I hear a DJ crank up an electric guitar and belt out, "All my troubles seem so far away..."

Stanley chokes on his food. "Once we leave Mumbai, Madam, your troubles will be far, far away."

I glance around the room and all eyes are on us, although the staring hasn't bothered us in ages.

On the contrary, Stanley reminds me of our past issues: the leaking tub, the broken windshield, the dead refrigerator compressor, and how I've managed to lower my standards. And your point is?

"Madam, I love you because you've conquered India!"

Hogwash.

Finally the new waiter delivers my entrée and it smells like chum.

Straight away, the DJ strikes a chord, "Every Breath You Take" by the Police, and I'm thinking, thinking, too much thinking every gulp of air I take in equals pathogenic bacteria.

I head to the loo and on my return Matthew is in the hands of our original waiter at the dessert station with pink, sticky, gooey cotton candy all over his shirt and in his hair. Grant is on the stage dancing.

After Stanley pays the bill, I grab my LV tote bag and collect the boys. I spot Rohit, across the street, asleep in the car. Stanley dodges three rickshaws and bangs on the window. He wakes up, starts the engine, and we cruise home.

I'm brainstorming ideas for Moe's trip. Friends since our freshman year in college, we've experienced a lot; however, the thing I fear the most, aside from his reaction to the homeland, is the Taj Mahal visit because of the aforementioned lack of flights to Agra.

Let's get real. You want to see the Taj, one of the Seven Wonders of the World? Then you go by train (schedule permitting), car (road conditions are hazardous), or by private jet (costly). However, he's giving up two prime vacation weeks—the least I can do is pull out all the stops.

Anxiously I pencil out an itinerary.

I need to go to Citibank. Rohit will drive me along with Naushad because the car washer is cleaning Rocket.

While headed back home, we pass a goods carrier truck. The tailgate reads: INDIA IS G-R-A-T-E!

Naushad points to the misspelling and I remind him Grant missed that word on his spelling test last week. I also remind him Boss doesn't think India is *ever* GRATE, but I do on days when things go my way.

We pull into the car park to see Neelam jumping into a rickshaw to take

Matthew to Little Butterflies. I call the Grand Hyatt and order salmon and Naushad arranges flowers in the brass *urlis* out in the foyer. Lolita arrives to scrub the marble floors and bathrooms and the newspaper delivery man drops off our dailies.

Naushad wraps up the *urlis* project and is ready to drive to Chhatrapati Shivaji International Airport. I take the lift down and climb into Rocket. As we turn onto Linking Road, my mobile beeps. It's a text from Moe: "Should I grab a taxi or are you picking me up?"

I show Naushad and we laugh out loud. I mean, the thought of letting Moe attempt to speak Hindi and flag down a taxi to get to Oberoi Crest never occurred to me.

We're parked outside the international terminal, but I'm hiding off to the side of the exit area because we want our new guest to experience sensory overload full throttle!

Finally, after standing for roughly ten minutes, I see him go from exhilaration into complete panic mode. He's staring, staring, too much staring at the Indian men feverishly waving and staring back trying to get his attention for a taxi ride.

I'm the only white person, Moe is the only black person, and we're surrounded by a sea of brown people. Moe has the deer-in-the-headlights look big-time. I sprint over, place a lei around his neck, and give him one gigantic hug. "Welcome to Mumbai!"

Naushad greets Moe with a firm handshake, and once the suitcases are loaded, we head straight to the Mini Marble Palace.

The first thing out of Moe's mouth as we pass a building with workers constructing the exterior walls of a soon-to-be-office complex, is, "That is *not* bamboo scaffolding…"

Yeah, it is.

Horns are honking, people are begging at the windows, rickshaws fly by, five people pass on one motorbike, and I watch Moe ponder what he's gotten himself into for the next fourteen days. We pull into the car park and take the lift up. Stanley wants to know what took us so long to get home.

Seriously?

Moe says after he collected his bags and cleared customs, he somehow ended up in the line to connect to the domestic terminal until he caught his mistake. I raise my voice as I hear his story from the bedroom and shout, "That was a test!"

Then I smile. *Trust me, it won't be the last.*

Later in the afternoon, Moe wakes up from a much-needed nap. The doorbell is ringing. In comes the plumber, in comes the delivery guy with water and Diet Pepsi, and in comes one of the Professional Security Guards delivering the mail.

"Unbelievable," he says. "You weren't lying when you said there's no end to people constantly disrupting your privacy."

The boys are happy Uncle Moe is in the Mini Marble Palace and that he dares to race them around the block in rickshaws before distributing candy and gifts.

He and I head out for cocktails at Vertigo and dinner at Olive after we share sunset drinks with Stanley on the balcony. We laugh about the rat story and as we stumble into Rocket hours later, I tell Moe, "Congrats! You just survived your first day in India."

The next morning, we're up at 6 a.m. because a wedding party has lit a case of jumbo firecracker strings in front of Oberoi Crest, and even Grant can't ignore the noise. Moe is petrified. He thinks the city is under siege. The pandemonium goes on for an hour, and then we all crawl back into bed.

After breakfast, we drive down south and tour the Gateway of India and visit shops in the Taj Mahal Palace Hotel. Moe is shaken by the traffic but more so by Naushad's ability to drive on the wrong side of the road to keep us moving.

We shop at Bungalow 8 and Bhaghem Bombay, where Moe blows his budget on twelve-dollar pillowcases and a king-sized bedspread, the first of many to come, and he meets Harry #2. I grin, knowing his family will receive Christmas presents from this holiday for the next three years.

Later, with Stanley in tow, we pass a burnt orange sunset over Haji Ali Mosque en route to The Dome Bar for cocktails. Then, after dinner at Shiros, we board Rocket for the fifteen-minute ride home. Moe can't believe it took us two hours to get down south but less than twenty minutes to get home. I whisper in his ear, "Well, you just survived test number two—the ability to withstand traffic without losing your mind."

Once upstairs, the guys sit down to discuss Austin and work. I'm walking out of the loo when I hear a piercing scream. Moe looks scared stiff.

"*Kya hua?*"

He's pointing to our "pet" fruit bat perched on the palm outside our balcony.

Austin's Congress Avenue Bridge is home to 1.5 million urban bats, so Moe's familiar with the only true flying mammal colony found in the capital city where he attended college. What he isn't expecting is that fruit bats in India grow to be the same height as Matthew.

The following day he and I are up and at the airport's chaotic domestic terminal. Our short flight to Jodhpur is delayed, but as we finally descend into the city, Moe notices the military tanks, anti-aircraft guns, fighter planes, and missile dense packs on the tarmac as he coughs back the DDT.

Welcome to Rajasthan!

Moe maintains his cool with the military presence, Laxman picks us up on time, and after a vegetarian lunch at the Four Hands house, we explore Jodhpur—the Sun City, so called because of the bright and sunny weather. It is also known as "the Blue City" for the vivid Indigo-hued painted houses owned by Brahmins. Moe freaks out when he sees a herd of goats ushered down a dirt street.

"Babe," I say, "You're in the country. We left the big city behind and you're going to see many, many fascinating things here."

Out of nowhere, a group of camels appear from a side street near our car and lazily walk down the middle of the road. Moe's camera is in overdrive and he can't take the wildlife shots fast enough. Laxman points out the lone stoplight in the place one and a half million locals call home.

By the time we buy saffron and his second bedspread, finish our private tour of the Mehrangarh Fort (built around 1460), and sip Sula on one of the balconies while the sun sets in the distance, I can tell Moe is starting to chill.

We thank Mr. Pratap Singh for inviting us into his home, a small stone structure that is part of the fort's complex. His balcony, four hundred feet above the city, has a breathtaking view of temples and the Thar Desert in the distance. His son, Magan Singh Rathore, escorts us to one of the seven gates and bids us farewell.

The following morning, Stanley lands in Jodhpur and we spend the afternoon relaxing at Cathy and Roberto's homestead.

The next day, we're up for a quick breakfast and then out on a Jeep safari. We snicker when we pull into a village and spot elders talking on mobiles. To our left is a medium-sized hut with a TV antenna on the thatched roof. I tell Moe they probably own a DVD player and a Nintendo Wii home video game console, too.

In the second village, the Bishnois locals do not have running water, but everything is spotless. Picture a group of round, thatched, white-painted huts made of dirt and decorated with wonderful designs surrounded by stacks of hay, a herd of goats, and cow-dung patties drying in the sun. A group of *sari*-clad women carrying jugs, their faces barely visible through the veil draped over their hair and face as a sign of respect to their husbands, scurry by to a small well.

Swiftly, we're ushered under a low-hanging roof and seated on beautiful-ly-crafted rugs where we're invited to participate in an opium ceremony. Our host is a little glassy-eyed and our guide offers to translate the ceremonial ritual.

An elder with a gigantic white moustache grinds small chunks of opium in a copper pot. Then the granules, dissolved in water, are strained several times through a sieve held up by an elaborate filtration apparatus. The mixture drips slowly into a carved wooden jug that resembles a topless Aladdin's lamp.

I turn to my left and Moe's eyes are glued on the sieve. Grinning, I say, "It looks like a dirty sock."

An elder with a salt-and-pepper moustache walks through a set of chants and makes hand gestures "offering it to the gods," according to our guide. I wonder if he's talking about us in third person since we're about to drink it, not real gods. The third elder stands, picks up the jug, and pours it into the cupped hands of the host, who peacefully offers it to Moe.

Stanley laughs so intensely he snorts like a pig. Moe looks at me with fear written all over his face.

"What hospitality!" I say.

We inhale. We exhale.

Moe hands me his camera and slurps down the bitter liquid.

"Not bad. Not good either," he says.

The sun begins to set, and as we start our one-hour journey back to Jodhpur, we drive to a third village where local artisans are making lac bangles and rolling turbans. Cathy calls to say the cook will make Mexican food for dinner. Moe salivates at the thought of chicken fajitas, queso, and Spanish rice because he's not an Indian foodie. At this point, he's craving McDonald's, Pizza Hut, you name it—he wants something non-veg that doesn't have masala in it, period.

The drive along the dirt road is relatively trouble-free, and once back on the main highway and back at the house, we shower and feast.

We spend the rest of the night playing cards before stumbling across the lawn to our respective bedrooms. Moe just survived another test—the ability to entertain oneself in a foreign land when there is absolutely nothing else to do. Up at the crack of dawn, Stanley flies back to Mumbai, but Moe and I are on our way to Pushkar, the world's largest camel festival.

Two words: road trip.

Naturally, I put Moe up front to see Rajasthan in all its glory. Indian roads are an adventure full of motorbikes carrying multiple passengers, herds of sheep, camels, Jeeps, rental cars, horses, tractors piled high with materials, Tata trucks, fleets of large Rajasthan State Road Transport Corporation (RSRTC) buses, and a perpetual concerto of honking. Two hours into the three-hour-and-thirty-seven-minute drive via RJ SH 21 and NH89 (a 188.2-kilometer trip), we stop at a *dhaba* (a roadside restaurant) for snacks and a potty break. Our driver shows us to the loos: two separate holes in the ground surrounded by plastic shower curtains.

I finish first and purchase two bottles of Himalaya water and double-check to make sure the seal isn't broken. I buy two bags of Ginnies chips: tomato mazaa and classic salted. Strong, spicy smells waft from pots boiling on an open fire where local men sit on *charpolis* (rope cots) and red plastic chairs.

"Moe, are you hungry? Do you want to try a *thali*?"

"A what?"

It's a rimmed plate containing a variety of food in small bowls—it's a taste of India. He shakes his head vigorously as in "No."

"Do you need *chai*? How about roti and samosas? They look tasty."

He snatches both bags of chips from my hand. "I'm good. Let's go, Rhon!"

We climb back into the car and buckle up.

I point out two signs. One reads: CHILD BEER. The second: WTF!? WOW, TASTY, FOOD.

"Wait, look at the sign on that Tata truck," I say. "IN TRUST WE GOD."

He laughs and crunches away, but Moe becomes silent when the driver begins to play chicken with the oncoming traffic going 100 miles per hour.

Suddenly, the road turns into a single lane with continuous two-way traffic.

"What happens if cows want to cross the road?" Moe says.

"Pray for dear life. All drivers brake for cows!"

I witness him tighten his seatbelt.

Speaking of which, our driver is now lost, so at an intersection he slows down to ask three skinny men in bright orange turbans and white *lungis* herding goats which way we should go.

We stare off into space as each uncle points in a different direction.

"Moe, the rule is to ask three people for a majority decision, but in this case, we're screwed."

Eventually, we reach Pushkar.

There are camels (more than 200,000 of them) as far as the eye can see. It's a county fair of epic proportions complete with snake charmers, magicians, dancers, musicians, and circus rides.

Our driver parks and heads off to eat a late lunch. We've got two hours to explore. First we're caught off guard by cries from ornery camels, then by the smell of thousands of goats, cows, and sheep combined with the sporadic whiff of *biryani* (a fragrant mixture of basmati rice, vegetables, yogurt, and spices simmered for hours) and *gujiya* (sweet fried dumplings filled with a mixture of nuts), which overloads our senses. It's dry, and dust fills our ears and lungs.

Moe wants to buy a camel and set it free. Prices range from fifty American dollars and up. I mean, this place was *the* place to be. An English-speaking tour guide leading a group near us tells Moe, "Camels are worth their weight in rupees and they live to be eighty years old. They're used for transporting materials and in agriculture, and they produce the white gold of the desert: camel's milk. When they expire, the tribe benefits from their hair, meat, leather, and bones." He adds, "Plus, the excrement is free fuel for cooking."

I study the line-up. The camels are dressed for show, embellished with silver bells, bangles, mirrored saddles, and hand-woven colorful harnesses. There's even a camel beauty contest for the best-bedecked camel.

Kinda. Dorky.

I join in the fun by sitting for *mehndi*, a temporary reddish-brown skin decoration on my arm. The dye will fade, but the memory of Moe's visit will stay with me evermore.

"Olonga!"

"Olonga!"

A group of locals with oily slicked-back hair dressed in tight black jeans and Digicel cricket shirts are waving to Moe who is taking pictures of camels next to him, beside him, and behind him.

A crowd of students from Delhi yell "Olonga" and wave.

Who is Olonga?

Turns out, Moe looks like a famous Zimbabwe cricket player named Henry Khabba Olonga, and locals think he's the real deal. Pursuing this further, an English-speaking guide tells us they think I'm the white girlfriend.

Moe says, "We can seriously take advantage of this gig," and we do. We wave. Moe signs autographs and we pose for photo ops for endless fans who holler and cheer us on.

It's time to leave the festival and head out for Jaipur three hours away. We're behaving like such juvenile delinquents that the driver has to pull over twice because we can't control ourselves.

The faster we go, the more we fill the car with laughter, and the more it rattles. At this point, we're delusional.

Entering the city center, I see a large grin appear on Moe's face. He's seen the bulbs lighting the McDonald's sign.

I motion for the driver to pull over and Moe screams with delight, "I'm ordering a Quarter Pounder with cheese!"

Bet you're not!

H-E-L-L-O!

"Moe, there's no beef at the Golden Arches, but you can purchase fries and the Maharaja Mac, a vegetarian burger."

Crushed, he opts for the only two non-masala items on the menu—fries and a sundae. We check into Bissau Palace outside Chanpole Gate, and Moe gets tense when the hotel manager hands me their version of the Great Big Book of Everything to sign, even though he's paying for the two rooms. I list our names as: Priyanka Erwin and Mohan Beswonee Singh, just for grins.

An employee escorts us to our suites, and we agree to meet at the rooftop restaurant within the hour. It's been a long day, and I'm impressed with Olonga's stamina; he's basically living on a prayer.

After I accept my room key, I hold out rupees, ask the clerk to order two large Domino's cheese pizzas, and leave to go take a hot shower. An hour later, I climb the maze of intricate tile stairs up to the roof.

Sipping cold Kingfisher and Sula, we make a toast to friendship.

When the pizza hits the table, guests want what we're having. However, they don't live in the homeland and don't understand anything is possible— for a price.

Moe and I exchange a glance across the table.

"You read my mind."

The gooey thin-crust slices are scrumptious.

He inhales. He exhales.

Moe concedes as he takes a sip of beer, "I lost my ass in the betting pool. I didn't think you could do it."

I raise my glass. "Never discount the girl from the North Side."

He chokes back his laughter. "You're living a thrilling life."

"Each day is an adventure, but it's not a permanent reality."

"Rhon, I'm truly impressed, but do you think India desensitizes you to human misery? The caste system and poverty are inconceivable."

"Moe, it's not possible to shut out humanity, but I'm able to find a peaceful balance. Maybe that's what visitors don't comprehend—that amid the chaos, there is a harmony."

Something did transpire during that ultimate champi Indian head massage.

The following morning, we dine on scrambled eggs and chapati for breakfast. After we check out, the clerk introduces us to our new driver who can barely speak the Hinglish because he's coughing too much.

I turn to Moe. "I hope he doesn't have typhoid fever."

He glares back at me while he puts our suitcases in the trunk. We squeeze ourselves inside the teeny tiny Indigo.

Our mission: the Taj Mahal.

With just four and a half hours to go, we crank out old-fashioned fun: I teach Moe how to do the head wiggle.

"This cranium shaking drives me nutty," he says.

I grin.

"Makes no sense to me," he adds.

The roads to Agra aren't as ghastly as I remember, but he insists the route should be named "the Highway of Death." I already know this.

I scribble a water drop and a faucet on my tablet and the driver pulls into a petrol station. Moe perks up in the car, and minutes later, he appears out of the storefront with his hands full of souvenirs. With Chips Ahoy! spilling from his mouth, he mumbles I should go in to buy a set of camel bone bracelets and Mentos, and I do as instructed. Back in the car, we race toward Agra.

Reaching our destination, the driver (with an endless hacking cough) weaves meticulously through the labyrinth of traffic, bazaars, and alleys. We park and he speaks Hindi to a teenage rickshaw driver in worn leather flip-flops, who pedals Moe and me to the entry line for the famous site.

We're behind forty locals dressed in their Diwali best when we're plucked from the procession and placed front and center at the ticket counter. I'm nervous a fight might break out. We purchase our tickets and are issued a free 500-milliliter bottle of water and shoe covers.

We don't comprehend our instant celebrity status until we're whisked through the south gate security check and respectfully escorted through the impressive red sandstone gateway inscribed with verses from the Quran.

"Olonga!"

"Olonga!"

"*O-l-o-n-g-a!*"

Oh. My. Lord.

I visited the Taj with Stanley and the WPO group last fall and it was lovely—but this is fantabulous. Local teens are taking photos of Moe. Women are putting babies in my arms, wanting family group shots.

Moe and I refrain from giving each other a high five, Michael Jordan-style.

The tour operator points out four sets of aunties and uncles speaking Hindi. "They say today is an auspicious occasion because they have never seen a white person *and* a black person together."

Isn't that special?

I look at my watch and we've only got thirty minutes left to tour the grounds. Why I felt the need to book an 8:30 p.m. return flight from Delhi to Mumbai I'm not sure, but that is the plan. Moe runs around, snapping all the iconic shots. We pose for photographs on Diana's bench, pretending to be a real couple, and one of the official Taj photographers races off and returns with a stack of printed shots of Olonga in front of the Taj, beside the Taj, behind the Taj, all over the Taj.

Kya daam hai? (Translation: What is the price?)

He mumbles, "One thousand rupees."

"I was here last year and you are cheating me on the cost," I say.

In perfect English he responds, "No, Madam. This good price."

Swarms of people walk past me. I wave my hand and dismiss the photographer.

"What are you doing? I want the photos," Moe says anxiously. "If it's just a few dollars, who cares?"

"You're a banker, right? It's the principle."

He's flabbergasted.

We exit the grounds and shoo away the teenagers shoving Taj snow globes and Taj alarm clocks in our faces. I see our driver waiting near the car. We walk 100 yards and surprisingly I hear, "Olonga! Olonga! Madam! Best price here, Madam!" It's the photographer running our way.

Moe is bowled over. I hand over 300 rupees and collect the prints.

In the car and back on the Highway of Death, the driver begins to cough again. I reach forward and slap him on the back. "Call in sick the next time you have whooping cough, damn it."

I text Stanley: "Headed to Delhi."

I text Naushad: "Madam/Moe to Delhi airport."

Have I mentioned India has pollution issues? On this particular Thursday, the pollution is so grim we can't see two cars in front of us. For three hours, we drive ten miles per hour and I'm certain we'll miss our flight. Moe is gripping the dashboard and grinding his teeth while the driver coughs up his other lung.

I had hopes for a lull in the traffic, but that doesn't happen because the driver takes the wrong way into the city to the opposite side of where the Indira Gandhi International Airport is located.

Moe looks at me. "He's lost."

We literally stop seven times to ask for directions, and, at one point, a derelict man wants to get into the car with us and personally escort us to the domestic terminal. *I don't think so.*

I'm not sure Moe believes we're going to get back to Khar West, and that plays into more jokes that keep us sane for the remaining tense time in the car.

Moe is learning yet another valuable lesson in India: patience is a virtue.

Moe's watch reads 8:35 p.m. Guess we missed our flight. "Rhon, it took us five hours to find the airport, and I can see the terminal 300 yards away. We can walk to our gate faster than riding in this crappy Indigo."

I agree. "Perhaps we can make the Jet Air 10:30 p.m. flight though and then we'll be home safe and sound."

It takes us—and I'm not making this up—fifty minutes to drive 300 yards. Had Moe not purchased another two bedspreads and six wooden elephants at a third rest stop on the way back, we could have sprinted to the terminal and carried our luggage.

The time on my watch now reads 9:25 p.m.

The driver parks the car and unloads our suitcases, but the airport security guards won't let us in because we missed our flight. Moe starts to lose it. I jerk my ticket from the guard's hand and march through the door, shouting to a Jet Air attendant for assistance.

She waves me in and over to a kiosk. I look around—Moe's stuck at the entrance. I turn, march back, grab Moe, and pull him past the guard and yell, "His name is Olonga and he's with me!" We waltz to the Jet Air counter and the young employee reviews our tickets and says calmly, "You missed your flight."

I swear, steam is coming out of Moe's ears. Welcome to my character-building world! The manager puts us on the waitlist. She says we have a decent chance to make the last flight out of Delhi because a lot of people no-show.

Hmm. I find a seat, but Moe is pacing. He's tired and hungry. He hasn't had enough caffeine and cold Kingfisher for the day. He's checking the departure board. He tells me to skip over to GoAir and put our names on the waitlist in case we can't get on the Jet Air flight.

At the counter, a young girl tells me they don't do standby and they don't sell tickets. The only way we can get on the plane is if two current ticket holders physically sell us their seats because they decided not to fly on the GA 10:45 p.m. flight to Mumbai.

I politely ask, "You mean to tell me if people are no-shows, you can't sell me their seats?"

"Yes."

"Can I pay you to sit in an empty seat?"

"No."

"Why would anyone drive in traffic to the airport and stand around to sell a ticket they don't want to use?"

She frowns and turns to the girl standing beside her and they start speaking Hindi.

Typical.

I walk back to Moe "Apparently when you need to go...you can't *go* on GoAir!"

He's reached his boiling point. In the end, a Hindu family of five flies to Mumbai, and we're left behind.

I ask about options and I'm told: eat at the airport restaurant upstairs, or go talk to the airport manager, or sleep in the airport.

Moe checks out the restaurant. It's closed. To get to the manager, you have to leave the terminal, but the security guards with the AK-47s won't let you out with your luggage that has been scanned, even though you missed your flight.

I decide to leave the bags with Moe and exit the terminal. The manager is holed up in a small government office beside the entrance. He wants to send us to the airport hotel for 400 rupees or we can stay in the check-in area until our 8 a.m. flight tomorrow.

I'm inhaling and exhaling.

I strut back into the airport and tell Moe, still mad at GoAir, the new options. We walk back towards the security guards from the first encounter and explain our situation. They're adamant we must stay put. All of a sudden, Moe channels the dark side of the force.

He begins to scream.

Now, under *no* circumstances will they permit us to leave. Moe is outraged! He begins to mouth off about how he has no idea why he ever wanted to visit India.

"Calm down."

He gives me one of his special go-to-hell looks I haven't seen since my sophomore year.

I lower my voice. "India really is g-r-a-t-e, and I can solve this nightmare."

I march over to the Jet Airways counter and inform the manager we need to leave and get a hotel, but the guards won't let us exit the terminal. Can she help? Swiftly, she walks over to a side security entrance where the armed guards are on a *chai* break. Then she pulls out the Airport Great Big Book of Everything, writes down our ticket and bag information with a Bic, and sets us free.

Just like that, we're liberated from the idiocy.

Outside, a man with one eye walks up holding a dirty cardboard sign that says "Msr. Ervine Airpot Hotal" in red marker.

Moe is terrified.

I shriek, "Go away! Far, far away!"

He says, "Manager send me, Madam!"

I squeal, "I don't care who sent you! I changed my mind!" I turn around to face Moe who is just standing motionless, afraid.

"Isn't this fun?"

But he's not in high spirits.

We assume we're out of the woods, but none of the prepaid taxi drivers will load our luggage. They don't want to drive black or white people tonight.

Seriously.

We finally see a worthy driver approaching the taxi queue, but a shady driver opens his door, pulls him out, and punches him in the stomach. A fistfight breaks out over us. The two men are pulled apart but continue exchanging harsh words.

I say, "Never, never go with the drivers who fight over you. That would not turn out well."

At last, we spot a clean taxi and what looks like a fairly nice driver. We jerk open his backseat doors and plop down our heavy bags. He's grumpy but we don't care. The Jet Air manager suggested we check out the Radisson seven minutes away, so off we go.

We hand over the prepaid slip to the driver, but he wants no part of it. I tell him to speed up, and he turns around and yells at me. We slouch back into our seats and play the quiet game. The driver instantly makes a sharp left turn around the corner, and thankfully we see rows of hotels. Maybe we're not going to end up dead in an empty lot. Before we reach any of the entrances, he asks how many rupees we paid the taxi attendant back at the airport.

"I don't know." Then I lie. "Our tour guide paid for us."

Out of nowhere the driver acts like he's not going to stop unless we give him a tip.

Moe looks at me. I put my finger up to my mouth and motion not to speak.

Other cars on the road are passing us. Thank the Lord Shiva he pulls into the Radisson car park and out we jump quick, quick.

"I want more rupees!" the driver says angrily.

I shout, *"Hell no,"* and Moe flips him the finger.

It's 11:45 p.m.

We sprint into the hotel lobby. Once inside, I notice Moe loves the Radisson by his strut. There is no pollution or smog to inhale, and the front desk staff greets us ever-so-sweetly. A handsome young male employee tells Moe they will hold our suitcases and we can spend the evening relaxing in the foyer, eating in the restaurant, or we can pay for a room—there are many choices. We can also get a free ride to the airport via the air-conditioned Radisson shuttle in the morning.

I exhale.

Leisurely, I walk to the bathroom and then head to the bar.

As I sit down, the waiter is delivering a tall, cold Kingfisher to Olonga, and I know he's going to be tolerable. He proudly shows me the menu and points to three words he's missed seeing—American-style hamburger. Now tears of bliss fill his eyes when a waiter promptly takes our order that includes artichoke dip, thank you very much.

"This is the best service I've had since living abroad," I say. "Now I know every little thing will be alright."

We slurp down the dip, and I notice John has sent me a Thanksgiving haiku from Houston.

I show Moe the text and he tells me, "This is the first time I haven't eaten turkey and dressing with my family."

OMG!

We'd completely forgotten it's Thanksgiving Day! We're sad but grateful our night didn't end someplace far worse than the Radisson.

After two more rounds of drinks, Moe begins to lighten up. Tipsy, he pays the tab in rupees and scribbles an "OLONGA" haiku on the bill:

> *Radisson Hotel*
> *It's a beacon in the night*
> *Saved my sanity!*

We land back in Mumbai the next day with the usual drop from the sky. Man, what a week it's been.

We watch a Bollywood movie and then walk over to 15th Road with Naushad to purchase *sev puri* from Somnat, who is holding court in his usual spot. When Moe finishes his *chaat*, he looks me in the eyes and says, "I'm done with Indian food, much less anything edible that has masala or cumin in it—forever!"

I snicker because he forgets it's exactly what Virgin Airways will serve on his flight back home to New York.

On Saturday, Moe participates in the Dharavi slum tour. He returns to the flat astounded. He tells us many of the locals thought he *was* Olonga—my, my, my, how he continues to roll as the celebrity. On Sunday, we dine at China House with Pinky. She says she's very sad to hear we're leaving in June and urges us to change our minds.

Moe says, "Pinky, Stanley bought the tickets and he's done with your country."

She looks at me mournfully.

"I know, I know, it will be upsetting to go."

We reach over and hug tightly.

By Monday, Moe crams his "Made in India" goodies, including a custom handmade tuxedo from Millionaire, into Rocket and we bid farewell. Naushad returns from the airport and calls from the car park.

"Madam, Boss Moe very, very quiet to airport," he says.

I bet he was.

"Madam, Boss Moe waved to me. He said, 'See you later, alligator!' But Madam, I asked him how and when I would see him again because he's never coming back to India, and he laughed at Naushad. I don't know this alligator talk."

"It's a figure of speech from an old song, but you're right—Moe will never return to the homeland."

Without warning, the lights go out on the Christmas tree we put up while Olonga was here, and Grant wants to know if the bad juju is back.

No. No bad juju here—just cheap made-in-China lights sold in India. Slowly, I take the dead strings off the tree and rearrange the remaining working strands.

On Wednesday morning, Naushad calls to tell me he overslept.

I'm livid because he knows Grant's class has standardized testing today.

I check downstairs and all drivers are out.

Back upstairs, I announce, "I'm driving Grant to school because he can't be late."

Stan says, "Are you kidding me?" I finally confess I've been taking driving lessons in case of an emergency. Stanley looks frightened.

With no time to spare, I stand my ground. "This *is* an emergency! The rickshaw school wouldn't let me enroll, so I spent my time learning how to drive Rocket. Look—we have no other choice and I can do it."

"When were you planning on telling me?"

"Not today. Not tomorrow. Maybe never."

I race down the stairwell and sprint through the lobby. The Professional Security Guards tell me in Hindi Naushad is not present.

I show them my car key. I point to Grant and make driving motions with both my hands and then point back to myself. They spring into action. The car washer pushes the side mirrors in on both sides of Rocket and backs away. Two guards open the car park gates and the third guard stands right in the middle of the street and stops traffic.

I say a small prayer to Lord Ganesha, drive forward out of the complex, and turn left. We're off!

"Grant, Mommy has to concentrate. Please play the quiet game."

"Okay, Madam," he says.

To my surprise, a small gypsy girl the same age as Grant taps my window at the traffic signal, then smiles and gives me a thumbs-up.

I drive the entire way to ASB with little trouble and a lot of honking. A driver about to leave helps me parallel park and I race Grant inside to his classroom.

When I reappear in the lobby, Naushad is waiting for me. "Madam, you too good. I saw you drive yourself!" He flashes an enormous grin.

Little do I know Pussycat barely missed us. He saw me turn the street corner past Khar Gymkhana and jumped out of a rickshaw and ran after me, yelling, "*madam, no madam, madam, stop the car!*"

When we return home, the guards cheer when they see Rocket survived my first solo run.

Another strand of Christmas lights is out, so I head off to the electric goods store with Naushad at the wheel to buy more lights and three power bars.

On Thursday, I visit Natasha at the salon, where it takes a record four hours to color and cut my hair. On the way home, I call Mary and ask her to pour me a glass of wine and set out a tray of cheese and crackers.

I. Need. To. Meditate.

At the stoplight, my mobile beeps. The text from Wendy reads: "Need2stranglemyself."

I call her.

"My parents are cooped up in my Modern Marble Palace. Dad continues to recover from the dengue fever he caught here, and I need out! Robin has been at work all week." We choke back tears and wonder if this country is finally going to break us. "I know in a couple of hours, if not days, things will get better like they always do. And India will be our love again."

I tell her about driving Rocket.

"Don't mess with Texas," she says, and the crying stops. We promise to get together once her parents return to the States.

Naushad and I drop Grant at swim lessons. On the way home, Naushad tells me he bought outdoor Christmas lights to decorate the balcony.

"Madam, I will put the lights up as soon as we get home."

The air feels chilly as we pull into the car park. I take the lift up, knowing this is our last Christmas in India.

Instead of a having a pity party, I transform the sad feelings into a positive and say, "We're lucky to have one more Kris Kringle event before we go."

After baths, I color and play Candy Land with Grant and Matthew. We enjoy a delicious Italian dinner Mary left for us to reheat, and then it's bedtime for the boys.

I pour a glass of Sula and join Stanley, who is sipping an Old Monk cocktail on the balcony. The neighborhood is quiet. I'm calm, admiring the amount of wiring and silver duct tape Naushad's used to secure thirteen new strings of multi-colored lights. He's outdone himself. The display is radiant, but if I make a wrong move, I'll be electrocuted.

Closing my eyes, I channel Yoga Hottie's wisdom, and breathe.

I am present; therefore, I only think of tonight.

29

Dash down Linking Road
In a broken metered rick,
O'er the tracks we go,
Laughing all the way,
Bells on cows do ring,
Making spirits bright,
What fun it is to ride and sing
A rickshaw tune tonight!

Chorus:
Namaste,
Namaste,
Riding all the way!
What fun it is to ride and sing
In an open rick tonight! Hey!

December is here and the Indian calendar is brimming with festivities. We skip the ASB Family Fun Day and spend the evening at the Grand Hyatt for the official Christmas tree-lighting ceremony. Santa rolls into the marbled courtyard in a tricked-out convertible rickshaw smothered in white lights, and the cold air conditioning dupes us into thinking it's winter.

Hark! The expat children sing
Glory to the twenty-five-foot tree!

After the boys are asleep, I wrap Christmas presents and review the grocery list:

- Cheddar from New Zealand, Rs 77
- Ham from Belgium (seven slices), Rs 100
- Mozzarella from Denmark, Rs 180

- Double-stuffed Oreos from Canada, Rs 290
- Cream of asparagus soup from Malaysia, Rs 75
- Ritz crackers from Singapore, Rs 90
- Pickles from Germany, Rs 120
- Baby corn from Thailand, Rs 70
- Chickpeas from Italy, Rs 60
- You'd Butter Believe It (instead of I Can't Believe It's Not Butter) from Ireland, Rs 250

Then I review the holiday selections from the Grand Hyatt and the JW. Each dinner includes chestnut or corn stuffing, potatoes, vegetables, gravy, rolls, and soup.

My two favorites:

- Boneless Honey-Baked Ham—a whopping $423
- Cherrywood-Roasted Christmas Duck with giblet gravy—$115

Stanley tells me to order the duck dinner.

"In your dreams."

An article in the newspaper last month detailed the flamingo-poaching epidemic in national parks. The meat is sold to shops as duck.

"Stanley, the only quack-quack meat I eat is the Peking Duck at China House because I can see the real deal hanging upside down in the rotisserie ovens."

He does the head wiggle.

For dessert, I can also order a "Yuletide" or "Festive" hamper with items such as marzipan stollen, dry fruit log, lebkuchen prune, panettone, mince pie, gingerbread, and sparkling wine. The word "hamper" frightens me because a hamper in Texas is a place we put dirty clothes.

Maybe it's best I purchase a turkey from HyperCITY, bake traditional sides in my Easy Bake Oven, and place an order for giblet gravy and crab bisque. Mary will have the day off.

The following morning, Wendy drops off two fancy gingerbread houses—one for Naushad's daughter and one for the Erwin brothers—and Christmas cookies from the Oberoi Hotel in Nariman Point. The sugar cookies in the shapes of bells, ornaments, and mittens are beautifully decorated with white icing. Grant and Matthew hug Madam Wendy, and Neelam and Mary are in awe that the items are edible.

Before leaving, Wendy spills the beans: she has visa renewal issues. "My only two options are fly to Houston and miss my trip to Thailand and Australia, or stay over eight days in Bangkok on the return leg and pray the Indian consulate processes my application in the allotted time. India is not my love, Madam Rhonda."

I agree.

The Indian company processing her visa didn't do its job. It makes me think of Mr. Sanjay, who still owes me seventy-five dollars because he didn't do his job either.

"Go for the second option and I will visit. By the way, I almost enrolled us in a Medication Camp the other day, but I read the sign wrong. Turns out it's a Meditation Camp. Since the swag bags won't have pharmaceuticals, I decided against it."

She giggles. "You're too much, Liz."

During the night, I wake up to a piercing scream. My head is spinning. I race down the hallway. Matthew is agitated and he can't see.

I jerk him out of the crib and take his temperature. It's 103.6!

Stanley isn't sure what to do.

Given the hour, I reluctantly call Dr. M, who says it sounds like pinkeye. I write down the name of the medicine he mentions and graciously thank him for accepting my call.

The two pharmacies within walking distance are closed, and Asian Chemists, which operates twenty-four hours, is located seaside from 16th Road. I can drive the car, but I can't remember how to navigate the four-lane road with a divider down the center to separate the two directions of traffic—not that there would be traffic at this hour. But I'm exceedingly nervous. Chances of getting a rickshaw are zero. I can jog to Asian Chemists, but I don't know how safe it would be at night.

I need my bodyguard. But instead, I reach out to Neelam. I can't believe my luck.

Within minutes, she and Matkar, her so-called "friend," walk into the car park. I hand him the keys and off we go, quick, quick, to Asian Chemists. Back at Oberoi Crest, I offer rupees as a tip for their services, but they decline. (For the record, I'm a better driver than Matkar—just saying.)

The power is off again and I have to walk up the stairwell using my mobile as a flashlight. The following morning, Dr. M and Dr. L are on the scene. Matthew has a cold and pinkeye.

Dr. L asks, "Where is Grant?"

"Uh-oh, at ASB."

Sternly he says, "Send Naushad to pick up Grant now. You're acting like an Indian mum. The Erwin family shouldn't be exposing the students and staff to pinkeye!"

Suddenly, I'm seven years old again and my grandfather is scolding me for letting my three-year-old brother get too close to the indoor gas heater.

As I hand over 1,500 rupees for the house call ($38.46), my mobile rings. It's the ASB nurse demanding I retrieve my son at once because he has pinkeye.

"My driver is on his way!" I say apologetically.

Instantly my mobile beeps. Before I can say goodbye, I see a school-wide text alert: "Warning! Warning! Parents and Staff: Student Grant Erwin has conjunctivitis. Please take precautions."

G-R-A-T-E.

Now the entire ASB community knows what a terrible mother I am.

No sooner do the doctors leave than Neelam storms furiously into the Mini Marble Palace.

"The guards told me my Matthew has pinkeye. Madam, the school is full of nasty children who spread germs. Please keep the boy home and he can play with me while I clean," she says adamantly.

I have a throbbing headache.

Hesitantly, I call Matthew's teacher to report his absence. She has to use a courier to deliver letters to all the parents about the health risk. She confirms pinkeye is a huge problem, but her hands are tied. Moreover, because Indian mothers pay the tuition, they think it's their right to send the kids to school even when they are not feeling well or sick.

Stopping at the main intersection where Turner Road meets SV Road, Naushad and I observe gypsies selling Santa hats and stockings. I grin when the kids start singing "Jingle Bells" at my window. They don't know all the words, but it reminds me of last year when a small gypsy girl sang to me and then gave me the finger because I didn't tip her.

Naushad is chatty, and we continue south toward the Gateway. He tells me his daughter's school project is to decorate a small cardboard sleigh and create a Santa Claus out of tissue paper and plastic. He and his wife don't comprehend the assignment.

"Did you find an adult who can decipher the directions in the English to help?"

He glances at me with a blank stare. I'm thinking, thinking, too much thinking—surely this isn't the first time this has happened.

His wife completed high school, but the curriculum was in Hindi. She can't read or speak English, so between the two of them, they make do for Firoza. I notice he picks up his mobile to make a call when I step out of Rocket.

Once inside Lifestyle, one of India's moderately priced leading department stores, I spot precisely what I need for the boys and Stanley. I'm keyed up there is gift-wrapping, and I love my India today. I watch the clerks carefully prepare each package with holiday paper and a bow. It's not Saks Fifth Avenue or even Kmart quality, and they don't use boxes for things that aren't sold in a box, but it's free.

Second stop is Big Bazaar. I score the usual grocery items I can't find in Khar West. Additionally, the eight-to-one ratio of employees to shoppers does not bother me because I'm on a stress-free roll now that I've knocked out the gift list. After I pay the bill and climb into Rocket, Naushad turns up the new Om Shanti Om disc I bought in Thailand from a street vendor.

"Madam, can I tell you something?"

I do the head wiggle.

"Madam, Swami call Naushad while you too much buying in Big Bazaar, and he's too mad at Crazy Madam. She stayed out late while Boss Nick gone. Drinking, drinking, too much drinking, Madam, and then walking to find Swami watching a DVD not answering calls," he says, giggling.

"Then Crazy Madam yelling, yelling, too much loud yelling, Madam. Swami give keys to her to drive herself." He slaps his thigh, snorting with laughter. "Crazy Madam too mad, then gives Swami 2,000 rupees to get in the car and drive her home. Madam, he did this drive home, but not out of respect."

Never. A. Dull. Moment.

In honor of the season, I purchase spare *chaat* and deliver it to the Alert Security Team at Le Gardenia. They tell Naushad they miss Madam and Boss. I inquire about Manu, Head of the Alert Security Team. We're told he "remains in his village, his uncle expired, and he won't return until January."

Okay.

Total cost to deliver esprit de corps: 180 rupees.

Tanu waves to me as she drives out of the car park with a new driver. I miss her. I look at my watch: 6:45 p.m. I've been gone seven hours. I'm tired. I tell Naushad to head home. He's drained, too. He lets me know his wife spoke to a teacher and now they know how to complete his daughter's project.

"*Theek hai,* Madam."

I exit the car and before I step into the lift, he hands me back the *Spider-man* DVD he watched during my shopping spree.

"Madam, this good movie. Very, very good movie, but I cannot believe this man exists. Have you seen this man in America?"

I squint to see if he put those opium drops in his eyes again and I step forward out of the lift and say slowly, "Naushad, this is a Hollywood movie and Spiderman is a comic book character. He's fiction. A writer made him up."

He lowers his head and gets quiet.

We inhale. We exhale.

He hits the elevator button for me again and as I step in, I turn around pursuing this further, "But you were joking with me, silly bodyguard!"

Rapidly, he says, "Yes, yes, Madam. You are correct." He adds, "Thank you, Madam."

It's Wednesday, and down in the car park Naushad tells me the service reassigned Swami to a new family.

"Crazy Madam said naughty words to service and wants Swami back," he says, "Madam, Swami had to switch numbers like this, like that, Crazy Madam too much calling him. Madam, she calling me, she bribing drivers for his number."

"Naushad, do drivers talk about her in Hindi?"

"Madam, she no understands. All drivers hate Crazy Madam."

"Do you ever talk about your Madam in Hindi?"

He winks. "Never."

We're on our way to pick up Wendy, and then Annette, and we're off to the potluck Christmas luncheon at the American Consulate for AWC and INDUS members. (INDUS International is an inclusive group founded to foster relationships between Indian (IND) and American (US) women. Each board position has both an Indian and American counterpart.)

Naushad drops us at the security gate and we take the oldest lift in the country up to the residence level and deposit our savory dishes on the kitchen countertop. In addition, we pay 100 rupees per person for wine punch.

Before we left Austin, I fantasized about wearing fashionable *saris* to galas and social soirees at the consulate every weekend. Two words: Not. Happening.

In other words, I have no society gatherings on my calendar—just AWC monthly coffee gatherings, potluck lunches, and board meetings. The galas and balls are held at the US Embassy in New Delhi and we're not on the invitation list, despite our social status back in the River City.

Wendy, Annette, and I quickly get to work at the check-in table.

When it's time for the luncheon to begin, we join hands and say grace. However, when the wine punch hits the table, the INDUS members are not elated we didn't label the dishes "veg" and "non-veg."

I whisper in Annette's ear, "This meal represents traditional American Christmas dishes and that's why we didn't skimp on the meat!"

I turn around and roll my eyes at Wendy.

She mouths, "More wine punch."

Before heading back to the north side of the city, we stop at Nature's Basket and hit the jackpot. We purchase grapefruits, wine from California, and candy canes, of all things. Who knew you would miss candy canes during the month of December?

In fact, their lights are up, they have a large decorated Fraser fir, and fake snow garlands hang from the ceiling. Plus, Mannheim Steamroller plays loudly through corner speakers.

"Girls, it feels like we're in New York City!"

It's Thursday morning. Wendy and I discuss shopping plans and logistics. We determine Naushad will stay behind to pick up the Erwin brothers from school. Rajesh and Naushad give each other an exuberant high five in the car park and we're off!

Wendy says, "Rajesh, you and Naushad have the best Madams in all of India."

He snickers. "Yes, Madam. Best Madams not in India, but the world."

We're set to meet Binaka for lunch at East Pan Asian, the top Malaysian restaurant in town, down south.

Meanwhile, sitting in traffic, Wendy has her *Easy Hindi for the Tourist* book out and we're pronouncing phrases.

"Kitne paise lagte hain?" (How much does it cost?)

Rajesh agrees. "Very, very good phrase for best Madams in the universe."

Then Wendy says, "Rajesh, *Tum samajhte ho ki, main lakhpati hun?*" which means "Rajesh, do you think I am a millionaire?" and we giggle. Rajesh is laughing, laughing, too much laughing at us trying to speak Hindi.

Suddenly we stop at a traffic signal, and the *magazine wallah* runs over to the car. He's selling the new December issue of *Elle*. We pay 500 rupees and the *magazine wallah* hands the two copies to Rajesh.

Like ladies of leisure, we open our magazines in sync. There, on page 184 is heartthrob Dino wearing a plaid suit. He's listed as one of "India's 50 Most Stylish" but he looks like he pulled an all-nighter before the photography gig. On page 194 is Robin's friend Rahul. Now, *he's* definitely stylish, wearing a bomber jacket, aviators, and boots in the magazine's indoor style spread. Wendy shoots off a text to Rahul giving him a hard time. I send a text: "Dino, not as cool as Rahul on page 194, but party on!" He immediately replies back: "How's my favorite Desperate Housewife of Mumbai?"

Rajesh almost wrecks the car when I show him the message, but he gains control and stops at the next signal. This time, a younger *magazine wallah* in a red *Elle* tee holds up the anniversary issue with a pin inside and points to the cost printed on the magazine: seventy-five rupees. He wants to make a sale.

No way! We got ripped off! Rajesh is in stitches and can barely breathe, much less drive, at the same time. He says, *"Yah bahut zyada hai!"* which translates to "This is too much!" "You two Madams too much. Too, too much for Rajesh."

I look at Wendy, "When did he start talking about himself in third person?"

TGIF! The official countdown to Christmas starts now.

Lolita is here to clean the bathrooms. She tells me in Hindi she's thrilled with the arrival of her new grandson—finally, a boy in the family. She explains that she touched Matthew's feet every time she cleaned the flat, and she went to temple every weekend; Lord Ganesha answered her prayers. Mary translates the entire story to me, just like she always does.

"Madam, please taste this casserole. I baked it with fresh spices from the Santa Cruz market," calls Mary. I walk into the kitchen and she holds out a spoonful of food.

"Why can't you taste it?"

"I'm fasting."

I grin. "Me too."

A courier delivers an invitation. Jiri, our talented artist friend and Caron's husband, is showcasing his new work at the Hyatt Regency. The reception invitation he designed is stunning.

My mobile beeps. Naushad is ready to pick up Grant from school. We cruise onto Linking Road with relatively no traffic and stop by Pukar Printing Press to pick up a stationery order. After I pay the bill, the Muslim owner gives me a free calendar and six notepads, thankful for my business. Naushad beams with pride when I show him the free stuff.

At the intersection, I remind him all the shop owners, whether Hindu or Muslim, like Madam, except for the Muslim Boss who runs the Something Special Shop on Hill Road and never gives me the correct change. Naushad shrugs. He is done listening to me rant over a few rupees. Now he wants to talk politics.

I say, "S-T-O-P."

"Don't stress out. America is full of C-H-E-A-T-E-R-S too." He peers at me in the rearview mirror.

We pull up to the traffic signal and there is Jolly Driver waiting for the light to change. I wave and Naushad rolls down his window and speaks Hindi. He got too scared of "The Don," who is back in Mumbai after his short stint in Pakistan, and does not drive for Miss T anymore.

Naushad delivers me to the ASB front entrance, where I walk in and pick up Grant. I ask if he wants to stop and get a snack at McDonald's. He tells me he's fasting.

Good. Grief.

Before driving home, Naushad pulls into Citibank because I need rupees from the cash bin. Grant leans over and says, "Mom, do you need to buy things?" Naushad starts giggling and then I have to laugh too. Then Grant can't control himself either.

"You guys think all I do is spend rupees?"

They're still utterly amused with themselves.

"Who do you think I shop for? Most of the time it's for you two meatheads!"

I swear, when we're back in Austin, Grant and Matthew will never remember I ran a household in a developing country and had an elephant delivered to our flat. They won't remember I found the only bakery that sold Pop Tarts. And, I guess they won't remember the countless hours I stayed awake at night praying that they'd never catch a deadly virus. What they will remember is that I shopped every day for jewelry and tunics.

An hour later, I change into my big girl pants, but they feel snug. I weighed at the JW and I'm not happy.

Wendy phones to see if the AWC board meeting is canceled.

"I don't care about the status of the meeting. What I care about is that I've gained six pounds."

She cackles, "Liar."

I'm not in the mood to joke. "Madam Wendy, I might need to take up South Indian food to lose weight."

"I've gained weight too, but I have a better idea—tapeworms from Crawford Market. I'll shove one into a vegetarian burger and another one into a non-vegetarian sandwich for you in honor of our INDUS friends from the consulate lunch. Either way, we'll get sick and lose pounds without having to diet."

Perfect. I phone Naushad.

"Pussycat, I need you to go buy two tapeworms from Crawford Market right now." He starts laughing, laughing, too much laughing, and he replies, "Madam, *Tum badmash ho*," meaning "Madam, you are a rascal," and hangs up.

Before the day ends, Boss and I go to temple. Heading home as the sun begins to set, we see our street is busy with activity, and Diwali lights still strung on buildings and at intersections shine bright. We see trees through windows in various flats adorned with ornaments and lanterns. We take the lift up and the boys race to greet us at the door.

"Madam, what did you wish for in the rat's ear?" Stanley asks.

"Global peace."

He does the head wiggle.

"Boss, what did you wish for?"

Without hesitating, he says, "The list is long...

- Please give us the ability to use tap water and not get polio.
- Can we have rupees without wings?
- Can we get lights in our flat that work?
- Can our landlord provide us with a full-time geyser you don't have to switch on daily to provide hot water?
- Can we get cable that works and provides something other than *Animal Planet*?
- Can you send visitors from America? (They don't even have to bring anything.)
- And, is it possible to get a surprise gift hamper containing six pork chops, two bottles of Jordan Chardonnay, a tube of AIM toothpaste, a large bag of tortilla chips, seven avocados, eighteen Taco Bell seasoning packets, a fire truck for Matthew, a portable DVD player for Grant, three boxes of Cheese Nips, and a case of double-ply Charmin?"

On Saturday we attend the last of the swim lessons for the year, and on Sunday we rest.

On Monday, Naushad and I pick up Madam Wendy before driving down Linking Road and turning northbound into traffic. Forty minutes later, he drops us at the entrance to HyperCITY. Inside, bird prices are now more than the hotel turkey prices. In fact, we see most of the items are cooked. Christmas is days away. Yikes!

Wendy and I venture into the gourmet area and the foul smell reminds me of the Koli fish and shrimp staples. A worker holds up a smoked chicken that looks like roadkill. Wendy grabs turkey loaf for Robin and exits the area, leaving me gasping for air. I nod "no" to the worker and call Hannah to inform her we cannot, under any circumstances, purchase food from Hyper-CITY for Christmas dinners.

After lunch, we drop Wendy at her building, make the block around Khar Gymkhana, and drive to Oberoi Crest. Boss calls me from his office, and I tell him to buy four Santa hats from the gypsies at the traffic signal on his way home. Grant needs one for the Christmas assembly and we need extras for photo ops.

It's Wednesday and on the way to Little Butterflies, we spot Father Christmas on a motorbike. Matthew screams, *"I want santa, Mummy!"*

Neelam and Boss agree to pick up Matthew and Grant: I'm on my last mission possible—gifts for teachers.

With list in hand, I jump into Rocket. Naushad has my undivided attention. He's talkative and I sneer when I notice he locks the doors and windows each time a *magazine wallah* approaches. We're passing a section of the city where they sell poultry—probably the same white meat Foodland sells, just in fancier packaging.

"Naushad, did you see what those chickens were eating?"

He smiles.

"My New Year's resolution is to go veg like Madam Wendy."

He laughs. "Madam Wendy smart, Madam." Then he says, "Madam, can I tell you something?"

What now?

He looks at me in the rearview mirror. "Madam, one whole year you say this and you still eat chicken. When are you *really* going to stop eating the small white bird, Madam?"

I inhale and glare at him. "Frankly, I've wondered that myself!"

When I exit the car at the entrance to Shopper's Stop, I say under my breath, "Gosh, my legs are like sausages in these jeans." I hear a chuckle in the background and turn to see Naushad holding court. I spin around and he freezes. "Are you thinking what I'm thinking, bodyguard?"

He laughs out loud in front of the Shopper's Stop security guards.

"Seriously, Madam," he says, flapping his arms like a chicken.

I race through the department store and purchase stocking stuffers and gift certificates. I stop by Citibank and the cleaners and pick up lunch at

Subway. Grateful to be done, we pull into the car park where Grant is riding his bike. "Little Boss, we saw Santa Claus on a motorbike driving along Bandstand Promenade."

He's confused by this announcement. He saw Santa at the tree-lighting ceremony at the Grand Hyatt and he doesn't understand why he's still in town.

"Grant, you've seen the construction in Khar West. Santa needs to stick around to figure out his flight plan, then submit it to the Chhatrapati Shivaji International Airport."

He interrupts me, "Momma, his cook needs to pack him a good tiffin because he will sit in traffic." He adds, "They better have new batteries for Santa or Rudolph won't be able to land the sleigh."

Friday is a key day for us. Naushad is off to celebrate *Eid al-Adha*. On this day, Muslims commemorate and remember Abraham's trials by slaughtering an animal such as a sheep, camel, or goat. Sacrificial goats around the neighborhood are blessed with colored powders in bright shades like green or pink.

The meat from the sacrifice is divided: immediate family and relatives get one-third, one-third is given to friends, and one-third is donated to the poor. The act symbolizes the willingness to give up things that are of benefit to them or meaningful in order to follow Allah's commands.

The day drags on because I'm not running errands or doing much of anything, because I have no driver or car. Mary serves a mediocre dinner. She's been consistently late all week.

"Mary, if you're searching for a new job, fine, just let us know so we can hire another person. Do not leave us hanging with two small children."

"Madam, I'm helping my sister who got fired find another job. She needs me."

"Mary, you must show up on time. You are getting a full salary for part-time hours. Plus, I don't like talking about food every day. Remember—you can take cookbooks home or make notes in Hindi to prepare daily menus."

"It isn't my fault I don't understand all the recipes. I worked for a Japanese family before you." Then she bows, says, "Konichiwa," and disappears into the kitchen. I glance around the flat to see if I'm on *Candid Camera*. She peeks out of the kitchen, breaking the tension in the room.

"Konichiwa means 'hello' and Grant says this to his classmate Satoshi from Japan."

"If you can speak and read Japanese better than English, then I'll order Japanese cookbooks from Amazon and have them shipped to future visitors for you to use."

She waves me off.

I skip to the loo and grab a hand towel and scream into it. Then I look into the mirror and smile at the girl I see. "Can't pull the wool over my eyes!"

I tuck Grant and Matthew into bed. Stanley's busy on a conference call.

I confirm reservations for Christmas Day brunch at the Grand Hyatt and check email. It's a note from Wendy. It reads:

> *Dear Rhonda:*
> *Rajesh is pointing out bad things that Muslims do each day because he's jealous Naushad got to drive to the airport to pick up Mom and Dad. He forgets he went to the airport with Robin at the same time but that is not the point. So, the past week he's been in rare form. For example, we stopped at the traffic signal and he saw a man stealing apples. He pointed and said, "Madam, Muslim right there, cheater." And then he pointed to a daily urinator, saying, "Muslim." Finally I told him we have Muslim friends and Naushad is an amazing driver. He must stop his crazy behavior. He persisted. So, we passed by Shah Rukh Khan's house yesterday and I pointed and said, "Muslim." SRK is his all-time favorite Bollywood actor. He freaked out and almost rear-ended a rickshaw. Rajesh was born in India and he knows SRK is Muslim, but it didn't deter him. I finally threatened to tell Robin on him. Then, yesterday on my way to Judy's flower-arranging class, he whispers to me while holding the car door open: "Madam, Shah Rukh Khan—non-practicing Muslim." I have one question that continues to elude me: where is the respect, and why aren't we getting any?*
> *Love,*
> *Wendy*

I shut down the computer and present Mary with a birthday present, a small Christmas bonus, and an Indian Barbie for her daughter before she leaves for the day. In return, she hands me an envelope containing 1,000 rupees to buy chocolates and gifts for the boys. Clearly overpaid.

Saturday is a blur of last-minute wrapping. Lolita shows up to clean the floors and when I present her with a gift from the boys, she kisses my feet again. She is thankful and as always, pulls out the front of her *sari* blouse and tucks the rupees into her bra.

On Sunday we take a rickshaw to the brunch at the JW Marriott and have the honor of meeting Bollywood actor Rishi Kapoor, a main character in *Fanaa*.

Back home, Grant says he's sad ASB friends are leaving to move to other countries, but he's thrilled about the three new students his class will welcome in January. We sort through holiday cards from Koke, Maddy, Emily, Ben, Isabelle, and Julia.

"Mom, I miss Austin friends," he says. Seven minutes later, he and Matthew return with packed suitcases full of toys and pajamas.

"Mom, we're flying to Texas for Christmas," they say in unison.

Speaking of flying, texts are racing across mobiles with season's greetings and farewells and final goodbyes as expats leave the city. Grayson and his parents left India last month to move back to the UK. Sophie's parents are leaving next week to move to Germany. In January, Crazy Madam and her family are headed to Panama. It's time to shift to other posts or return home, wherever that may be.

I love Wendy's message: "Just got the new Vogue magazine to read on the plane, and SRK's wife is on the cover. I showed Rajesh and told him Hindu woman married to Muslim man. See…Hindus and Muslims can get along. I got him! Merry Christmas."

My favorite text is from one of Stanley's employees leaving to visit family in Detroit. It reads: "Merry Christmas, Stain!"

It's Christmas Eve Day and Neelam shows up to work for a few hours. She immediately picks up Matthew and takes him into the kitchen to feed him rice and eggs. As I pass by on my way to Grant's room, I see him put his hands to his mouth to signal he's hungry. Then he says, *"Mujhe do,"* which means, "give me."

OMG! He just spoke Hindi.

I watch Neelam give him milk after he points to the refrigerator. He acts like the gypsy kids who beg for food. Gosh, I hope he doesn't break out into "Jingle Bells."

The next thing you know, he gets his little red chair and pulls it up to the counter. Then he points to the three pieces of apple on his plate and counts, *"ek, do, tin."* He just spoke Hindi again.

Neelam catches me watching. "Madam, I know they speak Hindi to him at school and I also speak Hindi to him. It's good for Little Boss."

Naushad calls. He needs *chai* and wants to know when I plan on coming downstairs because he's tired of waiting for me. "Madam, I worry you leave on June fourth," he adds.

I wonder why in the heck he's worried about something five months away; obviously he doesn't have much going on. He must have overheard me tell Wendy our departure date.

"Fourth unlucky day. Four peoples together on the fourth, I don't feel good about this departure, Madam," he says. "You change tickets and consult a monk or a guru before booking new tickets. You like guru talk like this, like that."

"Naushad, I consulted Boss and we're leaving at 2:30 a.m.—officially June fifth—so go have *chai* and stop worrying and calling me. I will get down to the car park when I get down to the car park."

The trash guy knocks on the door and collects the garbage. A Professional Security Guard knocks twice and I sign the Great Big Book of Everything. He hands over holiday cards sent from America.

Suddenly I realize I forgot to buy a nativity scene for Matthew—the one thing he seems interested in that Grant has in his room.

Naushad and I race up to Hill Road. When Naushad pulls Rocket over and rolls down my window, I ask the man selling manger figurines what the going rate is for his remaining inventory spread out on two pieces of plywood. He's confused and hands me a tree topper. I do the head wiggle.

Naushad speaks Hindi, talking over my English, and the man disappears behind a storefront and returns with ornaments. I feel like I'm in a Three Stooges comedy act.

Finally, I point to the manger and say loudly in my cheerleader voice, "Where is Baby Jesus and his people?"

The man grins and tells me slowly, "Jesus is gone Madam, and he won't be back until next year."

Good to know.

Naushad drives to Sante and parks while I run in to buy whipping cream and imported butter. When I walk out, I try to open the car door but it's the wrong Innova. I can't find Naushad.

I turn to the left and see nothing but locals walking down the street. I turn to the right and see Rocket 100 feet away, surrounded by approximately fifty men. I walk toward the group and Naushad and a drunken teenager are fighting. A Hindu uncle turns to me and says, "Your Muslim driver hit the Hindu guy first and the fight broke out."

Seriously? I push my way into the center of the circle to find Naushad choking the teen, but he stops when he sees me.

I shout, "*Kya bat hai?*" which translates to "What is the matter?"

Cars are honking and honking, too much honking, and now a hundred locals are staring at us.

I walk backward right into Milan's son, who has stepped out of Sante to check on the commotion. He tells me to get into the car and lock the door. The teenager walks away, but Naushad is shaking. He's embarrassed and mad. I've never seen him like this before. We drive off in silence. He finally speaks to me when he parks the car at Oberoi Crest.

"Madam, I needed to back up the car. I honked the horn like this, like that, and he not move," he says. "I laid on horn and he hit our brake light cover with a whiskey bottle and broke it."

Then he tells me when he got out of the car, there was pushing and an exchange of bad words. The guy pushed him down. Then Naushad got up and popped him. Then I walked out of Sante.

I take one look at him. His shirt is untucked and soiled, and two buttons are loose. His shoes are muddy and his hair is ruffled. He slams the door and tells me he's going home.

I exhale.

"You're not leaving. You need a beer because you kicked ass on Christmas Eve!"

He stands still, staring at me.

"V-I-C-T-O-R-Y! Victory is your battle cry!"

Slowly he grins.

"Look, a drunk teen will not ruin our day. It's a light cover, for crying out loud. Shake it off!"

I take the lift up and he parks Rocket.

Seven minutes pass and he walks through the flat door I've left open and removes his shoes and dress shirt. Neelam sews on the two buttons while he cleans up in the servant's quarters. He returns in his undershirt with hair coiffed, smelling like musk Axe Deodorant Body Spray. Stanley hands him a cold Kingfisher.

He accepts the beverage and kudos, but I sense he's uncomfortable drinking in front of Boss.

Neelam collects her gifts and says goodbye. While she waits in the foyer with Naushad for the lift, I tell her, "No more calling Naushad 'Pussycat' in my presence. He's skinny, but he has the eye of a tiger!"

After baths, I cook sides in the Easy Bake Oven and serve the pre-cooked Christmas Eve dinner items and the sliced smoked turkey from Sante. The boys, in pajamas, put milk, cookies, and reindeer food—colored rice—next to the tree for Santa to give to his staff.

We read *The Night Before Christmas* and tuck the boys in. The Mini Marble Palace is still. The Christmas lights on the balcony are glowing. Our simple tree is beautiful. I notice one strand flashes blue and green—the red and yellow lights have burned out.

I wave to the family on the fourth floor across the street, with a small tree lit up. They wave back. Someone has turned off the Bollywood tunes downstairs and "Silent Night" plays softly.

Climbing into bed, I pull up the crisp cotton sheets, lean over, and whisper in Stanley's ear, "Santa Baby, hurry down Linking Road tonight!"

30

With January approaching, a new beginning hasn't weighed this heavily on me since I graduated from college in the early nineties when job prospects were dismal.

The past year has turned out to be the most defining time of my life. I'm no longer a stranger in a weird land dealing with the extremes of vulnerability.

Freedom lit a fire. It forced me to let go of mistakes and cut myself some slack.

So, with four days left in the year, I take stock. I do something I've never done before: set achievable goals—which is powerful and uplifting.

Brrrrring, Brrrrring. Wendy is calling from Bangkok. "How was Christmas, Madam?"

"Santa brought gems, Stanley got a trip to Nepal, and the Erwin brothers got toys sold in Crawford Market. But my most-loved gifts were a text from Mr. Carpenter Man saying 'Marry X'Mas From=Carpenter'; a bundle of day-old orchids from Matkar with a card that said 'To: Rhonda 'N' Family, Marry Criesmas, From: Matkar' (the only person who can spell my "good name" correctly); and a hot apple pie from Milan at Sante.

"The Lord Ganesha delivered too: we've got guests. Steve, one of Stanley's business college fraternity brothers, and his significant other Tim, from Colorado, will be spending the next few days exploring Mumbai before they fly to Jodhpur with Boss. They'll shop for furniture and bring in the New Year at the grand party held at the Mehrangarh Fort."

"What will you and the boys do?"

"We'll celebrate Neelam's fortieth birthday and lie low. I ordered a cake from the JW bakery, and I bought a pair of gold hoops and a new tunic for the boys to gift her."

"How does she feel about turning the big four-O?"

"Resigned—another year of singledom; too old for an arranged marriage."

We're catching up on our sleep, eating delicious seafood, and breathing unpolluted air in sunny and rustic Bali.

Once again, we forgot to check the weather. It's monsoon season. Light showers early in the mornings or late in the evenings consume our days. Grant and Matthew sprint freely on the hotel's pristine green lawns and putt-putt course. Matthew spends most of his spare time raking the sand traps, but the staff doesn't seem to mind. In addition, they're delighted to discover *Blue's Clues*, *Dora the Explorer*, and *The Backyardigans* on TV in English.

I catch Neelam making the beds. Gently, I remind her about housekeeping as I watch her stash the usual haul of toiletries into her suitcase—and that is how Neelam rolls at the Ritz Carlton.

Over breakfast one morning, we remember the National College Championship game will be televised. Right away, I send a text to friends in Texas: "What time is kick-off?" hoping to find out the network sponsor and game time. Neelam doesn't understand why we flew to Bali to watch cartoons and football.

At the pool we meet an American couple and they join us for midday conversation and cocktails.

I inhale. I exhale.

The boys are content splashing in the pool.

Lathering on sunscreen, I hear my mobile beep. It's a text from John: "Now."

I reply back, "In Bali. Got cable. What channel?"

"Fox Sports."

Ruh-roh!

We get Fox News.

I send another text: "Out of luck."

Our drinks arrive and my mobile beeps again.

It's a text from John about the NCAA game: "10-3 for OSU; 2:21 left in first quarter."

This is mind-blowing. I feel like I'm in outer space receiving a text from earth.

Our new friends from Indiana are thrilled to hear the news too. The rest of the people at the pool—Russians, Germans, Australians, Chinese, and Japanese—couldn't care less.

Stanley and William discuss sports and Jennifer asks if we socialize with diplomats at the embassy.

"The American Embassy is in New Delhi. We only party at the consulate," I say.

Not.

We order starters and John sends a text: "LSU: 24; OSU: 10; half."

The afternoon showers stay at bay, but it's humid. The sun is blistering. Stanley and William ask for the third quarter score.

I check my mobile.

I text: "Are you there?" but get no reply.

I check the time.

John Boy is night-night.

An hour later, on the way into town, my mobile beeps: "LSU: 38; OSU: 24; Final. Fell asleep."

The markets are hectic, and it's fun to explore the island. On our way back to the hotel, Wendy sends a text. She's chillin' in Bangkok, hoping her Indian visa comes through, binging on retail therapy.

Two days before we leave, a driver picks me up in the lobby to take me to the Sicilian Spa thirty minutes away for a deluxe treatment. Stanley, off to play eighteen holes with William, assures me he researched spas before we left Mumbai. The Sicilian is top-notch.

The first sign of danger: the driver wants to wait for me. He doesn't think it's "smart idea to leave Madam."

Regardless, I pay the cheap fare, get ready for the complimentary welcome drink, and wonder how bad it can be.

The second sign of danger: no drink.

The salon attendants speak English and nervously hand me the Great Big Book of Available Spa Treatments, and then burst into a fit of laughter. It reads:

> *Wide Range Services, Better & Best Price. Eye Brow Shaping, Body Painting, Detoxification/Ear Candle, Full Body Wax, Body Whitening, Bust Tighten, Infant/Baby Massage, Style/Coil for Hair, Cream Bath, Thai Massage—and my favorite—Slimming Massage.*

Now it makes sense why he didn't book a spa treatment at the Ritz. Stanley wants me to purge the pounds I've packed on.

Take a moment and visualize over the course of two hours lying on a vinyl table in a non-air conditioned straw hut, while a robust, beastly woman slaps, whips, and openly massages and washes your entire body against your free will. Now imagine wanting to yell for help but not, for fear of retribution when you notice bamboo sticks nearby on a chair. *Are those party favors?*

At one point, I can't feel my body from the waist down, but thankfully I can manage to move all my fingers. I will need them to strangle Stanley and poke his eyes out.

Gingerly, I pay the bill, wave down a taxi, and return to the hotel.

Total cost for the Molestation Massage and Skin Stretch Treatment at the Sicilian Spa—$7.89.

Spotting my target at the bar, I yell, "Maybe you had decent intentions, but when the masseuse rode me, then flipped me over on my back and grabbed my breasts, I blew a gasket!"

I call Naushad to check in and see how the car and flat are holding up. He doesn't answer, which surprises me because there is only a two-hour time difference. Hours later, I try to call again but still no answer.

Hmmm.

Lounging on the beach, I discover a Kingfisher Airlines advertisement, (they now fly to Agra) in the December issue of *Elle* magazine, and I make a mental note to email Moe.

Grant interrupts my train of thought. "Momma, we love the water slides, the hot dogs, and the pool. Can we move to Bali?"

I receive a text from Kate. She's in London but is worried the AWC newsletter didn't get delivered over the Christmas break. Wendy is the first to respond. She's headed to the spa and has no idea if the newsletter got delivered. I respond and say I'm in Bali, and yes the newsletter went out before I left. Immediately, an email follows:

> *Hi Gals,*
> *I have to laugh. Wendy's in Bangkok, Kate's in the UK, Rhonda's in Bali, I'm in Arizona but flying to Chicago tomorrow. Our newsletter writer is in Mississippi. Amazing. So, it sounds like the newsletter did get sent out. Aren't we the international bunch? It is funny, isn't it? Do you think there is anyone in Mumbai at the moment? I'm eager to hear about your trips!*
> *Safe travels!*
> *Gail*

I call Naushad again and still, no answer. I had Steve and Tim give him the keys to our flat before they left. I send a text: "Stop having a prayer rave in the flat and call me."

Nothing.

"Call Madam or Ms. Harwani is going to call the police."

Silence.

"Should I be worried?" I ask Stanley.

"He's your driver, and I don't get in the middle of you two."

I exhale.

Now, I'm furious. I remember when the Fat Family at Le Gardenia went out of town and left the flat key with their driver—he threw a party. I know because I was invited. I actually went up to the eighth floor where the drivers and the Sleepy People were drinking Kingfisher and watching cricket while the cook prepared *aloo ki tikki* and lamb curry.

Immediately, I text Yoga Hottie and ask him to stop by the flat if he's in Khar West. Lastly, I call Matkar and let Neelam speak Hindi to him. He's going to call Naushad and go by the building.

Twenty minutes pass.

Straightaway, I get a call from Naushad gasping, "I'm sorry, Madam, very sorry. These numbers no know. Please don't be mad at Naushad."

"You better be telling the truth."

I get off the phone, and Stanley says, "He didn't recognize the number—no big deal. He wouldn't do anything to you because you made it clear at the airport that you would *kill* him if anything happened. Even I was scared."

"He's playing those Jedi Driver mind games with me again."

Boss does the head wiggle. The internet is up and working in the business center so we check email and there is a hysterical note from Liz and Spencer, who visited last fall, which reads:

> *We thought about you a lot this last week while we were in Sri Lanka. We were there for a week and decided it's a lot like India, and your emails over the year made us laugh that much more. Lots of head bobbles, things take forever, there are big books of nothing everywhere, poverty, lots of curry, lots of talking and talking and more talking, even Sleepy People! The main differences are it's much more orderly, has significantly less people, and is a lot smaller. One thing very similar was the smells. We hired a sweet, kind, wonderful driver to take us all around the country for six days in a great car and be there for us on a moment's notice, all for $50 a day (including gas, car, his room/board). The downside was this did not include a shower! By the fourth day, it was unbearable. He smelled SO bad. Spencer and I had a long conversation about who would discuss personal hygiene if we were going to proceed for two more days together. We kept wondering, what would Rhonda do? Spencer adamantly said, "You know Sula Sister would just tell it like it is—'You work for Madam, you must shower.'" So he tried to pull it off: "You work for Spencer, you must shower!" He took one for the team and told him slowly in English, with a lot of sign language he needed a bath. We even bought him a bar of soap. Spencer did a game of charades showing him how to wash his upper body. The next morning he smelled like a spring day—seriously (just like you always say).*

School starts back with a bang: Naushad, tired from celebrating Muharram (New Year's Day on the Islamic calendar) until five o'clock, oversleeps Monday morning.

"Madam, I stayed late at mosque," he says. I hang up on him. Frantically, I help Grant get dressed and head down to the car park.

When I hold up the car keys, the Professional Security Team opens both gates and turns in the side mirrors. Cruising down Linking Road, I spot construction near ASB. I have no clue how to go the back way to reach the campus.

Gosh darn it. I don't panic and follow a Skoda carrying five local kids—they must be heading to DAIS. In the end, we're ten minutes late. Ms. Sally, Grant's teacher, is impressed I can drive. On the other hand, I'm frazzled and wait for Naushad to drive me home. I don't have the energy to get back on the road. When he knocks on my car door asking for the keys, I say, "No more praying on school nights!"

Things are quiet this time of year. Slowly, we begin to schedule after-school activities and coordinate holiday plans for upcoming months, which will include a visit from Stanley's brother. I schedule tennis lessons with Krishna and weight-training classes at the JW, where for 170 rupees, Amol can train me on the circuit weights.

Bye-bye Pravin.

I'm determined to lose weight, since birthday month is around the corner.

There was sunshine in Bali, but winter is here. Long-sleeve tunics and pashminas are out in full force. Yesterday I saw Karishma Kapoor in a fancy scarf and boots at Little Butterflies.

Neelam reports for duty and I hand over her passport. She doesn't think twice about telling me how fat I am or how tired I look, but she completely doesn't care how I write her "good name." I've been spelling it wrong: it's "Nilam." I haven't even noticed until now.

"Why didn't you correct me?"

"No one cares, Madam."

The American Women's Club meeting is being held today in my Mini Marble Palace. I set the table, and Mary helps me display the assortment of mini quiches, fruit salads, and desserts. We're serving mimosas, coffee, juice, and tea. Finally, the five-year-old tea set from Russia is coming in handy. The boys are at school. Mary and Nilam are serving the group. The meeting is long but there's wonderful news: an AWC ball will be held in May.

Wendy stays behind to visit and catch up. She tells me about her trips to Bangkok and Sydney. I love hearing about the Parsi wedding she and Robin attended. She shows me photos of her beautiful *sari* and a party pic of Robin in a turban. "You do know I was the only person wearing costume jewelry!"

"We thought about Pinky while we were in Bali. I'm glad she canceled her wedding, but the reception would have been over-the-top."

Annette returns from kickboxing and we spend the afternoon talking, talking, too much talking about the social ritual we initially endured. All but a few existing expats and mothers at ASB judge you on anything from your style to club memberships to careers. In the end, it makes no difference. Circles are broken and we disperse. Annette will relocate to Hong Kong, and Wendy will move back to Washington—yet despite our differences and histories, we feel a genuine bond. We're part of a handful of women who deal with the pressure and refuse to take ourselves too seriously.

Thursday is here! I'm flying to Jodhpur with Hannah to meet up with Wendy and Baby B for one last girl's trip before our youngest AWC member leaves in February.

Hannah and I land first and gather our bags.

In comes a text from Wendy: "We had a layover in Udaipur. Passengers with chickens needed to deplane!"

Ah, the joys of flying Air India!

Thursday night we sit on the roof of Mehrangarh Fort, drinking Sula and watching the sunset. Out of nowhere, the Royal Mehrangarh Heritage Brass Band appears and serenades us. Wendy and I can't resist the music; and waltz into the middle of the circle the musicians have formed and we boogie down. Laxman joins us to show off his fancy moves. It's a dance party I won't forget.

On Friday, after a day full of shopping, Cathy and Roberto pick us up to meet Bozzo and his first cousin, Princess Baijilal Shivranjani Rajye, at Umaid Bhawan Palace for drinks and dinner.

Over dessert, we tell Cathy we've spent our whole lives referring to ourselves as princesses, but now we know the real princess—the one who lives in a fancy palace and is sitting with us at the table. The night is wonderful and in the end, the princess did what royals do—pick up the tab for the common people.

Saturday is packed with visits to warehouses selling textiles, furniture, and spices. Ishpal, the Four Hands cook, picks up Chinese food and delivers it with lots of Sula to the warehouse we've invaded.

I exhale.

In honor of Republic Day, India's most important national event celebrated on January 26, we break for lunch among the hand-painted trunks, chairs, mirrors, and cabinets and raise our glasses and vegetarian eggrolls to toast the homeland. On this day in 1950 the constitution of India came into force and India became a truly sovereign, democratic republic.

My fortune reads: *Go for it. You never know whom you might run into.*

Cathy calls to confirm dinner reservations and we head back to the Four Hands house to shower. In our haste to leave the city, we forgot to check the weather, not realizing this time of year it's freezing in the desert. The temperature is forty-eight degrees—the coldest day in Jodhpur in forty-five years.

The night before, Wendy and Binaka had discussed attending a Parsi wedding wearing *sari* blouses with sleeves like the grandmothers and aunties who were in attendance. The modern women wore sexy Bollywood tops baring lots of skin. Wendy told the group, "We looked like the girls from the village." And, after drinking too much, she began to introduce herself to guests late in the evening as "Wendy from the Willage," and that is how my

Sula Sister rolls at Parsi weddings.

Consequently, I've borrowed a sweater and a scarf Wendy wore on Friday. Binaka is fashionable, wearing a long-sleeve tee and socks with ballet flats, and Wendy has two pashminas wrapped around her torso. Hannah has on a men's jacket and a hat she bought in the market.

Two hours later, Laxman drops us.

The second the princess sees us, she says, "Oh look, it's the girls from the village again."

The Nepalese cook prepares an incredible meal under the stars. During dessert, we meet one of India's 50 Most Stylish—Raghavendra Rathore, (page 189 from the December issue of *Elle* magazine) and his beautiful wife Kavita, who arrived late from a wedding.

The cold weather is here to stay. Back in Mumbai, Monday rolls around and Stanley leaves for Canada and Texas. The week flies by with food orders, the geyser leaking onto the dryer, water leaking in the bathroom from the ceiling again, and the washing machine breaking down.

When Stanley calls to check in, I say, "I've got Carpenter Man hanging new artwork, Mr. Plumber Man rigging the geyser with string, Lolita cleaning the bathrooms, Mary testing new Junior League recipes, Nilam ironing tunics, and the Chotu Veg Guy delivering asparagus. Naushad is out filling up Rocket with petrol. Matthew is snoring and Grant is working on a Lego project. Also, the consulate issued a warning of possible terrorist attacks, urging Americans and Canadians to stay put, so the cable is out and internet services continue to go down."

I add, "Nilam and I filled up the bathtub and four buckets with tap water."

He promises to be home in seven days and is in a rush to hang up. Nilam makes *chai* and my mobile rings.

Again.

Caller #1: An expat friend ranting about living in India. She's lived down south for five years.

Caller #2: An ASB mum furious over her broken dishwasher. I tell her I don't own a dishwasher and to use common sense, and buy some paper plates, order out, and call Vijay Sales.

Caller #3: A neighbor. I don't pick up. Nilam and I shake our heads—she's dialed my number fourteen times. "Maybe she likes listening to my hello tune from Om Shanti Om?" I say. "For now, I've had enough. I'm taking a walk around Khar Gymkhana. I need to get away from the morons calling to whine day in, day out."

"But Madam, now you're going out with millions of morons on the streets."

Nilam makes me laugh.

I turn left out of the car park and head down 16th Road. I pass three cows and wave to the man who fixes the zippers on our suitcases. A gypsy woman I don't recognize approaches me, begging for rupees. I show her my pockets are empty, and a young Muslim boy in *kurta* pajamas at the bus stop yells at her in Hindi to leave me alone. I'm not a tourist.

All the roads around my street are torn up and construction workers are working slowly to fill potholes. I make the corner and the Nepalese owner in the shanty snack shack on my street corner holds up eggs and bread. He speaks Hindi to me. I make a flipping motion with my hand so he understands I'll be back tomorrow to buy the items. The Diet Pepsi Man—the one who can afford a vacation with his family in Kerala due to my caffeine addiction—waves from his storefront.

Namaste.

My train of thought drifts off to the sound advice Caron gave me after I told her about the debacle at the spa: "If you're mindful of lessons of failure, you can make every day better than the last."

You can say that again.

I love the analogies she likes to use—that India is a mirror, a window, and a door. Mirrors offer self-reflection—we see ourselves better, in angles we otherwise might not see. Windows open our eyes to new opportunities—for careers, families, and individuals. Doors open to give us a chance to act on opportunities.

I continue walking and notice there's a dharmic center. Monsoon rains washed the dirt off the sign.

Brilliant. Who needs meditation camp when you can race over to the dharmic center for an alignment?

I walk into the car park and the society manager is baiting traps. I take the lift up. The boys, using one of the buckets of water, are taking sponge baths. I dig around in my nightstand and find a journal I packed in the crate.

I flip through the pages until I discover a favorite quote by Bob Moawad: "The best day of your life is the one in which you decide your life is your own. No apologies or excuses. The gift is yours—it's an amazing journey, and you alone are responsible for the quality of it. This is the day your life really begins."

31

At five o'clock in the morning, dawn begins to break and the sound from the mechanical muezzin signifies the call to prayer. It's February 1, birthday month. Last year I was the Devil Wearing a Burning Sari, and this year I'm the Devil Wearing Knockoff Chanel Winter Wear.

Stanley is halfway around the world and I can't stop thinking about the Tex-Mex he's consuming. It's just not fair.

However, on Monday after yoga, I no longer crave nachos or barbacoa tacos. I switch gears and make a list of items I want to buy to take back to Austin. First up, a custom order with Mr. Tailor Man to create a designer Bollywood Christmas tree skirt on his sewing machine—the same model my grandmother used to make clothes for me in elementary school. Naushad speaks Hindi and with my perfected Pictionary skills, we design a masterpiece. Delivery time: one week.

Naushad drives over to Swami Vivekanand Road and I pop into the VJ Sales electronic store before heading home. The Sikh manager, who knows me, calls a technician to figure out why the washing machine isn't working. Twenty minutes later, he's in my flat and discovers one of the pipes isn't aligned, which is why the water can't drain into the basin.

"It's under warranty, Madam," he says.

I'm astonished.

Nilam, who is in the living room vacuuming, yells, "Madam, you must give him something!"

Of course.

I call Naushad upstairs to water plants on the balcony.

Within two minutes, he's done.

Nilam shrugs. "Well Madam, he killed all the plants while you were on the train trip. It doesn't take long to water the three plants Lolita borrowed from Le Gardenia."

Mr. Coconut Man is at the door. He holds his hand out to collect $2.56 to prune the palm trees.

On Tuesday, I walk four miles seaside towards the Taj Land's End and back. It's chilly. Turns out February will be the coldest month in Mumbai. If I didn't know any better, migratory birds appear to doubt their sense of direction and the only locals smiling—other than the *firangi*—are the Tibetan vendors selling wool items in the markets. The boys wear jeans to class and long-sleeved shirts as the air conditioning units gather dust.

Channing sends a note:

> Dear Birthday Madam,
>
> I'm sending two horoscopes. Number One reads: Aquarius (January 20–February 18): You've got the big picture of your life in focus, and the decisions you're making are directing you down a more secure track. What will require extra scrutiny this month, though, will be new business arrangements. With Neptune entering your financial angle, you need to put the details under a microscope and find out exactly what others intend. Get away this February if you can; with Venus in Aries you're bound to have some brilliant adventures. Number Two reads: These next few years are going to be good, though your occupation fluctuates like a barometer in Texas. Moments will happen when you feel your life is charmed by the gods. It's time to bring plans to fruition.
>
> Only you can know what this means, water bearer.
>
> Write to me, and don't forget to commemorate your big day in style.
>
> Love,
> Chan

My reply:

> Dearest Channing Darling,
>
> Birthday month is always bittersweet. However, this year I intend to celebrate with grace. I'll email when I'm older and wiser.
>
> Love,
> Madam

Wendy's Modern Marble Palace is full of fresh flowers, and we visit with Annette about the AWC Ball in May she's spearheading. We also spend some minutes discussing the unusual assortment of coats, hats, mittens, shawls, boots, socks, and pantyhose our neighbors are showcasing, men included.

"Before I left, Lolita stopped by to clean the bathrooms," I say. "She was on the verge of hypothermia, so I gave her two sweaters and a scarf."

Annette says, "Have you seen the locals wearing leg warmers on the courts at Bandra Gymkhana?"

I nod.

We say in unison, "*Flashdance!* What a feeling!"

The next day, Wendy treats me to lunch at Elco and over *sev puri* and *pani puri* I tell her Naushad got locked inside his mosque again during his latest prayer rave.

"Now he's back to a five-cigarette-a-day habit," I say. "He would smoke more if he could afford it."

Back in the Mini Marble Palace, I remind Mary she didn't put ham in the quiche. When I leave the kitchen, I hear Nilam speak Hindi, "*Maidam janmadin maheene ke dauraan rasoiyon aag ke lie pasand karate hai*," which translates to, "Madam likes to fire cooks during her birthday month."

There's knocking at the door, and in comes a painter with two of my antique figurines: a small woman in a *sari* and a blue-baby Krishna we honored for *Janmashtami*. I'm stunned. "Who gave this guy my people?"

"Madam, these nasty figurines look better fresh, Nilam says."

I. Don't. Think. So.

"Matkar found a painter who works during Ganapatti. You pay nothing, it's birthday surprise."

Worried by the look on my face, Mary calls Naushad.

Nilam is discussing my collection of antique gods displayed in front of the foyer mirror with the painter, who is giving his opinion in Hindi on how to make each one look new again. Unexpectedly, my bodyguard appears like a vampire and escorts the painter firmly out of the flat. Nilam leaves for the day, but not before I say, "No more touching Madam's things without asking."

Naushad steps back into the flat, "Madam, can I show you something?"

What now? I follow him downstairs and he motions me to get into Rocket. I do as instructed and he climbs in the front seat but doesn't start the engine. Instead, he turns from the driver's seat and hands me a plastic bag wrapped in duct tape. I open it and count $2,000.

"Madam, momma gave me this cash. I'm too scared to put in Indian bank."

I'm inhaling and exhaling.

"Madam, I use this money to buy Rocket, I think. A small down payment." He can see I'm stressed. "Madam, you take time. Maybe you need medication."

I pinch myself hard to make sure I'm not dreaming.

"You mean meditation."

We take the lift up to the flat and count the rupees together. I make him sign a sheet of paper after I record the amount, and then I put the bag in the safe. I call Wendy and ask Naushad to speak to her over the phone, confirming our transaction.

Yvette drops Grant off from ASB.

He and I discuss his field trip to the Maharashtra Nature Park on the edge of Dharavi, on the banks of the Mithi River.

"Momma, the park is a forest and we saw snakes and birds," he says. "The butterfly garden with lots of flowers was pretty but smelly like number two."

On second thought, maybe I do need medication.

Rohit sends a text: "Got Boss + bags."

It looks like Stanley and his two hundred pounds of contraband made it home. Exhausted, he enters the flat an hour later. I put the items away and after an early dinner, the boys are in bed and we retire to the living room.

"I can't believe this weather," he says.

"Hey, bet you can't believe this! So two days ago I stroll to Le Gardenia to give Lolita her weekly rupees. The Marble Palace remains empty with water damage and the building next door is now complete. The construction nightmare we heard for nine months is over."

He walks to the kitchen, mixes an Old Monk cocktail, and sits back down on the sectional. I hold up the new *Love Mumbai* book I discovered at Crossword on Chapel Road.

"It has a wonderful inventory of things to do and places to see. It's perfect for the Madams who actually love India."

"At some point, you should stop talking about yourself in third person."

On Monday, Yoga Hottie shows up after I drop the boys at school. We sit. He can tell my mind is racing. "Tell me," he says. "Better you say now."

I smile. "I've been thinking. When you turn older, you get to revisit parts of yourself. You can re-evaluate whether you should make changes, upgrades. Normally I'm vulnerable, critical about aging, especially considering there's more of me to love—"

He cuts me off. "You will lose the weight, *jaan*."

We laugh. "What I'm trying to say is, for the first time, I'm not holding on with an iron grip to stop the clock. I've changed. I feel a significant shift, as if the universe is speaking directly to me, and it's saying, "It's time to give yourself a hefty dose of self-compassion which will allow you to see more clearly the endless possibilities going forward, Madam!

"It sounds like a cliché, doesn't it?"

He does the head wiggle.

"As you age, you have choices, and choosing the life you want is powerful. A change today makes for a different tomorrow." He adds, "You're a strong person."

"You mean stubborn and bossy?"

"*Jaan*, do not put words in my mouth. It is not others who must change, but you. When you open your mind and accept spiritual freedom, the noise stops. You have the willpower."

I sit peacefully and relax. "Thank you for having faith in me, because I have changed. I'm not the same person I once was—nor should I be."

After lunch, Annette and I participate in a group lesson with Krishna. Standing next to a plastic bucket full of balls placed on an old wrought iron flower stand and serving like I'm at Wimbledon gives me joy. When Krishna signals a timeout at the net, the gymkhana manager races over with a Diet Pepsi in a glass bottle with a straw. Then he hands Annette an entry form for the upcoming badminton tournament; he's been watching us play.

Back at Oberoi Crest, the flat door is unlocked. Mary, presiding over a cake, hands me a small, wrapped gift. Then Naushad walks out of the kitchen with forty roses and a wrapped shirt box from Shopper's Stop. Mary's gift is a red necklace and matching earrings she bought on the train for eighty rupees. "Madam, you wear this with your red *sari*," she says.

I love the inexpensive glass jewels.

Naushad's present is a black-and-orange *kurti* pajama set with a *dupatta*—exactly my size and beautiful.

Nilam interrupts our exchange on her way to Grant's room, mumbling, "Not appropriate for drivers to give Madams gifts." Then I hear her talking Hindi to Matkar on her mobile.

A storm is brewing.

Later in the evening, Mary drapes my *sari* in a record time of twenty minutes. Then Stanley and I head out to Aurus for a romantic dinner while the sun sets over Juhu beach.

Tuesday's alarm rings in a setting of chaos. Naushad hasn't called. I throw on a kaftan and race down through the stairwell. I search the car park. Rocket is gone.

My mobile rings. "Madam—" he says out of breath.

I cut him off. "Tell me you have the car."

"Yes, Madam."

I shout, "Are you a doofus?"

He grunts.

Stanley and the boys are upstairs sleeping.

"Madam, these drivers too much drinking Kingfisher with me, making me in honor of my madam's birthday. I drive home because I miss my train."

I scream, "Never take the fucking car after you've been drinking alcohol! If you kill a person or a cow, we can never leave this country."

Click.

Luckily, Kate, one street over, gives us a ride. I'm sitting on the curb outside ASB, waiting for Naushad to pick me up. I'm in workout clothes with no makeup. A ghost of Vinay lurks in the shadows, making me feel unsuitable.

Naushad shows up and honks the horn. He sees me sitting and fuming, but makes no move to properly collect me.

I flashback to ninth grade, when Tony Cooper pulled into my parent's driveway and honked for me to get into the car for a double date with friends. One of the few things my father ever did right was to tell me firmly, "If young men don't have the respect to walk to the front door to greet your parents and escort you to the car, they don't deserve to be with you."

I stay put. Naushad honks again. I don't budge. Finally, he gets out of the car, opens my door, and I walk slowly to Rocket and climb in.

I put on my sunglasses and recline the seat.

We cruise down Linking Road, pull into the car park, and sit.

"Are you mentally deranged like Crazy Madam?" I say.

He does the head wiggle.

"If you steal the car again, I'm going to the police station."

On Thursday morning, we fly to Kerala. I can't believe my eyes when the hotel driver appears in my Indian dream car—a shiny white Ambassador—to take us to the Leela Kovalam hotel. I've loved these historic cars since day one and now I know where the government is hiding the remaining fleet.

Trucking along the pitted roads, passing palm trees, dodging farm animals and uniformed schoolchildren, I see that Kerala is paradise. The backwater and a chain of lagoons and lakes are relaxing. But the forecast is hot, hotter, and hottest throughout the first day. On day two, before a shopping spree in one of the markets, I'm floored to find more brass *urlis* I've been searching for in one of the makeshift shops near the hotel.

On day three, we swim and bike down dirt paths, and the pace is slow. Unfortunately, during the holiday, Nilam shows her true colors.

She acted upset when we sent her and Matthew to the Kid's Club each day. She was short-tempered and pushy. Plus, she threw a hissy fit when her mobile ran out of minutes and she couldn't contact Matkar. I have a feeling we are in for t-r-o-u-b-l-e.

Wendy sends a text thanking us for letting her and Robin use Naushad to pick up Robin's dad and stepmom from the airport. Rajesh had been sent home early to avoid potential Hindu/Muslim conflict. Later in the afternoon, Naushad calls. "Wendy and Robin best Boss and Madam in the world." Then he coughs back his blunder. "Well, after you and Boss, Madam."

After I hang up, Naushad sends me a text in all caps: "NEXT TIME RAJESH SEE ME, HE KILL ME, MADAM."

My official day, the sixteenth, is here! I'm exhausted, since I've been on a celebratory roll since the first of the month.

I work out during the morning then join the boys for lunch and pool time. Stanley surprises me with a cake in the hotel library where the Leela staff sings "Happy Birthday."

Yet I notice Nilam is huffy when I unwrap a gold and diamond tennis bracelet Stanley bought from Harry the Grand Hyatt Jeweler.

I hear her mumble, "*Goras* spend too many rupees on jewelry."

The nerve! Gold jewelry is a huge part of an Indian wife's life, her dowry.

Nilam is not married, and therefore she has no gold except for the pair of hoops we gave her.

The following day after lunch, Nilam tells me, "Madam, I've only been on one excursion outside the hotel—the small boat ride—and I didn't like it. What else will we see in Kerala? I'm ready to go."

Instantly, an image of Fiona comes to mind. I tell Stanley after we send her to pack, "We've been too generous, and it's gone to her head."

Our landing back in Mumbai is unusual: the plane glides onto the tarmac with perfection. I text Naushad, and he drives up to collect us. Usually, Nilam and Naushad joke in Hindi during the ride home, but this time they sit in silence.

On Tuesday, Naushad and I drop the boys to school and drive to the flower market to shop. When we return to the flat, Nilam cusses out Naushad in Hindi in front of me.

"*Kyon tum use baajaar ke lie le gae the?*" she says.

Naushad snaps back, "*Main use sabhee baajaaron ke lie le jaega.*"

Then, "*Aap phool khareedane par use dhokha.*"

Finally, he shouts, "*Mujh par gussa mat hona, kyonki aap ek chor hain.*"

I haven't mastered Hindi at this point, but I think he's accusing her of cheating me when she buys the weekly flowers in the market. From what I can gather, she's pissed he took me to the crime scene.

Normally, Naushad ignores her sly remarks, but this time he stands firm. When I walk into the kitchen, Mary looks scared.

When Nilam leaves for the day, I wait a few minutes and then open the front door. I catch her in the foyer speaking harsh words in Hindi to Naushad, who looks angry.

"Go home!" I yell.

I call Stanley, "I don't like Nilam's foul attitude. It isn't getting better, and I'm nervous she might steal something or hurt Matthew."

He agrees but points out, "You're the property manager. You take care of it, not me."

This is the part about having servants I dislike. You allow people into your home and treat them as family, and it comes back to haunt you.

Once a therapist told me, "When people show you their true colors, believe them."

Naushad steps back into the flat, and I call Mary from the kitchen into the family room.

"Listen—if you don't spill the beans, I'm going to the police station with Pinky to report all three of you."

Naushad gives me a smirk since I threatened him with the same thing when he stole the car. Then there is talking, talking, too much talking in Hindi, and I can't comprehend a single play of the game plan.

I witness lots of head wiggles and fast-talking.

Finally, I shout, "*Ya he tenido suficiente de ambos. Di la verdad en inglés ahora!*"

Mary and Naushad are surprised. They don't know I speak Spanglish. But I have their full attention.

"I want the truth or you won't receive the bonus for staying until the end or a recommendation either. You make the call."

God, I hate acting like a bitch during birthday month, but enough.

I hold my hand up to signal a pause in the conversation. The boys are watching Hindi cartoons on the TV in Grant's room. I turn up the volume ever so slightly and shut the door. I don't want to alarm them.

Then Mary and Naushad stand and deliver:

- Nilam cheats me on flowers by ten to twenty rupees when she buys them each week. *(We're talking a few cents, and I don't have to waste petrol to go get them.)*
- Nilam washes Matkar's clothes during the day. *(Bizarre.)*
- Nilam gives Matkar bottled water and Diet Pepsi from the refrigerator. *(Their caste doesn't drink bottled water or soda because they can't afford it.)*
- Nilam makes ugly faces at Grant and Matthew when they don't do what she wants them to do. *(I don't like this, but Grant's never said anything bad about Nilam. Therefore, I don't know if this is true.)*
- Nilam eats our food. *(She's fatter than when she started.)*
- Nilam says Boss pays her to spy on me each day. *(Funny.)*
- Nilam says we're divorcing because we argue from time to time. *(This amounts to telling lies, and it's causing unnecessary drama and conflict.)*
- Nilam says we don't pay her enough because she works harder than Fiona. *(It's none of her business what we pay or have paid other staff.)*
- Nilam says the visiting friends should tip her when she washes their clothes. *(Not sure who she thinks she is.)*

I hold my hand up and take a loo break.

I grab a towel, twist it, and scream to high heaven like I've done time and time again.

When I return to the living room, I make a mental note to call Cathy and Caron for support.

Naushad says, "Madam, are you fine?"

Cutting him off, I demand, "Why didn't you relay this information to me two or three months ago?"

No one speaks.

"Naushad, on days you take Rocket to get petrol, I know you keep the extra rupees to buy *chai* for the building staff and the drivers. You're the cheapest guy in the city and I know you don't use your rupees for goodwill." (I don't care, because once a month I buy Kingfisher and pizza for the Oberoi employees and drivers.) "Mary, when I order asparagus, you take a hefty portion home, because we don't eat the full bundle."

They don't say a word. I'm beside myself. "Both of you leave for the day and we'll talk tomorrow."

The next morning Nilam steps into the dining area, and Naushad sits stiffly at the table.

"I need your phone and house key."

She looks surprised but acts proud placing the items on the table.

"Nilam, you're a liar and a cheater."

She starts bawling.

"I'm tired of your bad behavior."

She points to Naushad speaking Hindi frantically and I channel the inner head cheerleader of my youth once more: "Shut up! Stop believing your own bullshit!" I add, "You're in trouble because of your attitude in Kerala. You did this to yourself. And tell Matkar to stay away. If he makes threats, I'm going to the consulate."

She shrugs as if my words don't matter. I do not know the Nilam before me.

Then, I hit below the belt. "Get out of here. I don't want to see your face again."

She leaves with nothing. I slam the door behind her and stare at Naushad. *"Ap ne samjha ki, main ne kya kaha?"* which means, "Do you understand what I said?"

He pouts. "Yes, Madam."

I'm frustrated. I remember the day she showed up to the Marble Palace asking for employment, and I've been her champion since day one. We've been through the good, the bad, and now, the ugly. I take a deep breath.

By calling her the assistant property manager, I gave her unearned power, and she abused her authority. Mary reports for duty and tells me Matkar is calling repeatedly, threatening to do mean things to her. Naushad's mobile begins to ring. It's Matkar, but Naushad doesn't answer. I'm speechless. I pour a Diet Pepsi and return to the living room.

My mobile beeps. It's a text from a foreign number: "Killl YOOU."

I show Naushad and delete it.

Instantly, a second text follows: "Watch."

I cannot believe this.

I call Matkar, who is very cordial to me on the phone, despite his evil advances, and tell him to send Nilam over at 11 a.m. on Thursday to pick up her stuff. We hang up peacefully.

Mary is terrified. "Nilam did say you like to fire people during your birthday month."

I laugh so hard I race to the kitchen and spit out Diet Pepsi into the sink! "Adios, Nilam!"

Stanley calls, but he's oblivious to my situation, as usual. He's never had the pulse on domestic life. His focus has been on local work and international travel.

Naushad drives me to Little Butterflies. We both go up and I show photos of Nilam and Matkar. The teachers now know they're not allowed on the property. Then I contact ASB to revoke Nilam's security badge.

Back in the car park, my bodyguard speaks to the Professional Security Team, the society manager, and the drivers, who declare Matkar's shady presence is not welcome at Oberoi Crest. They form a coalition, stand united, and assure me they will protect the boys and me.

Yoga Hottie shows up for weight training. I tell him about the situation with Nilam. He declares, "She must go."

After lunch, Naushad collects two boxes from the stairwell to gather Nilam's things. In Matthew's bathroom is a cabinet Nilam uses as a chest of drawers. I go through each shelf, throwing shirts, pants, toothbrushes, floss—items we've given her or she's accumulated on trips—into the containers. She's amassed quite the stash, and Naushad can't believe the amount of freebies.

Finally, the cabinet is empty when something catches my eye. I reach into one of the front corners and pull out a small plastic bag wrapped in old newspaper.

"Madam, you put down now!" Naushad shouts.

I do what he tells me to do. I set it on the floor and then I just stare at him. He's dead serious and reaches for the newspaper and opens the packets. You can tell it's been in the cabinet for some time. There is a pile of yellow powder and a pile of red powder.

He's shaking.

He sprints to the kitchen and returns with Mary.

"Madam, this powder not good powder. This powder for black magic," he says.

Mary is just as serious. "Evil Hindus practice black magic and these colors are put in areas where you want bad…" She can't think of the name.

I say, "Juju," and they shake their heads side-to-side double time and add that indeed, it is put in places when you want bad things to happen to people.

"Okay then. Let's put it in the trash can in the stairwell, and the juju will be gone."

They're spooked.

"Listen, the holy water cleansed the Mini Marble Palace, remember?"

Naushad takes the packets of powder to the trashcan while Mary makes *chai* in the kitchen.

We drink up and walk back into Matthew's room to get the boxes, and there on the floor we see a brand new 100-rupee bill. Immediately they drop down to their knees and begin to pray.

Naushad prays to Allah and Mary prays to God.

"Have you lost your minds?" They stop praying and look at me.

Mary speaks. "This is a sign from God." Naushad says, "This is a sign from Goddess Lakshmi. The bad juju is gone, Madam. Money is a good sign and now money has come back into the flat. We are fine now."

I look around. "The money probably fell out of the cabinet or a pant pocket."

"No, Madam," Mary says.

Naushad pipes in, "No, this sign from gods, Madam."

"The bad juju we had is because Nilam cracked the glass while using the vacuum cleaner in Grant's room. Then, the windshield broke because Naushad parked it under a palm full of coconuts. Lastly, we've been ill because viruses run rampant in the neighborhood. I do not, I repeat, I do not believe for one minute these things happened because Nilam wished bad juju on us. Now, get up."

I send a text to Stanley: "The circus is in town."

On Thursday, Nilam shows up downstairs. She's surprised the Professional Security Team will not let her up to the flat and that Matkar must stay on the street.

Naushad calls, and I walk down with her savings, final salary, and passport. We hand over the boxes, and I look at her and say, "You're a liar with nothing better to do but cause problems. I know what you did. I contacted the consulate and you will never work for an expat family again."

She refuses to make eye contact with me.

"I found your powder. Now the bad juju is back onto you double because you're fired."

She wipes away tears and remains unapologetic. (Mary told me to say the part about the bad juju, because it's really gruesome if you wish bad juju on someone and they find out about it, and then they put it back on you.)

She collects the stuff and exits the car park.

I never see her again.

In spite of my failed attempts to fit Nilam's idea of how a proper Madam should act, she did teach me something important about myself—courage doesn't always roar.

Mary reports to work the following day. "My mother-in-law says for bad juju to work, the powder must be swallowed."

"WTH?" I spout. "You think she put the powder in our food?"

Mary is thinking, thinking, too much thinking and she says, "Beef is the only thing you and Boss eat. No one else eats it, not even the boys. I think she put it in the beef, Madam, that you still serve sometimes."

She adds, "One time I go to the loo, Madam. I come back and I find two spoons in the beef instead of one spoon."

She sighs.

"Nilam did not like holy water in the flat. Then she got angry when I hung the rosary from John."

I jump up from the living room sofa and call Naushad up from the car park. I drag the trashcan into the kitchen from the stairwell. We empty the contents of the spice cabinet and the refrigerator.

"No more talk about Nilam."

Days fly by, and despite the recent drama, Stanley's brother Kevin lands late Thursday evening. The next day we're up and out the door touring Mumbai. It's refreshing to have a guest.

One morning, he rides with me to Little Butterflies to drop Matthew. "Is that woman working in a construction zone with bare hands and flip-flops?"

I smirk. We drop him back home, and I make a pit stop at Siddhivinayak Ganapati Temple to pray to the Lord Ganesha for divine consciousness.

Hours later, we're raising our glasses over sunset cocktails on the rooftop at The Dome Bar because bad juju is the last thing on my mind.

Next stop: Trishna.

We're throwing back crabs dusted with butter, garlic, and pepper when Kevin says, "It's unbelievable people think you're living the high life with servants, but you're slumming it."

"Excuse me," I say. "Dharavi slum *is* ten minutes away from our flat and our address clearly states we live in Khar West, Kevin. And while I don't live in 'the' Palace in Jodhpur where the real princess lives, I love my Mini Marble Palace nevertheless."

He laughs. "You can sugarcoat it all you want, but you live in a shithole."

You don't see what I see.

The following day, Stanley and Kevin fly to Delhi for four days and then head on to Vietnam and Bangkok.

As it stands, the Professional Security Team is more alert, and Naushad and Mary acquire new mobile numbers. Naushad is sleeping in the small driver's quarters every night, but Sabal, Crazy Madam's former driver, won't stop sending me text warnings: "Nilam telling drivers bad things to happen to you. Be careful. You favorite Madam but careful."

Seriously? I show it to Naushad. "Madam, I'm your bodyguard, and nothing will happen to you."

I peer into his eyes, looking for any trace of opium. "Listen, I'm more worried about you and Mary than myself. The norm is for people to act insane when they get caught."

Naushad interrupts my train of thought. "Madam, Sakina, the cook who stalked Crazy Madam, months later still wondering why she can't find work and talking, talking, too much talking bad words about Crazy Madam."

Birthday month begins to wrap up and the black cloud over the Mini Marble Palace lifts at dawn on Friday when I hear Mary say, "I will cook and take care of the boys until you go, Madam."

I exhale.

In the end, I discover Nilam stole four things: a broken light cover, ninety rupees, one of Grant's favorite books, and a $200 golf jacket. Stanley and I got off cheap. It could have been a disaster.

Lolita shows up to clean the bathrooms, and I ask her to remove the plastic bottles, newspapers, glass, wine bottles, and plastic bags. There will be no more hoarding.

On Saturday, parents melt at swim lessons. I want to jump into the pool with the kids. But before Naushad drives us to Hard Rock for lunch with the air con on full blast, I ask him to stop at Siddhivinayak Ganapati Temple one more time. I feel the need for prayer today. I leave the boys in Rocket and sprint inside.

Long after I clear the queue to collect my *joolis*, I notice a sadhu I don't recall meeting before outside in an orange toga and cool vintage bracelets. I walk over and bow.

"*Ta-da!* I'm a year older and hopefully wiser."

He gives me the once-over and grins.

"Well, you made it this far, Madam; why not keep on going?"

Exactly.

32

As the days become warmer, I find myself walking faster with a spring in my step. It's the beginning of March and a cricket match is underway at Khar Gymkhana. The broad-beamed, high-intensity, artificial lights shine brightly onto the field, and flashbacks to Aldine Mustang football games at W.W. Thorne Stadium flood my memory bank.

I dodge a taxi and hurry past a chunky uncle on a WWII motorbike with a sidecar stuck in a pothole. A group of filthy gypsy kids race to push the bike free, and he sputters away. Keeping my stride, I cross the street and pass a man with a bonnet macaque monkey. He doesn't ask for rupees because I gave him a large donation last year when he appeared in front of Oberoi Crest on the day we selected a flat.

A cool breeze whips strands of hair around my neck, and I notice a man sleeping under a sign that reads: "Keep Mumbai Clean." I see the low-caste servants in Nehru suits, *kurta* pajamas, and cheap *saris* on their way home colliding with the middle class in designer tunics, skinny jeans, and fashionable wedges. It's a clash of castes in the city of hopes and dreams—now a staggering population of twenty million people.

The walk gives me time to escape the banging, banging, loud banging, Karishma's construction crew continues to perform upstairs at all hours trying to fix her water issue. I turn into the car park rejuvenated, skip the lift, and sprint up the stairwell to the Mini Marble Palace.

Stepping through the door, the original Erwin brothers call from Vietnam en route to Varanasi.

Before disconnecting, I tell Stanley, "According to Cathy, Hindu tradition dictates that after you expire, you're cremated and sent to the spiritual capital. Don't forget, you'll witness life, death, and Lord knows what else. Prepare yourself mentally. May the Force be with you."

Back in Khar West, Naushad refuses to leave my side and Matkar continues sending threatening texts on a daily basis. They show from an unknown number, but it's him, no doubt. I've had talks with Mary and Naushad, but their confidence is shaken. Naushad continues to sleep every night on the premises because he's scared Matkar will pick all four locks on our two doors and break into the flat to harm me.

"Madam, this bodyguard Costner protects Madam Whitney. I do this for you."

I inhale.

He says, "Madam, Boss kill me if you die. Madam Wendy kill me, too."

I'm hosting the AWC board meeting. I've splurged on flowers galore and I'm using the Easter décor Kevin graciously gifted. The menu: crustless pimento cheese sandwiches, deviled eggs, homemade chocolate chip cookies, smoked-salmon-and-cream-cheese toasts with chives, fruit salad, mimosas, tea, coffee, and pecan tarts (you can't get pecans in India). I mean, this is how the AWC board meetings should roll every month.

Gail exclaims, "You did all of this for us? What a bunch of work!"

Then Wendy snickers. "She's bored. Stanley's out of town."

Ah, the joys of finding ways to entertain oneself when there is absolutely nothing else to do.

After the meeting, Wendy and I are heading to Nail Bar when we pass Rajesh, who is walking to the train station. He's headed to his village—his arranged marriage waits. Naushad slows Rocket down and we cheer out the window, "Remember—turban straight, don't be late!"

Naushad adds, "Forever, long time."

One morning Naushad says to me at the traffic signal, "Madam, can I tell you something?"

I do the head wiggle.

"Madam, last night you heard noises and called Naushad, I told you things are fine. I tell you no one break into your flat like you think, but they break into first- and second-floor flats."

I scream, "No way in hell!"

"Maybe Matkar trying to get to fourth floor but not possible, Madam?"

Sure enough—these are the days of our lives.

"I did hear mysterious things while I was on the computer. Several times I jumped up to look around the flat and peeked out on the front balcony. I couldn't find anything, but I kept hearing noises in Matthew's bedroom after I tried to sleep so I called you. You said the building was secure."

"Madam, you right, something bad happening. This means burglars two floors down drinking while Matthew two floors up sleeping. This you hear."

The next day I learn the Professional Security Night Guards are in the Bandra Police Station because the Khar West Police Station is full.

"Madam, burglars took nothing from first floor. They reach second floor balcony and enter through big sliding door." He stops and laughs. "They eat and drink while Boss, wife, and three servants sleeping."

Then, he says, the following morning the husband found the empty beer, Sula, and vodka bottles and food wrappers on the ledge. They stole a Black-Berry and a small 18-kt gold Ganesha.

"Madam, I not want to tell you this terrible robbery. Boss is gone."

A small part of me can't help but wonder if Matkar and his low-caste Hindu brothers are up to no good. Several days later the drivers tell Naushad the wife stole the BlackBerry because the husband works long hours, and the servants think painters stole the Ganesha.

What can't be explained is: who left the empties? Speaking from experience, you should never, ever over pour the Sula or the Indian whiskey, because it makes you do cockamamie things you'll regret.

To my dismay, Naushad says, "Madam."

I know this look.

"What now?"

"Boss is a spy, Madam. He travels to America and Canada many times and Matkar is spreading this gossip to everyone."

I blurt out, "Who is everyone?"

"Madam, the people—drivers, maids, nannies, car washers, security guards, vegetable vendors—anyone who will listen."

Once again, the servants are talking, talking, too much talking in Hindi at Foodland, ASB, birthday parties, DAIS, hotels, shops, markets, among themselves on trains, and spreading rumors about other people's business they know nothing about—and this is how servants roll in the city.

I wave off the gossip and change the subject. "Naushad, you should wear your earbud 24/7 to look official."

Funny thing is, he appears the next day sporting a military haircut.

Stanley and his brother call from Agra to check in. I relay the contents of the rumor mill.

Kevin says, "If my brother was a spy he would have known Nilam washed Matkar's clothes and gave him your Diet Pepsi—right?"

Of course.

"How was Varanasi?"

"Well, we tasted things we never want to eat again. We smelled mysterious things, and we've got a peculiar funk on our shoes that won't come off."

Stanley wishes me a Happy Women's Day. I remember this occasion from last year when we celebrated the economic, political, and social achievements of women in Albania, Armenia, Belarus, Cameroon, China, and Serbia. Do females have equal rights in these countries?

After dinner and baths, I kiss Grant and Matthew goodnight. Before my bedtime, I touch my Elephanta God in the foyer. I give thanks to Lord Ganesha for gracing Stanley with much-needed brotherly bonding time—nothing like going to a place where corpses are burned to appreciate loved ones.

Even though the drama continues, Mary cooks more Junior League recipes, and Naushad is content. In fact, I bought them a second set of new SIM cards and abruptly, they're free of all the relentless harassment. After yoga with Amol, I venture out the door to purchase eggs, bread, and buy vegetables. Naushad joins me.

"Madam, you no need to leave," he says. "It's too hot."

"Then what would I do for the rest of the day?" I add, "You know it gets so dry in Texas, cows produce evaporated milk?"

He giggles. "Madam, Naushad knows nothing of this talk."

We backtrack to the building, climb into Rocket, and turn on the A/C. It's too hot to walk.

Then, casually, Naushad says, "Madam, can I tell you something?"

I peer in the rearview mirror since I switched to my regular seat and I'm thinking, thinking, too much thinking, *What can it be now?*

He clears his throat.

"Grant roll down his window little bit for fresh air. We got to school, it not go up," he says. "Madam, Little Boss got scared and looks at me, says, Momma is going to be real mad we're having glass issues again."

Wow.

He adds, "I leave the window, just like so, showing me with his hand where the window got stuck and when I return from walking Grant into class, it went right back up after I hit the door with my fist."

Meanwhile, we cruise down Linking Road to finish errands.

"Madam, Sabal tell me he can help Naushad buy a car, but he needs down payment," he says. "I gave him 100,000 rupees, but I change my mind. I want the rupees back…Seriously."

I inhale.

I pick up my mobile to text Yoga Hottie but stop. *Wait a minute.* I've spent months meditating, stretching my yoga knowledge. I focus. I breathe. I flex. I visualize a happy place and remain calm. Amol doesn't want my drama.

I exhale.

"Madam, you need medication? Sula?"

"No, stop it! I need to resolve this pronto."

He frowns.

I text Sabal: "Please pay N or he goes to police."

Instantly, Sabal returns my text: "Meet KW Police Station now."

I send a second text: "You my fav driver. Pleeeese return rupees for me. Luv, R."

I show Naushad the text before I hit SEND.

"Naushad, maybe the 'fav' and 'luv' will do the trick. He's a pushover with the expat Madams. But, I'm real mad at you."

For five minutes we sit in silence.

I meditate.

Instantly, my mobile beeps: "8 p.m. deliver to OC."

After a trip to the salon for highlights, I return to the Mini Marble Palace and Mary makes *chai* while Naushad chases Matthew around the flat on his plastic airplane scooter. Realizing we have too much on hand, I send the rest down to give to the Professional Security Team and the other drivers—eight cups total, after I mix it with plenty of milk and sugar. Naushad makes the delivery and returns to the flat. Clearly he wants to remain in the air conditioning.

Ten minutes pass.

Knock, knock, knock on the door. It's one of the window washers returning all eight cups, spotless. He tells me in perfect English, "Good *chai*, Madam, but next time, more sugar." Mary and Naushad screech with laughter.

Later I meet Wendy for dinner at Olive. We're seated at one of the best tables—front and center. There's no Rosa, Saif Ali Khan's ex-girlfriend, dining tonight, but the Gladrags Unisex Pageant and The Hottest Model Hunt in India are under way, which translates into many young men wearing sunglasses at night, vying for attention.

Wendy and I decide the only thing "hot" in the room is the room. The A/C units don't seem to be functioning properly. Dinner is scrumptious; we pay the bill and leave. On the way home, Naushad takes the long way past SRK's bungalow and Salman Khan's flat and we yell, "We love India's version of Tom Cruise and Charlie Sheen, and that's how Muslim actors roll in Bollywood!"

I unlock the flat door. Stanley and Kevin are home, and Mary is sitting at the dining table counting a pile of rupees.

Lovely.

"Madam, Sabal delivered here," she says. "Also, you owe me 120 rupees because I paid the refrigerator repairman to replace the bulb. And I missed my train. Naushad should drop me?"

With the clock ticking, I feel as though I've lost all authority with the staff.

I call Naushad up and seal the rupees in an envelope. They initial it, and I date it. After I lock it in the safe, I learn Mary knew about the car deal but didn't tell me.

When Kevin returns to the living room, dressed after a hot shower, I hand him a cold Kingfisher.

"I saw white powder on most of the Indians at the Taj. What's up with that?"

"Um, darker skin is associated with lower castes because the poor are exposed to the sun during manual labor. Locals can't afford soap, deodorant, and often shampoo. Baby powder is a cheap alternative to take the edge off body odor." I add, "You do know every Indian woman has mastered the skill of rinsing herself through her *sari*, right?"

"What's the high-pitched sound I hear in the mornings? It reminds me of nails on a chalkboard."

I grin. "I didn't know this until Nilam explained it to me. It's the *chowki-dar's* whistle and each vendor learns a specific 'call' per product."

"What's up with no PDA?"

"Well, Public Display of Affection between men and women is a no-no and discouraged. It's been difficult for me because I'm a 'hugger.'"

He asks, "Why do I need to remove my shoes when I enter a building?"

"You walked in Varanasi?"

"Yeah."

"When they burn corpses, the ashes rise and fall—onto the ground. Here in Mumbai, men spit and urinate on the sidewalks and in the streets. There you have it!"

"I bought a Taj Mahal clock in Agra and the cashier used carbon paper to write up three receipts."

I laugh. "The first time I used carbon paper was 1978 at my grandparent's house, built in 1952. Having said that, two days ago I signed on the carbon dotted line to buy a photo frame at a government shop. It's the norm."

I grab a glass of Sula in the kitchen and turn on STAR TV to watch India's version of the Oscars. Karishma, in a beautiful white *sari*, sits in the audience, cheering Kareena's Best Actress win for *Jab We Met*, my second-favorite Bollywood film.

It's that time again! Students are studying to get good grades to earn top-rate, high-paying jobs in order to take care of their parents. On the way to Little Butterflies to pick up Matthew, Naushad points to chalkboards posted at major intersections with messages announcing, "Good Luck on Exams!"

Back in Rocket, Laxman calls. "*Namaste*, Madam Rhonda."

"Hi Laxy!"

"Reporting for duty, the final furniture shipment from your girl's trip in Jodhpur will be delivered the day Brett visits Mumbai."

I hesitate. "Frankly, my dear, I don't give a damn!"

"Madam Rhonda," he laughs. "I don't know this saying."

"Lax, we've waited sixteen months for Brett to visit and you want to deliver furniture on the same day—no, not happening!"

He mumbles in Hindi and agrees to call me back.

Later in the afternoon we visit Mr. Tailor Man and pick up my Bolly-wood Christmas tree skirt. It's not perfect, but when I drag it out during the holidays, the fond memories will rush in.

After ASB pickup, we approach the hotel entrance to pick up a jewelry order from Harry and the Grand Hyatt Security Team stops to check for bombs under the hood and underneath the car.

"Madam, do security teams check like this in Texas?"

"No," I say. "What you've got here are crummy security guidelines because the bomb is in my LV tote bag. Why would terrorists put the bombs where they always look?"

The next day Amol shows up at 10 a.m. for yoga and to return DVDs, asking to check out more, no doubt watching all 400 flicks we packed in the crate.

Brett calls. After business in Delhi, he'll stay in Mumbai two days to visit us before flying to Singapore. I ask if he's energized to be in India again.

"Yes. Are you eager to move back this summer, Madam?"

"It's bittersweet. I finally got my act together and now I must leave."

"But the homeland has made you stronger."

"It hasn't been all rainbows, but I don't want to go. I can't fathom living without color. This country changed me."

"Rhonda, darling, I'll give you advice I was gifted when I created Four Hands Home: success is not final, failure is not fatal. It is the bravery to continue that counts.

"I'll wrap up business in Delhi, visit with you and the family in a few days, then I'll see you on the other side. Chin up, mate."

Instantly, I think about the mishap at the Taj Exotica, as well as a number of similar scenarios that have taken place. I've come full-circle with Ritvik's wisdom to live with purpose.

On Sunday, Naushad insists on working, which translates into his wife wanting him to do things he doesn't want to do, and we drive to the Hard Rock Cafe for lunch. At the traffic signal, a *magazine wallah* approaches the car and Naushad locks the windows. The seller holds up *Vogue* India with Kareena on the cover. Before I can open my mouth, Grant shakes his head side to side and says, "Nay, nay, Madam has it."

Before the light changes, a young boy walks over selling strawberries, and Matthew says, "Nay, nay," shakes his head side to side, and says, "*Chale jao*," which means "go away."

Meanwhile, Wendy sends a text from the Dollar Store. First of all, the conversion rate fluctuates daily; therefore, it's never going to be a real Dollar Store, but the owner got a deal on signage made in America. I send the usual auto-reply: "Bubble bath plez."

Today, Brett's flight lands at the domestic airport. An hour later, Naushad drops Stanley and Brett at the flat for lunch. The boys are elated another visitor from America is here, but they're confused by his British accent. However, it doesn't stop them from sprinting around the flat and showing off.

It's great to see a friend from Austin and we discuss "our" India. Mary and Lolita are introduced, and after lunch we race south to The Dome Bar. Traffic is horrendous and we watch the sun set over the Arabian Sea from the backseat of Rocket, sipping roadies.

At the hotel, we converse over more cocktails.

"I can't wait to move back to the States," Stanley says.

Brett looks in my direction, but I don't say a word.

Sensing my anxiety, he says, "Rhonda, darling, you will respond to things in your life going forward with more patience, generosity, and compassion—our India teaches this to those who want to learn."

I know this.

The tab lands on the table, we pay the bill, and I text Naushad.

Rapidly, we're off to Saltwater Grill for dinner. I show Brett and Stanley the "sexy" description in which the *Love Mumbai* book describes our destination: "Goa relocated on Chowpatty Beach." On the drive down, Brett is in awe of the Queen's Necklace, the C-shaped boulevard that resembles a string of pearls at night.

When Naushad deposits us in front of the property, we're instantly smitten with the hammocks and dining canopies on white sand under palm trees. Wendy and Robin recommended Saltwater Grill because they're big fans as well.

We scan menus and tables nearby—the food looks yummy.

We place our order and witness the power go out, leaving the area in a blackout.

I peer at the guys, scanning their silhouettes under the moonlight, and whisper, "Who tripped on the cord?"

They cackle, "Here's to India always keeping us in the dark!"

After dinner, we cruise down 15th Road to show Brett our former Marble Palace.

There in the driveway is Jakdeesh, a driver we know, smoking a *bidi*.

Naushad speaks Hindi, urging him over, and he greets us. I roll down my window and say, "Hello, *ap kaise hain?*"

He looks at me, glances at Stanley and Brett in the backseat, scans my face, and speaks Hindi rapidly to Naushad.

When Jakdeesh peers down again into the front seat, the guys begin to wail.

"Did he just say I'm fat?"

No doubt, there's laughing, laughing, too much laughing at my expense.

"I'm not fat! I wear a size four." (Okay, for the record I'm wearing size six capri pants, but they're loose in the waist.)

The next morning, on the way to school, the first thing out of Naushad's mouth is, "Madam, Jakdeesh say you not fat. He said Madam move to India she too skinny, too fragile, and too white. Now she brown and has a little fat on her bones and she looks good—she looks like Indian Madam."

Why are the people still talking about me?

After Mary cooks lunch, we bid goodbye to Brett. Naushad returns to the car park and then up into the flat for *chai*, extremely quiet.

Intrigued, I say, "Boss Brett dropped to airport, all good?"

He ignores my question, "Madam, he talks to someone named Lover

Bird. Does he own a Love Bird bar in Austin?"

"No, he doesn't own a brothel. He owns a furniture company and Julia is his partner, love interest."

"Are they married?"

"No."

"Why, Madam?"

"They live together. Julia is his girlfriend and they call each other 'lover,' like the Veg Choctu Guy calls me 'Bobbi.' It's a term of endearment. It's sweet talk."

The bottom line is, Brett wasn't aware Naushad speaks and understands the English, meaning whatever is spoken in the car is fair game unless we speak quick, quick.

Once again, the people are talking, talking, too much talking but also, listening, listening, too much listening to things that don't pertain to them.

"Stop eavesdropping on people's conversations or I'm going to fire you."

"Madam has three more months and she is not going to let her body-guard go. She needs him."

The parrot across the street wakes us at six o'clock, squawking at a stray cat in a neighboring tree. Then I hear my mobile beep: no yoga, *jaan.*

After breakfast I take the lift down to the car park.

Naushad checks his mobile while waiting for me to lace up my running shoes.

He says, "Madam, you and Boss have two good friends."

"We have more than two friends, Naushad."

Frustrated he shakes his head, "Madam, you and Boss have *too* good, too much good friends come to our India."

"I agree."

"Mr. Brett, very nice boss, Madam. Moe, nice talking and looks too good with no hair."

I smile. He's on a roll and has my undivided attention.

"A favorite is Julia, what you say...um, Brett's lover bird, very pretty. Big Boss Jim and Madam Carole fun and nice manners, important, Madam; Steve and Tim, Madam, too crazy peoples but they give big tip and American cigarettes. Madam, best family is husband and wife with son same name as our Matthew."

"The Gore Family?"

He nods.

"Madam, the sweetest friend is the madam who likes drugs who was here with the husband that doesn't work, do nothing, like you."

I look away and then over at Naushad and think to myself: this is my reality.

Slowly I say, "Liz and Spencer?"

And he responds, "Yes, yes, Madam."

"Naushad, I've known Liz for years, and I'm not aware she's a junkie."

He cackles, "No, Madam, too much funny story, Madam, too much." I squint into his eyes, wondering if he put opium drops in before boarding the morning train.

"Madam, when I take Liz and Spencer to airport, she tells me she needs drugs before leaving Mumbai. I was in shock. I tell her, Madam, I didn't know where to buy drugs. I don't know people who sell drugs.

"Madam Liz insists she really needs drugs. She tells me if I can't find drugs, she will show me where to get drugs herself. But, Madam, I thinking she in India one time and how does she know where to get drugs?"

He begins to snort and slap his thigh, snorting more, "Madam, she points to the chemist store...she was talking about medicine because Spencer might be sick, Madam. Too much funny."

This week is full of festivities. Thursday, Matthew and his classmates celebrate Mahashivratri, a Hindu holiday honoring Lord Shiva. Good Friday allows Christians and Catholics in the area to commemorate Jesus Christ's passion, crucifixion, and death with long church services and special meals while ASB students shower one another with water and non-toxic multicolored powders during an early Holi party. Saturday, locals ring in the official Holi festival honoring the triumph of good over evil.

Plus, Naushad celebrates *Eid Mubarak*, Mohammad's birthday, by sporting black *kurta* pajamas, a black *topi*, and black Lancôme eyeliner—priceless!

Wendy sends a text from Seattle: "Don't be angry, it's Holi!"

Later in the evening, I send her an email:

> *Dear Madam,*
> *Happy Eid and Happy Holi! Participated in a Muslim prayer rave (sorta), thanks to Naushad, via tapes in the car for seventy-eight hours, a preamble to his festival this weekend. By the way, ran into Norrine at the corner store and we decided to skip purchasing Holi colors and stay indoors. We remembered she lived with blue hair for five months after partaking in Holi 2007! Currently watching a makeshift fire from our balcony (larger than the Texas A&M Aggie Bonfire) in the building car park across the street right under low power lines. Wish you were here.*
> *Much love,*
> *Priyanka*

On the way home from Easter brunch (dressed in Indian clothes) at the JW, Grant discusses our planned egg hunt.

Naushad interrupts. "Little Boss, a large bunny delivers eggs like this Santa Claus delivers toys, and how does he know where you live? People in Mumbai do not celebrate this." He adds, "Explain Easter."

"It's a Christian holiday about Jesus," Grant says.

Naushad looks scared. He lowers his voice, "Is he real, Madam?"

"Is who real? Jesus?"

"The bunny, Madam. The big white bunny." Seething, he says, "Spider-man isn't a real person, but you want Naushad to believe a rabbit gives choc-olates to children?"

Mary is busy cooking *chapati* for Matthew, who's sitting on a stool, imi-tating her moves. I watch him put his hand to his mouth and say, "*Mujhe do.*" Our little guy loves Indian food, but what he's currently craving are the Chicken Vienna sausages Robin promises to bring back from America within days.

Mary asks me a question about a Junior League recipe she's cooking for lunch just as the power goes out. She grabs her mobile and uses it to find the flashlight in the cupboard. Frantically, we open the drapes. The block is dark on this particular cloudy day. Six minutes later, the power returns.

I decide to retrieve a package out of Rocket and walk into the foyer and step inside the lift. The doors close, I hit the ground floor button, and the lights flicker.

Then I hear the power shutting down again.

Damn it!

I'm stuck. I check my mobile. "No service" glares back.

Forget *Matkar*! This is the day this *country* will defeat me!

I begin to inhale and exhale, and the first thing I notice is that it's quiet.

I glance at my Tag watch glowing in the dark. Where on earth is my bodyguard? I call out for Naushad. No answer. I yell for Stanley. No answer. I start to panic, but I stop myself.

Fifteen minutes pass; then twenty. I start to meditate and I visualize myself out in the foyer, not stuck in the lift. Then my mind twists. I open my eyes. *Yep, still in the dark.* More important, I'm aware of the underlying meaning darkness has for me: the unknown.

This may be precisely how I landed in Mumbai, but it's not the way I'll leave.

Dare I confess I've come full circle? *Crisis does not build character, as Caron says—it reveals it.*

The cage shakes, and I hold on for dear mercy, instinctively crouching down in a sumo squat.

It does not freefall, but slowly descends and hits bottom.

I stand up and push every button like a five-year-old. The door budges open an inch and a Professional Security Team Member who was off the night the burglars broke into the building sees me. I've landed on the lobby level.

Immediately, Naushad, a driver, and a window washer leap into action. With everything they've got, they manage to pry the doors apart. I squeeze out. Within seconds, the doors slam shut again.

I'm shaken, but I graciously thank them. Naushad escorts me through the dim stairwell and I begin to sob.

"Madam, you fine. You okay."

I'm overcome—one of the few times in the homeland.

He opens the flat door and we enter. I turn around and encounter a shortness of breath.

"Naushad, what if the building had caught fire while I was in the lift?"

Sweetly, he grins. "Madam, you too much thinking, thinking, thinking like this. What you say all times, not seriously, but the other thing...?"

"India is g-r-a-t-e?"

"No, Madam."

"India is *my* love?"

Instantly, the power supply returns.

33

Dear Channing,

My apologies it's taken so long to connect.

I've spent the past month hatching an exit strategy! What I can also tell you is I've done a ton of soul-searching, and now that I'm older and wiser, I've come to terms with the past.

Guess what?

Moving forward, I've decided to no longer waste time trying to salvage what isn't meant to be. In other words, a bad day or a failed relationship won't tie my wings. Seriously, I've taken time to reflect on my youth. Growing up, I wasn't allowed to have needs because everyone else's needs were more significant. Through the years, I had to validate my worth to my family, and accept it when they couldn't handle the truth.

You've known me for a long time, and you know the perfection demon took its toll on me alongside motherhood and exhaustion right before our big move. I was barely breathing. My surplus was depleted.

During birthday month, particularly after St. Valentine's Day, I understood change must happen for reasons only our heart can determine. So please know I'm in the right place at the right time. The stars aligned in my favor—and the internal negative voice undermining my motives—no longer exists.

During a temple visit, I felt a profound presence. India said, "It's time for a reboot, Madam!" And she was spot-on because I feel magic in the healing that's occurred—and I say this with utmost sincerity.

On another note, I hope you're sitting down. Perhaps I'm becoming soft in my late thirties. Maybe it's because I'm a parent and a child's trust is fragile—I would be devastated if Grant and Matthew lost respect for me—so here goes: it's time for me to forgive my mother's favoritism toward my younger brother and my financially absent, alcoholic, and abusive law enforcement father and put the past behind me. I'm no longer handicapped by the embarrassment and shame they caused me in my youth.

As a result—this may sound completely radical—I'm no longer afraid to die, because let me tell you, girlfriend, I've been livin'! It's been mind-blowing. (By the way, Mr. Sharma, who read my palm again in Jodhpur recently, told me he saw my life span continue until eighty-six or eighty-seven years of age; consequently, there is no time to rest. I told him eighty-seven had a nice ring to it because I graduated in 1987 and an extra year to go places and say goodbye to friends in person would be phenomenal.)

Stunned by the depth of enlightenment I've received? Me, too!

After all, who knew the control freak could hit the release button and let go. Actually, India did it for me, and I've learned it takes discipline in order to focus on what's really important—living in the moment, present tense.

On the marriage front, the friction Stanley and I have suffered living in a developing country continues to test our marriage to the nth degree, but ultimately we've chosen to exempt each other for the horrible things we spewed to one another during the move abroad and the actions we displayed that weren't up to par. Living the expat dream is a series of highs and lows, plain and simple.

As a sidenote, Stanley's intuition proved to be correct: this year was disastrous for real estate. However, his ability to forecast the market last year saved the company millions of dollars; hence, the return to Austin. Since the company sold Trammell Crow Meghraj, they've decided to spend the billions of dollars investing in real estate elsewhere.

The clock is ticking, and it's difficult to swallow that I will leave this life for another in a matter of two months. Honestly, something inside of me lingers, and it's the feeling I may never feel this alive again.

But I know nothing happens unless we jump into the game—there's no action on the sidelines. And I'm no benchwarmer! I fully intend to take my zest for living in the moment and Zen with me when I go—as carry-on luggage, of course!

Yesterday, I ordered takeaway from China Gate and my fortune read: Age can never hope to win you while your heart is young.

Hallelujah, sister; looks like this girl born in Texas City finally learned faith trumps fear.

Love,

Rhonda

P.S. In a moment of clarity, I decided to delete Mr. Sanjay's mobile number from my contact list and pardon his insanity. Cheers to wisdom!

34

According to an article in the *New York Times* News Service, in the blink of an eye India has gone from faith, prudence, and chastity to…Brandi, Amber, and Tiffani.

Seems on Sunday, a team of Washington Redskin cheerleaders landed in Bangalore to help create India's first cheerleading squad. According to the Redskins' website, the cheerleaders will conduct a national audition. The aim of the exercise: to set up a squad of indigenous pom-pom wielders for the Bangalore Royal Challengers, one of eight teams that will play in the IPL.

A current member of the squad is quoted as saying, "Cheerleading has unique American spirit and the fact it's now a bridge into India and their national sport, cricket, speaks to the world vision of the Washington Redskins."

I wonder if this person even knows where India is on a map, and…do the Washington Redskins have a global vision encompassing the homeland? When Boss finishes reading the rest of the article to me, I say, "Two, four, six, eight, who do we appreciate?"

"You know, there is hope for you, Madam. This will give you and Madam Wendy something to do in early expat retirement. You Madams can return in a few years and coach professional cheer squads and make your junior and high school cheer coaches proud."

I spin around with a glare. "You're the boss, Tony Danza"—the new nickname Wendy and I started calling Stanley.

The American Women's Club held its annual general meeting at the Grand Hyatt in late March and just as quickly as the year flew by for current board members, myself included, the membership elected a new slate of officers ready to take the reins and move forward.

It seems the Mumbai Hillbillies took note and decided to move onward as well. We gave our move-out notice to the landlord, packed our bags, once again didn't check the weather, and set sail for Bangkok, arriving at one of the hottest times of the year for spring break.

We spend every day riding the tram, visiting the food courts, touring Ocean World, scouring the malls, swimming in the hotel pool, ordering from the tailor stores, and shopping in the night markets. No wonder Liz and Spencer love the city.

My goodness! We have fast, reliable internet service, fresh vegetables you don't have to soak in bleach before you can eat them, and scallops and ahi tuna galore—the seafood section in the grocery store literally makes my eyes water. Overall, the trip is outstanding, but things keep happening to show us no matter how hard we try, India is always with us.

Grant and I are in the lift one evening when it stops on the seventh floor. In steps a Hindu family of eight, including the papa. It's obvious they'd been shopping at the Emporium Mall near the Emporium Suites Hotel. As the door shuts, the papa accidentally leans against all the buttons, thus causing us to stop on each floor. When his nine-year-old daughter quickly calls out the error, he apologizes to us.

I say, "*Kya hua, Papa?*" which means, "What happened?" and everyone is in shock I speak Hindi.

Suddenly, we land on our floor, the doors open, and we exit.

Grant says, "*Achchha,*" which means "Goodbye," and says, "Momma, they must be on spring break too. Looks like everyone wanted to escape."

Over the weekend, we take the boys to an indoor play gym with a three-story ball pool at Siam Paragon Mall. They enter eagerly along with two small Chinese children who are enamored of our little boss with gorgeous blue eyes who speaks Hindi. But within minutes of nice playtime, they start stalking and bullying Matthew. We call out over and over again for Grant to help his little brother, but he can't hear us over the other children's voices.

Matthew hides from the stalkers, but they hunt him down and harass him again and again. We feel helpless. For the fourth time, the siblings tickle Matthew and squeeze his chubby cheeks, repeatedly yelling at him in Mandarin.

All of a sudden, Matthew takes control. He stands up, looks them right in the eye, and says, "*Kya karun?*" which means, "What shall I do?" and begins *kung fu fighting!*

Seriously.

Then Matthew pulls a wad of the girl's hair, bringing her down to her knees, and kicks the young boy in the balls with his right foot. He unleashes Hindi and punches them in the stomach, slaps them across the face, and karate chops their ears. Needless to say, they run away crying.

I'm a tad bit self-conscious, but a Hindu mum standing next to me breaks into laughter and says, "*Main ispar wishwas nahi kar sakta,*" which translates to, "I can hardly believe it." Matthew is half the size of the two culprits, but he mastered three simple rules I remember Muhammad Ali practiced when I watched his fights as a little girl with my grandfather: stick and move, the best defense is a good offense, and fight tight, yet relaxed.

I tell her he attends a Hindu Montessori school in Mumbai and she says in return, "No wonder he knows how to take care of himself. Indian parents don't discipline their children, especially boys."

I look over at Stanley. "Guess we don't have to worry about Matthew defending himself anymore. I think he might have to protect his older brother from here on out."

One afternoon after pool time, the boys are watching cartoons in Thai when a text rolls in from Wendy: "Naushad wrecked Rocket. Gave rupees to fix."

What?

"Stanley, Wendy said Naushad wrecked the car!"

He laughs. "April Fools, Madam. They punked you!"

Good grief.

I can play this game, too.

I send a text back: "I hope you're kidding because I fell down the stairs in the tram station and broke my left arm."

Now flurries of texts are flying across my mobile from Naushad and Wendy. I sit back, watch the spectacle of missed calls, and grin. Two hours later, Madam Wendy sends a text: "Naushad crying, crying, too much crying you're hurt."

I reply: "Gottcha back, F-O-O-L-S!"

On Friday night, we stay in, and Mary cooks Japanese vegetable stir-fry for dinner while the boys play board games. Just before bed, I receive a text from Wendy.

She and Robin are at Olive sitting next to Saif Ali Khan and Kareena Kapoor. Wendy confirms Kareena is a size zero, which must be from all the power yoga she endorses. What I want to know is why Wendy and I participate in power yoga with Amol and *we're* not a size zero.

The boys crash from exhaustion, but Stanley and I stay up to pack and go for seconds on the stir-fry and rice wine. Late at night, an onslaught of texts continues to come in from friends in Mumbai, and when Boss zips up the last bag, we look at each other—mission possible.

Overall, being in Bangkok was like being at Burger King. We had it our way and loved it.

Returning to Mumbai I feel ambivalent. The flight home was surprisingly smooth and on time, but as we stroll through the new international terminal, Stanley looks over and whispers, "Madam, this is the last time you're going to take this walk. The next time you visit the airport, you're going to be leaving this godforsaken place."

I burst into tears, drop my suitcase, and race to the loo.

Uh, not ready to start the countdown just yet, Tony Danza, because in life,

I see the glass half-full, not half-empty.

After we unpack, we benefit from a long, relaxing weekend before school starts by planning dinners with friends, and I schedule tennis lessons for the rest of the month with Krishna and Annette. The next day, when Naushad and I roll out of the car park to drop the boys to school and run errands, I can't help but notice how quiet it is.

Things aren't normal.

Naushad reads my mind and tells me, "Madam, it's No Honking Day."

Stop!

"Madam, seriously like you say all the time. Today no honking in India."

"You must be pulling my leg. It's not possible!"

"Madam, I don't know this talk," he says, laughing. "The peoples on the radio declare today, Monday, No Honking Day."

I think we heard three honks total while out and about. It was eerie to get on down the road relatively noise-free.

The light changes and we drive by Gloria Jean's Coffee. Naushad dodges two pedestrians in *saris*, pointing and telling me how excited Madam Wendy is to see this coffee shop.

"Does the sign say Gloria Vanderbilt Jean's Coffee?"

"Like Starbucks, Madam." (How does he know about Starbucks?)

I don't drink coffee, but maybe they will have something unique to sample. Then, back to the flat. Naushad calls the bottled water guy and places our usual order.

Stanley sends the mass exodus email to our friends, and our mobiles ring at warp speed.

Undoubtedly, we'll have plans every night. Sadly, most couples we'll never see again, because Tony Danza will be gone twenty-one days in May and we leave the country in the wee morning hours of June 5.

Sunday rolls around—time for our last expat brunch. My mobile beeps with a text from Wendy: "Robin in gym with Indian cricket team at ITC Sheraton. Running late."

Traffic is dismal to the JW. We spot Craig and Amy in the lobby. No sooner do we sit down than Wendy and Robin sashay in.

Wendy jokes, "The police had to storm the building to physically remove Robin from the workout room, because he refused to stop lifting weights with the cricket team present."

Then Craig surprises us with news they may be moving to London. Brunch is yum yum, and afterward we head to the Grossgart flat for Wii golf action until it's time for Naushad to drive Stanley to the airport. He's going to Texas for ten days. No, no, no food lists this time—or special requests. We're on the home stretch, making do.

Matthew is down to one pair of shoes that fit and the boys have outgrown most of their clothes. Plus, I've got one last bottle of Liz Claiborne perfume to my name.

If we weren't the Mumbai Hillbillies before, we officially are now.

The next morning, Wendy and I decide to run errands together. We crawl down 16th Road with Naushad to Gloria Jean's Coffee. I order a mixed fruit berry chiller and when they ask for my "good name" I say, "Priyanka."

The cashier stares at me. "Really," she says in perfect English.

Then the cashier takes Wendy's order, and Wendy says her "good name" is Ayesha. When my order is up, they shout "Priyanka" loud and clear, and as I walk up to get my drink despite the staring, staring, too much staring from the expats and locals, I can't but help smile big time. I'm absolutely going to miss these moments.

Ah-h-h, the joy of entertaining yourself...

All I have to say is that from now on, whenever Wendy and I visit the new coffee shop, we're known as Priya and Ash and that's how we roll at the Gloria Vanderbilt Jean's Coffee House (as we like to call it) on Pali Hill.

I finalize social events and playdates until the end of May. The last orders are confirmed and placed for rattan furniture, kid's bedding, picture framing, and the moving announcements. Lastly, I make one final call to the packers, who are set to arrive May 27. Stanley emails he's working on his own list of things that must happen before we return to Austin, and every day the list grows. His top priority—purchase cars.

The boys and I wake up to running water again. Three air conditioning units are leaking. I call Naushad up to the flat and we take them apart and clean them together with toothbrushes. However, the main living area unit still won't work properly, so we call Mr. Hunchback Electrician Man to fix the problem with his expertise and proper tools.

While we wait, I hear the *mango wallah*'s whistle as he walks down our street, calling out to anyone who might want the popular fruit. Mango season is in full force, but somehow they don't taste quite as sweet since I'm moving on. Besides, the only fruit I now crave is the Mixed Berry Chiller at Gloria Jean's Coffee—which is, stunningly, ninety-seven percent fat-free. Finally, something sorta fat-free in Mumbai.

Wendy calls to see what's on the agenda for the day but I tell her I have to wait for Mr. Hunchback Electrician Man before I can leave the building.

"Madam, there are four Indian times. When someone tells you they will be there in five to ten minutes, it means they will show up in two hours. When someone tells you they will arrive around 2 p.m., it means they will arrive at 8 p.m. or show up the next day at 10:30 a.m. Or, when someone tells you the work will be completed in twenty to thirty days, it means it will take six months to a year to complete the project.

"And finally, when a person or the government says the work or project will be completed in one to two years, it's never going to happen."

Stanley calls from Dallas to describe the Mexican dinner he wolfed down with Uncle Jim. He's trying to get me to admit I don't love India anymore because he's so done. I ignore him and hang up the phone, pretending there's a bad connection.

On Tuesday, Naushad and I take Grant and Matthew to ASB for a parent–student conference.

Linking Road is spooky.

Naushad says, "Madam, do you notice anything different?"

OMG!

No rickshaws are on the streets. Naushad says, "The government wants rickshaw owners to purchase new meters, but Madam, these meters 6,000 rupees a piece. Drivers are on strike. No one has rupees to do this new law. I had to walk from the train station this morning. My rick driver refused to start his engine."

I do admit I saw hundreds of rickshaws parked on Linking Road. Drivers, napping or sipping *chai*, are sprawled across rick backseats, sweating to death.

Stanley, who's returned from his business trip and is working from home while I'm at the JW gym, calls to inform me, "It's hot and the air conditioning units are barely functioning. It's agonizing."

"Deal with it."

He says, "Now do you want to leave?"

"No." I add, "The weather this time of year in the River City is hotter."

Brrrrring, Brrrrring, Brrrrring. Wendy is calling to let me know Rajesh got in a motorbike accident after his wedding, and he's at the hospital.

"Maybe marriage didn't agree with HR?" I say.

"I'm sad I may never speak to him again," she says. "Thank the Lord Ganesha his bride wasn't riding sideways in her *sari* on the motorbike."

"Hire Naushad to drive for two months after we leave."

And that made Wendy happy.

While the boys watch Mary cook, I race to Christiaan Georgio Salon (the ultra-chic establishment for men and women in the Grand Hyatt) for highlights, since Natasha is out of town.

Once I enter the salon, the handsome Christiaan compliments me on my perfume.

I crack up.

We discuss hair products and color and then he gets right down to business. Halfway through my appointment he says again, "Your fragrance is magnificent."

We share stories about living in Mumbai, and no sooner do I take a sip of Diet Pepsi than he says, "I must know the name of it."

I more or less spit soda out onto the mirror. I murmur, "I can't tell you the brand name."

Throughout the appointment, he goes on and on about Bollywood but also about my scent. Finally he says, "Why can't you tell me the name? It's killing me. Do you buy it at Target?" And, then I really lose it.

Here I'm thinking, thinking, too much thinking...I wish I could buy it at Target.

"No, it's just that I've worn it since seventh grade, but time after time I get compliments on it—no matter where I am."

"Well then, you must be doing something right."

He leaves to mix color and I rapidly text Wendy: "Christiaan complimented me on my fragrance. Can you believe it?"

She immediately replies back: "HELL NO!"

As I check out, he runs off to his next appointment and I leave his tip in an envelope with a signed note:

> *Thanks for the laughs and fabuloso color treatment.*
> *Hugs,*
> *Liz*

I return to Oberoi Crest in record time and Mary heads home for the day. I put the boys in the bathtub for a short scrub and then after story time, into bed. While running a bath, I get exactly six minutes of water. Then a text comes in from Madam Wendy: "Saw CG at GH while picking up salmon. He sends kisses to LC."

Grant stumbles down the hallway disgruntled, "Momma, I forgot to find out how many breaths we take in a day for school. Can you text Yoga Hottie?"

Did he just say *text* and *Yoga Hottie* in the same sentence?

After I re-tuck Grant back in bed, I contact Amol.

Immediately my mobile beeps: "We take 22,000 breaths a day, *jaan*."

And on that note, the flat is peacefully quiet.

With pajamas on, I reflect on those cheerleaders coming to India. Hindus are perplexed at what to call them. There is not a word for cheerleader in Hindi. I think they'll be referred to as "*utsaah-utpaadak naari*" which means "a woman who generates enthusiasm," or Indians will have to incorporate the word cheerleader into their lexicon.

Already there is talk of planned demonstrations outside the cricket stadiums by women's groups and Hindu fundamentalists about the anti-In-dianness of it; although it's comical how this pales in comparison to the broader lesson. With cheerleaders on Indian soil, we can safely declare that British cultural influences have suddenly been replaced by American ones.

I brush my teeth, reach for the newspaper, and climb into bed. The article ends by saying, "India's relationship with the U.S.—economic, strategic, and cultural—is now its primary external alliance, with a complex nuclear deal at one end of the spectrum and twelve cheerleaders and two choreographers at the other."

I sit up, turn out the lamp, and when my head hits the pillow, I say aloud, "Two bits, four bits, six bits, a dollar...all for the cheerleaders, stand up and holler!"

35

What time is it? (Clap, Clap, Stomp, Stomp)
It's time!
What time is it? (Clap, Clap, Stomp, Stomp)
It's time.
It's T-I-M-E. It's time—for me to leave!

Well, May is here and despite the drizzle, Mumbai continues to sizzle. Temperatures soar despite early showers, and the hot cheerleaders continue to make headlines.

Right after the squads formed and the chants began, the morality police swarmed in. Immediately, cheer uniforms are replaced with drill team costumes. The girls sport tights, and people can't stop talking about how cricket games have turned into dance bars and gambling dens.

Headlines scream:

"GEORGE W. BUSH WAS A CHEERLEADER!"

"STATE EXEMPTS CHEERLEADERS FROM 'ENTERTAINMENT TAX' AND LOCALS ARE MAD!"

"BOLLYWOOD DESIGNERS REWORKING THE DRESS OF CHEERLEADERS!"

"COVER-UP, MUMBAI!"

While I see the urinators out in full force on our way to a cricket match in Wankhede Stadium, the city is torn—to show skin or not to show skin—during matches.

Stanley, barely home for a week, repacks faster than a speeding bullet and flies to Nepal to trek to Everest Base Camp—a dream come true. Grant and Matthew have no inkling Daddy is gone for twenty-one days. Friends and family are in shock he's pursuing such an extreme bucket-list item. As far as I'm concerned: have passport, will travel.

With Stanley hiking Everest's daunting summit, I plan our exit strategy and indulge in Sula Sister bonding time.

For starters, the AWC Ball occurs the first weekend of May. Mary lends her *sari*-draping expertise, so Madam Wendy and I get dolled up together. Before we leave to pick up Robin and Raj (his friend from college who is living in the city), there's a knock on the door and in walks Naushad in a black *sherwani* suit, black Lancôme eyeliner, and a red turban.

"Whoa! Look who's bringing sexy back to Khar West!" Wendy says.

Mary says sternly, "Madam, something is wrong with his eyes."

Naushad stands tall.

Wendy explains, "He's using make-up instead of opium drops."

Why not?

The drive south isn't bad, and unpredictably the only drama for the night is when Madam Wendy's right heel breaks on the red carpet. We thought you could get anything you wanted in India, but we were wrong. Who knew you can't get cheap shoes bought on Linking Road fixed at eight o'clock on a Saturday night. Regardless, Wendy did what we Mumbai Hillbillies do—rolled barefoot.

Sunday morning, even though the Sula Sisters are parched, Naushad slowly drives us near the Taj to attend the *Elle* Breast Cancer Brunch and Fashion Show—compliments of Chef Max. Society ladies are in abundance and pop-up shops sell fashion wares to benefit breast cancer research.

Grabbing two flutes of champagne from a white-gloved waiter's tray, I spout, "Wendy, I just scored a Priya rhinestone pin I plan to wear to Gloria Jean's the next time I order a Fruit Berry Chiller."

She laughs, then waves me into the photo booth. The photographer snaps a shot of us officially on the cover of *Elle* magazine. Patiently, we wait for the print-outs, when a waiter refills our large glasses with pink champagne—priceless.

What a day!

From those fun events forward, the days drag on. Grant and I spend a lot of time participating in after-school activities and volunteering. Matthew continues to learn Hindi, bond with classmates, and attend birthday parties.

Moreover, we begin to notice dark clouds in the sky and heavy rains loom.

Stanley calls. He rambles on about needing more water, oxygen, and buying extra wool mountain attire in the market because hikers coming down from treks warn about big snow ahead.

"Well, it sounds like you've got your Halloween costume."

My mobile rings again. It's a fellow expat discussing Naushad's credentials. In the end, she decides his salary is too costly. I call Naushad up.

"Apparently, this person didn't comprehend our ad." He sulks. "We'll help you get a job before we leave," I say, "With a person who can read."

Truth be known, I've received dozens of phone calls from families wanting to hire my driver/bodyguard, but he's too picky. He refuses to work for a local family or for expats who smoke.

Harry the Grand Hyatt Jeweler sends a text asking to meet. I returned a bracelet and need to settle the bill. The following day, after Naushad takes the boys to school, we pick up Wendy and drive to the Grand Hyatt. After passing through the security checkpoint, we decide to lunch first at Celini, the Italian restaurant.

When the menus appear, so does Christiaan Georgio. "Hello, Gorgeous and Beautiful," he says, giving me a firm squeeze and Wendy a kiss on the cheek.

Instantly, Madam Wendy says, "Do you ever work? Whenever we see you, you're speaking Greek on your mobile in the hotel rotunda outside the salon."

I chime in, "You're not turning hair orange like Seth, just looking hot talking on your mobile?"

He shakes his head, "Liz, you girls are too much."

We bid goodbye and order up. After a brilliant lunch, the manager visits our table to announce Mr. Georgio has paid the tab.

Wendy says, "Madam Rhonda, it was the perfume."

Day turns to night, and the next morning I'm scheduled to meet Yoga Hottie in the building workout room for weight training at nine o'clock with Madam Wendy.

He knocks, leaves his shoes in the foyer, and enters the flat.

"I'm starving and need *chai, jaan,*" he says, heading to the kitchen.

Hindus eat *dahi,* the tart-flavored yogurt, but he knows I buy the creamy imported French yogurt from Sante and Nature's Basket because the texture is better and he's hoping to have some. Mary pours him the last cup of java made from Café Coffee Day beans.

After the amusing workout session, I pick up Matthew from school and we visit Siddhivinayak Ganapati Temple to pray.

Then, later in the evening, Naushad calls to check on us. When I pick up, he says, "Madam, it's raining a little bit in Colaba. I think your temple wish will come true."

How does he know what I whispered in the rat's ear?

Mango season continues and local hotels are advertising mango soup, mango chicken, and mango ice cream. In addition, Indian researchers have uncovered a new mood phenomenon: soaring temperatures cause tempers to flare.

All my friends have been fighting, fighting, too much fighting with their drivers *and* spouses because it's humid.

Friday is a perfect example: I wake up at 7:30 a.m. and hear water running. I hope our dirty windows are getting a power wash, but it's not a rainstorm. It's one of the geysers leaking on a toilet.

I grab towels and clean up the mess. I glance at the clock and see Naushad is late.

He calls my mobile and even though I don't recognize the number, I answer. He overslept and missed his train. Funny how his irresponsibility used to annoy the heck out of me; now, it's carte blanche.

After breakfast and a change of clothes, I grab Matthew out of the crib and we race down the stairwell with Grant leading the way.

The lift is out because the power is off. The New and Improved Professional Security (NIPS) Team, who replaced the Professional Security Team Who Might Have Stolen Things, springs into action. They supervise Madam putting Matthew into his car seat, shut Grant's door, pry open the gates, and stop traffic.

Hell hath no fury like a Madam scorned when her bodyguard sleeps in.

I cruise down 16th Road heading for Linking Road. I beat the light, position the wheel for a right turn, and downshift into second gear. Rickshaw drivers scurry out of my way like school mice. Matthew waves to Muslim neighbors headed to mosque. I pull into the ASB car park before the bell rings and walk Grant into class.

My mobile rings with an unrecognized number as I exit the security checkpoint. I answer, thinking it could be Stanley. Once again, it's Naushad informing me he sees Rocket and he will drive Matthew and me back to Oberoi Crest.

"Kiss my grits."

"What, Madam?"

"There's a new sheriff in town!"

Click.

My patience has run out.

The minute I see him walk across the lawn, I buckle Matthew in his car seat, jump in, lock the doors, and drive off, leaving him in a spray of dust.

I'm drinking a Diet Pepsi and reading the daily out on the balcony when Mary shows up in the car park sideways on a scooter with a cute Indian gentleman at the helm. After using her key to enter the flat, she sees me sitting on the balcony. I've seen her driver. When I open the sliding glass door, she wants to speak to me.

"Madam, I can explain my situation."

Peacefully I say, "Your state of affairs is none of my business. I'm not judging you." Once more, everyone is talking, talking, too much talking to me regarding their personal lives and involving me in their drama.

Then her mobile rings loudly and it's Nisha, Naushad's wife, calling—she's in the hospital with a broken leg. I skip downstairs to search for Naushad who is next door in one of the glossy evergreen trees knocking down green mangos with a machete.

I'm outraged.

"Get the hell off the neighbor's property, Naushad!"

Casually, he crawls down the tree after knocking more mangos to the ground. The NIPS Team scrambles for the fruit and deposits it into a nearby wicker basket before standing at attention.

God Almighty! I'm in charge of a team of idgits and I just confirmed in an email that Naushad is a responsible person.

Before I can break the news, my crazy Muslim driver cuts several shavings of unripe mango with a rusty knife and sprinkles them with salt from a small paper pouch. Leaning forward, he gently offers them to me on a page torn from an old *Time* magazine.

Ruh-roh.

Since I humiliated him in front of the drivers and the NIPS Team, he's paying me back. Under no circumstances do I want to throw back raw mangos. This is one of those driver control tactics, and I have no choice but to taste the pieces and swallow gracefully. I love Sour Patch Kids soft and chewy candy, but I can barely choke down the third slice. My eyes begin to water. My throat is on fire.

My bladder is going to implode in less than an hour, and I pray whatever loo I can stumble in has a sprayer. My expression alone takes down the crowd—including two delivery boys—into a fierce shriek of laughter.

Game over.

I wave my arms, dismissing the audience and resume yelling at Naushad about climbing in our neighbor's trees for mangos. Then I give him the news about Nisha's broken leg. He sprints into the street, flags down a rickshaw, and heads to Khar Railway Station.

An hour later, I'm told I can pay twenty dollars for pills or ninety dollars for a cast, medicine, and a follow-up visit. Quickly, I inform the doctor the rupees will be delivered and ask to continue services.

I check email and there is a note from Madam Wendy. On Tuesday, Robin stopped by Gloria Jean's to grab a coffee and they asked if he wanted to use his frequent patron card. He told the staff he was positive his wife had one, no need to open a new account.

When they inquired about his wife's details in order to pull up the card number to obtain the house discount, he described her as a tall blonde who frequents the shop with a short friend named Priya. Instantly they shouted,

"Ash," and gave him the reduction.

Harry the Grand Hyatt Jeweler calls Madam Wendy, saying we need to pick up orders we had placed from his shop. Mary, who is busy cooking and baking, will pick up Matthew from Little Butterflies at noon. Grant will attend a birthday party after school until five o'clock.

So at 11:45 a.m. Naushad drops me and Wendy at the Grand Hyatt, where we pick up our purchases and once again lunch at Celini. Seated at a four-top in the back corner, we place our usual order and visit with the staff.

Ruh-roh!

"What's wrong?" Wendy whispers.

"Guess who is talking on his mobile five tables over to my right?" I whisper back. "I'm embarrassed we're eating and drinking again."

She gives me a stern look and replies, "What do you think he does all day—cut hair, eat pasta, cut hair, and talk in foreign languages on his mobile?"

Thankfully, the Italian grape juice lands on the table and we indulge.

Returning from the loo, I see Christiaan is now at our table chatting with Wendy. I head in their direction, but before I can sit, he picks me up and gives me a twirl. "Little Liz, I'm going to miss you and Wendy," he says. I'm mortified. He must have the strength of Hercules to lift my fat ass.

He gently puts me in my seat, gives us each a hug-hug, kiss-kiss, and then races off to the salon.

Madam Wendy and I have a fantastic lunch reminiscing about our youth and college. She's an only child, but had many cousins to play with growing up. She tells me that at an early age, she realized her grandparents favored her over the other kids.

I say, "How did you know?"

She says, "They gave me my own room with a plaque on the door that read 'Wendy's Room' and refused to let my cousins sleep or play in it when they were in town for visits." She adds, "Even I felt bad for them."

Seated next to a Hindu family whose younger son is celebrating his ninth birthday, we're quite the spectacle. Wendy shares another funny story and we get so tickled red wine spills out of Wendy's mouth and I cross my legs to keep from wetting my pants like Crazy Madam.

I'll admit we are making a bit of a scene, but we can count the number of lunch guests on two hands. And, why is the boy not in school? We request the check and reapply lipstick. Moments later, the Celini manager informs us Mr. Georgio has once again paid our tab and tip. Wendy looks at me. "Liz, your perfume is dangerous!"

On our way home we collect Grant, and Chef Max sends Wendy a personal invite on her mobile to his private Italian wine tasting and food party in conjunction with Opera Consortium at Olive.

She shows me the text. "Priyanka, is it possible we can dress up and continue to gorge ourselves?" I do the head wiggle and we laugh all the way down Linking Road.

Later that night as we dine on starters, red wine, and seafood, we rub shoulders with Bollywood starlets and actors Shenaz Treasurywala, Zeba Kohli, and AD Singh. At one point, we pinch each other and toast, "Our last time to live the high life, *grazie!*"

We adore Chef Max. When he leaves the sexy Russian models to hang with the Willage Sisters, the cameras begin flashing, flashing, too much flashing and for a brief moment, we're stars in our own *Desperate Housewife* minds. We thank him profusely for the invitation, and then he kisses us on both cheeks and leaves to go entertain Bollywood newcomers.

Tonight of all nights—*Mera Bharat Mahan* (My India is Great!).

We collect the complimentary gift bag of imported wine, a chef's apron, and an Olive discount card, and depart.

Pulling into Madam Wendy's building compound, Naushad opens her door and bids goodbye.

We inhale. We exhale.

Wendy shouts, "Madam Priya, today is epic—it's the first time we did not spend a single rupee."

The next morning at eight o'clock, the sun peers through the drapes. I hear Matthew tossing in his crib. My mobile beeps. It's a text from Caron: "Nice photo of you and Wendy on page eight." I frantically toss back the duvet. I jump out of bed, sprint down the hallway to the front door, and grab the newspapers.

It's not page six in the *New York Post*, but I grin with pride.

I flip through the *DNA* pages and find the AFTERhrs section. In full color, we're in the midst of the models and movie stars in the society section. Every person is mentioned by name except for us. Our caption reads, "CHEERS: Guests getting a refill of wine." I crawl back into bed and text Wendy the news.

She's received a dozen phone calls from friends, but has no paper trail.

"Well, first, it isn't the best photo of us. Second, we look like Holly Hobbie and Betsy Clark next to the glamorous actresses on either side of our mug shot. Third, the kicker is the caption. It states we were going in for a refill, which implies we've already been to the bar! But, major points scored for former cheerleaders making headlines!"

While the boys are in class, Madam Wendy and I work out, clean up, and hit the streets. We stop at Sante after lunch and purchase chicken ham. We also run by the photo shop, Elite Tailors, and remember to pick up our framed orders from Painted Rhythm Art Gallery.

As we get back into Rocket to pick up Grant, I lean forward and whisper to Naushad, "*Jane ka wakt hua hai?*" which means, "Is it time to go?" and he refuses to break a smile. The days have begun to fly.

Wendy and I continue on our self-inflicted food and wine tour while Mary babysits. Robin is in Chennai, Tony Danza remains in Nepal, and we're craving sushi from Wasabi by Morimoto. We climb into Rocket and head south for dinner in the Taj Mahal Palace Hotel—precisely where my India experience started and where I dreamt of living.

The traffic flows and we enjoy a gorgeous sunset along Marine Drive, but the car begins to smell funny, and Wendy and I start to feel ill. I look at Naushad in the rearview mirror and he's pale. We ask him to roll down the windows but it doesn't help the conditions. It only attracts the *magazine wallahs* and the gypsy kids whenever we stop at intersections.

I had asked him earlier if he was feeling okay and he confessed to climbing in the mango trees again. Now there's rumbling in his tummy and no public bathrooms along the route.

Naushad's biggest fear is coming true: his two favorite Madams are in the car, and there's a decent chance he might have to pull over and go in the ocean or on the rocks—along with other daily urinators.

Wendy, sitting beside me, sends me a text: "It stinks. Need to heave."

I text back: "Two words—raw mangos."

She sends a text back: "Make it stop!"

Wendy slips out of her seat onto the floorboard in a fit of giggles. Tears are rolling down my cheeks. Poor Naushad, gripping the steering wheel, swerves to miss clipping a taxi. We love he's lost control.

Madam Wendy sends another text: "Can we stop and buy gas masks in Crawford Market?" I howl.

Thankfully, we escape the flatulence finale when Naushad pulls up to the Taj. Passing through the security checkpoint, our hair resembles bird nests and we are drenched in sweat. Inside the fancy marble bathroom, we salvage ourselves and then head into Wasabi.

While dining on incredible sushi and sipping sake, in walks Christiaan Georgio. Wendy says, "How is it possible he's here in the flesh?"

We look at one another and mouth, "Stalker."

Once he finishes dinner with a client, he sits down at our table. We talk shop and I wink at Wendy, hoping she's thinking what I'm thinking: *Please pick up our bill.*

An hour later, Christiaan bids goodbye and leaves to meet friends at a new hip music venue called Blue Frog. A bit deflated, we pay for dinner and move to the bar. We reminisce over cocktails and more sake, but as karma would have it, the bartender informs us our spirits have been paid for by none other than Mr. Georgio.

Muah!

On the way home, Wendy and I discuss how moving reminds us of college graduation when the party is over, reality sets in, and it's time to get on to the next phase of your life.

I tell her that friends back home don't care to hear about our adventures—like the time we danced on the roof of the Mehrangarh Fort under the light of the moon while serenaded by the royal band.

"Re-entry will be lonely because people can't fathom what we've encountered and endured."

Wendy agrees. "Think about the women who complained 24/7. What a waste of time. I even feel sorry for their staff."

We pick up our handbags, I text Naushad, and he collects us at the hotel entrance. He's feeling better and confesses it wasn't a good idea to eat raw mangos.

"I used the driver's loo behind the Taj and blew out," he says.

Wendy looks my way. "Wonder where he got that expression, Madam from Texas?"

"Hey, Naushad, Madam Wendy and I are going to host a tag sale to make extra rupees to spend on new stuff before we leave," I say.

He does the head wiggle.

I turn to Wendy. "I forgot to tell you. I spoke to a white-bearded sadhu the other day at Temple and he told me to free myself from all the material things I own. Our sale is just the beginning I need."

Wendy says calmly, "Baby steps, Madam, baby steps."

The boys miss Daddy, but continue on with the ho-hum of our daily routine. Despite regular clouds overhead, every day is hot, hot, and getting hotter. You can tell the difference by the amount of traffic. People stay indoors to keep cool.

Luckily, I've pre-sold some of my bigger furniture pieces like our sectional and the dining room table, but there are a hefty number of bookcases, textiles, chairs, nightstands, clothes, and kitchenware remaining. Monday evening, Wendy brings over her stash of things.

Mary is cooking dinner while we begin to price and group items. This is also the evening we waltz into the kitchen and lay our eyes upon two fancy opened bottles of wine. Stanley brought them from our cellar in Austin and has been saving them to drink at poker night when he gets back. One bottle is a 1989 Silver Oak.

"Zoinks!" says Wendy. "Mary, Boss is going to fire you for opening them and strangle me and Madam Rhonda for drinking them."

"I'm sorry. I forgot to ask. Can I put the corks back in the bottles? Can I save them?"

"Sadly, it doesn't work that way," I tell her.

Wendy cheers, "We have no other choice but to drink them!"

There's a knock at the door and in walks Pinky, returning DVDs she's borrowed. She's in shock the Mini Marble Palace has turned into a boutique. She gladly accepts the invitation to join our exclusive wine fest. Wendy is delighted to finally meet our favorite Bollywood gal.

Stanley calls bright and early the following morning and talks to the boys. When I tell him about the wine, he explodes into a fit of rage.

Once the boys are at school, I get dressed, eat breakfast, and make last-minute preparations for the big day.

Nine hours later, we nail the tag sale. Mary kept the mimosas flowing, Naushad carried larger purchases down to restless drivers in the car park, and Grant kept the starters circulating when he got home from school. There's nothing like inventing ways to entertain oneself while making a lot of rupees on the side.

Grant and Matthew turn in early. I lower the air conditioning, sit down in the recliner, and sip a glass of the good stuff. I look around the flat in the evening light and try to imagine what it will be like once we leave Oberoi Crest.

Panic lurks, but I let go of the tension.

I know there will be moments in my future when I slip on one of my Lucknow hand-embroidered tunics from Neemrana, or slide the designer bangles from Tempus Gems onto my wrist to attend a dinner party, or meet a girlfriend for lunch, and I will remember what an adventure we had in the homeland.

I think about Amol and Caron—their kind words of encouragement that pushed me onward. I think about Pinky, my Indian sister from another mista, as well as the voice inside my head that is at peace. I now know how it feels to be guided by unforeseen things. India made me feel empowered. In essence, she gave me time to understand autonomy.

I take another sip of Silver Oak. *Gosh, this wine is delicious.*

At its best, this country inspires us to be better versions of ourselves long after we've left.

Naushad, with typed references in a Word document, is off to an interview with the head of Lehman Brothers.

It's not an ideal time to seek employment because school is out the first week of June and most, if not all, expats leave to avoid monsoon. Wendy and Robin have offered to hire him to drive during June and July, but he might have to wait until August when school starts to get a permanent job. Or he'll have to work for a service again, which he dreads. He's continued to receive offers, but he's holding out for an American expat family.

The days are speeding by and I charge onward, marking things off my to-do list as they are completed. Wendy and I shop at HyperCITY one last time. I buy toys for Grant's birthday, and she purchases departing gifts for her cook's children.

We remember to stop by Trésorie to buy cute votive candle holders but quickly regret our decision. One person rings up the items. I scoff when we then move to the left while another person swipes our credit cards. Then we sign the slips. Then that same person stamps the written bills the first person generated and then staples the two receipts together. And if this isn't enough, we must walk four steps farther to the left to a counter while the sales associates wrap our items in plain brown paper and white string. At last, we're asked to hand over the receipts every employee in the store saw us get to a person at the opposite end of the counter who stamps, stamps, double stamps it with the date, and then initials the slips with a blue Bic.

Hold on! Finally, we must show the receipts to the security guard at the front door—who has witnessed the entire transaction—before we can leave with our packages. Not going to miss that ultimate five-star shopping experience.

Naushad picks us up for salon appointments, and I can't take him seriously in the aviator sunglasses Wendy bought him. He paid for his own haircut this month—another short military style, channeling Kevin Costner.

We return to Oberoi Crest and spend the rest of the afternoon pricing items for *one more final* tag sale Wendy convinces me to host. I know it sounds cuckoo, but we still have things to purge and it provides entertainment.

Grant helps organize the clothing and jewelry section while Matthew spends most of his time rearranging the price tags. We send out yet another invitation to the ASB and AWC members comparing our event to the likes of an estate sale. Once it floods inboxes, mobiles buzz with cash offers.

When Naushad leaves the next morning to drop the boys at school and camp (Little Butterflies school year calendar has ended and the summer schedule is underway), the expats rush in—buying, buying, too much buying the remaining inventory. The last customer leaves at 3 p.m. We easily make another $3,000. Leftover items are given to the servants and charity.

Tag sale—out!

The end of the week approaches. Wendy and I attend an expat event at The Dome Bar. It's an interesting change of scenery, although we feel attacked by fellow expats from Germany, Denmark, England, France, and Canada who persist on questioning us about the election in the United States. Every foreigner wants to know who will win—Hillary or Obama. Despite my fondness for the northern half of America and its ten provinces and three territories, most of my fellow neighbors have wacky political opinions.

Moreover, we're smart cookies, and keep our mouths shut, learning long ago it's better to avoid opinionated discussions whenever possible. Living on this side of the sphere really does put things into perspective. It makes you understand how sensationalized issues are back in the States.

On the way home, I tell Naushad and Wendy I smell the rain coming.

"I'm not sure if it's the new morning dew I can see or if it's the arrival of slightly cool afternoon breezes, but something is developing."

Wendy will get to experience the torrential downpour in full force and doesn't want it to arrive a second earlier than predicted.

"Hey, Madam Wendy and Naushadie, I promise to do an item number— the thirty-minute song routine in every Bollywood movie where the actors sing and dance in the rainstorm or jump out from behind a tree—in the middle of the road before I go."

They smile, considering they've witnessed my dancing skills.

On Saturday, we drive Grant to swim lessons again at ASB. After Naushad parks the car, he graciously remains in the play park area to help babysit Matthew, who sporadically dashes around the pool, watching his big brother.

Naushad and I are standing near the jungle gym with fifteen minutes left in the lesson when we witness black clouds gathering overhead. Out of nowhere, fierce winds begin to thrash the trees and rainwater pelts down furiously. The coach gathers children from the pool.

Naushad grins. "Madam, Lord Ganesha is doing this for you." Immediately, the temperature drops and then things get quiet. I step out from under the covered jungle gym and let the water hit my face. The other expats stoop under the patio covering.

Something inside of me has irreversibly changed. My head is in a different place. My heart allowed a country and people I had never imagined in. And at that very moment, the rain washed away any remaining despair and unmet expectations.

The parents and staff are silent, wondering if the thundershower would keep falling, falling, too much falling, or stop.

Imagine their relief when the clouds disperse.

Mary has the day off, so we return to the flat, change clothes, and pick up Wendy for lunch down south at Ruby Tuesday. The traffic isn't too terrible and we witness a little shower along the way. Reports are saying this monsoon is going to be a big one.

On Sunday, the boys and I walk over to a small makeshift temple at the end of our street. We wait in a short line to bestow our offerings. Grant tells the Lord Ganesha he's ready to move, but he will miss ASB friends, Naushad, and the rickshaws.

I whisper in the rat's ear, "Please make sure our crate arrives in July."

And lastly, Matthew whispers in the rat's ear for more cheese balls from Foodland.

On May 21, Boss lands at the airport minus twelve pounds. The Erwin brothers simply do not recognize their father channeling his inner Grizzly Adams standing in silence, reviewing our empty Mini Marble Palace.

"You made a 360," I say. "You just camped on Everest. Sleeping on the full-size mattress we're giving to Mary on the marble floor under a dripping air conditioning unit will be a piece of cake."

Dog-tired and delirious, he showers, brushes his teeth, and collapses into a deep sleep for forty-eight hours.

I send a late-night text to Caron, Wendy, and Annette: "Sula Sister 911, SS 911—forget tapeworms. Everest Base Camp=weight loss."

Grant turns six on May 22. Stanley and I read books to his class and bring in cupcakes, party hats, and goody bags. Moreover, Boss blushes when he's congratulated on climbing to the top of Mt. Everest, the biggest mountain in the world. We set the record straight and depart ASB for lunch at Pure Restaurant inside the Taj Land's End.

Friday flies by and Grant is thrilled to be six years old. Our go-to babysitter Alex and Wendy stop by with presents for the birthday boy. After many jabs at Stanley about his luxury "camping" venture, Wendy leaves to go pack for her trip to Bangalore with Robin, and Alex heads back home to meet her parents for an early dinner. The boys take a bath while I cook Mexican food.

Sitting down at the table, Stanley says, "Rhon, with the heat and the wet season approaching, we're in the right mindset to go."

I don't want to admit that once the furniture left the Mini Marble Palace, the floodgates released the moving kraken. I think back to the conversation I had with the sadhu about material things.

"It feels wonderful to purge our possessions. It's just stuff other people need more than we do. And as far as the memories go, I've tucked them away where I can't ever lose them—in my heart."

Mid-morning, we meet up with the moving company's Hindu representative, Austin. He delivers our contract and once our hour-long meeting is complete, I tell Stanley, "If that isn't a sign from the Lord Ganesha, what is?"

Later in the day, I go to school and collect Grant and his friends for a birthday playdate. The boys are charming as they dance to Ashkay Kumar's "Hare Krishna" Bollywood song in the car as we cruise down Linking Road.

On Saturday, we wake up extremely early to new construction noises. Naushad calls from the train station and tells me to look out my living room window—there's a light rain. He will be late because he's waiting for the commuter tracks to be cleared. Three people were crushed during the early morning's rush hour. Grant needs to get to ASB for his last swim lesson so I announce, "I will drive Rocket."

Stanley glares in my direction. Then he announces, "It's my turn to drive!"

Seriously?

This person just spent the last month on Everest, but is in competition with me because he has never driven in India?

Twenty minutes later, Stanley calls from ASB telling me he rear-ended a rickshaw while turning off Linking Road. The second I hang up, Naushad calls.

"Madam, where you?"

"In the flat."

"But then who drove the car, Madam?"

"Boss."

Aghast, he stutters, "Oh-h-h-h-h, shit. Oh, so sorry, Madam."

Clearly one of the drivers saw Rocket leave the car park and called Naushad to tattle on us.

Sure enough, thirty minutes later Naushad calls back.

"Madam, Boss did hit a rickshaw, I see new scratches on the front bumper."

An hour later, I take the lift down and jump into Rocket with Naushad. We need chicken ham from Milan and eggs from the corner store. Naushad stops at the traffic signal.

Knock, knock, knock on the door and there's the girl with no tongue wanting rupees. No. Not going to miss seeing the people missing body parts begging for money. If India can fix me, why can't it fix the racketeering?

Back at the flat, Boss finishes reading *The Times of India*. "Madam, I'm not going to miss the dust and dirt, and the high cost of dull food, and imported wine."

"That's all you're not going to miss? I thought there would be a much longer list!"

He hesitates.

"Did I mention I won't miss paying for things in cash? I won't miss the deceit and I won't miss the diarrhea."

Calmly, I reply, "Tony Danza, visualize India in your rearview mirror."

He yells, "Madam, you do know Tony Danza wasn't the boss? He thought he was the boss on *Full House*, but he wasn't."

I laugh so hard I spit tea all over my *salwar kammeez*.

Quickly, I sneak down the hallway to the bedroom, change my outfit, and send Wendy a text: "TD just got it."

My mobile rings. It's Raj from TCM. The company wants to show our flat to an expat couple and I tell him next week will work. He hangs up and our doorbell rings.

Deepak, Raj's counterpart, smiles and announces his presence with two potential clients.

Stanley mutters, "Really, India?" under his breath.

Deepak and the husband-wife team enter and boy, do they get an eyeful. The guest bedroom has mold growing on the wall because the shower leaks. Three toilets run. Four kitchen cabinet doors have fallen off. Mold is growing sporadically on the ceiling in Grant's room. Boss has clothes hanging in Matthew's bathroom on the shower rod, since the shower head stopped working during Diwali. The owners never replaced the wiring in the ceiling or in the geyser, so we turned it into storage space.

The bottom line is, the place looks like a fraternity house after a Saturday night rush party. Deepak pathetically thanks us for allowing them to intrude upon our family time and they exit.

Craig calls to say London is not in the future for the Grossgart family. They'll be in Mumbai one more year.

After lunch and games in the park, we return home.

Finally, Austin calls.

The movers will appear on Wednesday.

On Sunday, Laxman calls saying he'll be in Mumbai for two days on business and will stop by to see us. Grant and Matthew are happy they will get to say goodbye to Uncle Laxy in person. On Monday, Wendy and I enjoy lunch and spa treatments at the Hyatt Regency compliments of Caron and Jiri, and then Naushad drives us to Penne Restaurant.

On Tuesday, while Stanley and I spend most of the day prepping for the movers, Naushad and Wendy run errands until evening traffic dies down. When they return to the car park, she joins me in the kitchen for a final glass of Sula. She's headed to Chicago to attend a wedding and to Dallas to visit Baby B. At the last minute, she asks me to ride to the airport with her. The boys are asleep and Stanley waves us out the door.

We leave the flat and step inside the lift. Once down in the car park, we climb into Rocket with Naushad at the helm.

This is our last high life moment together in India, with my driver escorting us and Murlie, Robin's company driver, following close behind with Wendy's gargantuan suitcases. Traffic is nonexistent until we pull up to the international terminal. Naushad maneuvers the car closer to the entrance and we stop.

Wendy hands me a card and a gift. "I don't do goodbyes, Priya, because we're friends forever. You're stuck with me now."

Thank God we had each other. The minute she disappears into the airport, I break down. When Naushad turns left on 16th Road, he pulls over and stops the car. He hands me a Kleenex from the glove box.

"Madam, don't cry. You will see Madam Wendy again. I know this."

Laxman's train from Jodhpur is surprisingly on time the next day. He's shocked at the condition of the flat. It's ironic, he was the first to arrive at the Marble Palace two and a half weeks after we landed to help with our Four Hands Home delivery.

Now, he's in the midst of the packing, packing, too much packing, instead of the unpacking, unpacking, too much unpacking. We have a pleasant visit and it's helpful he's on-site to speak Hindi to the team of thirty movers.

The rest of the week is a blur of errands. The few of us remaining AWC members gather and lunch at China Gate on Friday to say goodbye to a British member moving to Singapore. Afterward, while we're waiting outside the restaurant for our drivers, an AWC member driving by sees us. Her driver rolls down her window, we race over, give kisses, and then she says, "I probably won't ever see you again—but have a nice life."

The minute the light changes, she disappears into traffic.

At that instant, I too grasp that I might not ever see these women again either.

Tick. Tock.

The following day, I play tennis one last time with Krishna. It's humid, but it feels good to sweat out the large amounts of Sula I've been consuming and to play like no one is watching—except for the thirty-five construction workers, four trash attendants, two building rats, three bald eagles up in a tree, and seven club personnel putting up the bamboo scaffolding in preparation for one last paint job before June.

We aren't really keeping score, and I'm not sure if he let me win or if I really did play well. We had an extraordinary final lesson. I gather my racket cover and tell Krishna he can keep my winning balls.

"Madam, you are funny," he says.

Naushad pulls the car up to the club entrance and I hand Krishna a gift bag full of diapers and clothes for his baby boy that I purchased at Mothercare. I wave to the Attendant Troll sporting a frown and open the car door. As Naushad pulls away from the curb, I hear Krishna shouting at the top of his lungs, "Madam, Madam, remember to practice your forehand!"

On Friday, Amol arrives on his motorbike and meets me downstairs in the building gym for our final workout session. He's giddy about his first trip out of India to Thailand for yoga and Thai massage training.

An hour later, we wrap up our session. I give him my Bangkok map, a Lonely Planet guidebook, and a huge hug goodbye. Yoga Hottie has been a rock when emotions floundered. I'm going to miss him, but we will keep in touch.

Saturday morning we're in a brawl with Writer's Relocation who has yet to finalize the estimate and paperwork. They want to increase our shipping costs despite the fact we're taking back fewer items than what they previously accounted for within the estimate.

Firmly, I tell Boss, "Only in this country does your stuff get packed and leave your hands without knowing how much it will cost to get it back, wherever it went. I told Dinesh, one of the managers, not to go too far because we haven't agreed on the fee and he might have to bring my things back in two days to unpack."

Stanley takes Grant and Matthew to the JW pool to meet several other dads and classmates for lunch and a swim. Naushad takes me to my appointment to see Dr. Kathiwalla, one of the city's top dermatologists. On the way, Naseem sends a text that she needs twenty more minutes. A patient was late. To kill time, we stop at Gloria Jean's Coffee House and I grab two ninety-seven percent fat-free Mixed Berry Coolers—one for me and one for her—plus a cookie for Naushad.

Home for dinner, Stanley orders pizza and I insist Naushad stay. He's nervous eating in front of Boss, but we pig out on carbs and Kingfisher. The boys play trains with him and wrestle around in the empty flat after dessert.

Grant says, "Thank you for being sweet and for letting me sing and dance in the car. Thank you for building Legos with us and for being the best driver."

Matthew runs over and holds up his arms for Naushad to pick him up. He hugs both boys tightly then leaves with Stanley for his last poker night in the Lapsara building.

When Naushad returns to Oberoi Crest, he calls me.

"Madam, Boss in great mood. Saturdays best winning poker nights for Tony Danza."

Lolita arrives for her final cleaning. Naushad escorts her up and speaks Hindi. Mary is late.

The day races by and we meet Laura and Brooks for dinner and yummy California red wine. (They obviously perfected the importing we were never able to do.)

Tuesday afternoon, I say goodbye to Harry the Grand Hyatt Jeweler and for dinner we dine with Jiri and Caron at Stax, the incredible Italian restaurant at the Hyatt Regency. The South African wine goes down smooth. They will head to Istanbul in a year and we promise to keep in touch and visit—somehow I know this is a commitment that will be kept.

Naushad reports to duty Wednesday morning with a skip in his step. He's been hired by an American expat family for a two-year contract, and will begin in July when Madam Wendy leaves to move back to Seattle. The family has two small children under the age of four and the new madam is eight months pregnant.

As a bonus, the family lives in Colaba, near his homestead. The family hired him based on recommendations from the Sula Sisters after he spent one day driving for the new madam.

Mary waltzes into the foyer, and I open the door. "Madam, can I tell you news?" I nod. "The window washer, who got our former window washer we liked fired, is giving Nilam gossip about our family."

No way!

"Yes, Madam. She can't find a job and he and Matkar have nothing better to do but gossip about the spy family in Khar West."

"We're not spies, remember? Listen, I have an idea! Let's spice things up! Tell the window washer we're taking you and Naushad back to Texas with us." She grins. I'm happy no one has Naushad's new job information, nor do they know where Mary will work once we're gone.

Naushad is in such a grand mood he lets me drive Grant to ASB for his last day of school. In fact, he sits up front in the passenger seat with his seat-belt on tight. We experience little traffic congestion on Linking Road, but once I approach the traffic signal, there is Jolly Driver with Tanu in the back-seat of the car in the left lane.

Naushad rolls down the window and there's an exchange in Hindi.

"Madam, the Don wasn't able to find another driver for his daughter. He looked fifteen days, got desperate, and called Jolly Driver and gave him a raise. Now the Don is in Pakistan hiding. Tanu happy to have her driver again."

Seems the Sleepy People at Le Gardenia made sure every new driver candidate understood exactly whom they were working for and what he could do to them if something went wrong (like wrecking a car).

When the traffic signal changes, Jolly Driver waves me on and gives me a thumbs-up.

I park the car at ASB and Naushad remains seated while I walk Grant into his classroom. Heading out the glass school doors, a woman approaches me and grabs my arm.

"Can you give me advice on how to survive India? I've got my information packet for the new school year, and I'm furious at my husband for moving our family here. I *hate* this country! I *hate* Indian food! I was told you're on the ASB Parent Welcome list. The office staff said you're one of the parents I can call on for assistance."

This woman is very uptight. As she loosens her grip, I step back.

"Listen, appearances can be deceiving. I leave tonight and the most important information I can give to you is that India can be all you want it to be or you can be totally miserable—the choice is yours. In my darkest days, my mantra became 'India is my love,' and this alone helped me see the positive in everything around me. This place will teach you a lot about yourself. I hope you're ready."

She glares at me, unable to speak. I begin to walk away, and as I push the glass door open, I turn back to see she remains right where I left her.

"And two words for you to remember, and I mean commit to memory, while you're here: character building."

Back home, Laxman's movers collect the gifted items going to Jodhpur, a local friend buys the Pottery Barn baby crib, and I grasp the game is over—mission accomplished. Stanley has the boys at a friend's flat and I'm alone.

I step out onto our balcony and a drop of water hits my right hand, then a light shower begins to cool things down a bit. I peek over the railing and call down to Naushad. He looks up, grinning, from the car park and waves. He points up to the gray clouds over Khar West and leisurely lights a *bidi*.

I pretend I'm puffing away on an imaginary cigarette and he does the head wiggle. I take one long deep breath of polluted air and burst into tears. Oh my God, I cry. I can't stop. I step back from the railing so my bodyguard doesn't see his Madam crying.

A tidal wave of emotions hits me like a ton of bricks. I'm weeping because I witnessed firsthand the dark side of the human race: stabbings, robberies, assaults. I wipe the tears away. I know these emotions from my youth and the respectable news is that they no longer control me.

I center my core and feel stillness. I pause and reflect. I've been humbled by holy men and starving gypsy children on evening walks. I've laughed with drug dealers, swapped stories with prostitutes, and cursed with thieves. I have felt intense euphoria and kindness from complete strangers over and over again.

India willed me to put the past behind me—an essential part of growing up and getting on with life.

Going forward, I will live life with passion.

Namaste.

My mobile beeps. It's a text from Pinks. She's waiting outside our gate. I freshen up and take the lift down.

"Thank you for allowing me to be a part of your family," I say. "I'm the luckiest of the lucky."

She flashes a Miss India smile, "We created enormous memories together and I learned a lot from you—we all did."

And on that note, off to Gold's Gym she goes!

One by one, Naushad lifts the boys into the backseat for the last time. Stanley climbs into one of the bucket seats and I sit up front, for old times' sake.

Quickly, Naushad disappears into the driver's loo and then reappears in a navy-blue shirt that reads: "THANK YOU FOR NOT COOTCHIE-COO-ING ME."

I giggle.

"Did Madam Wendy give you that tee?"

"Madam, I bought this in the Crawford Market to make you laugh. Don't be sad."

Once the doors are locked, we pull out of the car park, and Naushad hits the play button. My favorite song from the soundtrack of Kareena Kapoor's movie *Jab We Met* hums through the speakers. (*Jab* in Hindi means "when," as in "When We Met.")

I'm sporting shiny black ballet flats because Naushad took them to the *shoe wallah* to be polished so Madam could wear the same shoes she arrived in.

Who knew my bodyguard was this sentimental?

Then he takes the longest route possible to the airport and that's g-r-a-t-e with me. I make mental notes of rickshaws with signs saying "WOMEN EMPOWERMENT" and "KEEP DISTANCE."

I blink back tears. I want to stay present.

Unexpectedly, raindrops hit the windshield. I smile, thinking about all the water I've dealt with since I moved. It was raining when I left America, and showers appeared when I landed. It poured again when I left the flat last summer, and it rained on me four weeks straight in Texas. When I returned to the city in July, the precipitation continued through September. Now the sporadic forecast is appropriate.

The wet weather forced me to slow down and reevaluate what wasn't working in my life. Actually, with each cascade, I better understood why the universe put me in the homeland—to give myself permission to let whatever happens, happen, and not feel so directly and vulnerably tied to outcomes.

I think about my grandmother, who lit the spark in me to seek out new places. I would have made a lousy meteorologist—her dream—since I forget to review the forecast before any trip. But she would be proud I've maintained the spirit of the frontier—opportunity, liberty, and tenacity.

Naushad pulls up to the terminal and parks Rocket. He begins to unload the suitcases when frantically, Stanley jumps out of the backseat and races to the entrance with Grant and Matthew, while two clumsy attendants drag trolley carts over to collect our stuff.

He screams, "Bye-bye, India. I'm FREE!"

Oh, Tony Danza. You chose India.

Naushad, smelling of Axe Deodorant Body Spray, opens my door and picks me up when I step out and gives me a big hug despite the staring, staring, too much staring from the hundreds of onlookers. I'm in shock he can lift me, considering chicken remains a staple in my diet. Once he collects himself and sets me down, I grab my LV tote bag and begin to walk away.

Mr. Cootchie-Coo is left standing beside the car, crushed. Instantly, I turn back and walk up to him.

We're face-to-face.

I bow. "*Namaste.*"

"No, Madam. I bow to you."

Then, his tears flow.

"Remember when you move here, Madam. You thought you need Naushad more like this, like that, but I needed you, Madam. No one cared about Naushad but you, not in my whole life, Madam." He clears his throat. "Madam, we both needed each other."

The rain pelts the ground and I hear thunder in the distance. He quickly grabs the umbrella out of the car and races around to place it above my head so I don't get wet.

"Naushad, you were more than a driver to our family. I pray Allah continues to bless you with health and success.

Then I say quietly, *"Main Phir Aunga,"* which means, "I shall come back again."

He giggles.

"You too good, Madam. You tricked Naushad. You really tricked me, Madam. You know Hindi—seriously."

We're standing in the middle of the car park, two blubbering fools, and the floodgates are now fully open.

"Madam, India is totally crying because you leaving."

I inhale.

"Naushad, it was fate that brought us together."

I exhale.

He does the head wiggle.

"I will always cherish our time together."

"Me too, Madam."

I give him one massive squeeze, knowing he grounded me. He hugs me back two-fold, grabbing my right hand tightly and whispering, "India will always be your love, Madam."

I strut toward the airport entrance, stop, and perform a few sassy dance moves, mindful that the gods gave me strength for the next chapter in my life.

Showing the security guard my ticket and passport, I step inside.

It looks like the Lord Ganesha granted my final temple wish, after all—monsoon.

◀ GLOSSARY ▶

Aap kaise ho: You're welcome

Ab ja sakte ho: Now you can go!

abhyanga: anointing of the body with oil. Often infused with herbs and usually warm, the oil is massaged into the entire body before bathing

Achchha: Goodbye

agni: the third eye *chakra,* the seat of concealed wisdom, our ability to focus on and see the big picture

Ayurveda: the ancient holistic approach to the mind-body connection

balasana: Sanskrit words *bala* and *asana,* meaning "child" and "pose" respectively

bidi: a popular tiny hand-rolled cigarette. Tar and carbon monoxide deliveries are high because of the need to puff harder to keep it lit

bindi: a decorative mark worn in the middle of the forehead by Indian women

biryani: a fragrant mixture of basmati rice, vegetables, yogurt, and spices simmered for hours

chaat: savory snacks, typically served at roadside stalls or food carts; street food

chakra(s): centers throughout our bodies in which energy flows (tailbone area, lower abdomen below the navel, upper abdomen in the stomach area, heart, throat, forehead between the eyes, the very top of the head)

chai: a traditional Indian drink made by a blend of black tea mixed with milk, sugar, and cardamom; the Hindi word for "tea"

Chale jao: Go away!

champi: Indian head massage

chapati: a flat, baked, pancake-like bread made of *atta* (Indian wheat flour), salt, and water

choli: a short, fitted top with short sleeves worn underneath a sari *chor:* thief

chutney: a spicy condiment made of fruits or vegetables with vinegar, spices, and sugar

dahi: a yogurt created by boiling milk, then cooling it to room temperature and adding the previous day's acidic curd

dhaba: a roadside stall where food is sold

dosha: the three energies that define every person's makeup: *pitta* (fire), *vata* (air and space), and *kapha* (earth and water)

dupatta: a long multipurpose piece of material worn as a scarf or head covering

firangi: foreigners, especially Westerners

gand: ass

gujiya: a sweet fried dumpling filled with a mixture of nuts

hakka: a Chinese preparation where boiled noodles (rice or wheat flour) are stir fried with sauces and vegetables or meats

howdah: a seat for riding on the back of an elephant or camel

jaan: sweetheart

jootis: traditional Indian leather slip-on footwear

kalava: a red sacred Hindu thread tied by a monk or priest on the wrist (right hand for males and left hand for females) to invoke a blessing

karigar: artisan

Kitne paise lagte hain?: How much does it cost?

kurta: a traditional loose-fitting shirt worn by men or women that falls just above or somewhere below the knees

kurti: a traditional loosefitting shirt worn by women that falls just above or somewhere below the knees

kurta pajamas: a comfortable clothing set comprised of a long, tailored, knee-length top worn with loose-fitting leggings or bottoms

Kya bat hai?: *What is the matter?*

Kya daam hai?: *What is the price?*

Kya hal he?: *How are you?*

Kya hua?: *What happened?*

Kya karun?: *What shall I do?*

lei: a flower necklace

lungi: a two-and-a-half-yard piece of cotton or silk cloth folded around the body and tied at the waist

maharaja: ruling prince or king

Main ispar wishwas nahi kar sakta: I can hardly believe it!

masala: a varying blend of spices used in Indian cooking

mehndi: a traditional art of painting (usually cherry-red to brown color) decorative designs on the hands, feet, or body with a paste made from the powdered, dried leaves of the henna plant

migas: a Mexican dish consisting of fried corn tortilla strips, scrambled eggs, diced onions, tomatoes, and cheese, as well as salsa or pico de gallo

muezzin: in Islam, the official (from the minaret of a mosque) who proclaims the call to prayer on Friday for the public worship and the call to the daily prayer five times a day: at dawn, noon, mid-afternoon, sunset, and nightfall

Mujhe do: Give me!

naan: a popular Indian flatbread, usually baked in a tandoori oven

Namaste: a respectful form of Hindu greeting, usually spoken with a slight bow and hands pressed together, palms touching and fingers pointed upwards, thumbs close to the chest

nimbu-mirchi: a lemon-chili on a string used for keeping your family safe from evil spirits; generally hung on or in a vehicle

Om, Mani, Padme, Hum: Mantras (a word or sound that is repeated during meditation that is capable of creating a transformation of energy or a vibration of divine qualities); a Buddhist common prayer (containing all the teachings of Buddha) used for enlightenment

paan: a popular chewing mixture of areca nut and tobacco

pandal: a fabricated structure, either temporary or permanent, used in a religious event such as a festival or wedding that gathers people together

pani puri: a round crisp hollow disk (puri) stuffed with chickpeas, boiled potatoes, and mung (legume family) beans. First it is dunked in a sweet tamarind chutney and then in ice-cold, thin, watery, mint-flavored liquid spiked with chilis called "pani" and eaten in one mouthful

puja: prayers

Raksha Bandhan: a Hindu religious and secular festival; means "bond of protection"

rakhi: a bracelet, ideally made of silk or silk with gold and silver threads, beautifully crafted embroidered sequins and/or studded with semi-precious stones

ruko: Stop

sabat soorat: an item of headgear (turban) associated with Sikhism; asserting the public commitment to maintaining the values, ethics of tradition, including service, compassion, and honesty of the Sikh culture

sadhu: sanskrit for "accomplished" and refers to any religious holy man who has renounced caste, social position, money, and authority

salwar: a pair of light, loose, pleated trousers tapered to a tight fit around the ankles

salwar kameez: traditional dress consisting of a *kameez* (shirt) and *salwar* (trousers)

savasana: a pose usually done at the end of a yoga practice, in which practitioners lay flat on their backs with heels spread as wide as the yoga mat and the arms rest at the sides of the body, palms facing upward

sev puri: a mix of crushed *puris* (deep-fried disks of flour), puffed rice, *sev* (fine crushed crispy chickpea noodles), diced onions, boiled potatoes, coriander leaves, and green chillies. It's tossed with one of three chutneys: sweet tamarind, red garlic, and spicy green chili

sherwani: a popular long garment worn over a *kurta*; the lower part of the dress consists of a *salwar*

Skoda: Czech car-maker, one of the fastest growing companies in the Indian automotive industry, who reached Indian shores in 2001

surkha: another name for *lungi*

tandoori: a method of cooking using a clay oven

thali: an Indian style platter, made up of a selection of various dishes, used to offer the perfect meal: six different flavors of sweet, salt, bitter, sour, sharp, and spicy

Theek hai: Okay or That's fine

tilaka: a mark worn on the forehead and other parts of the body for spiritual reasons

topi: a type of round headcovering or "prayer cap" worn by Muslim males

Tum samajhte ho ki, main lakhpati hun? Do you think I am a millionaire?

wallah: a surname in India of a person indicating their profession

Ya he tenido suficiente de ambos. Di la verdad en inglés ahora: I've had enough of both. Speak the truth in English now.

Yah bahut zyada hai: This is too much

Ode to Bollywood
Dance and sing on film
Girls from India are hot
Goal is not a song!

Ode to The Dome Bar
Your chips are from God
Your view like a necklace
Rooftop bar with smog.

Ode to Chips at The Dome Bar
Crispy and spicy
Taste on hands for seven days
No dip for this chip!

Ode to Stan's Elephants
What are they made of
Bone, marble, silver, or stone
Can you say lucky?

Ode to Stan's Elephants
What are they made of
Bone, marble, silver, or stone
Is it over, no!

Ode to Stan's Elephants
What are they made of
Bone, marble, silver, or stone
Maybe one more, yes!

Ode to Stan's Elephants
What are they made of
Bone, marble, silver, or stone
Will he buy again?

Ode to Rhonda
I will not do it
Not today or tomorrow
How about never!

Ode to Go India
A discount airline
Cheap fares throughout India
No brains at the top!

Ode to Opium
Drink or smoke, your pick
The elders use a filter
Wax body for job.

Ode to Green Wine
A smell from my past
To drink a joint I would try
Shave the body down.

Ode to Pushkar
Pushkar Fair was fun
Rhonda pulled stickers from feet
Camel sales were swift.

Ode to the Taj Mahal
Taj Mahal by car
Twelve hours on a two-lane road
Should have flown this time!

Ode to Beef
Buffalo or steak
Best meal I've had in four days
Who cares, it was great!

Ode to Kingfisher
You are tall and cold
I have loved you from the start
Kingfisher is beer!

Ode to an Indian Rest Stop
"Exit here" it says
Promising food for a king
More stuff to buy, yes!

Ode to a Driver
English was not good
Sneezing, coughing all day long
Airborne bath for us!

Ode to an Indian Massage
Ouch, what did he do?
Kama Sutra or Yoga?
Popped more than a knot!

Ode to Indian Food
Curry is the base
Too many dishes are thee
On a plane, not fair!

Ode to a Shart
A mistake are you
An unexpected surprise
Just air—oops! Who knew?

Ode to an Air India Landing
Like a rock we fell
Boom, then boom again, oh my!
Yep, I'm awake now!

◀ ABOUT THE AUTHOR ▶

Rhonda Erwin, avid traveler and writer, received her Bachelor of Arts degree in journalism from Southwest Texas State University in San Marcos. She has been a public relations director, an advertising account manager, and a special events planner. When she's not traveling to India, Cuba, Japan, and beyond, Rhonda loves to run with her Shih Tzu, who suffers from "little dog" syndrome.

◀ ACKNOWLEDGMENTS ▶

Naushad—Best Bodyguard In The World—I could not have survived without you. (Thank you for *not* cootchie-cooing me.)

Wendy—Soul Sister. You have an indomitable wit. I'm blessed by your friendship and I will never forget our adventures.

Caron Kobos—A Lighthouse In Any Storm. You taught me the value of believing in my own revelations. I'm a better person knowing you.

Mike Aviles—Superman. You suggested I take my aspiration to the next level, trusting my voice.

Harrieta y Emiliano Meisel—Trailblazers. You showed me how expats should roll.

Renee Barnes—Mother Theresa. You're the first person to tell me to keep a journal and turn my memories into something precious and tangible.

Trammell Crow Company (TCC)—the catalyst for my journey and responsible party for lots of teeth gritting. Kudos for sending the best expert for the job.

I'm grateful to my papaw—for unconditional love and telling me I was his favorite grandchild.

Big LOVE to India, who changed me. Plus admiration to Lord Ganesha, Lord Shiva, Hanuman, and Allah.

And most of all, I want to thank Stanley, who moved me across the globe and upon our return to the River City, told me continually over the years—with affection but harshness—F-I-N-I-S-H the book! Thank God, I finally listened to you.

As a sidenote, writing isn't easy. It's a job full of self-doubt and tears, but ultimately, pure joy when the result is complete. Therefore, between connecting the 411 dots and the 911 sips, I'm blessed to have loyal friends like Cathy Nieddu, Moe Benson, Annette Beeches, Channing Wiese, Naseem Kathiwalla, Sally Metcalfe, Sheri and Bob Myer, Tammy Belisle, Cindy Valdez, Amy-Beth Morrison, Aileen Aviles, Bridget Glaser, Amy Dolce, Lori and Mark Osborn, Amy Peng, Megan Overland, Annika Franco, Carrie Biggar, Becky Heston, Kim Ray, Brett Hatton, Debra and Rex Gore, Pinky Harwani, Laxman Chand, Christiaan Georgio, Dick Anderson, Jan Heaton, Sonia and Sandy Shah, Bozzo Singh, Jane Vanisko McCan, Liz Williams, Debbie and David Arnow, Mark Burns, Linda and Tommie Charrier, Ken Lewandowski, Victoria Nygren, Mike Fleischhauer, Graciela Rapallo, Steve Ruff, Quynh Pham, Terry Balderach, Blair Burke Kaine, Michele Aucoin, Marcia Meier, Amy Hufford, John Metzger, Clint Greenleaf, Don LaPierre, Mark Norton, Amir Ramos, Kelsey Grode, Charlotte Lillywhite, Sally Garland, and Matthew Briggs, who have all, in different ways, contributed to this book.

The END.